THE CAMBRIDGE COMPA:
THE HISTORY OF THE

Throughout human history, the world's knowledge and fruits of the creative imagination have been produced, circulated and received through the medium of the material text. This *Companion* provides a wide-ranging account of the history of the book and its ways of thinking about works from ancient inscription to contemporary e-books, discussing thematic, chronological and methodological aspects of this interdisciplinary field. The first part considers book cultures from local, national and global perspectives. Part two, organized around the dynamic relationship between the material book and the mutable text, develops a loosely chronological narrative from early writing, through manuscript and early printing, to the institution of a mechanized book trade, and on to the globalization of publishing and the introduction of the electronic book. A third part takes a practical turn, discussing methods, sources and approaches: bibliographical, archival and reading experience methodologies, as well as pedagogical strategies.

LESLIE HOWSAM is University Professor in the Department of History at the University of Windsor. She is author or editor of seven significant books and numerous articles, most notably *Old Books and New Histories: An Orientation to Studies in Book and Print Culture* (2006) and *Past into Print: The Publishing of History in Britain 1850–1950* (2009).

A complete list of books in the series is at the back of this book.

THE CAMBRIDGE
COMPANION TO
THE HISTORY OF
THE BOOK

EDITED BY
LESLIE HOWSAM

CAMBRIDGE
UNIVERSITY PRESS

CAMBRIDGE
UNIVERSITY PRESS

University Printing House, Cambridge CB2 8BS, United Kingdom

Cambridge University Press is part of the University of Cambridge.

It furthers the University's mission by disseminating knowledge in the pursuit of education, learning and research at the highest international levels of excellence.

www.cambridge.org
Information on this title: www.cambridge.org/9781107625099

© Cambridge University Press 2015

This publication is in copyright. Subject to statutory exception and to the provisions of relevant collective licensing agreements, no reproduction of any part may take place without the written permission of Cambridge University Press.

First published 2015

Printed in the United Kingdom by Clays, St Ives plc

A catalogue record for this publication is available from the British Library

Library of Congress Cataloguing in Publication data
The Cambridge companion to the history of the book / edited by Leslie Howsam.
  pages cm – (Cambridge companions to literature)
  Includes bibliographical references and index.
ISBN 978-1-107-02373-4 (hardback) – ISBN 978-1-107-62509-9 (paperback)
  1. Books – History. I. Howsam, Leslie, editor.
    Z4.C26 2014
    002–dc23
    2014021021

ISBN 978-1-107-02373-4 Hardback
ISBN 978-1-107-62509-9 Paperback

Cambridge University Press has no responsibility for the persistence or accuracy of URLs for external or third-party internet websites referred to in this publication, and does not guarantee that any content on such websites is, or will remain, accurate or appropriate.

TORFAEN COUNTY BOROUGH BWRDEISTREF SIROL TORFAEN	
01669308	
Askews & Holts	27-May-2015
002.09	£19.99

CONTENTS

List of illustrations — page vii
List of contributors — viii
Chronology — x

1. The study of book history
   LESLIE HOWSAM — 1

PART I BOOK CULTURES, LOCAL, NATIONAL AND GLOBAL

2. Books in the library
   KAREN ATTAR — 17

3. Books in the nation
   TRISH LOUGHRAN — 36

4. Books in global perspectives
   SYDNEY SHEP — 53

PART II THE MATERIAL BOOK AND THE MUTABLE TEXT

5. Materials and meanings
   PETER STOICHEFF — 73

6. Handwriting and the book
   MARGARET J. M. EZELL — 90

7. The coming of print to Europe
   ADRIAN JOHNS — 107

CONTENTS

8 The authority and subversiveness of print in early-modern Europe
CYNDIA SUSAN CLEGG — 125

9 The industrial revolution of the book
JAMES RAVEN — 143

10 The book in the long twentieth century
ALISTAIR McCLEERY — 162

11 The digital book
JON BATH AND SCOTT SCHOFIELD — 181

PART III METHODS, SOURCES AND APPROACHES TO THE HISTORY OF THE BOOK

12 Book history from descriptive bibliographies
MICHAEL F. SUAREZ, S.J. — 199

13 Book history from the archival record
KATHERINE BODE AND ROGER OSBORNE — 219

14 Book history in the reading experience
MARY HAMMOND — 237

15 Book history in the classroom
LESLIE HOWSAM — 253

Glossary of technical terms used by bibliographers and historians of the book — 268
Guide to further reading — 273
Index — 281

ILLUSTRATIONS

2.1 Book containing British Museum sale duplicate stamp and a manuscript note by Augustus De Morgan. Reproduced with permission from Senate House Library, University of London. *page* 31
3.1 'The Press Descending from the Heavens'. Reproduced with permission from the Bancroft Library, University of California, Berkeley. 37
4.1 Modelling situated knowledges in book history. Reproduced with permission of Sydney Shep. 66

CONTRIBUTORS

KAREN ATTAR is Rare Books Librarian at Senate House Library and Fellow of the Institute of English Studies both, University of London.

JON BATH is Director of the Humanities and Fine Arts Digital Research Centre at the University of Saskatchewan and a member of the Implementing New Knowledge Environments (INKE) research team.

KATHERINE BODE is Senior Lecturer in Literary and Textual Studies in the Centre for Digital Humanities Research at the Australian National University.

CYNDIA SUSAN CLEGG is Distinguished Professor of English at Pepperdine University.

MARGARET J. M. EZELL is Distinguished Professor and the Sara and John Lindsey Chair of Liberal Arts in the Department of English of Texas A&M University.

MARY HAMMOND is Associate Professor of English at the University of Southampton.

LESLIE HOWSAM is University Professor in the Department of History at the University of Windsor.

ADRIAN JOHNS is Allan Grant Maclear Professor in the Department of History and Chair of the Committee on Conceptual and Historical Studies of Science at the University of Chicago.

TRISH LOUGHRAN is Associate Professor of English and History at the University of Illinois in Urbana-Champaign.

ALISTAIR McCLEERY is Professor of Literature and Culture at Edinburgh Napier University and Director of the Scottish Centre for the Book.

ROGER OSBORNE is Visiting Fellow in the School of Humanities and Social Sciences at the University of New South Wales.

LIST OF CONTRIBUTORS

JAMES RAVEN is Professor of Modern History and Director of the Centre for Bibliographical History at the University of Essex; he is Senior Research Fellow of Magdalene College, Cambridge.

SCOTT SCHOFIELD is Assistant Professor of English at Huron University College in Western University. From 2011 to 2013 he was a postdoctoral fellow with Implementing New Knowledge Environments (INKE).

SYDNEY SHEP is Reader in Book History and The Printer, Wai-te-ata Press, Faculty of Humanities and Social Sciences at Victoria University of Wellington.

PETER STOICHEFF is Dean of the College of Arts and Science and Professor of English at the University of Saskatchewan.

MICHAEL F. SUAREZ, S.J. is Director of the Rare Book School, University Professor in the Department of English and Honorary Curator of Special Collections at the University of Virginia.

CHRONOLOGY

c. 70,000–80,000 BCE. First recorded evidence of human marks made purposefully on a material base – flint knapping on stone and bone, coloured with ochre. In the Blombos Caves in modern South Africa.
c. 40,000–50,000 BCE. Until the discovery of the Blombos evidence, cave paintings in Lascaux, France, were thought to be the earliest record of human marks. Pictographs and petroglyphs were painted and incised on stone from about 10,000 BCE in North, Central and South America, Australasia, Asia, Africa and Europe.
c. 3200 BCE. Beginning of written language in both ancient Mesopotamia (using clay as a writing surface) and ancient Egypt.
c. 3000 BCE. Papyrus (made from reed grown in Egypt) first used as a writing surface.
c. 1200 BCE. Beginning of written language in ancient China, using bone and tortoiseshell, later silk, as writing surfaces. Diamond Sutra the first dated book, 868 CE.
c. 1000 BCE. Writing on palm leaves in ancient India; palm leaf books called *sutras*.
c. 800 BCE. In Assyria, introduction of the wax tablet as a writing surface.
c. 600 BCE. Beginning of written Mayan language in ancient Mesoamerica.
c. 300 BCE. Foundation of the library of Alexandria, in Egypt.
c. 100 CE. Paper first used in China.
c. 100–200 CE. In Europe, parchment (sheep or calfskin leather) first used extensively as a writing surface; about the same time, appearance of the first codex, beginning to supplant the papyrus scroll.
c. 220. In China, first printing using woodblock technique, on cloth.
c. 1000. In Korea, first printing with moveable metal type.
1074. First European paper mill established in eastern Spain by Muslims – paper made from linen rags.
Medieval Europe. Bibles, Books of Hours and other works published in manuscript on parchment, later on paper.

1403. Foundation of the Stationers' Company in London.

c. 1456. A printed bible issued from Mainz by Johannes Gutenberg using moveable type and letterpress technology (on parchment *and* paper).

1450s–1500. The incunabula period, when printing spread from Mainz to other European cities, beginning with Venice, Paris, Krakow and Flanders. Caxton's first press in England established 1476.

1522. Luther's German bible issued from a press in Wittenberg.

1534. Foundation of the Cambridge University Press; first book printed in 1584.

1536. Press founded in Mexico.

1593. Press founded in the Philippines.

1638. Press founded in British North America (Cambridge, MA).

1662–95. Licensing Act controls printing in England.

1666. Royal Society (London) founded; publishes the periodical *Philosophical Transactions*.

1710. Copyright Act in England, recognizes rights of author.

1725. William Ged develops stereotype plates, in Scotland, for printing whole pages of type (technique was reinvented and made commercially viable in 1804 by Stanhope).

1730. Benjamin Franklin official printer to the state of Pennsylvania.

1751. Diderot begins publication of the *Encyclopédie*, circulating Enlightenment ideas in France.

1751. First printing press in Canada (Halifax).

1798. Nicholas Louis Robert invents a papermaking machine; 1804 Henry and Sealy Fourdrinier purchase the patent.

1798. Lithography developed as a printing technique.

1803. Stanhope builds first iron press in England; manufactured New York 1811, Germany 1815.

1810. König's steam-powered press patented in England (used to print *The Times* newspaper 1814).

1813. First handpress made of iron.

1820s. Beginning of binding with book cloth.

1842. Copyright Act implemented in Britain.

1843. Wood pulp begins to replace rag pulp in papermaking.

1847. Introduction of the rotary press by R. M. Hoe.

1851. First lithographic power press introduced.

1879. First machine to sew book bindings (but handwork by women continues).

1870s. Introduction of offset printing.

1886. Berne Convention establishes reciprocal international copyright law.

1886. Linotype machine introduced (automates typecasting and composition).
1890s. End of the three-volume novel in England (since the 1820s).
1891. Chace Act in the US ends literary piracy by Americans.
1892. Foundation of The Bibliographical Society (London).
Early twentieth century. Widespread use of paper made from wood pulp, rather than rags.
1903. Offset printing developed (lithographic technique using three cylinders).
1904. Foundation of The Bibliographical Society of America.
1926. Book-of-the-Month Club founded, US.
1935. Launch of Penguin Books in England by the publisher Allan Lane initiates the 'paperback revolution' (1939, Robert DeGraf launches Pocket Books in the US).
1937. Xerography introduced.
1950s. Beginning of photocomposition.
1961. Publication of D. F. McKenzie's first book, *Stationers' Company Apprentices 1605–1640*.
1969. Invention of the laser printer; introduced commercially by IBM in 1976.
1971. Project Gutenberg begins converting books to digital format.
1979. First publication of Eisenstein's *The Printing Press as an Agent of Change* and of Darnton's *The Business of Enlightenment: A Publishing History of the Encyclopédie*.
1983. Foundation of the Rare Book School at Columbia University; it moved to the University of Virginia, Charlottesville, VA in 1992.
1991. Foundation of the Society for the History of Authorship, Reading and Publishing. First conference New York, 1993.
2001. Development of e-ink and e-paper, and other new technologies (supports) for making texts available to readers.

1

LESLIE HOWSAM

The study of book history

The history of the book is a way of thinking about how people have given material form to knowledge and stories. Knowledge and stories are intangible; it is their material forms that make them accessible across the barriers created by time and space. But those forms vary. It is difficult to find two old books that are exactly alike, while new media too are remarkably unstable in their ways of capturing texts. The variations among copies and editions, and among conventions and practices, are the result of human agency: of political and personal choices, of belief and aesthetics, of economics and marketing. Studies in the history of the book discover and analyse the connections between the people who used books as readers, and those who wrote or compiled them. These relationships are often revealed indirectly, by focusing upon the contribution of the mediators between reader and author. Those who make, sell and save books – the scribes, printers, editors, publishers and retailers, the librarians and collectors – are essential figures in what is sometimes called a book culture. Their interactions make up a web of connections, each person influenced knowingly or unknowingly by the actions of the others. Commerce becomes involved; so does state authority, and so might literary art, entertainment, scholarship, piety, polemic or instruction. Thinking about old books gives us access to traces of the past, and reminds us that new books embody concrete evidence of the practices of our own time.

The history of the book is a field of study with extraordinary academic and popular energy. Many readers, aware of the changes occurring in contemporary publishing and bookselling and of the digital reading experience, are newly intrigued by the Gutenberg moment and the ways in which print and writing were disseminated in earlier times. Undergraduates find book history an accessible introduction to literary and historical approaches to knowledge and culture. Scholars are discovering, or rediscovering, its specialized skills of paleography and bibliographical analysis. This *Cambridge Companion to the History of the Book* is addressed to general readers, to scholars seeking an overview and to university-level students. The aim is to offer a good high-quality, wide-ranging coverage of the topic, with up-to-date further reading ideas. Readers will learn that the history of the book is an interdisciplinary field of study. Some of the disciplines in question are: literatures in various languages; history and its sub-disciplines; bibliography (which may connect both to literatures and to rare-book librarianship); communication studies; cultural studies; digital humanities; publishing studies; library and information studies. Scholarship in these fields, as in most humanities and social science disciplines, has been challenged to interrogate its Eurocentric biases and aspire to be transnational and transcultural. While this *Companion* includes extensive discussion of western literatures, historiographies and bibliographies, the ambition has been to show the book, and people of the book, in global perspective. Chapters address the traditional European questions and methods, while demonstrating their particularity and difference from practices that have developed in other parts of the world, and the chronology and glossary address key events and complexities of terminology.

What is the book?

Despite its undisputed materiality, 'the book' is a more flexible and abstract conceptual category than many people imagine, and it is this very quality that makes it interesting. There were books before printing, and the manuscript practices that reproduced texts before the use of printing still flourish generations after Gutenberg. There were scrolls before codex volumes, and the scroll form, too, persisted in some cultures (it has metaphorically taken on a new life in the way we respond to digital texts on computer screens). Before there was paper, there were animal skins, papyrus rolls and clay tablets, and these and other surfaces continue to serve as the base, or substrate, to carry texts across the limits of time and space. The history of the book extends beyond the western alphabet, to many different kinds of marks on a material base, used in various cultures as a means of communicating knowledge or stories. *The book* is an awkward and ambiguous term by which to convey all this diversity, but it is the only one we have. Most dictionary definitions of 'the book' are, moreover, unabashedly Eurocentric and modern. The *Oxford Dictionaries Online*, for example, refers to 'a written or printed work, consisting of pages glued or sewn together along one side and bound in covers'. For the book historian, such a definition presents several problems. Not every book is a 'work', whether of literature or of some non-literary genre. Some of those pages glued or sewn together contain writing that does not fall within the purposeful-sounding parameters of the term, while other 'works' appear on pages (or on non-page supports) which are neither glued nor sewn, and which may be bound or bundled together, rolled or gathered up, in a bewildering range of ways. Unbound, its pages wrenched one from the others, its words spoken aloud or repurposed in digital form, a book is still a book – but what is that?

For the book historian, then, the dictionary definitions (which tend also to be the definitions commonly used in journalism and the popular culture) can be problematic. They refer only to the codex, a specific form of the book introduced in Europe in about the second century CE, which began to be challenged (although not defeated) in the second decade of the second millennium CE. When a text is loaded on a digital reading device, it remains a book, although not a codex. There were books before Gutenberg started printing with moveable type in central Europe – manuscript books where he lived and printed books in China and Korea. Since the eighteenth century, a magazine or journal, if not exactly a book because of its periodicity and hybridity, has been very much part of the book culture in which it is published. So has a pamphlet, a comic, a blank form or an edition of the sacred text of any one of the world's religions. In ancient India, a palm leaf could carry the text of a poem and the same poem can be published, collected and read in print. In central Canada, the wampum belt used by First Nations people to communicate memory and story was a book of sorts.[1] In Mesopotamia, the clay tablets that have survived (where other more fragile forms of writing got lost) are books too. And so are the papyrus sheets of the Nile Valley, the sheepskin vellum that made sense in Europe, and the rag-based paper first used in China. In one sense, the mission of the history of the book is to unsettle conventional definitions of its very subject.

The objective of the present volume is to help readers recognize the lineaments of book history. To that end, definitions in terms of research practice and scholarly findings may be of more utility than sketching the range of possible book forms and formats. In one sense, 'the history of the book' is a narrative constructed to emphasize change over historical time and hence an argument about the past. But the history of the book is also something more abstract: a way of thinking about how forces within the media culture of any era have acted upon the authors and compilers who produced the works that became books and periodicals during that era. The approach includes consideration of how those works were reshaped to make new books and periodicals for succeeding generations of readers. The history of the book is also a field of academic study, although it is not an autonomous academic discipline. It draws upon a range of literary, historical, bibliographical and social science approaches to do its work. Although none of the four aspects analysed below can be separated from any of the others, it is nevertheless useful to think of the book (and the periodical) as a text, an object, a transaction and an experience.

The book is a *text*, which may or may not be a literary work. Texts are the business of both authors and readers, and scholars have shown that the same text was interpreted differently by different readers. Literary criticism considers texts without necessarily assessing their social and economic context, but the history of the book makes a vital contribution to criticism. Scholars investigate what can be found about an author's intentions and about how those intentions were thwarted – or enhanced – by the actions of those who were involved in its production, multiplication and preservation. Editors interpolate; typesetters misprint; publishers consult the bottom line; and authors respond. Charles Dickens, for example, was once disparaged because he wrote for money, not for literary art. Robert L. Patten has shown, however, that Dickens's art was to create his own persona *as* the author, using (and modifying) the tools of the print culture emerging around him in early Victorian England.[2]

The book is a *material object*. From the literary and historical perspectives, the materiality of books is often overlooked, so powerful are their texts and the impacts of those texts upon their times. But bibliographical scholarship demonstrates that the book-as-object holds the evidence of its own making; it carries not only the obvious text on its pages but a further 'text' in its format, materials, design and impression. The periodical is also an object, whose material text reappears, repeatedly and systematically, bearing a different written text each time. Such design elements are sometimes called the 'paratext', a useful concept introduced by the literary theorist Gérard Genette. Paratextual elements (bindings, blurbs, design and so forth) supplied by editors and publishers can affect the meaning of the text they embellish. Moreover, since books are reprinted, reissued, edited and excerpted, pirated or plagiarized, they also contain the evidence of their remaking, and point to the agents of revision. It is the combination of textuality and materiality, perhaps unique among human-made artefacts, that gives the book its power to convey a sense of its past. The New Zealand and Oxford scholar D. F. McKenzie showed how a playwright's typographic disposition of his plays crucially affected the way in which eighteenth-century readers understood them. McKenzie spoke of bibliography as a kind of 'sociology of texts' – a way to embed the study of material texts in the human and social contexts from which those texts emerged and within which they circulated.[3] Bibliographical scholarship in practice is highly specialized, like the knowledge of physicists. But (like the knowledge of physicists) its findings can be interpreted for a lay audience; and (unlike most scientific knowledge) bibliographical scholarship is accessible to new practitioners in the form of workshops and master classes.

The book is a *cultural transaction* – a relationship of communication and exchange (often commercial exchange) that operates within a culture and a political economy. The concept of the book as a transaction includes the nexus between one reader and another, as well as the interplay between reader and writer implied in every act of reading.[4] It includes the agency of the book trades, a complex set of practices that can easily be overlooked because the names and roles of the agents have changed with shifts in materials and technologies. In Europe's middle ages, for example, the key figures in book culture were the stationer (who controlled the trade in materials and whose shop was an intellectual centre) and the scribe (whose scriptorium was set up to reproduce texts needed by the major institution of his time, the Church). For three centuries after Gutenberg, that key agent was the master printer, an entrepreneur and intellectual as well as a craftsman. A scientific, medical or literary author who wanted to ensure accurate reproduction of a text was careful to work closely with a trustworthy printer. In Britain and early America, the term 'bookseller' referred to a dominant entrepreneurial figure in the eighteenth century, but to a less powerful retailer later on. In the nineteenth century, when printing and papermaking were made cheaper and faster by new technologies, the key agent became the publisher; printers and booksellers were less influential, and the gateway was controlled by this new figure. The roles of both entrepreneurial publisher and retail bookseller are being challenged in the twenty-first century and it is unclear which agent has become the more powerful.

Another element in the concept of the book as a cultural transaction is the agency of librarians and other collectors, including the power of institutions such as libraries and archives to shape a tradition or define a heritage. Many more books and periodicals were published than have survived, and survival has often depended upon the decision to put something in a library – and keep it there.

Some scholars have adopted methodologies addressing a wide-ranging or 'macro' analysis to capture the role of books in social and cultural transactions. The Annales school of historians in mid-twentieth-century France introduced methodologies for tracking the numbers of titles, editions and copies in circulation of certain books. Aspects of this methodology for quantifying and visualizing the penetration of significant works into their cultures (sometimes called 'historical bibliometrics') have been adopted by scholars using database methodologies and continue to be remarkably fruitful.

The book is an *experience* – the reader, the collector and the scholar, in their different ways, all react emotionally as well as intellectually to the books in their purview. Such responses are based on material and commercial factors as well as factors associated with content and genre. Although reading is a private activity, leaving little trace on the historical record, its importance has led scholars to investigate the evidence that remains. Letters and diaries sometimes yield valuable insights into the response of actual readers. Another source for the responses of early-modern readers is the commonplace book and more generally the copying practice known as 'commonplacing'. H. J. Jackson has demonstrated how scholars can use the notes made by readers who used the margins of a book to converse with the author and (as it happens) with posterity.[5] To collect books can be a passion. Collectors range from the wealthy investor in incunables or first editions, to the Book-of-the-Month-Club member, to the adolescent 'book geek' who is keen to gather a full set of graphic novels. What collectors have in common is a response to books *as* books, with all their materiality, multiplicity and variability. They are moved by the replication of some specific, idiosyncratic amalgamation of text and object and respond by seeking to possess a complete set. Some aspects of the scholarship in the history of the book attempt to capture this elusive phenomenon, recognizing that intangible emotional responses may be part of the reason why the book form has survived for millennia as a medium of communication. And some of the new scholarship in the history of the emotions has used as evidence the sentimentality of literary genres arising in the eighteenth century.[6]

That the history of the book draws upon all four of these approaches may go some way to explain how difficult it has been clearly to define 'the book' in a few words. But people who think in terms of book history share two key principles: the book is mutable (both text and material format keep changing, and much of our scholarship serves to document those changes); and the book is the product of human agency (despite the importance of technological innovations and impersonal forces, what we are interested in is the way human beings have used those innovations and responded to those forces).

What is the history of the book?

The opening paragraph of this chapter defined the history of the book as 'a way of thinking about how people have given material form to knowledge and stories' in the past and in our own time. At least five aspects of this way of thinking can be identified, and serve to illustrate what these words really mean in everyday practice.

Chronology

The most conventional and straightforward approach to the history of the book might be to start at the beginning, continue to present time, and then stop – on either an up beat or a down beat according to one's level of optimism about the future. In Europe-based scholarship, that chronology most often begins with clay tablets in Mesopotamia and moves on to writing on papyrus, then parchment, then paper. The focus switches from writing surfaces to book formats, citing the transition from scroll to codex about the second century CE. Rather than unrolling a papyrus scroll, readers turned a parchment or paper page, and scribes began to leave spaces between the words. Scholars of premodern Europe regard this turning point as even more significant than the next one, from manuscript codex to printed codex, about 1450 in Mainz, Germany, personified in the compelling figure of Johannes Gutenberg.[7] For the next three and a half centuries, printing and publishing were adopted enthusiastically throughout Europe and the world, but with virtually no change to the mechanism of the hand press. That technology was robust enough to support 'the birth of the novel' in eighteenth-century Europe as well as a vast output of newspapers and other periodicals. A further transformation occurred in the first half of the nineteenth century, beginning in Britain, where printing and related trades became industrialized – paper was cheaper, and machine-made; bookbinding was mechanized; steam power was applied to the press, and publishers made use of steam-powered shipping by rail and sea to distribute their products worldwide.[8] Further technological innovations were introduced throughout the nineteenth and early twentieth centuries, most notably linotype and photocomposition. In the mid-twentieth-century decades the innovations applied to marketing, when paperback binding and mail-order book clubs acted to further commodify books that were aimed at a new 'middlebrow' readership.[9] In the first two decades of the twenty-first century, it is the e-book that seems to be a significantly different way of delivering words on the page. The page, however, remains virtually the same as it has been since the codex was introduced a millennium ago.

Whether oriented to substrates, materials or genres, these compelling and coherent (though oversimplified) chronologies highlight similarities as well as differences. But they are all Eurocentric. They do not allow for the history of the book in Asia, where pictographic writing systems have meant different developments in relation to printing and to genre. Nor do they apply to any situation where scholars want to take into account the writing or notation systems used by indigenous peoples.[10] And there is an inherent problem in the teleological notion of progress, which might seem to imply that something called 'the book' has 'evolved' from a primitive to a more sophisticated way of preserving knowledge and stories. Fortunately, the study of the history and culture of books complicates this sort of developmental paradigm, because it embeds changes in book form, technology and practice in the cultures where they were used.

A circuit of composition, mediation and production

Perhaps the most influential piece of writing in the study of book history is a 1982 article by the historian Robert Darnton, where he sketched out a 'communication circuit'. Impressed by the range of methodologies for approaching book history, but troubled by the tendency of interdisciplinarity to 'run riot', Darnton offered a tentative model. It showed the book moving around on an oval track from author, to publisher, to printer, then on to the shipper, then the bookseller (both wholesale and retail) and on to the reader. The reader, he argued, 'completes the circuit' because the writer is also a reader. It was a compelling way to capture the complexity of a book's trajectory through space and time, and to demonstrate the influence of the book trades on the way in which readers interpret the work of authors. Darnton's own research has focused on eighteenth-century France, and the circuit he drew reflected that time and place, but the circuit can be modified to illustrate the processes in use elsewhere.[11]

A number of scholars have critiqued Darnton's circuit diagram, recognizing that it still captures only a narrow slice of the life of a book. It fails, for example, to demonstrate the movement of a single text through decades and centuries, and among various textual and material forms. There is no way to show the interplay in a literary culture, between purists and profiteers, perhaps characterized in gender terms as men of letters and women who are mere 'scribblers'. Scholars who focus primarily on the book as a material object have criticized the abstract nature of the 'book' characterized by Darnton, substituting a 'map' that identified the five events in the life of a material book – publishing, manufacturing, distribution, reception and survival. Darnton himself, in a 2007 article, recognized this shortcoming, and also admitted that he hadn't left a space for the survival of the book as an object, collected and collectible, enduring in libraries.[12] But the strength of the original model remains its emphasis on human agency in the making and use of books, and its potential for showing the relationships between those two functions.

Disciplinary boundaries and interdisciplinary opportunities

Another way of characterizing the history of the book is by identifying the intellectual formation of the people who research and write about it. Many scholars in this field can be located in one of three disciplines and related perspectives. As delineated above, but now from the perspective of disciplines: bibliographers look at the book primarily as an object; literary scholars think of it in terms of text; while historians conceptualize the book as a cultural transaction. It can be difficult to integrate the circuit of authorship, publishing and reading with the three core disciplines, since each process can be approached through several disciplinary perspectives, and each discipline prioritizes the various processes in different ways. In any case, it is impossible to separate any of these three aspects of the book from either of the others. The bibliographical object and the literary text are two sides of the same coin, and when the book is conceptualized as is a transaction, the biblio-coin becomes a currency, used for exchange.[13] Every scholar whose work includes book history uses all three of these approaches, but the set of assumptions drawn from each person's core discipline is likely to dominate.

The contemporary culture of the book, however, is not the purview of those disciplines looking into the distant, or even the recent, past. Plenty of people want to know more about the authorship, publishing and reading of the books we read today. Certainly the insights of book history are relevant to the study of contemporary publishing, where the mutability of texts in contemporary society, and global media, is a dominant theme. The marketing of a phenomenon like J. K. Rowling's Harry Potter books is a case in point: a biographical narrative of the author made her an attractive figure; titles and stories were widely known to have been revised for a transatlantic audience; and the popularity of the series became inextricable for a time from pedagogical and parenting discourse about boys as readers. The disciplines looking at contemporary culture and communications have found the interplay of production and reception inherent in book history useful for studying such phenomena as the adaptation industry, and transmedial authorship.[14]

Categories, genres, formats

Another useful way to structure the history of the book is to think in terms of how works are categorized – by the trade, by librarians and by scholars. Such designations affect the way books are written, made public, received and preserved. From a literary perspective, the term 'genre' addresses some, but not all, of the variables. The original, classical, genres are poetry, drama and prose (the latter subdivided into numerous sub-genres). In the contemporary publishing business, however, 'genre' has become a term for categorizing books for the purposes of marketing. 'Genre fiction', for example, differentiates mystery, sci-fi, romance, fantasy and horror, while 'self help' and 'biography' are two of several forms of 'non-fiction'. For book historians, however, it is often more interesting to work with subject categories, looser groupings such as literature, science, history, philosophy etc. These subdivisions might perhaps be characterized as *genres of the material book*. The disciplinary proclivities of people who embrace the history of the book are often reflected in the categories of the books on which they work. In Anglo-North American book history concentrated on the modern period, the overwhelming majority of studies are about works of literature, by literary scholars; there is a substantial minority of impressive monographs about scientific books and periodicals, by historians of science; a handful of studies, by historians, discuss the publishing history of history books, but few scholars have focused as yet on philosophy or mathematics as book-historical categories. Another category, again sometimes called a genre, is the material format in which a text appears. Such labels may relate to the anticipated readership or target market of the book: some of the distinctions include hardcover (versus paperback) edition; trade (as opposed to mass-market) paperback; comic book (versus graphic novel); various kinds of periodical (as opposed to monographs); and manuscript book (versus print-book or e-book). Scholarship in the history of the book is attentive to the ways in which historical actors, both producers and consumers, thought in their time about how books were categorized.

National and transnational approaches

To scholars oriented to national canons of literature in particular languages, and to national historical narratives, it has been of compelling interest to study the history of the book from the perspective of one country. Following the lead of the history of publishing in France appearing in 1986, national libraries, major publishers and prominent scholars initiated ambitious projects to chart the trajectories of the book in Britain, the US, Ireland, Scotland, Canada and Australia, to name a few. In most cases, a combination of chronological and thematic approaches was adopted, and strenuous efforts were made to fill lacunae in the research record. The bibliographical record associated with each national library was a key source document, as were the archives of publishers and the records left by authors and readers, libraries and booksellers. The similarities revealed by this new canon of book historiography are striking; but the differences are more interesting. The practices of composing, making, distributing and reading books have differed from one place to another and those variations derive from differences of geography, population and economy. Still, the national approach forced researchers to ask a new question. In an industry where the raw materials, the producers, the products and the customers all routinely cross national boundaries constantly, why should 'nation' be the paradigm in any case? Transnational and postcolonial approaches began to yield rich results, such as Isabel Hofmeyr's study of how that quintessentially English book, Bunyan's *Pilgrim's Progress*, attained its status in England as a result of how it was read and used in Africa. It became apparent that the nation state approach is also about theory, a theory of nationalism. Many scholars, both within and outside the history of the book world, have been strongly influenced by Benedict Anderson's idea, that readers form an 'imagined community' whereby they define themselves in national terms because they think of themselves as reading the same novel, or the same newspaper, as someone else in the same town, or the same country. Now the book history approach is being used to critique Anderson's compelling ideas.

The chapters that follow have been commissioned to showcase the history of the book in the way that scholars have come to understand the subject in the twenty-first century. Part I considers book cultures from the local, national and global perspectives, beginning with books in the library, where collections and individual volumes are preserved, catalogued and made accessible (Chapter 2 by Karen Attar). At the level of countries, the historiographies of printing, of the nation state and of modernity itself have become fused in a compelling but problematic narrative that has become book history's task to rewrite (Chapter 3 by Trish Loughran). Moving out to the transnational level that transcends nation and yet embraces locality, a focus upon the book's habit of travelling across the boundaries of time and space (undergoing transformation as it goes) has been captured in a challenging new model of 'situated knowledges' (Chapter 4 by Sydney Shep).

Part II is roughly chronological, with its seven chapters organized around the dynamic relationship between the material book and the mutable text. The first fundamental question concerns the way in which the surfaces (or substrates) upon which text is preserved – and the formats in which such materials are arranged – have worked over the centuries to convey meaning (Chapter 5 by Peter Stoicheff). Next comes handwriting, which in relation to the history of the book includes the persistence of manuscript as an effective medium of publication, not only in the European context before Gutenberg but in certain cultures long afterwards, indeed until the present day (Chapter 6 by Margaret Ezell). The coming of print to Europe appears midway through the volume, and the remarkable experiments made by Gutenberg are balanced against the equally important narrative of the means by which his contemporaries came to terms with the new technology (Chapter 7 by Adrian Johns). The following chapter lingers in the early-modern period to emphasize the dual character of the new 'print culture' in early-modern Europe, where the new medium undeniably exercised institutional authority but at the same time enabled subversive ideas (Chapter 8 by Cyndia Clegg). The industrial revolution of the book incorporated not only the new technologies that appeared in the nineteenth century, but also the new management processes that began to be established during the eighteenth century (Chapter 9 by James Raven). The book in the long twentieth century found publishers discovering and coming to terms with the complexities of intellectual property law and the possibilities associated with conceptualizing the book as a marketable commodity (Chapter 10 by Alistair McCleery). And bringing the study of the book up to present-day concerns, the scholarship of book history, working in collaboration with that of digital humanities, is helping us to understand the e-book (Chapter 11 by Jon Bath and Scott Schofield).

The study of book history is full of promise and excitement, but it is also rigorous and exacting, because much of the scholarship is based on the interpretation of empirical evidence. Part III is concerned with methods, sources and approaches to book history. The chapter on book history from descriptive bibliographies introduces a highly technical field of study from the perspective of the user, in order to help students of book history to interpret these useful (but often challenging) resources (Chapter 12 by Michael Suarez). Bibliographical analysis is crucially important because, often, the book itself contains all the evidence that survives about its own making. The essay on book history from the archival record, however, offers practical advice to the researcher who has either author–publisher correspondence or book-trade statistics to deal with (Chapter 13 by Katherine Bode and Roger Osborne). If it seems difficult to find evidence for the idiosyncrasies of printers, or of the motives of publishers, how much harder must it be to discover the responses of readers? Researchers have learned how to read the margins, as well as engaging with other evidence of the reading experience (Chapter 14 by Mary Hammond). And because none of this rich scholarship will survive unless it is conveyed to the next generation in a meaningful and attractive way, the final chapter examines the question of teaching and learning the history of the book (Chapter 15 by Leslie Howsam).

The book you are reading has a history, too, commissioned as it was as part of the reputable and popular series of *Cambridge Companions*. That commission, and the investment behind it, itself indicates the significance of this field of study in the second decade of the twenty-first century. It is the editor's book as well as the publisher's – another authority in the field might have designed a very different plan for a volume on the same subject. Each chapter was instigated by an invitation to contribute to the editor's larger design, and shaped by the publisher's guidelines, but at the same time each speaks with the contributor's individual voice. The *Cambridge Companion* does not claim to be exhaustive, or to offer the final word on the subject. Rather, it seeks to engage vigorously in the conversation that is the history of the book.

NOTES

1. G. Warkentin, 'In Search of "The Word of the Other": Aboriginal Sign Systems and the History of the Book in Canada', *Book History* 2 (1999), 1–27.
2. R. L. Patten, *Charles Dickens and 'Boz': The Birth of the Industrial-Age Author* (Cambridge University Press, 2012).

3. D. F. McKenzie, 'Typography and Meaning: The Case of William Congreve', in P. D. McDonald and M. F. Suarez (eds.), *Making Meaning: 'Printers of the Mind' and Other Essays* (Amherst: University of Massachusetts Press, 2002), 198–236. See also McKenzie's *Bibliography and the Sociology of Texts* (Cambridge University Press, 1999, first published by the British Library 1986).
4. L. Howsam, 'Book History Unbound: Transactions of the Written Word Made Public', *Canadian Journal of History* (April 2003), 69–81.
5. H. J. Jackson, *Marginalia: Readers Writing in Books* (New Haven: Yale University Press, 2001).
6. W. Reddy, *The Navigation of Feeling: A Framework for the History of the Emotions* (Cambridge University Press, 2001), 325.
7. R. Chartier, 'Frenchness in the History of the Book: From the History of Publishing to the History of Reading', *Proceedings of the American Antiquarian Society* 97:2 (1987), 310.
8. A. Fyfe, *Steam-Powered Knowledge: William Chambers and the Business of Publishing, 1820–1860* (University of Chicago Press, 2012), 55–64, 79–87.
9. J. Radway, *A Feeling for Books: The Book-of-the-Month Club, Literary Taste, and Middle-Class Desire* (Chapel Hill: University of North Carolina Press, 1997).
10. G. Warkentin, 'Dead Metaphor or Working Model? "The Book" in Native America', in M. Cohen and J. Glover (eds.), *Colonial Mediascapes: Sensory Worlds of the Early Americas* (Lincoln: University of Nebraska Press, Spring 2014), 50–82.
11. R. Darnton, 'What Is the History of Books?', *Dædalus* 111:3 (1982), 65–83. Reprinted with slight variations in *The Kiss of Lamourette: Reflections in Cultural History* (New York: W. W. Norton and Co., 1990), 107–35.
12. For the various models, see L. Howsam, *Old Books and New Histories: An Orientation to Studies in Book and Print Culture* (University of Toronto Press, 2006). R. Darnton, '"What Is the History of Books?" Revisited', *Modern Intellectual History* 4:3 (2007), 495–508.
13. Howsam, *Old Books and New Histories* and 'The Practice of Book and Print Culture: Sources, Methods, Readings', in E. Patten and J. McElligott (eds.), *The Perils of Print Culture: Book, Print and Publishing History in Theory and Practice* (Houndmills, Basingstoke: Palgrave Macmillan, 2014), 17–34.
14. S. Murray, *The Adaptation Industry: The Cultural Economy of Contemporary Literary Adaptation* (New York: Routledge, 2011).

PART I

Book cultures, local, national and global

2

KAREN ATTAR

Books in the library

Books in a library differ fundamentally from books anywhere else in that each one is part of a collection, an aggregation that imposes its own meaning derived from the decisions and accidents that went into its formation. Administration is an essential part of the difference, as librarians acquire, describe and arrange books, and make them available to multiple users. Still more crucial is the survival and transmission of knowledge which can extend far beyond the life of the individual library; when this knowledge is lost, the sense of cultural devastation is palpable. This chapter explores some aspects of these institutions, from the ancient world to the present day. It is based primarily on western (especially British) libraries, with particular emphasis on national and large academic libraries. These are the repositories with the largest numbers of books and the greatest responsibility for preservation. While technological progress renders a certain focus on the modern period inevitable, an historical perspective reveals that the basic principles of collection, preservation and the provision of access have transcended time and space.

Storage

The earliest libraries consisted of clay tablets kept on shelves, sometimes in receptacles (as in jars in Ashurbanipal's library in Nineveh in the seventh century BCE). The papyrus rolls forming the books in ancient Egyptian libraries were kept on open shelves or in pigeonholes in storage areas. The Romans introduced the armarium ('chest') as a receptacle for books used well into the Middle Ages. These were cupboards divided vertically and horizontally to house rolls, or by horizontal shelves only for codices, the norm from the fourth century CE. Books lay on their sides. With the increase in the size of libraries in the fourteenth or fifteenth century, sometimes from a few hundred to a few thousand books – a process encouraged by the advent of printing in the 1450s – armaria gave way to library rooms; some early-fifteenth-century purpose-built libraries were at Bayeux, York and

Rouen Cathedrals. The standard late medieval ecclesiastical and academic library, intended for books and readers, was rectangular, three or four times longer than it was wide, with high ceilings and large, high windows to maximise natural light, and stone walls, floor and ceiling to protect against fire. Libraries were on upper floors to protect against damp and floods. Books were kept on lecterns, or sloping desks, on spaces between the windows, perpendicular to the side walls, on either side of a central aisle. Some lecterns had a shelf approximately nine inches below the desk and/or a narrow shelf at the top to accommodate books. In some places such as Cambridge and Leiden, and generally in France, readers stood to read; elsewhere (notably Zutphen in the Netherlands) they sat on benches, with one or two benches between each pair of desks. Books were chained, attached to a bar at the top of the desk, and were kept facing outwards. Following the lectern system came the stall system, similar except that books were kept on short double-faced bookcases above the desktop (which might be hinged), with books beneath and benches at which to sit between.

The 'wall system' of bookcases against walls, allowing more storage, began at the Escorial Library in Spain (completed in 1584) and was soon adopted throughout Europe; in England, the eastern wing of Oxford's Bodleian Library (completed 1612) was an early example. Unchaining in Britain and concomitant storage of books with their spines outwards occurred largely by the second half of the eighteenth century. Some books still show how they were stored by signs of chaining where a staple was removed or by a title written on the fore-edge.

Selection and acquisition

The kinds of books in libraries vary according to aspiration and purpose. The desire to collect comprehensively dates back millennia. Ashurbanipal in ancient Mesopotamia, the Ptolemies at the Alexandrian Library (fl. *c.* 300 BCE–*c.* CE 270), the royal library in Cordoba in Muslim Spain (founded in approximately CE 850), Pope Nicholas V, founder of the Vatican Library, Charlemagne at Aachen and Sir Thomas Bodley in Oxford, all sent emissaries across Europe or (for the ancient libraries) the known world in quest of texts. Medieval monasteries contained primarily religious works, with the emphasis depending on the order (for example, church fathers and Franciscan commentaries in Franciscan libraries; sermons, canon law and rhetoric in libraries of the mendicant orders), and some practical ones (medicine, agriculture and so forth) required for the everyday administration of the monastery. Medieval academic libraries typically held works of grammar, logic, rhetoric, theology, medicine, law, philosophy, astronomy and some science, including mathematics. Both types of institutions contained primarily works in Latin. Since the Middle Ages, school and parish libraries have existed, as have professional and special libraries – for law, for medicine, for heraldry – to serve specific groups. Fee-paying subscription and circulating libraries originated in the eighteenth century. Commercial circulating libraries dealt chiefly in fiction (and were sometimes reviled for their demoralizing influence); subscription libraries were more serious, with titles in politics, religion, natural sciences and philosophy. Later, municipal libraries stocked both fiction and non-fiction, with frequent tension between the demands of education and entertainment. Some countries developed libraries to serve ideological purposes: Russian public libraries in the twentieth century were intended to inculcate the ideals of Communism, and German public ones during the Third Reich to further National Socialist views.

Books in libraries have not always been those that were wanted. Much acquisition in the manuscript period was by copying, which implies choice, and, much later, members of subscription libraries pooled resources to select what they wanted to buy. But most libraries were largely donation-driven until well into the nineteenth century; the university library at Göttingen in the eighteenth century was exceptional precisely for its purchasing capacity, with an acquisitions budget of 400 Taler a year from its foundation in 1737. Victorian British public libraries were as badly placed in this respect as academic libraries on both sides of the Atlantic, as the acquisition and upkeep of buildings devoured the available funds. Bequests were likely to be a generation behind scholarship.

Single major gifts or purchases frequently created or transformed important libraries: the Bibliothèque Mazarine in Paris, based on the personal collection of Cardinal Mazarin; the Biblioteca Marciana in Venice, based on the founding collection of Cardinal Bessarion; the Staatsbibliothek zu Berlin (State Library of Berlin), from the library of Frederick William, Great Elector of Brandenburg; the Sloane, Harley, Cotton and Royal collections at the British Library; the personal library of Thomas Jefferson at the Library of Congress, to name just a few. Early public libraries absorbed the entire holdings of mechanics' institute libraries.

The significance of books in libraries changes over time, as the content moves from up-to-date knowledge about a subject to sources for the history of that subject. Books now valued as history were once discarded as merely out-of-date. Manuscripts which were once carriers of knowledge are now preserved in libraries as artefacts and are studied for their paleographical, codicological, art historical or transmission value. Incunabula, also originally carriers of knowledge, have since the seventeenth century been acquired rather as specimens of early printing: fine collections of incunabula at the university libraries of

Oxford and Cambridge result not from century-long survival, but from aggressive purchasing in the nineteenth century. German National Socialist textbooks acquired for doctrinal purposes have now become historical witnesses to the Third Reich and warnings to future generations.

Access

The book in the library is a shared resource, open to members of a particular geographical area from parish to national level, professional or religious group, educational establishment, or other community or (for subscription libraries) those able and willing to pay. Access has never meant unrestricted or unlimited access. Lack of full-time library staff and reliance on natural light (for the centuries when artificial light depended on flame and was a fire hazard) combined to limit opening hours to only a few hours a day or even week. As an extreme instance, rules for Harvard (America's largest college library during the colonial period) from 1769 decreed that the library was to be open 9.00–11.00 on Fridays, with students entering singly. Commercial circulating libraries in Britain, on the other hand, opened for up to twelve hours a day, precisely because they were business ventures and the books commodities. By the end of the nineteenth century, most American college libraries (but not European university ones) were open for six or seven days a week from morning to night. Evening opening access was essential in taxpayer-supported public libraries, whose working-class clientele could not visit otherwise. Moreover, numerous libraries from antiquity onwards have been, at least in part, reference rather than circulating collections. Loan conditions have not been generous, as when medieval English Benedictine monks, in accordance with decrees handed down by Archbishop Lanfranc around 1070, borrowed a single book for a year at a time, exchanging books formally on a designated day. Political factors have hindered access and research, as when the progress of the *Gesamtkatalog der Wiegendrucke*, based in East Berlin, was crippled between 1940 and 1972 through world war and the Iron Curtain. The e-book has revolutionized access by enabling multiple simultaneous use of a single volume.

Sharing resources extends beyond single loans. The monastery at Fulda, founded in CE 744, lent numerous manuscripts to monasteries in France and Germany. An official system of interlibrary loan existed in the US and Canada from 1876, Italy from 1879, Prussia from 1893 and internationally from 1937. Linked with interlibrary loan is cooperative acquisition, whereby libraries maximize resources by a group of libraries deciding that each will specialize in certain areas and borrow from the others. Mass digitization projects of library holdings are a significant way of sharing books and knowledge of book history. Major projects include Early English Books Online (EEBO), of books printed in the English language or in English-speaking countries to 1700 (1998) and its continuation to 1800, Eighteenth-Century Collections Online (ECCO, 2003), both subscription databases based on the holdings of multiple libraries; mass digitization projects agreed between Google, Inc. and major American and British libraries; and the Bayerische Staatsbibliothek's undertaking to digitize all its incunabula, the world's largest collection of fifteenth-century books in terms of copies. Apart from the obvious benefit of providing access to numerous early texts and their layout, such databases enable comparison between a copy in hand and the digitized one, thereby exposing variations in early printing. They do not replace actual books because they cannot reproduce physical features such as watermarks, and do not always reproduce features they could, such as preliminary leaves showing evidence of provenance. Moreover, images are of one copy only: other copies may vary in elements ranging from mispagination or ornaments to the replacement of text, as when a description of scriveners being 'so rude, grosse, clownish, ignorant, that you would wonder', and one in particular being a 'rich vilaine, without learning, ciuilitie, humanitie & courtesie, whose face sheweth that he is always shiting' (copy at Senate House Library, University of London) turns with the substitution of a gathering to a commendation of M. X., 'a verie skilfull man in his trade' (the Harvard copy, reproduced by EEBO).[1]

An implication of books as a shared resource is a long-standing need to ensure socially acceptable treatment through rules and curses against theft, mutilation or the over-long retention of books. As long ago as 668–627 BCE, tablets in Ashurbanipal's library bore threats such as: 'Whoever removes [this tablet ...], may Ashur and Ninlil, angered and grim, cast him down, erase his name, his seed, in the land'.[2] Library rules attached to front pastedowns may testify to a book's past. Marks of institutional ownership are a security measure helpful in tracing provenance, from the manuscript 'ex dono' or 'ex libris' to bookplates, known from late-fifteenth-century Germany, and blind and ink stamps. Further sophistication may apply: the colour of British Museum stamps indicated whether a book was acquired by legal deposit (blue), gift (mostly brown or yellow) or purchase (red or black, depending on the year).

Cataloguing

A large collection of books requires a key to what is there and where. Libraries have catalogued their holdings since ancient times, as shelf-lists on walls, as at the library at Edfu in Egypt, or on clay tablets, as kept by the Mesopotamians: two lists of brief titles have been found at Nippur, dating to approximately 2000 BCE. By the thirteenth century BCE records sometimes noted the extent of a work, as evinced by catalogues found at Hattasus, e.g.:

'Three tablets on the spring festival of the city of Hurma [...] First and second tablet missing'.[3] Medieval catalogues were essentially similar, starting as brief lists of titles arranged by subject, author or donor. The late-twelfth-century catalogue of Christ Church, Canterbury, was the first to include location symbols. Thirteenth- and fourteenth-century catalogues recorded the opening words (incipits). Following a practice employed at Dover (1389) and Durham (1391), it soon became common for medieval catalogues to record the opening words on the second leaf of a manuscript ('secundo folio'), to identify a book if the first leaf had been lost, and to differentiate between different copies of the same text. Physical features, such as decoration, were sometimes also recorded to assist identification. A subject arrangement predominated. Catalogues of printed books were short-title catalogues, stating the author, title, edition, place and date of publication and format. Short-title catalogues arranged by subject or author, depending on preference, remained the norm until the end of the nineteenth century.

The French government issued the first national set of cataloguing rules in 1791. The British Museum Cataloguing rules devised by Anthony Panizzi (1841), Charles Ammi Cutter's *Rules for a Dictionary Catalog* in the US (1876) and the Preussische Instruktionen in Germany (1899) followed and helped to standardize descriptions between libraries, especially when instructions intended for one library were adopted by others. Globalization began with the issue of the first edition of the Anglo-American Rules in 1908, and leaped forward with Paris Principles of 1961 and the International Standard Bibliographic Description (ISBD), the first volume of which, for monographs, appeared in 1971. ISBD was the standard behind the various national cataloguing codes. It introduced international library punctuation, such as a colon between the place of publication and the name of the publisher in the imprint, so that users could discern the elements making up a book description without comprehending a particular language.

Catalogues were normally printed until the late nineteenth century, when, except for catalogues of manuscripts, the guard-book catalogue, sheaf catalogue and ultimately the card catalogue took over. The printed catalogue became a more specialist feature for subsets of library collections such as books of a certain age or printed in a certain country, like the series of short-title catalogues for books of various European countries printed to 1600 in the British Library, books acquired by a particular collector or books on a certain subject. The later-nineteenth-century dictionary catalogue merged subject and author into a single sequence. Automation from the late 1960s led to online public access catalogues (OPACs) from the 1980s which rendered arrangement redundant, as searching could be by multiple index points – subject, author, title, classmark or (where relevant) International Standard

Bibliographic Number (ISBN) – or by keyword. Moreover, the computer screen ended the restriction for descriptions to fit on to a card typically measuring three by five inches and thus allowed for much more detail. Inevitably much of this detail pertained to the history even of machine-press books, such as when the previous edition appeared, and whether the book was a translation.

In the 1990s a drive began in Anglo-American libraries to emphasize copy-specific features of older books, such as provenance, bindings and annotations. The new practice was clear in the level of copy-specific detail both in printed catalogues such as the three-volume *Catalogue of Scandinavian Books in the British Library Printed before 1801* (2007) and Lotte Hellinga's *Catalogue of Books Printed in the XVth Century Now in the British Library. BMC Part XI: England* (2006), and especially electronically. It transformed the function of the library catalogue. Hitherto the functions of a library catalogue had been those defined by the Harvard librarian Charles Ammi Cutter in 1876: to enable a user to find a known item, or to see what was in a library in what edition by a given author or on a given topic. Now the provision of extra details, combined with sophisticated electronic search methods, enabled the library catalogue itself to be used as a research tool. For example, the indexing of former owners enabled the reconstitution of dispersed libraries. It also made possible analyses of a particular owner's books by subject, date, author or even (depending on the level of copy-specific detail supplied in the catalogue and the application of vocabulary control) by how many of his books he annotated. Provided that libraries had entered the information, readers could furthermore locate publishers' advertisements and ascertain such things as what books had been given as Victorian school prizes, or how different copies of the *Eikon Basilike* were bound as an indication of how owners regarded them. The mere availability of online records revealed knowledge hitherto buried in printed or card catalogues about the history of books, particularly with respect to dating: for example, we can date Pablo de Santa Maria's *Scrutinium Scriptarium* (ISTC ip00201000) to 'not after 1470' on the basis of a rubricator's date on the copy held by Eichstätt University Library.

The concept of shared cataloguing emerged in the seventeenth century, when interleaved copies of the 1674 Bodleian Library catalogue were printed as a starting point for custodians of other libraries to create their own by annotating what they had and adding books held which were not in the Bodleian. Implicit was a notion of excellence and comprehensiveness against which other libraries could match themselves. In 1901 the Library of Congress in Washington, by then America's legal deposit library, began to sell cards of its holdings to other libraries in a large-scale effort of cooperative cataloguing; other libraries could simply add their own classmarks. The development of the machine-readable cataloguing (MARC) computer format in 1967–8, a division of the elements of book description into fields and subfields that enabled international sharing of catalogue records, revolutionized cooperative cataloguing. The introduction of the world wide web was a further revolution, and OPACs are now the norm.

Realization that it was useful to have an overview of the contents of several libraries together came by the thirteenth century, when the Cistercian abbey of Savigny listed the holdings of four other libraries in Normandy as well as its own. A particularly ambitious medieval union catalogue is the early-fourteenth-century *Registrum Librorum Angliae*, a list by Oxford Franciscans of the holdings of ninety monasteries in England, Scotland and Wales; John Boston of Bury added twenty new libraries in the early fifteenth century. Only in the twentieth century did printed catalogues (now also available online) attempt this again – the *Gesamtkatalog der Wiegendrucke*, begun in 1904; *A Short-Title Catalogue of Books Printed in England, Scotland, and Ireland and of English Books Printed Abroad, 1475–1640* by Alfred Pollard and G. R. Redgrave (first edition 1926), based on the holdings of four main libraries, but with additions from nearly 150 more; and later the *Verzeichnis der im Deutschen Sprachbereich erschienenen Drucke des 16. Jahrhunderts*, started in 1969 and taking the holdings of 152 libraries in eight countries into account. The advent of computerized cataloguing facilitated union catalogues: Copac in the UK, launched in 1996; the Catalogue Collectif de France (1997); the Online Computer Library Center (OCLC)'s WorldCat (1971); and the Research Libraries Information Network (RLIN, founded in 1980 and merged in 2006 with WorldCat) in the US. An outstanding example is Germany's Karlsruher Virtueller Katalog (1996), which in addition to allowing a search across libraries in German-speaking countries provides a portal for the union catalogues of other countries. In the most global manifestation of the union catalogue, books in libraries merge to form international bibliographies, such as the Incunabula Short Title Catalogue (ISTC, istc.bl.uk) begun in 1980 and the English Short-Title Catalogue (ESTC, estc.bl.uk) of books printed either in the English language or in English-speaking countries to 1800, begun as the Eighteenth-Century Short-Title Catalogue in 1976 and extended in 1987 to include earlier books.

Yet in addition to divulging the history of books, in some ways libraries obscure it. Catalogues invariably include a degree of librarianly interpretation, old printed ones by paucity of detail, newer ones by certain rules. Unlike bibliographies, library catalogues make no attempt to reproduce the appearance of a title page. Although specific rules for early printed books dictate accounting for every page in a volume, more general codes ignore unnumbered pages. Until 2007, the main Anglo-American code for early printed books,

Descriptive Cataloging of Rare Books (DCRB), recommended recording the date of publication in arabic numerals, whether or not it was in roman numerals on a title page; ISTC similarly interprets dates by standardizing those expressed in the publication in terms of a saint's day. Most rules provide for omitting the names of publishers after the first or third in a publishing syndicate, for omitting publishers' addresses given in imprints and for omitting the qualifications or other information about an author given on a title page. Libraries do not necessarily indicate when their copy of a title is a reprint, although reprints enhance our knowledge of book history, indicating popularity and sometimes evincing non-textual changes such as a price increase or new dustwrapper design. Catalogues are liable to confuse authors with identical names living at the same time, such as Edward Edwards, the pioneer of English public libraries (1812–86) and his contemporary Edward Edwards, a compositor. Retrospective cataloguing, namely the keying in of catalogue records or copying of other electronic catalogue records from sketchy card descriptions, can result in the wrong book appearing on the catalogue, especially in the case of variant editions. Copy-cataloguing perpetuates mistakes, as one library uncritically adopts erroneous records produced by another.

Libraries can obscure the history of books in other ways, such as by removing dustwrappers (which can contain advertisements and information not recorded elsewhere in the publication), rebinding books or pasting bookplates over indications of previous ownership. Private collections have been dispersed when entering institutional libraries. The books in libraries are not always the books as they entered libraries: institutional owners follow the practices of private owners in binding discrete items together for convenience, and composite volumes have been broken up, for example, to separate manuscripts from printed texts.

Classification

Like cataloguing, library classification has been practised, albeit crudely, since ancient times. Ashurbanipal (r. 668–627 BCE) is known to have kept a different subject in each room of his library. Roman libraries divided their stock into two sections by language, Latin and Greek. In the Middle Ages, books were classified broadly by subject, sometimes including those of the medieval university curriculum, the trivium (grammar, logic, rhetoric) and quadrivium (arithmetic, geometry, music, astronomy). This could be in simplified form: when the Bodleian Library opened in 1602, it did so with books in four categories – theology, law, medicine and arts – divided by size. Within broad subjects, books might be arranged alphabetically by author, as in Roman libraries, or subdivided hierarchically by the perceived level of importance. A shelfmark system predominated. Bookcases were lettered, with subjects grouped together under a particular letter, and books were assigned numbers according to their position on the shelf: for example, H.2.4 indicated the fourth book on the second shelf of bookcase H. Such shelfmarks can still be found in parts, at least, of some major libraries, perhaps most famously among the Cottonian manuscripts in the British Library, where each bookcase was known by the bust of the Roman emperor which adorned it, such that the *Beowulf* manuscript, for example, has the shelfmark Cotton Vitellius A.xv. When they can be traced to particular libraries, old shelfmarks are a valuable element of provenance research.

Classification as we know it, whereby broad subject areas are divided and subdivided and books are assigned codes which describe their relationship to each other rather than a fixed point on a shelf, began in the third quarter of the nineteenth century. It became prevalent in conjunction with the increase of open access to shelves in public libraries from the 1890s to facilitate subject browsing. (Previously readers had selected books from catalogues.) The first classification system to be published was the Dewey Decimal Classification, devised by the American Melvil Dewey for the library at Amherst, Massachusetts, which appeared in forty-two pages (twelve each of introductory material and tables and an eighteen-page index) in 1876. It was a numerical system which divided knowledge into ten broad classes, broken down further by tens: for example, 000 'Computer science, information and general works'; 090 'Manuscripts and rare books'; 092 'block books'. Dewey's system rapidly became popular. A second edition, expanded to 486 pages, was published in 1885; the twenty-third edition was published in four volumes in 2011. Classification helped to internationalize books in libraries: whereas with a shelfmark system the notation for a particular book would be unique to the holding library, a book classified by a particular scheme would theoretically have the same classmark (or call number) as the same book classified by that scheme anywhere else in the world. By 1927, when a *Survey of the Libraries of the United States* was published, Dewey's system was employed in 96 per cent of American public libraries and 89 per cent of college and university ones. The system reached the UK by 1878, when it was adopted by the National Library of Ireland and, by the time of the 1927 survey, was thought to be used in more than five hundred libraries in England. Today it is the most prevalent system in the world, used in more than 200,000 libraries in 135 countries. The Universal Decimal System, developed in Belgium, first published in 1904–7, and used in some 125 countries, derives from it. The Library of Congress developed an in-house alphanumeric system of classification with twenty-one main classes from 1897, proposing a provisional outline and beginning publication in 1901. First used in Britain by the National Library of Wales in 1913, it, too, is now used worldwide, especially in national and academic libraries. Smaller classification schemes have distinguished books nationally. Two faceted classification schemes, S. R. Ranganathan's Colon Classification (1933) and the second edition of the Bliss Bibliographic Classification (of which the first volume was published in 1977) have been welcomed as theoretical developments, but are applied almost exclusively in Ranganathan's native India and in England (the country where the Bliss system was developed) respectively.

Use

The importance of cataloguing and classification is that they facilitate use, for it is in being used that books gain their meaning. While private collectors such as Robert Cotton in Britain and Cardinal Mazarin in France have opened their libraries to scholars, it is primarily the book in the institutional library that has had a major impact on knowledge and research from the earliest times onwards. Callimachus used the library at Alexandria to compile his extensive bio-bibliographical *Pinakes*, 'Tables of Persons Eminent in every Branch of Learning, together with a List of their Writings', covering all Greek writings. Multiple holdings of the writings of Homer were used at the Alexandrian library to compile what was considered to be the definitive account. Jerome in the late fourth century CE used the early Christian library at Caesarea to write his Latin Vulgate and other works. Bede relied upon the monastery libraries of Wearmouth and Jarrow in the eighth century to compose his *Ecclesiastical History of England*. The scholar-printer Aldus Manutius based many of his early-fifteenth-century Greek classics on manuscripts from the Biblioteca Marciana in Venice. Karl Marx did much of his research and writing in the round Reading Room of the British Museum Library. Institutional library holdings are the basis for retrospective national bibliographies, and to a large extent for censuses of specific works detailing the history of copies of texts as diverse as Shakespeare's First Folio, the Kelmscott Chaucer and the first and second editions of Copernicus's *De Revolutionibus*, the latter based on the holdings of libraries in thirty-one countries. A list of eminent users of the British Museum Library provides a glimpse into the research value of institutional libraries, with names ranging from the philosophers David Hume and Jeremy Bentham to the historian Edward Gibbon, mathematician Charles Babbage and economist Walter Bagehot.[4]

Acknowledgements in numerous monographs and the access provided by edition or other reissue of printed books and manuscripts from institutional holdings indicate further use. A rich example for the English-speaking world is the edition of Chaucer's *Canterbury Tales* (1775) by Thomas Tyrwhitt, considered to be the founder of modern Chaucer editing: of the twenty-six manuscripts he consulted for his text, nine were at the British Library, six at the Bodleian Library, one at New College Oxford, two at Cambridge University Library and two at Trinity College, Cambridge. It is when books reach institutional libraries, moreover, that historians of reading are enabled to see how famous intellectuals have interacted with them through marginal notes, scribbled legally before the books became institutional property or illegally afterwards. Examples include Thomas Carlyle's notes on his books about Oliver Cromwell and Frederick the Great (at Harvard University) and Martin Heidegger's on books at the University of Freiburg.

Wider implications of libraries

Reading and research are the *raison d'être* of books in libraries, but their impact is more widespread. The book in the library has had, and continues to exert, an influence on publishing patterns. Most notably, the circulating libraries' support of the three-volume novel in Victorian Britain enabled its continuation after the single volume became common: when Mudie's and Smith's decided in 1894 to stop purchasing the so-called three-decker, it collapsed. The decision by Mudie's to buy or not to buy a novel in bulk could make or mar an author's prospects. American school district libraries originated in New York State in 1838 and acquired 400,000 books over three years, providing several publishers with a ready market for cheap books which the publishers sold on commission through local representatives. Sales of scholarly monographs and journals today are driven by the academic institutional market. The social impact of books can be yet wider: the historian George Grote, Vice-Chancellor of the University of London from 1862 to 1871, used the regular presence of 'a considerable number of females' reading and writing in the British Museum library to argue in 1862 that women should be permitted to take University of London degrees, an innovation finally agreed in 1877 which made his University the trailblazer of tertiary education for women in England.[5] Arguments for and against the establishment of public libraries supported by the taxpayer in England focused on such factors as the power of the book to stir up discontent among the working classes on one hand and its ability to educate them and entice them away from less salubrious haunts (public houses) on the other; the same arguments that were used across Europe for and against the inculcation of literacy.

Moreover, books in libraries confer status on authors, on collections and on library owners. For classical authors, acceptance of works they donated was a sign of validation, much as authors donate their books to libraries today to promulgate them and thereby enhance their reputations and (depending on the retention policy of the library) to immortalize themselves. Conversely, exclusion from a library was a mark of social disapproval, demonstrated when the Roman poet Ovid, banished from Rome to Tŏmis, lamented the removal of his works from the public libraries of Rome. While the quantity of holdings overall and in particular areas, typically early printed books, has been a status symbol, digitization from the 1990s onwards has been an equalizer. It enables numerous libraries, large and small, to offer the same journals and early printed books in electronic form. With further books from the holdings of such major collections as Oxford and Harvard being made available electronically and freely via Google, Inc., emphasis has turned to what libraries can offer that is unique or 'special', with particular stress on books given added significance by their context, such as their place within named special collections, and on copy-specific features.

Status extends from the library to its owner, sometimes with political overtones. Ancient libraries were located in temples or palaces. Ptolemy I is thought to have founded the library at Alexandria in order to stabilize Greek culture in Egypt. The library at Pergamon was established in the second century BCE to compete with that at Alexandria; a large statue of Athena and busts reinforced the message of dominating culture. Trajan's library, dedicated in CE 112/113, contained lavish stone and marble decoration. Outstanding large and airy later examples include the Vatican Library, begun in 1475, with marble, frescoes and some stained glass, and Michelangelo's Bibliotheca Medicea Laurenziana in Florence, opened in 1571, with a carved roof, patterned floor, walnut bookshelves and stained glass windows featuring the arms of the ruling Medici. The Escorial Library near Madrid, commissioned by Philip II, had walls and a high barrel vault roof painted in fresco, fluted Doric columns and large mahogany bookcases inlaid with ebony, cedar and other woods: magnificence which redounded to the monarch's glory. That the large, domed Viennese court library, finished in 1735 with space for 200,000 books, was designed to show state power is evident from a fresco on the ceiling depicting Karl IV (1685–1740) as a warrior. Closer to our own time, the Library of Congress was built 1886–97 in an Italian Renaissance style with a gold-plated dome and plentiful use of granite and marble. It was adorned inside with sculpture and paintings as a cultural monument intended both to link the US to European Renaissance learning and to demonstrate American wealth, culture and technology.

Preservation and loss

A reason why libraries are integral to the history of the book is their instrumental role in its preservation. Texts in ancient libraries were periodically 'refreshed' by being recopied onto new clay tablets. Preservation microfilming began in the US with the microform publication in 1936 of the *New York Times*, 1914–18. The microfilming of other newspapers soon followed, as did that of early printed books (the first unit of Early English Books appeared in 1938), and subsequently other items which provide an insight into book history, such as marked-up auction sale catalogues. Large-scale digitization, combining preservation and access, began in the 1990s.

Sheer acquisition is another element of preservation. The function of national libraries is to collect and preserve all publications emanating from or pertaining to the respective nation, as well as a selection of other important literature. They have been assisted in this by laws requiring the deposit of one or more copies of every title printed in a given country in a particular library or libraries of that country. To an extent the collection policy of national libraries has rendered preservation a national preserve. Practical considerations (readability) reinforce the national aspect. A library in an English-speaking country will probably have foreign translations of an English writer's work only as part of a special collection (often based around an author and designed to include as many manifestations as possible of the chosen writer's work), whereas the translations are the norm in libraries in countries where the language of the translation is spoken. A full picture of a book's history might thus be acquired through manifestations of that book in libraries in several countries. But as demonstrated by reference to the ambitious acquisition policies of people like Ashurbanipal and Sir Thomas Bodley, books have always travelled, and sometimes books emanating from one country are present only in another. According to an analysis done in 2002–3, 12 per cent of Italian editions of incunabula were not held in Italy, for example, and roughly one-third of incunabula with imprints from the Low Countries were present only outside them, while 10 per cent of British imprints 1476–1800 were not held in Britain and 628 items with American imprints were to be found only outside the US.[6]

This latter point draws attention to a less positive feature, the failure of libraries to preserve books. The quantity of books apparently surviving in very few, unique or indeed no copies testifies to this: an estimated 27 per cent of the 28,000 editions recorded on the Incunabula Short-Title Catalogue (ISTC) are recorded in unique copies, while possibly more editions have been completely lost than have survived.[7] These are not the only printed books, not to mention manuscripts, to have disappeared without trace. Cheap, small, ephemeral publications which were read to tatters, such as chapbooks and schoolbooks, were particular victims. The first English ABC book, Thomas Petyt's *The BAC* [sic] *Bothe in Latyn and in Englysshe* ([1538]) is known from a single copy held at Emmanuel College, Cambridge, while numerous

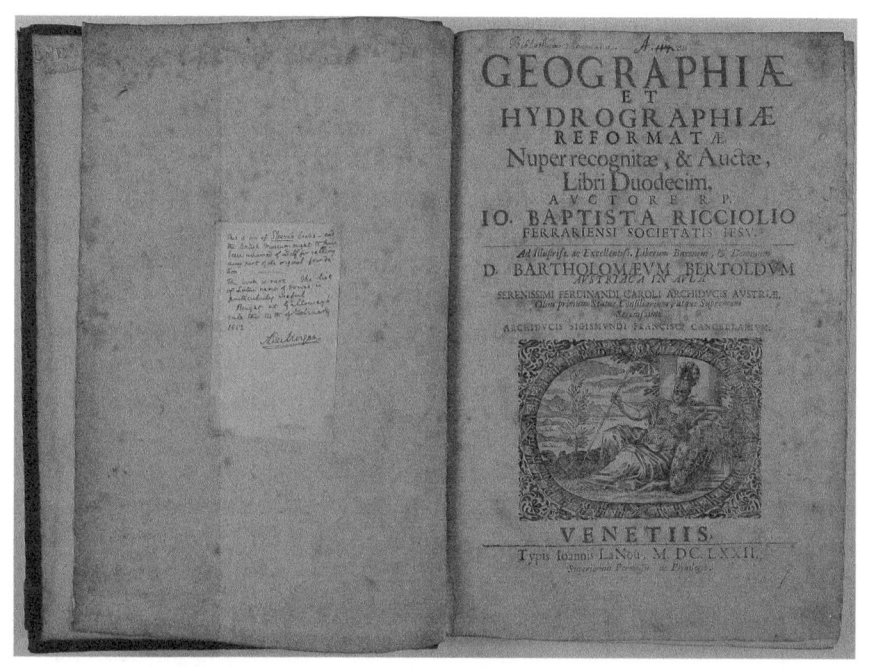

2.1 Book containing British Museum sale duplicate stamp and a manuscript note by Augustus De Morgan: 'This was one of [Sir Hans] Sloane's books – and the British Museum ought to have been ashamed of itself for selling away part of one of the founding collections. The book is rare. The list of Latin names of towns is particularly useful. Bought at Galloway's sale this 14th of February 1852. A. De Morgan.' Title and facing page from *Geographiae et hydrographiae reformatae, nuper recognitae, & auctae, libri duodecim*, Giovanni Battista Riccioli, 1672. Reproduced with permission from Senate House Library, University of London.

entire editions of staple textbooks published a century and a half later have disappeared. John Garretson's *English Exercises for School-Boys to Translate into Latin* was being printed in a twenty-fourth edition in London in 1777, yet no copies of the first, second, fifth, sixth, eighth or ninth editions are recorded, and the third, fourth, tenth, eleventh, twelfth, thirteenth, seventeenth, eighteenth, twentieth and twenty-third editions are known only through single copies at seven separate libraries in England and the US. The only three extant Dublin editions (the twelfth, twentieth and twenty-first) are similarly known from unique copies. This is no isolated example: Michael Suarez has estimated that up to 10 per cent of eighteenth-century editions are not known to survive.[8]

Legal deposit, intended to preserve books printed in a particular nation or region, began in France with the Ordonnance de Montpellier of 1537 (requiring that a copy of any published book be deposited in the king's library), and took over two centuries to spread over Europe, being introduced in Belgium in 1594, in England, to the Bodleian Library, in 1610, in Spain in 1619, Prussia in 1624, Sweden in 1661, Denmark in 1697, Finland in 1702 and in Italy in 1743 (in the Grand Duchy of Tuscany) and 1788 (in the Duchy of Milan). It was not always upheld, such that, for example, although 693 new items were published in 1800 in London alone, Cambridge University Library received just over fifty publications from that year, at least twenty-two of them provincial. Only when Cambridge University Library and the British Museum undertook prosecutions in the early and mid-nineteenth century respectively did British publishers observe it seriously. And even when publishers found it in their interests to observe legal deposit, libraries were cavalier: in the eighteenth century both the Bodleian Library and Cambridge University Library sold non-academic material to local booksellers. Libraries have ejected books in standard weeding processes in the interests of space and relevance, and in order to raise funds for new stock or other purposes. Only in national and major academic libraries is permanent retention a goal, and even the British Museum sold duplicate editions in major sales between 1769 and 1832. A vivid example is portrayed in Figure 2.1. The stock of dispersed libraries is known today partly through their ownership marks in books in other institutions.

Moreover, even when libraries were hampered in their acquisitions, they could decide what to exclude. Most Roman emperors before Constantine suppressed Christian writings, while some Christian bishops suppressed pagan writings. The great medieval Islamic libraries collected all subjects except the literature of other faiths. Mudie's Select Lending Library assured its Victorian readers that it stocked no books which could cause the slightest embarrassment when read aloud within the family circle. After the 1917 Russian Revolution collections were weeded for books containing undesirable information, and public libraries in Russia could acquire only books published in Russia or officially approved for Russian use. In Communist countries the state aimed to use libraries to propagate Marxist–Leninist philosophy and help people become better Soviet citizens. Public libraries everywhere supported the dominant political and social system, such that in 1928 the American Library Association cautioned, in its guide to periodicals for small libraries, against magazines with dubious political and social theories and undesirable fiction. The Association decided in favour of lifting censorship with a Library Bill of Rights only in 1939, with censorship lingering for children's books as a protective measure.

In more thoroughgoing censorship, Caliph Omar is reputed to have ordered the destruction of the Alexandrian Library in CE 640 on the basis that if the writings of the Greeks agreed with the Qur'an they were not required, and if they disagreed, they were not desired. Visitations to the university and college libraries of Oxford and Cambridge under Henry VIII (1535), Edward VI (1549) and Mary (1556–7) to purge the universities of heretical books, first Catholic and then Protestant, resulted in wide-scale conflagrations. The 1930s and 1940s saw the systematic removal and burning of writings by Jewish writers in German public libraries, and this was followed by the removal of Nazi propaganda from such libraries by the Allies after their victory.

Whereas censorship is focused, other forms of destruction have been less discriminating, and it is precisely the aggregation of books that makes them vulnerable. Some libraries, like Thomas Bray's British and American parochial ones, withered from neglect. Others across the ages have been the partial or complete victims of fire: for example, the Palatine Library in CE 64; the Imperial Library of Constantinople in CE 476/7; the Royal Library of Sweden in 1658; the Escorial Library in 1761; the University Library of Copenhagen in 1728; Harvard in 1764; the Library of Congress, most notably in 1851; the University of Virginia in 1895; the National Library of Peru in 1943; and the Academy of Sciences in St Petersburg in 1988. Floods have also wreaked havoc, for example at the Royal Library of Portugal (accompanied by earthquake) in 1755; at the Biblioteca Nazionale Centrale and other libraries in Florence in 1966, resulting in the loss of more than two million volumes; and in the Czech republic in 2002. Warfare has caused further wanton destruction, from Danish and Viking invasions of Anglo-Saxon England to the Peasants' War in Germany of 1524–5, the Thirty Years War of 1618–48, the First World War (including the burning by German troops in 1915 of the University Library of Louvain, founded 1425) and the Iraqi War of 2003. Air raids during the Second World War saw the loss of 250,000 books at the British Library alone. Italy lost two million books in air raids, Germany and Britain more (Britain is thought to have lost over twenty million volumes in libraries, bookshops and publishing firms), and over 100 million books are thought to have been lost between 1941 and 1944 in the Soviet Union. The dissolution of monasteries – in England in 1536–40; in Austria, France and Germany in the late eighteenth century; in Portugal in 1834; in Spain in 1836 – resulted in enormous losses, and the French Revolution led to the removal of books from the libraries of noblemen and religious institutions.

Sometimes upheaval has added new layers to a book's history, through its transfer from one institution to another. Duke Maximilian I of Bavaria sent thousands of manuscripts and printed books from the University of Heidelberg to the Vatican in 1623 to repay the Pope for his support during the Thirty Years War, and after Swedish conquests during the same war, books from Würzburg's university and episcopal libraries among others were sent to enrich the university library of Uppsala and the royal library at Stockholm. Archbishop Matthew Parker's salvation of manuscripts from English monastic libraries benefited the Parker Library at Corpus Christi College, Cambridge. Numerous books confiscated during the French Revolution made their way to the Bibliothèque Nationale and to new French municipal libraries. The Bayerische Staatsbibliothek in Munich was a major beneficiary of the dissolution of the German monasteries, although by no means the only one: via the individual German collector Georg Kloss, who garnered entire monastic libraries and whose books were sold by Sotheby's in London in 1835 and 1841, German monastic books entered institutional libraries throughout Great Britain and America.

The book in the library contributes to the history of the book not merely through its own artefactual value but through institutional records. Accounts provide information about chaining and unchaining; donors' registers and other accession lists indicate what entered a library when and from what source and possibly, if subsequently annotated, what was discarded when; library committee minutes reveal a library's treatment of and attitude towards books. Registers of users can suggest the influence of books in libraries, and circulation registers imply the popularity of particular books as well as their influence on specific people (although borrowing and reading do not always equate): an early example is the loan records of the endowed library of Innerpeffray in Scotland, whose loan registers go back to 1742.

In 1986 John Feather wrote: '[Book history and library history] are dependent upon each other, for the books whose history the book historian seeks to study are very largely the books that have been preserved for him by generations of collectors and librarians, while the library historian cannot ignore the books which are, after all, the *raison d'être* of the library itself. Just as the history of the book is a vital part of the history of our culture, so the history of libraries is a vital part of the history of the book.'[9] By digitizing holdings and by cataloguing books with growing attention to their history, libraries are making books increasingly available and research on those books increasingly feasible – among other elements, the history of reading. But for the history of libraries, it is the collection as a whole that compels attention.

NOTES

1. C. Hollyband, *The Italian Schoole-Maister* (London: T. Purfoot, 1597), leaf D4r.
2. L. Casson, *Libraries in the Ancient World* (New Haven and London: Yale University Press, 2002), 12.
3. Casson, *Libraries in the Ancient World*, 6.
4. See P. R. Harris, *A History of the British Museum Library 1753–1973* (London: British Library, 1998), 762–78.

5. A. Bain, *The Minor Works of George Grote, with Critical Remarks on his Intellectual Character, Writings and Speeches* (London: J. Murray, 1873), 167–8.
6. J. Goldfinch, 'The International Context of National Bibliography', in D. Shaw (ed.), *Books beyond Frontiers: the Need for International Collaboration in National Retrospective Bibliography*, CERL Papers, 3 (London: Consortium of European Research Libraries, 2003), 5–6.
7. J. Green, F. McIntyre and P. Needham, 'The Shape of Incunable Survival and Statistical Estimation of Lost Editions', *Papers of the Bibliographical Society of America* 105 (2011), 141–75, 154, 171.
8. M. F. Suarez, 'Towards a Bibliometric Analysis of the Surviving Record, 1701–1800', in M. F. Suarez and M. L. Turner (eds.), *The Cambridge History of the Book in Britain, Vol. V: 1695–1830* (Cambridge University Press, 2009), 40.
9. J. P. Feather, 'The Book in History and the History of the Book', in J. P. Feather and D. McKitterick (eds.), *The History of Books and Libraries: Two Views* (Washington: Library of Congress, 1986), 14–15.

3

TRISH LOUGHRAN

Books in the nation

The history of the book is that rare field that speaks simultaneously in two registers, describing epic transformations via small scraps of paper. The great titles of print history in particular announce themselves with fanfare. In 1958, Lucien Febvre and Henri-Jean Martin wrote of 'the coming of the book', as of some great sacral event. In 1962, Marshall McLuhan conjured 'the Gutenberg galaxy'. And in 1979, Elizabeth Eisenstein titled her massive, two-volume history of post-Gutenberg Europe *The Printing Press as an Agent of Change*, arguing that printing was 'an unacknowledged revolution' that had remade the world from 1450 forward. In each case, the historical model is one of impact (like an asteroid) or revolution (like a world-historical war). Even Benedict Anderson, in his more modestly titled study *Imagined Communities* (1983), insists on the seismic impact of what he calls print capitalism. All of these scholars imagine print, the printing press, the book and/or print capitalism as emanating from a singular point in time and space – from Gutenberg's press, which in 1450 first introduced moveable type in Europe and then seems to have exported it *everywhere*. The purpose of this chapter is to revisit that argument and place pressure on it from below, with special attention to the question of how, when and why two deeply European forms – the nation and the (Gutenberg) book – came to be synonymous not just with one another but with liberal progress and, indeed, with our ongoing idea of what it means to be modern.

The printing press cometh

Eisenstein's *Printing Revolution in Early Modern Europe* opens with an image titled 'The Press Descending from the Heavens' (Figure 3.1), which first served as the frontispiece to a much earlier history of print: Prosper Marchand's 1740 *Histoire de l'origine et des prémiers progrès de l'imprimerie*. As Eisenstein notes, the image depicts 'the spirit of printing ... descending from the heavens under the aegis of Minerva and Mercury', who offer an

Books in the nation

L'IMPRIMERIE, descendant des Cieux, est accordée par Minerve *et* Mercure *à l'*Allemagne, *qui la présente à la* Hollande, *l'*Angleterre, *l'*Italie, *& la* France, *les quatre prémieres Nations chés les quelles ce bel Art fut adopté*

3.1 'The Press Descending from the Heavens'. The frontispiece of both Prosper Marchand's *Histoire de l'origine et des prémiers progrès de l'imprimerie* (The Hague: Pierre Paupie, 1740) and Elizabeth Eisenstein's *The Printing Revolution in Early Modern Europe* (Cambridge University Press, 1983). Reproduced with permission from the Bancroft Library, University of California, Berkeley.

37

iconic hand press 'first to Germany, who then presents it to Holland, England, Italy, and France (reading from left to right)'.[1] Allegorical figures representing these different countries hold 'medallion portraits of master printers' (including the Germans Gutenberg and Fust; the English Caxton; the Italian Aldus Manutius; and the Dutch Laurens Koster). In this way, the image quietly makes a point that many of the foundational figures of modern book history were also making in the 1970s and 1980s: it implies a strong link between nation and print, evoking an orderly, isomorphic, proto-nationalist *series* of territorially delimited identities.

The image operates on two planes. It illustrates the top-down transmission of the hand press, first from the heavens to earth and then from royally garbed allegorical figureheads (very like kings or queens) to the mere men represented on each medallion. But it also figures (in its evocation of Germany, England, Italy and Holland) the horizontal spread of the liberal nation state as it exists geographically in real (European) space, with different countries spread out fairly evenly along a horizontal plane (though Germany is given a slight sense of vertical priority, as the site of printing's origin). It thus depicts something both mythic and mundane, commemorating a key moment of historical change in which the printing press is almost always present. We are witnessing here not just the divine transfer of a technology or its iconic object but what Karl Polanyi calls 'the great transformation' from feudal to capitalist culture. Eisenstein famously emphasizes this moment as a shift from antiquity (with its Greek gods) to modernity (with its earthbound humans). A number of book scholars after her would go on to intensify that account, describing the emergence of print culture as a shift from an old world order, in which objects, people and power are hierarchically organized in vertical tiers (as in dynastic monarchy) to another, more modern world order, made up of equals spread evenly across the globe (Germans, Englishmen, Italians, Frenchmen, Dutchmen), people whose only difference in the syntax of world history will be where each one appears in the unfolding narrative of what Marchand called 'progress'.

The image thus renders the Coming of Print as a story of European peoplehood – a geopolitical story, as the story of print inevitably must be, but also a modern and classically *liberal* geopolitical story with a representative human being at its centre (the Master Printer), who facilitates the emergence of the new order of the modern liberal state just as much as presidents and prime ministers do (and via the same representative logic). We are witnessing here not just the birth of printing but the birth of all the (western) things we habitually associate with print: Europe, modernity and the nation state itself, still tricked out in the trappings of monarchy but already embedded in the spatial logic of a new world inhabited by putative equals, whose difference from each other lies only in the material particularities of time (when each receives the gift of print) and space (where each lies on the European map, or in the syntax of the sentence of progress).

Placed at the front of Eisenstein's book, as it once sat at the front of Marchand's, the image serves as a kind of long Enlightenment *mise-en-abyme*, a wormhole that viscerally connects Eisenstein to her print-history precursor. Many scholars date the current practice of book history to work like Eisenstein's, but as her homage here suggests, her work is the Second Coming of something much older. The image works, for Eisenstein, both as an icon in its own right and as a more mundane archival example of how printers advertised their own importance. By placing it where she does yet assigning this circumscribed (even petty) function to it, Eisenstein does what print history has always done: she capitalizes on the depiction of a moment of transformation, a shift from this way of organizing the world to that, in order to evoke the longer history of western progress (or modernization), an unfolding series of events that places her, and the field she represents, somewhere far right (reading, like a book, 'from left to right'), out of the frame but still in the same unfolding sentence whose first uttered syllables were 'Gutenberg'.

Imagined Communities as universal history

Benedict Anderson's *Imagined Communities* – the most well-known and influential book to link nation and print – was built on the earlier work of Febvre, Martin, McLuhan and Eisenstein, just as theirs were built ideologically on accounts like Marchand's. Anderson's subtitle, in fact, uncannily echoes Marchand's. Where Marchand spoke in 1740 of 'The Origin and Early Progress of Printing', Anderson speaks of 'The Origin and Spread of Nationalism'. Writing in a period marked by renewed ethnic violence (in eastern Europe, central Africa and South Asia), Anderson was working, in 1983, to recuperate nationalism, taking the sympathetic position of the anthropologist-observer, whose conception of culture involves not just an expanded gaze across space but an equally comprehensive grasp of what is sometimes called modern history, a periodization that continues to start the clock on the world we live in today at or around Gutenberg-time: *c.* 1450. While the book historians who preceded him favoured smaller (national or continental) scales, Anderson's account is improbably and impressively global. He is very much a theorist of what Immanuel Wallerstein calls the world system, a well-functioning set of planetary processes that reach all the way (and yet *only*) back to the fifteenth century, the historical springboard from which western culture launches itself from Europe.

Anderson memorably defines the nation as 'an imagined political community', and this definition proves plastic enough to service his spatially far-flung but temporally staggered account of 'the origin' and 'spread' of the modern nation state.[2] Neither idea was new in 1983. Earlier scholars had already begun to place pressure on the idea of national antiquity, questioning the commonplace, racialized assumption that nations were the lineal descendants of ancient groups whose origins reached back to the deep recesses of ethnic or tribal history. Indeed, by 1983, scholars had already decisively denaturalized the nation state, showing that 'in spite of [its] claims to antiquity, nationalism was a late eighteenth-century creation' that 'owed its origins to [the] secularization of political thought generated by the Renaissance and the Enlightenment, to the egalitarian principles of liberalism, and to the conceptions of republicanism and citizenship popularized by the upheavals of the American and French revolutions'.[3]

Anderson intervened in this emerging consensus in two notable ways. First, he shifted the origin-site of nationalism from the Old to the New World, arguing that the nation-form originates in the Americas, where, between 1776 and 1830, 'the first substantial plurality of nation-states' emerged.[4] The US is thus given pride of place at the scene of creation (as Germany was in Marchand's engraving), followed closely by those Latin American states that forged themselves out of the debris of Spanish and Portuguese empire to the south. Anderson's second major intervention was his famous turn to print. *Imagined Communities* was, in 1983, a far more materialist approach to nationalism than had ever been theorized by political scientists, even as it offered a far more extended account of the decisive linkage between print and nation than any book scholar had yet produced. And though later editions of *Imagined Communities* extended its reach to institutions like museums and objects like the chronometer, it has been Anderson's turn to print culture – and especially to what, with enduring specificity, he calls print capitalism – that has most impacted existing scholarship, generating an enormous number of nation-based readings of print culture (and, conversely, print-based readings of nationalism) that all tend to share four premises. This scholarship generally assumes, first, that nations are *invented*, and they were invented rather recently, dating to the rise of global capitalism in the Renaissance in some accounts and to the late Enlightenment in others. Second, this body of scholarship understands nationalism to consist primarily of *imagined* connections between people who will never meet face to face yet who identify with each other as fellow nationals in ways meaningful enough to power life and death. Third, *printed texts* are agreed to be the primary mechanism by which this sense of imagined community-across-space is produced. And this means, finally, that modern citizens are understood to be readers, and vice versa.

Anderson's *Imagined Communities* is by far the most famous of these studies linking nation and print, all of which generally focus on the same momentous transformation depicted in 'The Press Descending from the Heavens'. But Anderson does something for book history that few others had done before him: he aggressively reorients Marchand's epic snapshot into linear historical time, in the process assembling a much more attenuated narrative history of print's spread across global space – a kind of morphology of modernity, in which print and nations will play equally important, mutually constitutive roles. Marchand's frontispiece emphasizes in one elegant freeze-frame the well-known antinomies of ancient and modern, mythic and historical, heaven and earth, the sacred and the secular, monarchy and nation state. For Anderson, however, this scene emphatically initiates a *series* of dialectical ruptures on a much longer timeline. *Imagined Communities* identifies four stages of nationalism in all, variants that are presented not as a static taxonomy (as we sometimes see in comparative histories) but that instead evolve at staggered intervals in a series of 'waves' that wash across the planet through the long arc of several centuries, moving from the western hemisphere to the east between the years 1776 and 1983, at which point the nation is said to have emerged as 'the legitimate international norm'.[5] The first of these four waves is Creole Nationalism, originating in the Americas between 1776 and 1820. The second is the class of popular ethno-linguistic nationalisms that spread throughout Europe in the mid-nineteenth century, borrowing from the first variant as they went. The third, again formed in reaction to what preceded it, is styled Official Nationalism (explicitly generated through state propaganda that was 'historically "impossible" until after the appearance of popular linguistic-nationalisms'). And finally, the 'Last Wave' completes nationalism's spread when it reaches the colonial territories of Asia and Africa in the twentieth century, as 'a response to the new-style global imperialism made possible by the achievements of industrial capitalism'.[6]

Just as nationalism is understood to have variants, print capitalism likewise has room to develop and adapt alongside these variations. Anderson's account of Creole nationalism, for example, is dominated by a small number of master printers and newspapermen; popular-linguistic nationalisms involve a much wider diffusion of texts; 'Official Nationalism' seizes these populist energies from the top down and rechannels them through propaganda; and the 'Last Wave' benefits not just from print but from numerous twentieth-century media, including radio and television. Anderson's argument thus depends on the fungibility of the term 'print capitalism', which works variably in different eras, but that is nevertheless very much an agent of a grand universal history. In this way, Anderson's account of print capitalism proves wonderfully plastic and contingent. Sometimes it's conceived of as something that materially circulates across space, creating fields of exchange. At others it's described (as in Eisenstein) as a technology that standardizes text and creates 'print-languages'. And at others it is merely the carrier of literary genres (like novels and newspapers, or philologies, dictionaries and grammars). For Anderson, each new 'wave' offers both repetition and difference – a framework for formal innovation that he calls modularity, in that each wave models itself on the previous one but also adapts the blueprint in order to bequeath a new model to the next wave. Successive waves of nationalists are thus dubbed borrowers, adapters and even pirates – with Europe positioned midpoint in the narrative between America and Africa, dethroning it from its conventional (more primary) position in other modernization narratives.

This overt attempt to provincialize Europe works best, however, only in an Anglo-American context (and especially from an American point of view). On the global scale on which Anderson's story takes place, the shift from Europe to the Americas hardly makes his history less European in deeper origin. Because the (American) colonies in this case are all some version of settler colonies, the Western Hemisphere winds up serving as a proxy for Europe rather than a decisive displacement of it. And though Anderson never says so, the revolutions that fabricate the nation-form are in this account all white revolutions, initiated by a class of settler-revolutionaries unironically dubbed 'Pioneers'. (The Haitian Revolution, which spanned 1791 to 1804, would be an exception to this racial rule, but Anderson doesn't explore it, making it a silent anomaly in his dialectical taxonomy of New World, Old World and Third World nationalisms.) The view from Port-au-Prince or Kolkata, Johannesburg or, indeed, from the Pine Ridge Reservation in Indian Country, is not likely to look that different, whether the nation-form originates with the white nation states of Europe or the white settler-states of the Americas.

Nevertheless, this model has proven compelling to scholars of both nationalism and print culture *because* it's a model – a flexible account that can be applied almost anywhere or any place we see print and nation collide on the world historical stage. It sees the nation state, like the Gutenberg press, as a kind of moveable *type*, positing 'the nation' as a modern, western form that starts in one place and then is exported in temporal and spatial 'waves' that spread like a Euro-American tsunami, as the culture of the Global North solidifies itself (first here, then there, there and there) and then slowly washes over the Global South. It thus reinforces a linear, western account of world history that is not just amenable to Enlightenment narratives of progress (like

Prosper Marchand's) but to Cold War – and today, post-Cold War, or neoliberal – narratives of progress. The fact that this story germinated during the Cold War and became a cornerstone of academic orthodoxy just as a new phase of globalization was getting under way is hardly a coincidence. Print-based accounts of the rise of nationalism do not, after all, simply theorize history; they take place in it.

Particularizing the universal: case studies across the timeline

The *Imagined Communities* thesis, which elaborated a link between nation and print that book historians were already gesturing towards in the 1960s and 1970s, triggered two successive waves of book scholarship. The first has tended to develop and affirm the link between nation and print (describing the rise of national print infrastructures, for example, in tandem with the rise of democratic polities), while the second has begun to test the limits of the imagined communities thesis and in some cases to dismantle it. And while this second school of thinking is a diverse and robust one, it's rarely one that approaches the question within the generalized framework I've described here. Historians – especially book historians – have generally contested the idea of the imagined community on the more local ground of different area studies, where it has proven easier to contest the shifting specifics of how print works in this or that setting, in this or that epoch (from sixteenth-century Europe to the eighteenth-century Americas to twentieth-century Africa and Asia). It is thus not unusual to see engagement with Anderson's core narrative across a wide array of regional or national studies within highly specific temporal brackets.

Scholars in early American studies, for example, have questioned the notion that New World print culture is directly linked to the rise of nationalism there. Ed White notes that this argument relies 'on a sleight-of-hand conflation of the American Revolution with the Latin American revolutions of a generation later, with a misleading caricature of print culture to the north'. Sara Castro-Klarén and John Charles Chasteen's *Beyond Imagined Communities* takes an even more local approach, insisting that Anderson's description of 'the operations of Creole printing presses' in Latin America is 'false' at 'virtually every step'. They cite François-Xavier Guerra, among others, whose research has shown that there was neither a newspaper nor a press in all of Chile until 1812, even though a 'local junta had already assumed power', well on their way to state-formation in the region. Even when newspapers did begin to circulate, many folded because of 'the narrowness of the reading public'. Though we have come to think of the newspaper as a critical material technology in the formation of New World nationalism, it was only in New Spain that 'real newspapers' flourished in the formative period, and scholars in the US context have argued much the same for North America. In both settings, local news was not the staple described in print-based readings of early nationalism, nor were newspapers. These scholars decisively show that print did not generate a sense of national identity in the materialist ways that someone like Anderson describes, if at all. To be sure, local and regional identities did exist in this period, but as work like Guerra's proves, 'periodical publications ... and the print market did not create those identities', and they were, in turn, 'not yet *national* in character'.[7] The same point can be made for the state of print culture in 1776 Philadelphia or New York.[8] The now well-known fantasy of a class of incipiently national printer-newspapermen is just that – a fantasy, largely based, Ed White suggests, on an overreliance on Febvre and Martin's hagiographic treatment of Benjamin Franklin in *The Coming of the Book*.[9] In fact, Anderson's belief in the universal utility of early modern print diffusion probably derives from the same source. He is especially fond of quoting *The Coming of the Book*'s diffusionist account of early European print culture and then extending that account out across other continents. 'From [1480]', Febvre and Martin declare, 'it may be said of Europe that the printed book was in universal use'.[10] And Anderson mistakenly assumes that this 'universal' process of diffusion is both accurate in its own right and infinitely extendable.

Scholars working in later periods and other locations continue to test the link between nation and print in ways that place pressure on the particulars of this universal history of diffusion. Shawn Frederick McHale has shown that in Southeast Asia, print was not as secularizing as we might expect, even in the twentieth century: in Vietnam, the 'imagined community' of print tended to reinforce, rather than replace, religious belief, and Buddhist and Confucian identity was far more important in twentieth-century Vietnamese print culture than political identity. In the African context, Christopher Miller and others have described a drive to use print capitalism to create a cosmopolitan African identity alongside nationalist ones. Finally, South Asian scholars like Rochelle Pinto and Anindita Ghosh have shown that nationalizing accounts of print culture tend to homogenize key differences between parts of massive continents (print means one thing in Delhi, another in Gao), even as they overstate print's ability to create national coalitions across class.[11]

In focusing on the relation between print capitalism and today's nation state system (an outcome that was never inevitable and is still only provisionally legitimate), the concept of the print-based (and highly modern) 'imagined community' minimizes all the other book cultures that flourished both before and after the coming of the hand press, before and after western-style literacies and consciousness had formed. Christopher Reed has shown that print followed a different trajectory in China and need not be linked at all to the rise of the global nation-form.[12] China, of course, is notable because it possessed indigenous print technology centuries before Gutenberg, but Reed shows that printing did not find a place in Shanghai until western lithography was imported in the nineteenth century, and even then it continued to be consumed by elites for many decades before 'print capitalism' in the modern sense could be said to have taken hold. The Gutenberg letterpress held little purchase in an elite calligraphic culture like Shanghai's, which for quite some time had no use for it, either before or after western-style presses arrived on the mainland. Scholars who work on Muslim book culture across Africa and elsewhere note much the same disregard for letterpress printing even in a culture in which all classes had access to the Qur'an. In Muslim culture, readers continued to prefer handmade books or, later, lithographic reproductions (as opposed to type) because in Islam, script is sacred.[13] Both China and Muslim Africa, then, are cultures that resist the modernization narrative as it pertains to print capitalism, not because they weren't or aren't modern but because their writing systems and book cultures were in fact already more highly developed than Europe's by the time the Gutenberg press arrived. In each case, a fixed set of cultural values was already well developed that the letterpress could not satisfy or revolutionize and certainly had no claim to modernize.

The nation and the book as derivative discourse

Still, it is not the specifics of any given nationalism that have made the idea of the imagined community so powerful but the putative symmetry and adaptability of the isomorphic nation-form – something that seems to have the ability to transcend language, culture and even power. Anderson repeatedly embraces 'the formal universality of nationality', noting that 'in the modern world everyone can, should, [and] will "have" a nationality, [just] as he or she "has" a gender'. In today's world, he writes, the nation state is the 'legitimate' and 'overwhelming norm', the very saturation of which makes it available to all. 'The ... idea of "nation" is now nestled firmly in virtually all print-languages; and nation-ness is virtually inseparable from political consciousness'. And while the temporal staggeredness and spatial spread of nationalism across the last three centuries has inevitably produced uneven effects in real time and space, the Andersonian narrative I have been describing here reads these gaps more as opportunities for collaboration and innovation than as part of the larger process of incorporation we call imperialism.

The same argument for isomorphic symmetry can be (and often has been) made for the codex book, which presents itself, in many accounts, as a similarly pure container for local differences. Perhaps it is not surprising, then, that Anderson's favourite artefactual emblem of national isomorphism is the bilingual dictionary, a printed text that, he writes, first became popular in nineteenth-century Europe at the height of the philological craze that was spurred by growing national consciousness and that later became the first object of study for would-be revolutionaries during the bilingual decolonization struggles of the Last Wave. Nineteenth-century bilingual dictionaries, Anderson writes, 'made visible an approaching egalitarianism among languages – whatever the political realities outside, within the covers of the Czech–German/German–Czech dictionary the paired languages had a common status'.[14] Convinced that the symmetrical form of the bilingual dictionary solves a problem of power, this account overlooks the ways that formal symmetry masks and often enables inequality. The first bilingual dictionaries and grammars, after all, actually far predate the populist productions of nineteenth-century Europe; such books were less the handbook of bourgeois revolution than the first thing printed on any imported press in colonies just about anywhere – a tool not of 'approaching egalitarianism' but of administrative empire in North America, India, South Asia, the Caribbean and Africa.

This is the problem with global readings that link print culture to modern nation formation. They read the liberal spread of national autonomy (and all the things that come with it: like dictionaries, novels and newspapers – and the western ontologies they carry) as a sign of freedom, rather than one of the cascading after-effects of empire. Nation-based accounts of print capitalism inevitably incorporate and coopt the cultural production of formerly colonized populations in liberated states (like India) even as they continually minoritize the writing of those indigenous and diasporic communities who continue to live in imperfectly decolonized spaces (like the US or New Zealand). When such accounts do consider how print capitalism was experienced and adapted by colonized populations (both slave and native) in places like the New World, that analysis is pressed into the service of a liberal master narrative to which such populations inevitably arrive belatedly. More often (as in *Imagined Communities* itself), such populations are not considered at all. Indeed, the borrowing and adaptation that mark Anderson's account occur along a dispersed timeline, not within a synchronous and fragmented (and still quite vertically organized but *contested*) space like, say, the nineteenth century Americas or contemporary Australia. Such spaces – the planet, we might say, at this or that particular moment – are instead naturalized in Anderson's modernization narrative as planetarily uniform (or worldhistorical). New World slavery and the rise of settler colonialism are linked phenomena that are rarely mentioned in grand narratives like *Imagined Communities*. This may be because nation and empire are understood, in such accounts, to be incompatible, the former rising up dialectically to decisively vanquish the latter. Anderson, for example, repeatedly describes great dynastic empires giving way to the flatter, more homogeneous and egalitarian form of the nation state. The doomed remnants of older empires (which persist in Europe and its dominions around the globe through the Official Nationalism period) are then, in his account, finally vanquished by the Last Wave of decolonization struggles – proof enough that the nation state is the political and spatial solution to the problem of empire, which is itself treated as a decaying remnant of premodern culture.

But neither nationalism nor print capitalism is a natural antinomy to empire. The Gutenberg book and the nation form are both western inventions, as is the story that links their global spread. Though the nation state is often treated as a universal, neutral and unmarked form, equally available to all, it is in fact, as Partha Chatterjee states, 'an export from Europe, like the printing press, the radio, and television'. And the implications of this 'export' are profound. 'In agreeing to become "modern",' Chatterjee writes, the postcolonial nation state 'accepts the claim to universality of this "modern" framework of knowledge' at the expense of its own history, its own tradition and its indigenous material (book) cultures, which forever after can and often are consigned to the realm of the premodern particular.[15]

In the end, however, all nationality is particular, and in the post-Gutenberg era it is also always already part of some larger colonial formation of identity. To think otherwise is to create a zero-sum historical condition in which all parts of the planet must either convert or be accommodated to the norm in order to be legible – or to survive as part of 'modern' history. Jean O'Brien has shown how a similar logic operated in the early Americas via the belief that 'Indians can never be modern': there, native cultures either assimilated to settler norms to prove their modernity (thus erasing their own cultures and their difference from the settler-state) *or* they were marked as primitively unassimilable and extinguished – either by forced 'removal' or by ethnic cleansing.[16] A similar sort of absorption-and-erasure is in play in many accounts of how the nation state – and print – finally came to the Third World. An excellent example comes again from *Imagined Communities*, where Anderson describes Ieu Koeus, a Khmer revolutionary, as 'a lineal descendant of the illustrious philologists of an earlier Europe, [who] ... designed a typewriter keyboard for the Khmer script and published a weighty two-volume *Pheasa Khmer* [The Khmer Language]'.[17] This example poignantly illustrates how postcolonial nationalisms are consigned to what Chatterjee has called a 'derivative' status – and it does so at the level of both language and print.[18] Ieu Koeus was, in fact, a radical anti-western revolutionary who sought to excavate his indigenous language and elevate it, through print, to a language-of-power. But within the framework of universal history, Koeus's philological work is not understood as either revolutionary or original but is instead styled 'a lineal descendant' of a model inherited from Europe – a derivative, last-wave knock-off. This is the dilemma faced by all postcolonial book cultures and indigenous writing systems that arise after Gutenberg – from Koeus's Khmer typewriter to the Cherokee syllabary to West Africa's Vai script – when understood within a model that naturalizes the universal diffusion of western forms, a model in which both modern book culture and the current nation state system are deeply implicated. Yet this is not a critique that has been taken up by book historians in the same way that it has been taken up by political theorists like Chatterjee. While book historians have chipped away at the facts and figures behind this master narrative, they continue to ignore the ways in which print capitalism is accepted not just as regional history but as universal history. But it is, in fact, the cult of Gutenberg – and our faith in universal diffusion – that we would do well to unsettle.

The challenge of decolonizing book history

Even today, with intense intellectual and economic pressure to recast the national in more global terms, the history of the book as a field has trouble *not* thinking about print as the agent of a western liberal tradition, with the nation state as its political cornerstone. David Finkelstein and Alistair McCleery cite no fewer than twenty-two multivolume but explicitly national publishing initiatives, most of them 'Anglophone ... surveys covering Australia, the UK, Canada, Ireland, New Zealand, Scotland, and the USA', all of which are devoted to showing 'the development of national print infrastructures' and all of which were first published, remarkably, between 1997 and 2010.[19] Even encyclopedias that take a more theoretically and spatially 'global' view – like Blackwell's *Companion to the History of the Book* (2007) or the *Oxford Companion to the Book* (2010) – often inadvertently reinscribe the viral logic of the liberal nation state in the kinds of stories they tell and the shape those stories take within their table of contents. The Blackwell volume, for example, aggressively emphasizes the Gutenberg book, with just two chapters on 'The World before the Codex' followed by six on 'The Book beyond the West' and culminating in eighteen on 'The Codex in the West 400–2000'.[20] The Oxford volume likewise shows a strong Anglo-American bias, with three chapters on Britain bookended on the other side with one on 'the History of the Book in America'. Within this stable Enlightenment framework, chapters on 'Sub-Saharan Africa', 'The Muslim Book', and 'The Indian Sub-Continent' stand as more premodern markers of difference – geographies that are either on their way to being imperfectly and belatedly absorbed into the existing system (like India) or that do the ideological work of serving as minority discourse within the volume at large.

Even as they attempt to include book cultures and writing systems from all times and places (from papyrus rolls to the undifferentiated 'Muslim world'), such global accounts cannot escape the recurring imprint of universal history – the idea that 'the book' has evolved over time, as has geographic space, which is often organized in such volumes within the categories of national area studies. Thirty of the fifty essays in the *Oxford Companion*, for example, deal with geographic areas and regions, most of them nations, and their titling employs a generic repetition that makes them parallel, very much like the recurring medallions that march across Marchand's frontispiece ('The History of the Book in Britain ... in Ireland ... in France ... in Japan ... in China ... in Australia ... in New Zealand'). That isomorphic repetition is the formal mark, the sign and syntax, of the nation state system, the Westphalian grid and grammar that so compellingly materializes, before our very eyes, as on a map, the international norm so central to modern book history. The lingering residue of area studies is all the more interesting in the case of the *Oxford Companion*, because it specifically imagines itself as a global antidote to western parochialism. The preface offers the project as a 'history of the book around the world, including the Muslim world, Asia, Latin America, and Sub-Saharan Africa' (a list that clearly expresses a postcolonial desire to go global) while reviewers from *Choice* have praised its 'global approach to the world of the book'.[21] Despite those ambitions, however, the Oxford volume, like the Blackwell volume before it, overwhelmingly rehearses a passion play about modernization, with a strong emphasis on narratives of liberalization and planetary development that is less postcolonial than what we might call neoliberal: a justification for the world as we know it that absorbs local differences within a totalizing picture of the Gutenberg book's global spread.

Though there are exceptions, this is what postcolonial book history tends to look like today. It is, as *Choice* notes, 'global' – but it's not yet decolonized. Book history today is dizzying in its diversity, filled with a seemingly infinite and quite ungraspable number of unique facts, figures and dates. But in more important ways, its encyclopedias and monographs often speak in unison. In particular, they almost all tell the story of modernization on the differentiated ground of this or that geographic locale. Ancient writing systems and book cultures in China, India, Vietnam and Africa are in each case described and then transformed by contact with both European missionaries and capitalism until all lie between Gutenberg covers. In fact, many encyclopedias focus on a diffusionist narrative that linearly traces the spread of book technologies *as* a kind of Andersonian spread (as, in other words, historically staggered, and hence uneven, geographic diffusion). It is a story that is sometimes told as a tale of materials (from palm leaf to papyrus roll to parchment to paper to computer screen), sometimes as a tale of format (from orality to manuscript to print to digitization), and quite often as a literal tale of cultural diffusion, of that which is and is not European encountering one another, in different sites across the globe, to one common endpoint: the endpoint of the present, the globalized world of today. This narrative has not, of course, gone unchallenged, but it's never gone away either. *Choice* hails the *Oxford Companion* as a guidebook for 'the world of the book', and in doing so concisely translates the incommensurability of geographic space ('the world') into the universal register of one object: 'the book'. The totality of that formulation is a problem as old as empire itself.

The challenge of decolonizing book history for the future will involve finding new ways to provincialize print capitalism, but this won't be easy. The Anglophone tradition of the history of the book has a quite specific set of historical strategies for containing difference, a method that yokes it to its own twentieth-century origins, regardless of which century or continent it looks (back) at. Susan Buck-Morss calls for scholarship that can work through 'the historical specificities of particular experiences, approaching the universal not by subsuming facts within overarching systems or homogenizing premises, but by attending to the edges of systems, the limits of premises, the boundaries of our historical imagination'.[22] Book history would seem a perfect location from which to launch such a trouble-making project because it's materialist, detail-oriented and historical. More than that, it's about the ways that people connect and communicate across the divides of space, time and language. Nevertheless, the fact remains: *there is no radical history of the book*, no comprehensively leftist or revolutionary or decolonizing tradition to speak of. There is no queer history of the book; there is no Marxist history of the book; and despite a massive global diffusion of the field, with production that ranges across every continent and in every known century, there is very little (in English) that we might truly call a postcolonial history of the book. The problem lies, I've suggested here, in how the field has historically mediated the universal and the particular – and to what ends. In this, the iconic picture of 'the book' (and in particular, the technology of print) is itself a major player, for the book *seems* like a neutral object but it's one on which we have grounded a number of core cultural fantasies about equality. And none are more important, today, than the stories we continue to tell about the book's relation to naturalized political forms like the nation state.

The non-Gutenberg variation of the book has existed for centuries in parts of the world that had no use for moveable European type before – and, in some cases, for a long time after – Gutenberg.[23] Why, then, can't modern print history quit Gutenberg? And by extension, why can't it quit the nation state and the linear logic of geographic diffusion that sustains universal history? Like Anderson, the field at large accepts both the Gutenberg variation of print *and* the nation as a 'legitimate international norm', and even as it tries to globalize its gaze, it continually falls into the zero-sum trap of chronological timelines and a closed world-system whose 'modern' origins are dated to 1450. This is hardly surprising, for as I've argued here, Anglophone book history is – by the standards of ancient book cultures – a fairly recent discipline, one that has its origins in the liberal western Enlightenment and its global spread, a process that is not ending but intensifying under twenty-first-century globalization. If this is true, it means that the field itself – from Marchand to Eisenstein and Anderson to the book you hold in your hand right now – is materially implicated in the postcolonial contradiction that Partha Chatterjee describes. Of the scholars cited in this chapter, only Chatterjee points out that the nation and the Gutenberg press are analogous (and contemporaneous) European exports, but his analysis of that connection is confined to a single sentence, and more work needs to be done to amplify that insight from within the domain of book history. Nationalism and print are two particular and connected 'manifestation[s] of a much more general problem', which Chatterjee identifies, in the end, as a problem of knowledge: 'a conception of knowledge, established in the post-Enlightenment period of European intellectual history, as the moral and epistemic foundation for a supposedly universal framework', a form of knowledge which pretends to be abstract, universal and 'independent of cultures'.[24] But knowledge is never independent of either culture or power. And neither are books, of any kind, in any world – but especially, perhaps, in the Gutenberg world.

NOTES

1. E. L. Eisenstein, *The Printing Revolution in Early Modern Europe* (Cambridge University Press, 1983), xi.
2. B. Anderson, *Imagined Communities: Reflections on the Origin and Spread of Nationalism* (London: Verso, 1983, rev. 1991), 6.
3. B. Anderson, 'Nationalism', in J. Krieger (ed.), *The Oxford Companion to Politics of the World* (Oxford University Press, 2001), 574.
4. Anderson, 'Nationalism', 575.
5. Anderson, *Imagined Communities*, 113.
6. Anderson, *Imagined Communities*, 109, 139.
7. E. White. 'Early American Nations as Imagined Communities', *American Quarterly* 56 (1): 50; S. Castro-Klarén and J. C. Chasteen (eds.), *Beyond Imagined Communities: Reading and Writing the Nation in Nineteenth-Century Latin America* (Washington, DC: Woodrow Wilson Center Press: 2003), 5, 6.

8. T. Loughran, *The Republic in Print: Print Culture in the Age of US Nation Building, 1770–1870* (New York: Columbia University Press, 2007).
9. White, 'Early American Nations as Imagined Communities', 57.
10. Cited in Anderson, *Imagined Communities*, 33, n55.
11. S. F. McHale, *Print and Power: Confucianism, Communism, and Buddhism in the Making of Modern Vietnam* (Honolulu: University of Hawai'i Press, 2004); C. L. Miller, *Nationalists and Nomads: Essays on Francophone African Literature and Culture* (University of Chicago Press, 1998); R. Pinto, *Between Empires: Print and Politics in Goa* (New Delhi: Oxford University Press, 2007); A. Ghosh, *Power in Print: Popular Publishing and the Politics of Language and Culture in a Colonial Society, 1778–1905* (New Delhi: Oxford University Press, 2006).
12. C. A. Reed, *Gutenberg in Shanghai: Chinese Print Capitalism, 1876–1937* (Vancouver: University of British Columbia Press, 2004).
13. G. N. Atiyeh (ed.), *The Book in the Islamic World: The Written Word and Communication in the Middle East* (Albany: State University of New York Press, 1995).
14. Anderson, *Imagined Communities*, 5, 71, 135.
15. P. Chatterjee, *Nationalist Thought and the Colonial World: A Derivative Discourse* (Minneapolis, MN: University of Minnesota Press, 1993), 9, 11.
16. J. M. O'Brien, *Firsting and Lasting: Writing Indians out of Existence in New England* (Minneapolis, MN: University of Minnesota Press, 2010).
17. Anderson, *Imagined Communities*, 131.
18. P. Chatterjee, *Nationalist Thought and the Colonial World*, 8–11.
19. D. Finkelstein and A. McCleery, *An Introduction to Book History* 2nd edn (New York: Routledge, 2013), 26.
20. S. Eliot and J. Rose (eds.), *A Companion to the History of the Book* (Malden, MA: Blackwell Publishing, 2007).
21. M. F. Suarez and H. R. Woudhuysen (eds.), *The Oxford Companion to the Book* (New York: Oxford University Press, 2010); *Choice* 48.2 (October 2010), 257.
22. S. Buck-Morss, *Hegel, Haiti and Universal History* (University of Pittsburgh Press, 2009), 79.
23. Reed, *Gutenberg in Shanghai*; R. Fraser, *Book History through Postcolonial Eyes: Rewriting the Script* (London: Routledge, 2008).
24. Chatterjee, *Nationalist Thought*, 11.

4

SYDNEY SHEP

Books in global perspectives

In his 1983 address to the Bibliographical Society, D. F. McKenzie remarked that 'what we much too readily call "the book" is a friskier and therefore more elusive animal than the words "physical object" will allow'.[1] Books as material artefacts can travel long distances, define different ideological spheres, negotiate new diasporic identities and transform cultures. Books as texts can be translated, repurposed, remediated, their intellectual content appropriated, adapted and transformed over time and space. Books as transactions chart complex and often fluid networks between authors and readers, producers and consumers. And books as cultural metaphors can provoke affective experiences, both sacred and secular, that inspire ritual and revelation, memory and renewal. This chapter discusses a number of ways in which books travel and transform, and takes as a starting point that the protean nature of books is one of their defining features. It engages with contemporary scholarship on transnationalism and postcoloniality. And finally, it concludes by introducing a new model for book history that repositions mobility at the heart of this interdisciplinary field of study.

The mobile and mutable book

When Samia Khatun visited a mosque in Broken Hill, New South Wales, Australia in 2009 to view what the locals proudly labelled a Qur'an, she found to her surprise and astonishment a well-thumbed Bengali *puthi*. How this five-hundred-page popular songbook printed in the port city of Kolkata in 1896 travelled from India to the remote settlement of Broken Hill, via networks of Afghan cameleers laying Australia's overland telegraph and Bengali lascars working the ships across the Indian Ocean world, is a compelling tale of intersecting cultures, multidimensional expressive forms and disparate reading practices.[2] The story of Khatun's *puthi* tells us certain things about book culture in Australia, both historically and in the present moment, but it does not fit neatly into a narrow nationalist framework. Instead, this story, like countless others, foregrounds the mobility of people, places and communication technologies (such as the book) and emphasizes the poetics and politics of information transmission. It also reflects Robert Escarpit's comment that 'when we hold a book in our hands, all we hold is the paper: the *book* is elsewhere'.[3]

Unlike cave paintings, stelae, totems or monuments, the material form of the book is a fundamentally portable communication technology. In their landmark *A History of Reading in the West*, Guglielmo Cavallo and Roger Chartier note that 'authors do not write books; they write texts that become material objects'.[4] Although there is always already an assumed physical or virtual instantiation, it takes the actions of various intermediaries (whether printers, publishers, distributors, librarians or educators) to place books in the hands and minds of their readers, and to complete, in effect, the communication process.[5] Book artists expose the bones of form and function, laying bare structural and intellectual skeletons in their creative entanglements with the medium. Mark Z. Danielewski's *House of Leaves* (2000) and *Only Revolutions* (2006) bridge the worlds of print and digital culture and construct highly interactive, self-reflexive works. The gradual miniaturization of these containers of information from the large folio lectern codex bibles of the Renaissance to the eighteenth-century Latin duodecimo classics printed by John Baskerville, and from the pocket railway edition paperbacks of the late nineteenth to the e-readers of the early twenty-first century, is predicated upon an increasingly mobile readership demanding ease and immediacy of use as well as the right to personal property and portable devices.

The intrinsic mobility of books transports ideas across physical, cultural, social and psychological boundaries. After all, the invention of moveable type in Korea in the thirteenth century enabled the unlimited reproducibility of the word and the potential industrialization of printing, even if it was not the preferred technology in Asia until the late nineteenth century. The reinvention of moveable type by Gutenberg in the fifteenth century and its adoption throughout Europe and beyond paved the way for the insertion of print into the spectrum of communication technologies. Print, however, was not necessarily fixed and immutable with an authority derived simply from multiplicity and reach: the technical language of state, impression and edition all attest to a variability that is a hallmark of the process. And the very status of print was contested from the start, particularly in scientific communities accustomed to different authority structures and modes of dissemination. Moreover, books and print can foment rebellion if not instigate revolutions, and are frequently the target of cultural genocide. In 1517, Martin Luther's

Ninety-Five Theses nailed to a church door in Wittenburg, Germany helped change the shape of European Christianity, empowering the faithful through the medium of print with vernacular translations of the Bible and hymnody, as well as placing individual and private reading practices at the heart of the Protestant Reformation. The emancipation of knowledge was furthered in the Enlightenment with the publication of dictionaries, encyclopedias and other reference works that shifted the gaze from the curiosity cabinet to the world encompassed between two boards.

In the long nineteenth century, the publishing industry responded to self-help initiatives promoted by the likes of Samuel Smiles, lifting the book out of the hands of the cultural elites and into the working class home. For figures such as the political journalist William Cobbett and the library-founding philanthropist Andrew Carnegie, knowledge was empowering and facilitated upward mobility and radical politics. It also provoked a questioning of authority as witnessed by the impact of Thomas Paine's *The Rights of Man*, engendered the trade union movement to protect workers' rights, and was a catalyst for the American, French and Indian Revolutions. An unassuming tome like *The Little Red Book* helped to consolidate the rule of Chairman Mao Zedong over Communist China during the Cultural Revolution. This book of quotations issued in pocketbook format with red vinyl covers was required reading for all party faithful. It was to be carried on one's person at all times and was the object of daily study. Much like a traditional Chinese almanac, it offered guidance and advice, codes of conduct and models of behaviour; in terms of power politics, it was the propagandistic expression of Mao's cult of personality. Yet, with over one billion copies printed between 1964 and 1976, a feat that singlehandedly stretched, reshaped and modernized the entire Chinese publishing industry, and translated into over forty languages, *The Little Red Book* galvanized the world's largest imagined community if not reading club.[6]

It is no wonder, then, that translation has become a key concept to understand the restless book. Embedded in everyday life are phrases such as to throw the book at someone, to be in a person's bad books, to bring to book or to speak like a book. Indeed, the legacy of bookness is manifested in the ongoing identity crisis of form and function in the digital domain: PowerBook, Super Book and Book Emulator join programs and applications such as MobilePress. Like metaphor, *translatio* is a rhetorical device predicated upon movement. Trading in translation rights, copyright and digital rights is big business at the Frankfurt or Kolkata Book Fairs. Linguistic translation, whether domesticated or foreignized, and what Roman Jakobson calls intersemiotic translation (the movement from one sign system to another, such as text to image), all place mobility at the heart of the enterprise.[7]

The industrialized book of the nineteenth century, colonial editions and other mass marketing ventures, plus the emergence of multinational corporations, all prefigure the era of e-books and innovative forms of online publishing, where mobility and mutability lie at the core of the user-generated experience. The 'unbound book' has become the mantra of writers, artists and publishers in the digital age.[8]

We often forget that an entire facet of industrial design is devoted to the systematic organization of unruly books and the cultivation of sedentary reading experiences. Bookshelves, revolving book wheels, desks and reading furniture such as armchairs, sofas and prie-dieus all accommodate the physicality of the book form. Bookmobiles, camel trains and saddlebags help spread the word and eclipse distance. That manuscript books in monastic libraries had to be chained to reading desks suggests both their intrinsic value and their potential promiscuousness. And while the power of the press – that fourth estate – might be more imagined than real, for the gatekeepers of knowledge the threat is unmistakable. The control of literacy through education systems and the control of production and dissemination through copyright are but two measures that constrain the protean book. In more extreme forms of censorship, the book itself becomes the victimized surrogate for an absent author, subjected to incarceration, burial, branding, mutilation or destruction by fire, most famously in ritualized burnings and burials in the Qin dynasty (213–206 BCE) or purges and pogroms in twentieth-century Nazi Germany and socialist Russia. Such forms of cultural genocide have been termed as variously *bibliocide* and *libricide* and documented the erasure of cultural memory and ethnic identity in the razing of the library of Alexandria, the bombing of cultural heritage institutions in Sarajevo, and the burning, then looting, of the National Library of Iraq under the eyes of the army of liberation.[9]

Despite the sheer weight of cast iron printing presses, lead types and ancillary equipment, printing itself is a surprisingly portable technology. Printing presses operated in the back lines of the Napoleonic and American Civil Wars, printing dispatches, notices and other battlefield ephemera. Even the guerilla tactics of the displaced Boers during the Second South African War included field printing on a mobile press ('drukkerij te veldt') and capitalization of their war effort through a mobile mint. If battlefields accommodated sites of print, troopships in the first and second world wars included printing offices for the production of magazines and newspapers on the high seas. Complementing shipboard libraries, such ventures gave outbound soldiers an opportunity to while away the time, promote camaraderie amongst and lighthearted competition between officer class and the rank and file, and craft a memorial of their journey should they not return. Shipboard printing and reading was also a distraction and entertainment for immigrants, documenting the transition between their past lives and their new spaces of settlement, or for members of the Hudson's Bay Company voyaging through Arctic waters on their way to outposts at the edge of the civilized world. The hunger for communication also arose in similarly ephemeral spaces: the goldfields. Newspapers followed the rhythms of boom and bust as temporary settlements sprang up around lucky strikes and equally quickly moved on to the next claim. Specially designed miniature print shops or parlour presses in the Victorian period shifted the production of books and print into the hands of private individuals and hobbyists, a sharp contrast to the highly structured, strictly gendered and rigorously policed trade training of the printing fraternity.

Printers, like many members of the book trades, were peripatetic agents, transporting and transplanting their skills and expertise along the road and into shops, offices and houses around the world. As embedded in the trade's traditional practices, successful apprentices became journeymen printers and were expected to travel before settling down. In the nineteenth century, however, this translated to a highly mobile workforce in a period of sustained technological change and global economic volatility. As tramping typographers, printers on the move followed established seasonal circuits, usually localized or regional.[10] Many became the equivalent of imperial careerists, following international and chain migration patterns, colony-hopping wherever opportunity and inclination led them. The result was the circulation of technological skills that added to the human chemistry of the print shop, linking printing traditions with localized practices, and enabling the development of new approaches to print in unfamiliar spaces.[11]

William Colenso, for example, trained in his native Cornwall, travelled to London to work for the British and Foreign Bible Society, then shipped out to New Zealand as printer for the Church Missionary Society in 1834. Lacking standard English-language typecases, he commissioned a local carpenter to fashion a lay that accommodated the Māori alphabet of ten consonants and five vowels. When setting texts in English, he had to fossick through extra letters still in their twisted paper wrappers strewn around the print shop. Moreover, he had to make do with a small amount of type for composing in Māori and use paper borrowed from missionary wives to print, in pamphlet form, individual books of the Bible delivered to him once their translations were signed off by head office. His original commission, to print the entire bible in Māori, was virtually impossible, with a non-existent workforce and a six- to nine-month wait for supplies. Even when completed, sheets had to be packed in casks and shipped to Sydney to be bound before being distributed to local Māori, whose rage for ownership meant walking days for a single copy or exchanging a Bible for a gold coin. Demand outstripped supply and eventually printing was repatriated to London, but not without structural changes to the industry. The British and Foreign Bible Society responded to market demand by issuing bibles in smaller, cheaper formats, using thin, tissue-like Oxford bible paper and industrializing their bookbinding practices, introducing case binding as a cheap alternative for a popular mass market. They also developed a transactional strategy linking buyers and sellers that cross-subsidised translations, enabled global distribution and promoted an international textual network.[12]

The part publication practice of mission presses was less a spiritual policy than one born out of necessity and survival. Part publication in the form of serialization was a more sustained business strategy that enabled publishers to gauge market viability for a lengthy novel before committing to book production. The demand for cheap novels and serialized bestsellers in the Indian market and the Canadian and Australasian colonies forced London and Edinburgh publishing houses to restructure their business practices from manufacturing right through to distribution.[13] Whether issued as colonial editions or serialized in magazines and newspapers, the international circulation and reception of literary works created an integrated reading zone, collapsing any real or perceived distinction between centre and periphery. Serialization also changed authorial practices. Charles Dickens, for instance, mastered writing on the instalment plan, producing his work according to the imposition rhythms of twenty-four or thirty-two pages. The mass market appeal for the next issue saw battles fought at the docks over incoming shipments, as well as various attempts to clone, repackage or pirate successful stories in local publications. In 1838, Henry Dowling reprinted *Pickwick Papers* in Van Diemen's Land (Tasmania), bringing the work out in an unauthorised part-issue format, followed by a single volume with pirated illustrations. The popularity of monthly and weekly magazines is evidenced by circulation figures which often belie the actual size of their readership, as well as by their global proliferation. *Punch, or The London Charivari* reappeared in well over a hundred guises around the world, spawning *Taranaki Punch* in New Zealand, *Melbourne Punch* in Australia, the Urdu *Awadh Punch* in India and many others that served local needs while retaining the satiric and iconoclastic spirit of the original. The now rare *Illustrated London News* Australasian Edition exemplifies what Law terms 'the ability for the periphery not only to select its own reading but also to write back'.[14] Newspapers with their cut-and-paste, snippet formula were a key player in the distribution of local and international news as well as literature in the nineteenth century and reflected the economies of scale possible for small, self-sustaining print shops that needed a diversification strategy to survive.

This atomization of the printed word was further emancipated by the reproductive technology of stereotyping which enabled texts to circulate widely and cheaply.

Books are powerful talismanic pledges in the legal arena, initiating the performance of truth telling, or attesting to the symbolic value of Abraham Lincoln's Bible upon which the Obama Presidency was founded. They are also key players in religious ritual, moving the spirit to realms beyond the mundane and diurnal. Whether it is the procession of the Christian Bible at the beginning of a church service, the enthronement of and obeisance to the Sikh Guru Granth in the Gurudwara (place of worship), the rituals surrounding the housing and reading of the Torah or the spinning of a Buddhist dharmic wheel and recitation of mantras to enact faith, religious texts instantiated in material form fashion the iconic book.[15]

The transnational and postcolonial book

Nineteenth-century evangelical Protestant missionaries used the book, termed the 'white man's fetish', to bring the light of faith and the civilizing power of empire to colonized peoples. Yet the transnational and translingual portability of *The Pilgrim's Progress* led to John Bunyan's story being naturalized in African tribal culture through multimedia and multilingual expressions of orature, performance and translation. Whether Bunyan is disaggregated and reconceptualized as image, illustration, photograph, postcard, magic lantern slide, pageant, sermon or hymn, Isabel Hofmeyr's magisterial study affirms that 'when books travel, they change shape. They are excised, summarized, abridged, and bowdlerized by the new intellectual formations into which they migrate'.[16] As a result, the 'radical historicity' of this particular book sets the stage for integrating the local and global into a web of nodes and links that constructs a transnational Protestant public sphere and dismantles the divided terrains and politicized imperatives of centre and periphery.[17]

Hofmeyr's latest work extends this transnational approach into a biography of Mahatma Gandhi's printing press established in 1904 at the Phoenix ashram outside Durban, South Africa. The main publication of the International Printing Press was a multilingual newspaper, *Indian Opinion*, an instrument of social and political reform that linked Indians around the world and promoted what would later be termed *satyagraha* or passive resistance. Gandhi's press became the hub of a utopian settlement run on Tolstoyan and Ruskinian principles, and 'constituted a kind of religion, the ideal for which settlers lived and worked'.[18] *Indian Opinion* had wide international circulation, fostered information sharing between disparate and diasporic communities and underpinned Gandhi's campaign for racial and social equality.

Linguistic and bibliographic translations serve as barometers of the indigenization and internationalization of books and printing, especially when religious and educational texts are rewritten. In his groundbreaking study *Book History through Postcolonial Eyes: Rewriting the Script*, Robert Fraser undertakes a highly nuanced, densely argued, comparative study of the technologies of the intellect – speech, gesture, writing and print – as they manifest themselves in South Asia and sub-Saharan Africa. In an exposé of the necessary rapprochement between book history and postcolonialism, Fraser counters the evolutionary telos of western print triumphalism, challenges alphabetic literacy as the universal litmus test registering the impact of writing systems and print technologies, and disputes an undifferentiated approach to the history of the non-western book. He argues that communication forms are multivalent, mutually constitutive, opportunistic and deeply implicated in their resistance to or adaptation of local cultural expressions. Whereas in South Asia 'the challenges facing print culture were the result of script complexity and diversification, in sub-Saharan Africa they were, to some extent at least, products of an orthography gap ... In one, speech gives way to a lengthy period dominated by script, leading eventually to the inception of print. In the other, oral communication gives directly onto print, with writing appearing principally as an intermediate, instructional mode'.[19] He also examines the adaptation of a wide range of classical and contemporary literary works from the *Ramayama* and *Mahabharata* to the works of Tagore, Ngugi wa Thiong'o and Ayi Kwei Armah as well as the role of the literary police force: those scholars, editors and censors who exercise their powers to delimit the motility of communication forms. Finally, in a parting gesture to the world wide web, the ubiquity of mobile technologies and the enduring if transformed age of the book, Fraser questions whether 'such confusing hierarchies of empire and post-empire retain any comprehensible, or barely relevant, meaning'.[20]

The mobility of books and the logic of empire are visible in the lives of individuals, such as the nineteenth-century book agent, Edward Petherick, who managed the London office of the Melbourne-based publisher and bookseller, George Robertson.[21] Petherick was instrumental in harnessing the potential of new transport and communication technologies (such as the steamship, the Suez Canal and the transcontinental railway, as well as the transatlantic, transpacific and overland telegraph cable services) to create an international book trade network that ensured readers in the Australian colonies could receive any book from anywhere on the globe at the right price and with little delay. Some antipodean contemporaries imagined these networks as a many-tentacled octopus or a water dragon linking northern and southern hemispheres. Petherick, however, understood their necessary social dimension. He conceived of the book trade world as a suite of connected ante-rooms populated by authors, publishers and booksellers who mingled and mixed, exchanging ideas and commodities that ensured the international circulation of books and print. Alison Rukavina has conceptualized these social networks as a series of fluid and elastic interconnections between agents – the producers and consumers of books – that are non-hierarchical, decentred and multidirectional. As such, 'books deterritorialize the world and the world reterritorializes books as they move through networks'.[22]

In order to understand the book without borders, book historians have increasingly looked beyond the nation state as the unit of analysis and beyond the notions of national exceptionalism that drove the proliferation of large-scale national book history projects. Many scholars investigating the circulation of objects and ideas across multiple sites of production, dissemination and reception have turned to new imperial history and postcolonial studies to challenge the distinction and hierarchy implicit in the spatial binaries of centre/periphery or metropole/colony, or to understand the role of print in the construction and deconstruction of race, gender, religion and class. Other scholars are interested in notions of a public sphere linked to the circulation and self-reflexivity of texts on a broader, more global scale than that proposed by Benedict Anderson whose concepts of imagined communities and print capitalism were originally tied to the formation of nation states.[23] The emergence of alternative frameworks (such as the transnational, the postnational and the translocal) are a salutary reminder that the essential characteristic of books is their mobility.[24] As the *Palgrave Dictionary of Transnational History* points out, the study of world history is based on the 'transnational connections and circulations, by people, goods, capital, ideas and tastes that are not always confined to any particular country or region of the world, nor are identifiable with states or governments'.[25]

The recent discourse around transnational and, indeed, international approaches in general has resulted in some quite compelling thinking about the always already embeddness of the transnational or 'elsewhereness' in the nation.[26] Studies of the print-mediated Scottish diaspora, of the development of Australian literature in a colonized market, of the Oxford University Press in India and of the Naval Kishore Press based in Lucknow, have all raised awareness of the interlocked empires of print and empires of the mind.[27] And yet, by continuing to invoke what Antoinette Burton referred to as 'the Inadequacy and the Indispensability of the Nation' – two questions remain unresolved: how do we model and understand the cross-border movement of books, technologies and people; how can we link and incorporate the individual case studies that have characterized much of book history scholarship to date within a larger historical narrative?[28]

Building a new model for book history

To help answer these questions, several perspectives are apposite: *histoire croisée*, new imperial histories, translocality and biography. Since 2002, Michael Werner and Bénédicte Zimmermann have advocated for a new model of history comprising empirical intercrossings, pragmatic induction and self-reflexivity, one that moves us beyond comparative history and transfer studies, into related modalities such as connected, shared or entangled history.[29] They argue that comparative history fixes the objects of study in synchronic relation to each other at the expense of the methodological asymmetries of analytic categories or nuances of historic specificity. Transfer studies assume a teleological, diachronic model of diffusion and adoption that 'studies the processes of transformation', but rarely engage with reciprocity or return. Werner and Zimmermann suggest that *histoire croisée* provides an opening to 'examine the links between various historically constituted formations' at the same time as those labile formations are interrogated by a researcher whose own subject position is acknowledged and examined. The concept of intersection is at the heart of a dynamic, multidimensional structure that deals with intercrossings of relationships, interactions, circulation, effects, repercussions, resistances, inertias and modifications.

The models underpinning the new imperial historiography are similar to the structure envisioned by *histoire croisée*, which similarly creates a nodal point, a clustering of interest and a density of relevance. In reviewing the revisionist historiography of empire, Tony Ballantyne has identified three interlocked approaches: 'the importance of knowledge production in the constitution of colonial difference; the centrality of cultural difference, whether gender, religion, or race, that shaped imperial cultural formations; and the concept of the web or network which displaces the binary of metropole/periphery and imagines the empire as a set of shifting, uneven, and often unstable inter-regional and global connections'.[30] Put another way, 'empire is now treated as an intellectually integrated zone in which developments are simultaneously shaped from different points in the imperial world'.[31] A fresh understanding of the kinetic nature of such spaces and places has led to a new appreciation of what have variously been termed 'meeting-up places', 'contact zones' and 'postnational geographies' or 'translocalities'.[32]

Like new imperial historians who foreground the constructed nature of empire, so too do translocal historians consider that 'locality is "produced" socially and culturally, often in contexts of heightened mobility ... and of transgression of boundaries'. Translocality has been proposed as both a tool for describing 'empirical phenomena that result from a multitude of circulations and transfers' and a research perspective to 'better understand and conceptualise connections beyond the local which are, however, neither necessarily global in scale nor necessarily connected to global moments'. Acknowledging the value of a *histoire croisée* approach and positioning translocality along a continuum that includes transnationalism and globalization, German scholars Ulrike Frietag and Achim von Oppen suggest that translocality enables different nuances, 'highlighting the fact that the interactions and connections between places, institutions, actors and concepts have far more diverse, and often even contradictory effects than is commonly assumed'.[33]

The three concepts of *histoire croisée*, new imperial histories and translocality foreground space, mobility and historiographical self-reflexivity but they also all wrestle with issues of scale and agency. Werner and Zimmermann emphasize that 'empirical objects relate to several scales at the same time', scales that are spatial as well as temporal, coextensive as well as codeterminant, products of the mutually constituted relationship between the objects of study and the observers' analytic frameworks. Both the translocal and the transnational scales illustrate this double logic:

> Within a *histoire croisée* perspective, the transnational cannot simply be considered as a supplementary level of analysis to be added to the local, regional, and national levels according to a logic of change in focus. On the contrary, it is apprehended as a level that exists in interaction with the others, producing its own logics with feedback effects upon other space-structuring logics. Far from being limited to a macroscopic reduction, the study of the transnational level reveals a network of dynamic interrelations whose components are in part defined through the links they maintain among themselves and the articulations structuring their positions.[34]

Such a dynamic process goes beyond a simplistic differentiation between macro- and microhistorical. Similarly, translocality encourages what Jacques Revel calls the 'systematic linking of different scales, both at the level of observation and at that of analysis. This "game of scales" also permits us to see the "local" and "global" not as two differing poles but rather as the intersection of connections and horizons of action and perspective of very different reaches'.[35] In other words, '"translocal" is one attempt to rematerialize not just the ideological and structural work of local and regional people and space, but to insist ... that the global is always already an act of positioning, used, if not designed, as a "signifier of difference"'.[36]

Human agency, or biography, is the fourth perspective to add to the mix. If both *histoire croisée* and translocality conceive of space as shifting layers of connectedness, the proponents of a biographical perspective also recognize the importance of tracking individual mobile agents through this arena of multisitedness. Perhaps the most eloquent expression of the role of human agency in this regard comes through two intersecting planes: David Lambert and Alan Lester's work on imperial careering and imagined geographies, in conjunction with Antoinette Burton and Tony Ballantyne's examination of gender and 'the dialogic relationship between space and body'.[37] These scholars recuperate life-writing and biography for the new millennium. As Ballantyne notes elsewhere, 'thinking through life histories is a powerful way of reconstructing imperial webs or networks and recovering the role of these connections in the making and remaking of imperial culture'.[38] Discounting the 'myth of personal coherence', Lambert and Lester explore a new 'mobile and decentred biographical approach' that maps neatly onto a 'networked spatial imagination' of empire. Informed by the work of James Clifford, 'life geography' becomes a 'narrative of transindividual occasions' in which 'individuals become meeting points for influences, no longer static but mobile, effusive, decentred, a process not a thing'.[39] Like books that travel and transform, so do human lives move through time and space, connecting and interconnecting people and events.

Modeling situated knowledges in book history

The convergence of *histoire croisée*, new imperial history, translocality and biography empowers book historians to think differently about our units of analysis, to account for a more nuanced picture appropriate to our field of study, and to introduce a measure of critical self-reflection that gets us closer to Eva Hemmungs Wirtén's call for a new kind of research that 'questions old truths regarding method and theory as well as the basic requirement of the nation state as our given investigative point of departure'.[40] If books are promiscuous and have no borders, how can we begin to theorize their function in society and culture?

Over the last thirty years, book historians have turned to models based on the classic electrical circuit to understand the production, dissemination and reception of books. Robert Darnton's 'Communication Circuit' from 1982 foregrounds the various historical actors involved at each step of the book trade process, from authors and publishers to paper suppliers and pressmen, from smugglers and colporteurs to readers and library borrowers. The economic, social, intellectual and political contexts in which these agents operate are positioned in the centre of the model and their influences are considered ubiquitous. 'A New Model for the Study of the Book' dating from 1993, by bibliographers Thomas Adams and Nicolas Barker, concentrates on functions rather than agents and invokes a life-cycle of the book that begins with publication (significantly omitting authorship), moves through manufacture and distribution to reception, and closes the circuit with survival. Again, the contexts are pervasive, but now visualized as 'the whole socio-economic conjuncture' surrounding the circuit. Two other, non-diagrammatized concepts of book history have emerged more recently. In 1997, literary critic Peter D. McDonald invoked Pierre Bourdieu's notion of fields of cultural production, both restricted and non-restricted, to create a three-dimensional Darnton in which the reconstruction of the 'predicament' of the book and the radically situated nature of its text is the necessary first step towards engagement and interpretation. In 2000, the historian of science James Secord used the analogy of a dividing amoeba and coined the phrase 'literary replication' to explain how texts and ideas can permeate society through reading, writing and talking networks. Such networks do not rely exclusively upon people having read the actual book(s) in question, but rather epitomise cultural formation in action.[41]

The field of publishing studies offers additional perspectives of interest to the book historian. The traditional publishing value chain is a linear rendering of the core book production functions, from concept to consumer, with each agent in the process adding significant value. More recently, South African scholar Elizabeth Le Roux has incorporated models from political sociology in order to understand the role of university presses under the apartheid regime.[42] By introducing a six-point spectrum from resistance to complicity, she has inserted Bourdieu's 'fields' directly into the value chain and conceptualized the politicization of the publishing industry as a continuum, thereby nuancing our understanding of the complexities of the industry. With paradigms shifting in the digital domain and contemporary publishers increasingly bypassing retailers in favour of targeting readers directly, the value chain is currently being reconfigured as a value network, a model more suited to the world of open access and e-publishing.

The agents involved in production, dissemination, reception and survival of books, the processes themselves, the fields of cultural production that situate books and readers and the ways in which books replicate themselves, have all been the subject of significant monographs. However, none of these approaches engages either explicitly or implicitly with the inherent mobility and mutability of books, whether physical or virtual. This intellectual blind spot can be addressed by modelling the field of book history as one of *situated knowledges*

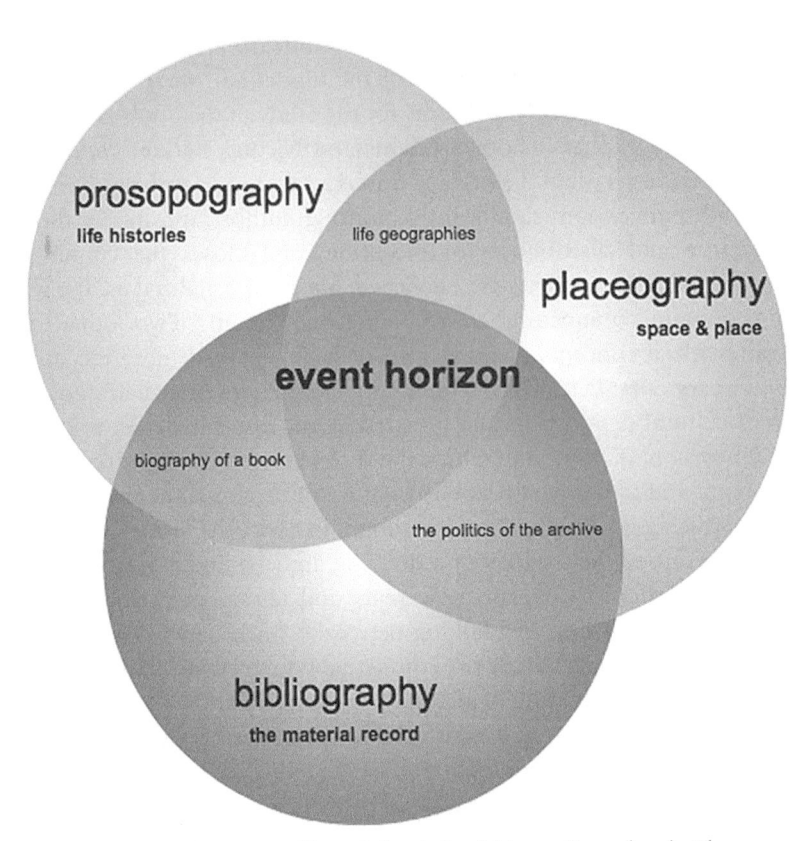

4.1 Modelling situated knowledges in book history. Reproduced with permission of Sydney Shep.

(see Figure 4.1). An examination of the complex, dynamic intercrossings between people (prosopography), places (placeography) and objects (bibliography) offers a quite different way of conceptualizing the ways and means by which books travel and transform through space and across time. Various nodes of intersection between adjacent elements suggest rich veins of contextual research, whether the life geographies of individual actors, the object biographies or 'it-narratives' of individual books and texts, or the politics of the archival spaces in which material records are deposited, described and discovered.[43] The three primary elements converge in a zone of investigation termed the *event horizon*. Adapted from general relativity and quantum mechanics, this multidimensional contact zone situates the book's historical research process as one of constant, energetic interplay between people, places and things. The 'event' is a unique node in the space–time continuum defined by links gravitating towards a horizon of significance. At any one time, depending on the research questions, the researcher's perspectives and the available evidence, the research activity may bend towards one particular element's event horizon more than another. However, the pull of the other elements balances the possibility of the researcher being captured by the potential black hole of a single domain. Such a model acknowledges the spatial turn in history in which space, place, site and location are critical factors shaping our understanding of the agency of material forms. It also moves us away from the current disciplinary orientation of book history being narrowly focused on literary criticism, history or bibliography, to a more comprehensive understanding of the interdisciplinarity that enables our field of study.

If this chapter began with the nineteenth-century movement of a Bengali songbook from India to the Australian outback, it concludes with a quite different, contemporary exemplar of situated knowledges. In 2001, Ron Hornbaker launched BookCrossing.com with the by-line 'If you love your books, let them go'. This social media and networking space encourages readers to read, register and release their books for others to enjoy. Whether on a train, in an aeroplane seat pocket or on a park bench, these modern-day messages in a bottle can be left and found. Their journeys are tracked through unique identifiers (BCIDs) glued onto endpapers, checked via their online mapping feature, or hunted down through titles registered on the website. Readers log their reading experiences, review books, establish communities called official book crossing zones (OBCZ), engage in random acts of BookCrossing kindness (RABCK), and contribute to the world's largest mobile library. 'Using books as the architecture and glue to facilitate the Great Conversation, there are currently 1,558,761 BookCrossers and 9,469,064 books travelling throughout 132 countries. Our community is changing the world and touching lives one book at a time'.[44]

The printer, inventor, library founder and politician Benjamin Franklin once said that 'All mankind is divided into three classes: those that are immovable, those that are movable, and those that move'. If people move and frisky bibliographic objects travel and transform, we should also recognize that spaces and places are fundamentally kinetic, articulating, sustaining and repositioning subjects and objects in an enduring engagement with cultural formation, reformation and deformation.[45]

NOTES

1. D. F. McKenzie, 'The Sociology of a Text: Orality, Literacy and Print in Early New Zealand', *The Library* Sixth Series 4 (1984), 334.
2. S. Khatun, *Camels, Ships and Trains: Connecting Histories from South Asia to Australia* (London: Hurst and New York: Oxford University Press, forthcoming 2015).

3. R. Escarpit, *The Book Revolution* (London: Harrap and UNESCO, 1966), 17.
4. G. Cavallo and R. Chartier (eds.), *A History of Reading in the West* (London: Polity Books, 1995), 5.
5. P. D. McDonald, 'Ideas of the Book and Histories of Literature: After theory?', *Publications of the Modern Language Association of America* 12: 1 (2006): 214–28.
6. O. L. Han, 'Sources and Early Printing History of Chairman Mao's "Quotations"', *BibSite* (The Bibliographical Society of America) www.bibsocamer.org/bibsite/han/index.html.
7. L. Venuti, *The Scandals of Translation: Towards an Ethics of Difference* (London: Routledge, 1998); R. Jakobson, 'On Linguistic Aspects of Translation', in R. Brower (ed.), *On Translation* (Cambridge, MA: Harvard University Press, 1959), 232–9.
8. 'The Unbound Book. Reading and Publishing in the Digital Age', Conference reports and videos. Amsterdam and the Hague, May 2011. e-boekenstad.nl/unbound.
9. R. Knuth, *Libricide: The Regime-sponsored Destruction of Books and Libraries in the 20th Century* (Westport, CT: Praeger Press, 2003); *Burning Books and Leveling Libraries: Extremist Violence and Cultural Destruction* (Westport, CT: Praeger Press, 2006).
10. E. Hobsbawm, 'The Tramping Artisan', *The Economic History Review*, new series 3:3 (1951), 299–320; H. R. Southall, 'The Tramping Artisan Revisited: Labour Mobility and Economic Distress in Early Victorian England', *Economic History Review*, 2nd series 44 (1991), 272–96.
11. I. Hofmeyr, *Gandhi's Printing Press: Experiments in Slow Reading* (Johannesburg: Wits University Press, 2013).
12. L. Howsam, *Cheap Bibles: Nineteenth Century Publishing and the British and Foreign Bible Society* (Cambridge University Press, 1991); I. Hofmeyr, '"Spread Far and Wide over the Surface of the Earth": Evangelical Reading Formations and the Rise of a Transnational Public Sphere – The Case of the Cape Town Ladies' Bible Association', *English Studies in Africa* 47:1 (2004), 17–29, rpt in A. van der Vlies (ed.), *Print, Text and Book Cultures in South Africa* (Johannesburg: Wits University Press, 2012), 74–86.
13. P. Joshi, *In Another Country: Colonialism, Culture, and the English Novel in India* (New York: Columbia University Press, 2002); G. Law, 'The Serial Revolution at the Periphery', in S. Frost and R. W. Rix (eds.), *Moveable Type, Mobile Nations: Interactions in Transnational Book History. Angles on the English-Speaking World*, Vol. X (Copenhagen: Museum Tusculanum Press, 2010), 85–97.
14. Law, 'Serial Revolution', 87.
15. J. W. Watts (ed.), *Iconic Books and Texts* (Sheffield: Equinox Books, 2013).
16. I. Hofmeyr, 'Metaphorical Books', *Current Writing* 13:2 (2001), 105; and *The Portable Bunyan: A Transnational History of* The Pilgrim's Progress (Princeton University Press, 2004), 2–3.
17. L. H. Liu, 'Introduction', in L. H. Liu (ed.), *Tokens of Exchange: The Problem of Translation in Global Circulations* (Durham: Duke University Press, 1995) (quoted in Hofmeyr, 'Spread Far and Wide over the Surface of the Earth').

18. I. Hofmeyr, *Gandhi's Printing Press: Experiments in Slow Reading* (Cambridge, MA: Harvard University Press, 2013), ch. 2, 'Printing utopia'.
19. Robert Fraser, *Book History Through Postcolonial Eyes: Rewriting the Script* (London: Routledge, 2008), 20–1.
20. Fraser, *Book History*, 188.
21. A. Rukavina, 'Social Networks. Modelling the Transnational Distribution and Production of Books', in Frost and Rix (eds.), *Moveable Types*, 72–83. See also Rukavina, *The Development of the International Book Trade, 1870–1895: Tangled Networks* (Houndmills and New York: Palgrave Macmillan, 2010).
22. Rukavina, 'Social Networks', 79.
23. Michael Warner, 'Publics and Counterpublics', *Public Culture* 14:1 (2002), 49–90.
24. S. J. Shep, 'Books without Borders: The Transnational Turn in Book History', in R. Fraser and M. Hammond (eds.), *Books Without Borders. Vol. I: The Cross-National Dimension in Print Culture* (Basingstoke and New York: Palgrave Macmillan, 2008), 13–37; and 'Imagining Postnational Book History', *Papers of the Bibliographical Society of America* 104:20 (2010), 253–68.
25. A. Iriye and P. Saunier (eds.), *The Palgrave Dictionary of Transnational History*, 2009, www.transnationalhistory.com/home.aspx.
26. S. Kamboureli and R. Miki (eds.), *Trans.Can.Lit. Resituating the Study of Canadian Literature* (Waterloo: Wilfrid Laurier University Press, 2007), x. See also Peter Mandaville, 'Reading the State from Elsewhere. Towards an Anthropology of the Postnational', *Review of International Studies* 28 (2002), 199–207.
27. B. Bell, 'Print Culture in Exile: The Scottish Emigrant Reader in the Nineteenth Century', *Papers of the Bibliographical Society of Canada* 36:2 (1998), 88–106; M. Lyons and J. Arnold (eds.), *A History of the Book in Australia 1891–1945: A National Culture in a Colonised Market* (Brisbane: University of Queensland Press, 2001); R. Chatterjee, *Empires of the Mind: A History of the Oxford University Press in India During the Raj* (New Delhi: Oxford University Press, 2006); U. Stark, *An Empire of Books: The Naval Kishore Press and the Diffusion of the Printed Word in Colonial India, 1858–1895* (New Delhi: Permanent Black, 2007).
28. A. Burton (ed.), *After the Imperial Turn. Thinking with and through the Nation* (Durham and London: Duke University Press, 2003), 1. See also in this collection, T. Ballantyne, 'Rereading the Archive and Opening up the Nation-State: Colonial Knowledge in South Asia (and Beyond)', 102–21.
29. M. Werner and B. Zimmermann, 'Beyond Comparison: *Histoire croisée* and the Challenge of Reflexivity', *History and Theory* 45 (February 2006), 30–50.
30. T. Ballantyne, 'The Changing Shape of the Modern British Empire and its Historiography', *The Historical Journal* 53:2 (2010), 429–52; 451. See also *Webs of Empire. Locating New Zealand's Colonial Past* (Wellington: Bridget William Books, 2012).
31. I. Hofmeyr, 'The Globe in the Text: Towards a Transnational History of the Book', *African Studies* 64:1 (2005), 87–103; 87.
32. D. Massey, *For Space* (London: Sage, 2005), 4, 9–12; M. L. Pratt, *Imperial Eyes: Travel Writing and Transculturation* (London: Routledge, 1992), 6–7; A. Appadurai, 'Sovereignty without Territoriality: Notes for a Postnational

Geography', in P. Yaeger (ed.), *The Geography of Identity* (Ann Arbor: University of Michigan Press, 1996), 40–58.
33. Appadurai, 'Sovereignty', 9, 5, 3; U. Freitag and A. von Oppen (eds.), *Translocality. The Study of Globalising Processes from a Southern Perspective* (Leiden and Boston: Brill, 2010), 3, 5.
34. Werner and Zimmermann, 'Beyond Comparison', 43.
35. Freitag and von Oppen, *Translocality*, 18–19. See also J. Revel, *Jeux d'échelles: la micro-analyse à l'expérience* [*A Game of Scales: The Microanalysis of Experience*] (Paris, Le Seuil-Gallimard, 1996).
36. T. Ballantyne and A. Burton (eds.), *Moving Subjects: Gender, Mobility, and Intimacy in an age of Global Empire* (Urbana and Chicago: University of Illinois Press, 2009), 337.
37. Ibid., 336.
38. Ballantyne, 'Changing Shape', 445.
39. D. Lambert and A. Lester, 'Introduction', in Lambert and Lester (eds.), *Colonial Lives Across the British Empire: Imperial Careering in the Long Nineteenth Century* (Cambridge University Press, 2006), 20–1.
40. E. Hemmungs Wirtén, 'Surveying the (Battle) Field: Book History, SHARP, and the Guerrilla Tactics of Research', *SHARP News*, 12:1 (2003), 4.
41. L. Howsam, *Old Books and New Histories: An Orientation to Studies in Book and Print Culture* (University of Toronto Press, 2006), 28–45.
42. E. Le Roux, 'Between Complicity and Resistance: University Presses in South Africa', PhD thesis, University of Pretoria, 2012.
43. L. Price, *How to Do Things with Books in Victorian Britain* (Princeton University Press, 2012).
44. See www.bookcrossing.com.
45. S. Ramsay, *Reading Machines: Towards an Algorithmic Criticism* (Chicago: University of Illinois Press, 2011), 33.

PART II
The material book and the mutable text

5

PETER STOICHEFF

Materials and meanings

Nature originally provided the surfaces, writing tools and media for any human communication that sought permanence, or at least presence beyond speech. Worldwide, the stone walls of caves, cliffs and boulders offered readily available means for attaching messages, some of which famously survive today in the form of the Lascaux caves in southern France and the pictographs of indigenous communities in the Americas. While stone itself offered a long-lasting surface – not only hardy but heavy as well – not all writing instruments and methods of inscription did. Increasingly exposed to light and human respiration, the dyed images in the Lascaux caves are now in danger of fading rapidly, and who knows what human messages, applied to exterior stones and with weaker tints and liquids, disappeared thousands of years ago due to nature's forces of erasure? Of the messages intended for impermanent inscription on such surfaces as sand, deliberately erasable, we know even less. We know relatively little about leaves, bark or wood, beyond the fact that they provided writing surfaces – few examples survive, yet they were used by peoples around the world for millennia. The materials of thousands of years ago were often robust, or heavy, or ubiquitous, but the marks made on them were usually mere molecules in thickness and are consequently lost to us.

Yet some examples do survive that reveal how for millennia indigenous peoples carved messages into stone surfaces (petroglyphs), painted on them (pictographs) and painted on or carved into bark and trees and other natural surfaces. These writing or ideographic systems were integrated with the immediate natural settings, the cosmologies and the oral traditions of their indigenous tribes. Instead of separate graphic systems such as alphabets, these forms of communication had meaning by virtue of their relationship with oral teachings, referencing shared ecological or spiritual or astronomical understanding. Surviving examples of American indigenous petroglyphs and pictographs are maps that describe hunting routes or geographic family boundaries; others contain ideographs describing abstract concepts of tribal harmony or conflict, interactions with the spirit world, ceremonies and contracts. Ideographic messages also existed on smaller, more portable surfaces such as the North American Mi'kmaq wampum, a woven belt of coloured shells communicating events of historical or ceremonial significance, treaty agreements or spiritual knowledge.[1]

Experimenting continues today with writing surfaces and materials that are permanent, flexible, accessible, readable, transportable and affordable. Versions of that combination have been sought for millennia, since the desire for inscribing communication outside of speech emerged. Each gradually evolving solution to that challenge helped determine the societies and civilizations that produced them, the book being one of the most successful.

The permanence of Egyptian stone hieroglyphics has instantiated their messages of power and the after-life, remaining to this day as the most enduring of inscriptions. Even with other means now at our disposal with which to secure the longevity of a message, we often still turn to the stone surface – when dedicating a prominent building or recognizing people or events in public spaces – to lend weight to the statement. Laws were inscribed in stone as were, and are, epitaphs. Any message that deserved protection from wanton change or destruction and to be understood for a long time merited capture in stone. Messages, too, whose meaning was inextricable from their location – pyramids near a river basin where many people gathered, caves and cliffs by animal migratory routes or other geographical attractions – were well served by the permanence of stone. Not surprisingly, the message and its medium reinforced each other. These forms of writing are not merely the most long-lasting we know of. They also shared an assumption that their purpose would be unchanging: the Egyptian after-life would always contain a 49-day interim period, buffalo would always pass by near southern Alberta's Head-Smashed-In buffalo jump.

Not all writing was motivated by the desire for permanence of message and material, or by location – those are merely the examples that, for those reasons, have survived for us to know them. We know Sumerians from the fourth millennium BCE used soft clay tablets that were erasable, reusable and portable – pretty well opposite to everything stone represented. Too, clay tablets required neither the labour-intensive dyes nor the rarer chiselling expertise required for communication by stone. Clay was not the Sumerians' material of choice so much as the material available and accessible to them. Its properties enabled a more private and transitory inscription and, if Sumerian advances in thought are any indication, apparently incentivized numeracy and literacy. Wet clay's flexible surface encouraged and enabled the development of cuneiform script, originally logographic and restricted in use but eventually syllabic and more easily learned in schools, encouraging literacy. Clay's fired and hardened surface also permitted archiving, and thousands of examples of clay tablet texts remain, excavated from vast systematized early libraries in Babylonia. The texts were not always flat and 'tablet'-like – formal documents are to be found on many-sided clay cylinders that once stood conveniently, accessibly and alphabetically ordered, on archival shelves. Though often meant to be an impermanent surface, some clay tablets were heated during invaders' fires and hardened for us still to see, unintentionally maintaining the daily thoughts and reflections of people targeted for destruction.

Not all surfaces intended for casual use by other societies and civilizations have met with the same serendipitous fate. We know bone and tortoiseshell were used in China from the eighteenth to the twelfth centuries BCE but few of the actual texts remain. Silk, too, was a writing surface in China, and increasingly popular by the first centuries CE, but it was expensive and, like bone and shell, intolerant of human writing error. Wood was used, at least by the Egyptians, earlier than that. Leaves were used by many peoples throughout Asia from at least the tenth century BCE to the nineteenth century CE. A popular technique involved palm leaves, cut lengthwise and inscribed with a sharp implement and dyed to give the text a visual contrast. The leaves were sewn together with lengths of twine through holes near each end, and held together with a stiff wood cover at the top and the bottom. The resulting palm leaf book usually contained *sutras* or aphorisms; the term elided the contents with the form of the object itself – it is derived from the root *siv* whence come the English words 'sew' and 'suture'. The perishable nature of the palm leaf material beyond a few centuries has meant that only a small number of the originals survive, though restoration efforts and digitization projects are now prolific. Bark, more durable particularly when varnished to highlight the text, was used until at least the sixteenth century CE in central America. Animal skins supplied writing surfaces for some three millennia after the Egyptians used them. Originally capable of inscription on only one side, and extremely labour-intensive to preserve in order to prevent swift natural decay, skins were nonetheless ubiquitous. Attempts to render them into an efficient writing surface would continue until the invention of what came to be called parchment solved the challenge in second century BCE Greece.

Standing alongside these two evolutionary stages of writing surfaces were papyrus and the wax tablet. Papyrus dominated the writing surface market in Egypt and the Mediterranean for centuries if not millennia until it was superseded by parchment. Papyrus was used for many purposes besides writing, such as the hulls of boats – important for a river culture – for baskets and for clothing. Papyrus was made from the stem of a plant readily available throughout the Nile basin. The stem was dissected into strips, which were dried and flattened and then woven, with the help of a glue of some sort, into a lightweight, thin and flexible mat. Its availability, relatively simple production requirements and longevity, combined with its portability and its ability to retain inks and to be legible, accounted for its popularity. It is perhaps not overstating the case to say that papyrus provided the surface upon which all Mediterranean civilizations at one time or another recorded themselves and evolved their thinking. Given the fibrous quality of the plant stem, papyrus was difficult to fold, and usually only one side was smooth enough to write upon. So papyrus was rolled into a scroll, which kept it intact for long periods. To solve the challenge of how to enable the eye to scan the papyrus scroll's otherwise long lines of letters, its text was arranged in vertical rectangular shapes of shorter lines called *paginae*, an early precursor of the page.

Although papyrus supplied the main writing surface in the Mediterranean basin for millennia, it was nevertheless a restricting medium. For one thing, its surface was rough and not easy to apply pigments to. For another, it was fragile, particularly susceptible to deterioration and unable to endure distribution through Europe's different climates. Too, its popularity – coupled with the Library of Alexandria's mission to copy all knowledge onto scrolls made of it – brought the plant itself to the brink of extinction by the second century CE, in the process driving up cost. Perhaps most importantly, it did not tolerate corrections well, nor could it be reused. Papyrus was able to provide a relatively formal vehicle for a finished writing product, but it was not conducive to the more transitory, but no less crucial, process of learning the skill of writing. And while it promoted the archiving of resolved thought and accomplished events, it was not quite adaptable enough to provide a widespread means of experimenting with provisional thinking and expression.

Those requirements were better met by the wax tablet, an innovative attempt to combine flexibility of use, portability, affordability and availability of material. It served a different purpose than the permanence of fired clay or of stone, and of papyrus. The wax tablet was made of a wooden frame into which a black wax was embedded that could be inscribed with one end of a stylus – metal-tipped and sharp – and erased with the broad opposite end. Probably originating in Assyria around the eighth century BCE, it swiftly gained popularity with Greeks and Romans, whose efficient alphabets and high literacy rates required a technology that sustained writing acquisition and use. And suitably framed in wood, wax tablets could be bound together with leather laces, as the Romans did – an early form of the book or 'codex' (the Latin word for a piece of wood) – to simplify the otherwise cumbersome access to specific *paginae* in the interior sections of the papyrus scroll.

The scroll's benefit, however, was the extended text it permitted (one version of the Egyptian *Book of the Dead* is 40 metres long, comprised of pieces pasted together) and, with that, more complex argument, thought and recorded history. Egyptian scrolls were rolled around a single central stick and had to be read by unfurling it in the one direction. The Jewish Torah has two wooden rollers (*atzei chaim*), one at either end, and could be more efficiently unrolled from either direction. The Greeks folded some scrolls in a pleated fashion, as did the Maya with their codices written on durable bark beginning around the fifth century CE. However structured, the scroll's potentially enormous yet storable length could contain the needs of a protracted narrative, of complex astronomical observations, of treatises and of encyclopedic social records and financial transactions. It was also relatively portable. Those architectural attributes were not about to be allowed to disappear due to the vagaries of papyrus. The scroll, that is, offered benefits too significant to lose, and if the properties of papyrus made it too fragile, if its scarcity and price had become issues, and if its geography was too localized for the expanding world of literacy and writing to sustain the technology of the scroll, some other material would have to take papyrus's place.

That material was animal skin, the other widely available surface whose provenance extended beyond the Nile basin (though not, for the potential purpose of writing, to Hindu cultures revering animal flesh). Like papyrus, animal skins were used for many purposes besides writing on – primarily clothing and building – and they were easily procured, if not so easily refined for inscription. Experiments with turning the familiar animal skin into a writing surface had been undertaken for millennia, and fragments of Egyptian texts still exist that were written on animal skin as early as the third millennium. Assyrian and Babylonian texts were sometimes written on animal skin as well, concurrently with the broader use of clay tablets and papyrus, from the sixth century BCE, and Greek texts on animal skin date from at least the fifth century BCE. But for most of that time, animal skin supplied a writing surface as compromised as papyrus – one-sided, rough, prone to disintegration and resistant to correcting and reuse, while requiring greater effort and expense than papyrus to create.

Improvements to the product occurred in Pergamon in the second century BCE, however, that remedied some of these weaknesses at the same time that papyrus was dwindling in supply and increasing in cost. Those improvements included tanning and liming to make the surface durable and foldable, scraping and dehairing to render it smooth and two-sided and stretching to render it very thin. Its thin, two-sided and foldable features essentially established the concept of the leaf and, influenced by the scroll's *paginae*, pages – and permitted many of them to rest together in a relatively compact space, efficiently bound by flat wooden covers. Parchment's treated surface gave it the capacity to hold ink accurately and permanently, and for corrections to be made by scraping. And the best animals for the purpose – sheep, cows, rabbits, goats, even unborn calves – were not found only in one region, as papyrus was, but everywhere the Roman empire extended.

The result was the most enduring and versatile writing surface invented prior to paper, and in some ways even after. Parchment from centuries ago exists in many libraries, some of it looking as if it were created yesterday. Easy to produce it was not, but its benefits would outweigh its arduous production process for well over a millennium and would make the popularity and influence of the book itself possible. Parchment's first use was as a writing surface for scrolls – large portions of the Dead Sea Scrolls are a famous example. But the period of parchment's ascendancy as a writing surface of choice was roughly simultaneous with that of the codex – identified by some as occurring in Rome in the first century CE, and others as being in Egypt or other northern African regions prior to that.[2] Although the book's pages could conceivably be made from material other than parchment – Egyptian papyrus codices survive from the fourth century BCE – parchment's unique qualities would provide the conditions necessary for the book to thrive.

For that to happen, though, a suitable process for accomplishing the many tasks involved in creating the parchment surface was required. Up to roughly the end of the medieval period, monasteries invented and practised an assembly-line system that effectively did just that, motivated by the desire to replicate and circulate not just books but *the* book, the Bible. Self-sufficient communities, monasteries carried out their own animal husbandry, vegetable gardening and mineral acquisition that provided them with animals, inks and dyes – the raw materials of book production. Combined with the intellectual raw material of Latin literacy and Carolingian script, monasteries controlled the making, selling, reading and circulation of books – essentially the entire European market – for the better part of a millennium.

Each stage of the monastic book production process required its own types of expertise. Sheep skins, for instance, were transformed into parchment through the laborious processes of liming, curing, dehairing, scraping and smoothing. They were also strategically cut to maximize the available surface area to produce as many leaves as possible – a complex geometric challenge. The resulting leaves, usually octavos, were passed to others for the addition of pencilled margins and lines. Lines were drawn from side to side, guided by a column of equally spaced small holes down the side margins made by a rolled pinwheel. The relative dimensions of margins were determined by various factors, and often by the golden mean or *sectio divina*. Examining a medieval page one can frequently see a height/width ratio of the text (not the page itself but the margined text within it) that approximates 1.618 (*phi*) or the ratio of 5:8.[3] Quill pens were made from the pinion feathers of many species of regionally available birds – swans, geese and turkeys were the preferred species – and the scribe held in his own left hand a small knife for both sharpening the quill end (our word 'pen-knife' has its ancestry there) and lightly scraping errors from the parchment. To prevent inadvertent rubbing during composition, spaces were measured prior to the scribe's work for the later addition of any illuminated initials in gold leaf or tints evolved from precious metals. By the seventh to twelfth centuries, book covers were made of wood or heavier leather to keep the parchment pages from swelling with humidity. Clasps were often used on the outer front edges of the covers to assist in keeping pages flat. Spines evolved from being stab-sewn, capable of accommodating a single sheet folded to form a signature, to a chain-link system that could accommodate multiple separate signatures. (Stab-sewn bindings are stitched together near the binding edge, whereas chain-stitched bindings allow groups of signatures to be sewn together through the fold.)

Add to these stages the arduous act of writing itself, often in cold and poorly lit scriptoria, and it is clear the entire activity of book-production was extremely labour-intensive. A single page prepared for the scriptorium could take a day or more just to inscribe, barring errors or other delays, tiring the body, mind and eyes. Some scripts are as small as one-sixteenth of an inch high, too small to be easily read with the unaided eye, suggesting the devotion was not in the act of reading but the act of the inscription into the parchment surface itself – literally making the word flesh. Digital enlargements of such scripts reveal an astonishing accuracy in the straightness of line, the height of script, and the shape and detail of individual letters.[4] One can imagine young scribes possessing a myopia ideally suited for the difficult purpose of repeatedly producing minute script, and gradually losing their ability – likely their sight altogether – much as today's high-performing athletes have relatively brief spans of prowess.

The monastery process was efficient enough to allow the production of an enormous number of books and thus their spread and influence throughout Europe until the invention of printing with moveable type in the mid-fifteenth century. The desired feature of portability, and the longevity of parchment and sophisticated inks, combined to make the book a formidable communication device. The assembly-line process and chain-link binding structure also meant that sections of a book – called 'peciae' – could be re-sequenced, inserted, extracted, edited or omitted altogether (the 'pecia system'), thus introducing a flexibility in the concept of the bible's canonical contents impossible for its predecessor, the scroll. This particular feature was crucial to the evolution of the Bible's canon, indeed to the very concept of the Bible's many reinforcing sections, narrative authorities and interpretations. The New Testament's twenty-seven books – the Gospels, Acts, Apostles' letters and Revelation – were recognized as canonical as early as the fourth century, and formalized as such in 692; the precise text and the inclusion of the Old Testament were not decreed by the Catholic Church until the Council of Trent in 1546, and even later by the Church of England. The flexibility in content allowed by the pecia system played an enormous role in the evolution of the Bible's canon. As the scholar-librarian Christopher De Hamel observes 'the Bible is not a single narrative but a series of often unconnected or loosely associated groups of short books. Those familiar with the text will know that even an exact definition of these individual components is not always easy'.[5]

The fact that the physical structure of the book permitted a flexibility of content had other far-reaching consequences as well. If the book could be a vessel capable of absorbing the evolving contents of the Bible, it could absorb all kinds of changing contents – and on demand. Monasteries took advantage of this by producing Books of Hours and other book genres tailored to the devotional preferences of private buyers. The market took advantage of this by turning bookmaking into a business enterprise that could respond to wealthy individuals' reading needs, and to the instructional needs of emerging universities. With the Renaissance and the rise of humanism came an increased demand for content that the flexible book could accommodate, indeed could drive.

Several technical challenges compromised the book's ability to achieve its potential in this regard, however. Of its many labour-intensive and costly features, the process of creating the parchment page was one of the most critical. The procedure for producing paper, invented in China roughly simultaneously with the emergence of the codex in the Mediterranean basin, reached Europe in the thirteenth century. It involved reducing cloth fibre to a watery pulp that could then be dried and stretched and thinned and bleached – slightly less laborious than the creation of parchment, but no longer reliant on animal husbandry, about one-tenth the cost of parchment, one-quarter its thickness and, crucially, capable of accepting ink more accurately.

The other part of book production that required so much labour was the process of inscription itself. Manual, time-consuming, physically demanding and inefficient, it meant a many-to-one, human-to-book ratio of effort. Gutenberg is widely acknowledged as the one who reversed that ratio, inventing a press that could produce many identical copies of a single text through the efficient reduction of duplicated tasks. Possibly others had the same idea. What turned the idea into a reality, though, was a combination of emerging technologies. Paper – cheap, thin and ink-friendly – was one. But Gutenberg himself crucially invented two others. One was new viscous printers' inks made from 'lampblack' (flame soot and varnish) that were darker, more permanent and more paper-ready than their water-based and vellum-specific predecessors. The other, drawing on Gutenberg's previous expertise in metals, was his invention of new metal for type, combining lead, tin and antimony to produce 'speculum'; it separated evenly from the mold into which its liquid state had been poured to make the letter type, and when solid it took and released the new inks efficiently. And of course – more conceptual than technological – was the inspired breakthrough that saw letters as individual, moveable objects, capable of reuse and repositioning. In Walter Ong's words, 'alphabet letterpress printing, in which each letter was cast on a separate piece of metal, or type, marked a psychological breakthrough of the first order ... It embedded the word itself deeply in the manufacturing process and made it into a kind of commodity' – something to be produced, sold, purchased and consumed.[6]

As with many transformative inventions, Gutenberg's printing press was inspired by familiar objects – in this case, olive and grape presses – and envisioned for a new purpose. Much was inspired by scriptorium precedent as well. The printing press process borrowed the manuscript's assembly-line sequence of people and tasks, replacing rulers and scribes and initialers with typecasters who cut type, printers who designed the page and the book, compositors who set the type in place, cutters who made woodblock prints for illustrations and initials, and pressmen who worked the press itself. Gutenberg began cutting type for the first printed Bible in 1449, composition of the pages began in 1452 and the printing of approximately one hundred 42-line Bibles was completed in 1456. Gutenberg printed his first thirty Bibles on parchment at a rate of 170 sheep per Bible; the one hundred Bibles he then printed on paper would have required, had they been on parchment, over 15,000 animals.

The intellectual and social and political consequences of the printing press are the subject of much debate. The nature of those consequences is attended to in the other chapters in this section. The transformative scale of those consequences cannot be questioned, however. Books became cheaper and easier and faster to produce, and as a result the numbers of copies of books, and of original texts to be copied, grew exponentially. Print was easier to read than cursive script, enabling more efficient silent reading. The pace of both the production of books (printing and selling) and their consumption (buying and reading) increased, leading to a self-perpetuating dynamic of greater literacy rates, greater demand and a greater ability to meet it. A book off the printing press consisted of paper pages that were relatively long-lasting, print that was clear, a physical structure that permitted varied contents, an efficiently transportable weight and size and a relatively affordable price tag. And the press itself was small and cheap enough that within fifty years of its invention Europe contained at least 200 of them, and they produced more books in that short time than had been produced by hand to that point in history. The printing press was so prolific, its technologies so transformative and efficient, that its fundamentals – a wooden hand-powered press, cloth-fibre paper produced in large sheets, new inks and metal types, an assembly-line production reminiscent of the scriptorium's – experienced only incremental change for almost three centuries.

Refinements would occur nonetheless and, not surprisingly, to the place of inscription itself, the paper page. Cloth-fibre paper sufficed, but it became increasingly costly because the raw materials – linens and rags – were themselves hand-made and, by the early eighteenth century, in short supply. Nature had always been making its own thin, light and very strong paper, though, by masticating wood fibre into pulp in the mandibles of the 'paper wasp' (*polistinae*). The French multidisciplinary scientist René de Réaumur recorded his observation of the wasp making its nest, and the potential impact for human papermaking, in a 1719 treatise. Wasps, he wrote,

> form very fine paper, like ours; they extract the fibres of common wood of the countries where they live. They teach us that paper can be made from the fibres of plants without the use of rags and linen ... If we had woods similar to those used by the American wasps for their paper, we could make the whitest paper, for this material is very white. By a further beating and breaking of the fibres that the wasps make and using the thin paste that comes from them, the very fine paper may be composed. This study should not be neglected, for it is, I dare say, important. The rags from which we make our paper are not an economical material and every paper-maker knows that this substance is becoming rare. While the consumption of paper increases every day, the production of linen remains about the same. In addition to this the foreign mills draw upon us for material. The wasp seems to teach us a means of overcoming these difficulties.[7]

Paper from wood pulp would prove, after refinements to the process by the end of the nineteenth century, to be whiter, thinner, better at absorbing ink, more legible, cheaper and made of more readily available raw materials, than cloth-fibre paper. It would also introduce perhaps the most environmentally destructive product of the industrial revolution, for it required access to vast amounts of flowing water in the form of rivers that conveniently carried away the poisonous chemicals required to break down wood fibre, congeal it into a paper-ready paste, purify it and, most damaging, bleach it – lye, hydrogen peroxide, chlorine dioxide, acetic acid, sulfur, sodium silicate and chlorine gas.

Notably, the reason paper was in such high demand, depleting quantities of linen and other cloth and causing Réaumur in the early eighteenth century to ponder the efficiencies of the wasp, was not books *per se* – it was newspapers. By the time of Gutenberg, the demand for the book required, and produced, the technologies necessary for its own advanced structural state. By the eighteenth century those technologies were, in turn, used in the service of newspaper production – the epitome of relentlessly paced and produced book-like efficiencies requiring all the current advances in type metals, inks, paper and mass production assembly lines. The material inventiveness that had gone into producing the book was, by the eighteenth century, redirected toward the purpose of the book's doppelganger, the newspaper. In return, the material and technological innovations that kept the newspaper in step with demand indirectly benefited the book and, most significantly, the novel.

The 1725 invention of the stereotype printing technique was a crucial example. For a text of any kind to be set for printing, prior to stereotype, each letter had to be set individually in place for each page, and any reprints had to repeat the composing process – a time-consuming and costly activity when undertaken for a book of novel length. Stereotype involved casting a mold for a complete page, releasing the type to be used for other printing projects and permitting the mold to be used for as many printings as necessary. This freed printers from having to guess how many reprints or editions a book might require, and meant newspaper printing could occur simultaneously on separate presses, reducing cost while increasing copies and speed of production. The consequences of stereotyping for the rise of the novel genre are difficult to measure. Guesswork regarding print runs and reprints still approaches an art form in publishing houses. In the eighteenth century when the novel itself was a new genre of the book and analyses of readership markets were centuries away, the many determinants of a novel's potential readership and market were virtually impossible to predict, leaving most printers no choice but to estimate conservatively and to spend the money to recompose and reissue when demand exceeded expectations. Due to their length, novels were costly to produce in the first place, and the average print run of 500–750 copies for seventeenth- and early-eighteenth-century novels meant a high price for the purchaser, preventing the mass readership the genre would later attract. The advent of the stereotype process, however, meant printers could reissue a novel on demand at considerably less cost than before. And if economies of scale in novel production meant that printers could benefit financially from print runs that responded to demand instead of to guesswork, it was logical that the best-selling novel would become an attractive commodity.

Other technologies emerged to ensure that happened. Until the beginning of the nineteenth century, the physical printing press was still operated by hand and manually fed with single sheets of paper. Each sheet was designed to be folded, and the folded sheet produced a set of pages called a signature. Bindings, too, were individually sewn and fitted to each book, necessitated by the irregular and imprecise dimensions of each signature or even each page, and of each unbound book to the next. These features impeded the pace of book production until the invention, in 1800, of the all-metal press by the Englishman Charles Stanhope, who exploited his country's improvements in metal casting to create a single-cast machine frame. Its increased strength and weight from the wood press of the day allowed a faster production time. The improvements in strength also meant that paper could be run through the press at a faster pace, opening the way for the use of continuous roll paper, invented by Nicholas-Louis Robert in London two years earlier, and first produced by machine there in 1807. Add to these achievements Friedrich König's fast steam-driven press that substantially reduced the need for manual labour, and the invention in the 1840s of the rotary drum press that pulled in continuous roll paper, and a virtually transformed book-printing assembly line existed to mass-produce books at an unheard-of pace.

That assembly line, though, originally served the purposes of the newspaper industry, not book printing. The first steam-driven press was built for *The Times* newspaper in London in 1814. But by 1840 the book printing trade in England had moved pretty well entirely to the new technology, accompanied by faster and more efficient, though still mostly manual, binding processes. By 1852 du Réaumur's earlier reflections on the potential for wood-pulp paper had caught the attention of the Englishman Hugh Burgess who helped design such a process, followed by chemical refinements to it by the American C. B. Tilghman in 1867 and the German C. F. Dahl in 1879. Dahl's contributions included developing a process that pulped one of the most ubiquitous tree species in North America, the pine tree. Prior to 1750, approximately one hundred new titles were published annually in England; by 1825 approximately 600 annually; by the end of the nineteenth century approximately 6,000. The increase in book production was accompanied by drastically reduced costs to produce them. Prior to 1800 the cost of paper accounted for over 20 per cent of a book's production cost; by 1900 it accounted for less than 7 per cent. American publishing firms such as Beadle and Adams, among others, took advantage of the swift technological evolution in printing capacity and the equally swift decline in production costs, and sold thousands of novel-length publications at a price of ten cents each. One of the first such dime novels, Ann S. Stephens's 1860 *Malaeska*, sold over 300,000 copies, an enormous leap beyond the average 500–750 copies from the previous generation of printing press technology. It was followed by a succession of American dime novels such as the Buffalo Bill stories by Ned Buntine (aka Edward Judson) and Colonel Prentiss Ingraham's *The Woman Trapper or Arkansas Sal and the Apaches* – one of over 1,000 novels and 'novelettes' he wrote.

The consequences for the book – and primarily the novel – of the press's improvements and of wood pulp paper's refinements were clearly enormous. It could be said that the physical structure of the book was not changed significantly from the period of monastic book production, but the technology-driven relationship among its principle stakeholders – printers, authors and readers – as well as what that physical structure could affordably contain, were transformed. Charles Dickens's *Pickwick Papers* remains a good example of all of that. Originally published in 1836 by Chapman and Hall in twenty monthly one-shilling instalments of 32 pages each, it sold up to 40,000 copies per instalment. The audience was not only enormous but, given the very low cost, more evenly distributed across income levels than before. A reader could purchase all the instalments for less than the complete novel would otherwise have cost. As important, it inspired a narrative design that Dickens would explore and develop throughout his writing career. The instalments would typically culminate at a point in the plot that created reader anticipation and thus reader demand, generating a plot and sub-plot motif that would come to typify the novel structure. That, in turn, gave Dickens the opportunity to develop large casts of characters to drive that structure, and to develop the many opportunities a now affordable long novel capacity would provide. By 1860, Dickens was selling 100,000 copies of *Great Expectations*'s weekly instalments in his new *All the Year Round* magazine. It was issued by Chapman and Hall in a three-volume set in 1861; five printings appeared in quick succession to encourage sales. Almost all of *Great Expectations*'s first 1,000 copies were purchased by Mudie's Select Library and were continuously loaned out. (As a result, a set in excellent condition is now hard to find, and can command upwards of $125,000.)

Charles Edward Mudie, like Charles Dickens, was an astute businessman. In return for purchasing large quantities of books from a publisher, Mudie would pay about half of what the publisher would charge for them on the market. He paid 15 shillings per copy for the first printing of Chapman and Hall's edition of *Great Expectations*, for example, which otherwise sold for over 30 shillings. He encouraged publishers to produce three-volume sets so that he could effectively supply three times the number of readers with one book (three readers could read the same book, at different stages, simultaneously) thereby attracting a larger membership to pay his annual one guinea fee. Mudie's libraries thrived well into the 1860s, after which time their influence waned as a result of the 1850 Public Libraries Act in England (which gave local communities the power to establish free public libraries). But until then, the result was that book prices were set artificially higher than most people could afford, ensuring Mudie's its corner of the subscription library market and publishers their bulk sales.[8]

The alternatives in England were its precursor to America's dime novels – 'shilling shockers' and 'penny dreadfuls' such as *Varney the Vampire: Or the*

Feast of Blood (1847, anonymous) or Thomas Preskett Prest's 1846 *Sweeney Todd, the Demon Barber of Fleet Street*. Mudie regarded such books as disreputable and refused to buy them. Ignored by him, made of cheap paper, poor bindings and sloppy printing, they were one-thirtieth the price of a three-volume Chapman and Hall *Great Expectations* and thus attracted enormous purchasing audiences. Too, by the last three decades of the nineteenth century, the sewing, gathering and covering of books became more automated – often called 'edition binding' – to keep pace with the automated press, and drove prices down even further. One result was that by and large the novel came to be regarded as a cheap commodity and, analogously, an aesthetically inferior genre of human expression. Henry James was responding in part to that view of the novel when he wrote in the 1884 'The Art of Fiction' that 'the old superstition about fiction being "wicked" has doubtless died out in England; but the spirit of it lingers in a certain oblique regard directed toward any story which does not more or less admit that it is only a joke'. And Mark Twain argued in his 1895 'Fenimore Cooper's Literary Offenses' that novelistic technique needed to be taken more seriously than Cooper did, whose work he evidently ranked with that of Prest, Buntine and Stephens. Like many inexpensive products of mechanical reproduction, the novel's artistic and monetary values were seen as one and the same; and the low production costs coupled with mass production capabilities opened a new market for attention-grabbing storytelling over artistic depth.

Or maybe it is the other way around: the wide currency of the novel, enabled by its technologized printing press assembly line, immersed more of the human imagination in the world of the book, opening the way for the explosion of novelistic experimentation and sophistication in the late nineteenth century and thereafter. The newspaper business once again obliged, driving further improvements to the printing process that increased speed (by the 1930s newspaper printers could produce tens of thousands of papers an hour) while reducing costs. Synthetic glues that replaced stitched bindings followed for book printers, along with the move from cloth or cardboard covers to thick paper covers. Together, these developments encouraged the development of the modern paperback. It had emerged in France and Germany in the mid-nineteenth century (particularly the Tauchnitz editions) to offer inexpensive reprints of popular authors, but in the 1930s it was redeployed by Albatross, Penguin, Mercury and others for first editions of such writers as Ernest Hemingway, Dorothy L. Sayers, Agatha Christie and Dashiell Hammett. The ultimate embodiment of consciously inexpensive and speedy book production, the paperback was a response to a massive demand for reading material that was otherwise met by newspapers and magazines. Priced to sell at sixpence (in the case of Penguin) and placed in drugstores and Woolworth outlets alongside newspapers and magazines, books from the high- to the low-brow were suddenly available in the form of paperbacks that were easily accessible as well as portable, inexpensive and disposable. Their rapid pace of production invited a writing production line of its own – formulaic fiction that kept pace with the consumption and production of the book, just as the newspaper kept pace with constantly changing events. Mysteries, romances, detective fiction, suspense, children's series and horror novels were some results (Albatross and Penguin colour-coded their different kinds of series) – impossible to imagine in the absence of the book's updated technologies of production, circulation and marketing. So too were encyclopedias, previously so large and compendious as to be unaffordable to most individual buyers since their eighteenth-century inception. With them, in fact, emerged the phenomenon of affordable access to reasonably portable archived information. Readers no longer had to move to where the information was – they could access it in their homes. In fact, they didn't even have to leave their homes to purchase it because salesmen brought it right to their door.

By the early twentieth century, the book had essentially achieved a technological equilibrium. It was a device that gave permanence to human expression; it could contain many kinds of information, from the novelistic to the encyclopedic; its physical structure provided easy access to that information; its quality of inks and paper and bindings made it readable; its size and weight made it comfortable to hold and portable; and its efficiencies of production and the availability of its raw materials made it affordable. Several factors converged to disturb that equilibrium, however. One was the cost of paper, in part a result of the unrestricted global depletion of forests that reached a critical point midway through the twentieth century. The depletion was not caused by the book industry alone but by all forms of commerce that relied on paper, from building materials to newspapers to office supplies. Recycling, a necessary response, increased the cost of paper as well.

The intrigue of digital reading environments became another factor. Whereas the development of the three-dimensional book was an evolutionary adaptation to reading needs, part of the move to electronic books has been a response to the possibilities inherent in the technology itself, not exclusively to greater demand for the book to be something more than it already was. Experiments occurred in the 1980s that involved exploiting the new medium of digital hyperlinks to replace the three-dimensional novel's authorially determined narrative structure with a more reader-oriented and aleatory one. The experiments, such as the 1990 *Afternoon: A Story* and *Disappearance: A Novel* by Michael Joyce, are fascinating, highly innovative reconceptions of narrative and of the reading experience that give the reader almost limitless choices for connecting narrative lines. In the process they overcome the fixed narrative sequences and authorially determined outcomes prescribed by the book's static printed form. Such hypertexts do not attract large audiences of readers, however, and remain a curiosity rather than a trend. As of 2011, Amazon.com has been selling more books in electronic format than it does physical books through the mail, but the contents of the electronic books are not, like Joyce's are, responses to their new technology – they remain in most cases uninfluenced by it, and their text remains the same whether read in electronic format or as a physical book. In fact, most are first produced as physical books and later, or simultaneously, as electronic texts. The authorial imagination, and the imaginations of readers, still seem to dwell in the world of the physical book, or the world of electronic books that are at most modestly changed versions of the physical book.

The evolution of the book prior to the advent of digital technology witnessed a symbiotic relationship between the contents of the codex and its technologies; human demand for written communication required technological responses that produced the book, and technological improvements to the book and its manufacturing processes opened the book to new audiences, genres and purposes. Digital technology has released the text from the book's physical structure, altering the conditions within which the book, in the form of electronic text, can be experienced. Electronic texts take the feature of portability to a new realm, reduce the reliance on the commodity of paper, offer easier access to the text itself via instant downloading capability, and provide more efficient dynamics of searchability, taking readers to the furthest remove yet from the time when, to access information, humans travelled to where it was inscribed, immoveable, in stone. The real revolution inspired by digital communication technology – computers and android devices that upload and download text and visual information accessed from everywhere – has transformed almost all communications media. We still, as of the time of writing, live within a period of technological overlap, during which one medium of communication coexists with its potential successor. Many years into the digital universe now, however, the physical book does seem to maintain a relatively stable position in the human imagination – a testament to its bestowal of permanence on a text, and its accessibility and readability and affordability.

NOTES

1. M. Battiste, 'Print Culture and Decolonizing the University: Indigenizing the Page: Part 1', in P. Stoicheff and A. Taylor (eds.), *The Future of the Page* (University of Toronto Press, 2004), 111–23.
2. For the argument in favour of Rome, see C. H. Roberts and T. C. Skeat, *The Birth of the Codex* (Oxford University Press, 1983); for North Africa as the origin of the codex see E. G. Turner, *The Typology of the Early Codex* (University of Philadelphia Press, 1977).

3. See J. Tschichold, *The Form of the Book: Essays on the Morality of Good Design* (Washington: Hartley and Marks, 1991), 44.
4. Otto Ege collection. 'Fifty Original Leaves from Medieval Manuscripts, Western Europe XII–XVI Century': Leaf 9, from a bible inscribed by the Dominican Order. University of Saskatchewan Library.
5. C. De Hamel, *The Book: A History of the Bible* (London: Phaidon Press, 2001), ix.
6. W. Ong, *Orality and Literacy: The Technologizing of the Word* (London: Methuen, 1982), 118.
7. Quoted in D. Hunter, *Papermaking: The History and Technique of an Ancient Craft* (New York: A. A. Knopf, 1947), 314.
8. R. L. Patten, *Charles Dickens and 'Boz': The Birth of the Industrial-Age Author* (Cambridge University Press, 2012).

6

MARGARET J. M. EZELL

Handwriting and the book

As is true for those working in many fields in the humanities, to write a chapter on 'handwriting and the book' would have been much more straightforward twenty or thirty years ago. Handwritten manuscripts then occupied a very specific position in the study of literary texts. If they were created after the establishment of the printing press in Europe in 1450 and the subsequent 'revolution' brought about by cheap print, manuscripts were understood as the first steps towards a printed book, drafts preceding print, of interest in understanding the creative processes and (if existing in multiple versions) supplying the variants to be compiled in preparing the best possible modern print edition. If they never achieved the status of a printed book, however, post-1450 manuscripts, especially those of the seventeenth through nineteenth centuries, were understood to have been created under adverse circumstances, whether that be official censorship by church or state, lack of access to a press, or lack of preparation by the author (traditionally imagined as a solitary individual) to engage with the world of print or fitness to enter the world of commercial letters.

The changing focus of textual studies and bibliography over the last twenty years has confirmed that handwritten texts and printed ones do indeed occupy such roles and relationships and these remain fruitful areas for further study. Nevertheless new scholarship has increasingly drawn our attention to the complexities of the relationships between the handwritten and the printed text and between the writers and readers of both, highlighting how the concept of 'manuscript' as a technology overtaken and made obsolete by print obscures the extent to which print indeed can generate, sustain and organize handwriting.[1] The habits of looking at post-medieval European and Scandinavian manuscripts in particular as somehow longing to be in print, and of looking at print as being a marker of commercial success and thus readership, obscure and oversimplify the complexities of not only the post-1450 physical objects themselves, but also the varied ambitions of a book's creators and readers and of the subsequent preservers of textual objects.

Medieval manuscript volumes and printed handwriting

The word 'manuscript' means quite simply 'written by hand', and the European medieval manuscript book produced between the fifth century and the late fifteenth century was the product of many hands.[2] A variety of scribal practices were involved in producing manuscript books, which ranged from such richly illuminated texts as the *Book of Kells* (the 340-folio work created by ninth-century Celtic monks) to plain texts of the bible done in a single volume in Paris in the 1200s (whose double-columned octavo format, use of thin paper and divisions into chapters still is the standard format for printed bibles today). The creation of such books involved the labours of the person who prepared the vellum or parchment paper, the scribe, a rubricator who added in the coloured inks and typically a separate illuminator.[3] Initially manuscript books were produced in monasteries in spaces devoted to the production of texts only. In the scriptorium, groups of monks produced copies of manuscript texts, usually for the monastery's library, or perhaps for presentation as gifts. By the fourteenth century, however, demand for these handwritten books had increased to such an extent that commercial scriptoria emerged, typically located in major European cities such as Paris and Rome and also in the Netherlands, those in Paris sometimes employing women as illuminators and scribes.[4]

The physical design of medieval, preprint manuscript volumes signalled their possible use and audience. Books that were created for medieval missionaries to help spread the Gospel, for example, were different from those created for the royal courts of Henry II and Charlemagne; prayer books created for use in a home were correspondingly different from those intended for a life in the monastery or parish church. The largest books, such as a lectern Bible from which the monks would read aloud to each other, required a very large piece of vellum, only folded once to make its pages. In contrast, Books of Hours were designed to be held in the hand and are frequently shown in medieval art as being read by ladies. Such manuscript books are typically heavily decorated with miniature scenes helping to guide the reader through the day. This was not a book used in the official Church services and the contents were frequently customized to suit the owner (for example prayers to St Margaret being associated with childbirth) and often the names and dates of important domestic events such as births, deaths and marriages were added to the individual book. The Book of Hours was, as critics have observed, 'the basic book for medieval household ... it was from the Book of Hours that children were taught to read', and it sold throughout Europe in 'immense numbers'.[5] Similar domestic manuscript books continued to be produced in England well throughout the nineteenth century.

As recent studies of medieval manuscript books have highlighted, 'the manuscript text is constituted by the individuals who created it: scribe, rubricator, corrector, illuminator' rather than by its subject matter alone, with the result that 'manuscript culture takes up its physical residence in that same world of variation, imprecision, and error' and 'each medieval "text" was as unique and concrete as the individual who copied or read it'. To attempt to read and understand a medieval handwritten book in terms of a single author or a stable text, John Dagenais asserts, is to deny the medieval practice of 'ethical reading' based on a process of the active reader's judgment and choice, the text changing through time with the addition of glosses, commentaries and marginalia into a different handwritten book from that which left the original scribe's hands.[6]

With the advent of print in Europe, early printed books (incunabula) were designed to look like handwritten ones, also signalling their possible use and audience. Studies of the development of type suggest that European printers in the 1500s were deliberately using formats already made familiar to readers from handwritten books, from the use of ligatures to link letters, common abbreviations, the formats of how the books began and ended and use of elaborate enlarged capital letters.[7] The printer Aldus Manutius (1449–1515) who founded the Aldine Press in Venice based the italic font used in his 1501 edition of Virgil on his own handwriting; his typefounder Francesco Griffo created the first roman type by modelling it after classical Roman carved capital letters. Aldus also invented the octavo format for printed books modelled on the private pocket notebook, a small volume that could be easily carried on one's person. Some incunabula have been described by literary historians as 'pseudo-manuscripts', or even as attempts to 'counterfeit' a handwritten text, a claim mostly rejected by recent book histories.[8]

The technologies of handwriting and of printing were both essential in creating these early printed books. This is highlighted in the practice of rubrication, or the addition to the page of passages done in coloured inks (typically red, but sometimes blue or green) often to announce the beginning or ending of a section, but also serving as decorative rulings on the page. The majority of incunabula, Margaret M. Smith has argued, 'did not issue from the press in a finished state ... [i]t is possible that hardly any incunabula was considered to be "finished" by its printer', but typically would require hand finishing, due, she argues, to the cost of printing with red or coloured inks.[9] Thus, from their origins, printed books have had a complicated and reciprocal relationship with handwritten ones and the technologies that produce them.

We find the self-conscious attempt by medieval printers to represent handwriting in print continuing well into the future. In seventeenth-century

England, news both foreign and domestic could be obtained by those living in the countryside by a subscription to a scribal newsbook compilation, such as those issued twice a week by Henry Muddiman (1629–92) in the late 1650s and throughout the early years of the Restoration. When Ichabod Dawks (1661–1731) created a printed version of the scribal form, *Dawks' News-Letter* (1696–1716), he had special type created, 'Scriptorial English no. 2', to mimic the appearance of the handwritten letter, and left a space blank at the top for a handwritten salutation to an individual subscriber. The printers of such news publications thus created the suggestion of intimate, inside knowledge about politics and foreign affairs being privately communicated by mimicking the appearance of handwriting and the format of earlier manuscript subscription-only publications.

The strategic use of script over print characters continued in the nineteenth and twentieth centuries, especially in publications which sought to distinguish themselves from more popular, commercial works. The use of handwriting suggested exclusivity as well as an artistic appreciation of the page. The modernist literary journal *The Neolith* (1908) published by the poet and popular children's writer Edith Nesbit (1858–1924) to which George Bernard Shaw, H. G. Wells and G. K. Chesterston contributed short stories and poems, was a magazine printed on folio-sized sheets. It used calligraphy by Graily Hewitt reproduced by lithograph, the technique of printing typically reserved for fine art drawings. Hewitt had the unenviable task of copying the contributions onto special transfer paper and organizing the layout of the page without knowing what else might be submitted. Not too surprisingly, given the amount of unpaid labour involved (only the printer was actually paid), this artistic magazine only ran for four issues.[10]

Handwritten culture, hybrid books and social authorship

The blending of two forms of book production, handwritten and printed, was often the result of the desire of the owner to create a unique and personal volume, but sometimes it was the result of collaboration between author, bookseller and reader. Books gained value, as historians of reading have pointed out, by the layers of handwritten glosses and marginalia added by their owners. Printed books during the early modern period well into the eighteenth century were personalized objects, with the purchaser buying only the gathered printed sheets, and then taking them to a bookbinder for an individually chosen covering. Owners were invited by the printer or the author to correct by hand the printer's mistakes listed on the errata sheet, and readers frequently drew up their own table of contents and index which they wrote in the end papers. Booksellers and published authors also provided the means for the purchase of individual handwritten copies, some published writers advertising their unpublished manuscripts in the backs of their printed works, urging readers to acquire the handwritten volumes directly from a bookseller (H. R. Woudhuysen documents this practice in the instance of Thomas Hill in 1571, for example) and there is evidence that booksellers were willing to lend manuscripts to be copied by compilers as a side-line to selling printed texts.[11]

Some early modern owners took the personalization of their books beyond selecting bindings and adding annotations, creating what are referred to as 'hybrid books', texts that fuse the individuality of handwritten volumes with the contents of printed texts. This practice continued in the nineteenth century in 'extra illustrated works', volumes in which the owner adds extra materials relating to the contents, often engraved portraits or scenes: in a New York rare book auction catalogue dated 1900, some of the items for sale included Item #34, James Boaden's *Memoirs of Mrs. Siddons* (1827) containing an 'autograph letter of the author, and numerous scarce portraits inserted', and Item #62, Colley Cibber's *An Apology for the Life of Colley Cibber* (1740), with 350 additional portraits, an autograph letter, hand-coloured drawings of eighteenth-century actresses and other supporting secondary texts including 'A Lick at a Liar, and other interesting data'.[12] The addition of personal writing and information, added illustrations, and decorations could thus transform a printed text into a unique book where print and handwriting illuminate each other within the volume's space.

As recent scholarship has highlighted, many early modern readers were keen to personalize the volumes they owned, not just with marginal annotations, but by creating *Sammelbände*, where multiple texts were bound together as one, creating personal collections sometimes combining printed and handwritten texts.[13] We find such hybridity in an early example, a small, leather-bound duodecimo volume with 'Life and Death 1600' picked out in gold on the spine.[14] It opens with a hand-drawn and coloured frontispiece, a familiar *memento mori* emblem of a small chubby angel, or putto, leaning on a skull, in a circular frame, with Latin verses on the opposite page signed 'Jeff Gilbert' done in a very fine italic hand. This is followed by fair copy verses in English and Latin, formally laid out on the page, on the topics 'Of Death', 'Of Man', 'Of Old Age' and 'Of Sickness', which lead to the interior of the book, the printed text of the Countess of Pembroke's translation of Philippe de Mornay, *A Discourse of Life and Death* (London: William Ponsonby, 1600).

The printed text, however, does not reside separately from its handwritten and decorated paratexts. The central printed device of the anchor on the title page is hand-coloured and there are handwritten Latin mottoes in gold ink rimming the title page's sides. On the blank reverse side of the printed title page, facing the first printed page, a small rectangular printed image has been pasted in and hand-coloured, a scene of two men viewing a funeral monument, to which has been added an ink inscription in English 'Time to live & Time to dy:/ God grant us live eternally'. Below that is a larger square pasted in, a printed image, also hand-coloured, of two figures, one old and one young, looking in a mirror as a skeleton watches over their shoulders; framing the outside edge of the image on all sides are numbered English verses: '1. Behold thy self in glass/ As thou art; so he was'. After the end of the printed volume, whose capital printed letters are decorated by hand, the book concludes with another section of manuscript verses, faced by more emblematic rectangular scenes. The bound volume closes with the repetition of the emblem of a putto in the circle, this time pointing at an image of Christ sitting in judgment at the end of time, with the inscription *'memoratoe novissima'* at its feet. At the very bottom of the page *'Post tenebras spero Lucem'* ('After darkness, I hope for light', Job 17:12), is added in gold ink. This small volume is both an original manuscript collection and a manipulation of a print text, incorporating the features of the printed book with the ornate embellishments of colour, image and the individual hand choosing the framing devices and additional poems.

It is possible that this hybrid book may have been intended as a gift. The fair copy handwritten book preserved its status as a gift object from medieval times onward. The young Princess Elizabeth created manuscript books as presents; when she was eleven years old in 1544, she copied *The Miroir or Glasse of the Synneful Soul*, translating it from French, 'as well as the capacitie of my simple witte and small learning coulde extende themselves', as a present for her stepmother, Queen Catherine Parr. The following year she created a manuscript book of the prayers of Catherine Parr and translated them into Latin, French and Italian, dedicating it to her father, Henry VIII.[15] Both volumes also demonstrate her skills as an embroiderer, the covers of the two books being elaborately wrought with silk tapestry patterns interwoven with silver thread: the individual books in their content, format and physical presentation announce the young woman's piety, filial devotion, intellect and appreciation of the book as a beautiful object.

The calligrapher and miniaturist Esther Inglis (1571–1624) created fifty-nine manuscript books known to have survived from this period, with the object of obtaining patronage from members of the royal family or people of rank and substance. As with Elizabeth's gift books, these texts were typically signed and dated and they were designed to demonstrate both the accomplishments of the writer and the virtues of the recipient. Inglis employed a variety of decorative scripts and many of her books feature a self-portrait done in colour; she also manipulated the concept of the book, creating miniature volumes, some measuring only 45 × 70 mm (1.7" × 2.75" or the size of a large stamp), with lines of script only a millimeter high, a measurement equivalent to the thickness of an American dime.[16] The larger books she made for the royal family are often bound in a richly embroidered cover, one 'A Book of Armes of England' created for Henry, prince of Wales in 1609, done in velvet with his royal crest in pearls, adding yet another layer of material meaning to the content of the text itself through her handwork.[17]

A whimsical continuation of this tradition of handwritten royal gift books can be seen in the miniature books created for Queen Mary, wife of King George V, in 1922. The 200 tiny books were part of a doll house library created by Sir Edwin Lutyens, and measure 4 cm by 3.5 cm; each of the books is an individual handwritten text; the collection includes works by Edith Wharton, Sir Arthur Conan Doyle and Rudyard Kipling. Other original miniature handwritten volumes in this group include 'The Doll's-house cookery book' by Agnes Jekyll (1860–1937) and E. V. Lucas's 'The Whole Duty of Dolls' calligraphed by E. R. Cross, playing off of the titles of earlier printed texts of domestic conduct.[18] The handwritten gift books, whether their contents were devotional, heraldic or entertainment, gain part of their value because of the labour of the scribe and the suggestion of personal connection between the handcrafted text, the writer and the reader.

In the nineteenth century we find an example of the creation of such tiny miniature handwritten texts serving slightly different purposes. The novelists in the Brontë family entertained themselves as children and young adults with creating manuscript books from sheets of folded notebook paper, about 4.5" by 3.5" in size. One of the earliest of these was by Charlotte, aged ten, written for her younger sister, Anne, entitled 'Young Men's Play' in 1826; brother Branwell and Charlotte not only produced miniature novels, but also 'published' a 'magazine' which they issued once a month, striving to look as much like print as possible. In her miniature novel 'The Secret', Charlotte aged seventeen dated the manuscript 27 November 1833 and signed with her own name, thus claiming the work as her own rather than a collaboration.[19] What this suggests is that although they grew up in relative isolation at Haworth Parsonage in Yorkshire and were mostly educated at home, they were nevertheless children raised in a literate and literary family, whose father had published his own poetry in 1811, and whose awareness of contemporary printed poetry and fiction led the 21-year-old Charlotte to write to the Poet Laureate of England, Robert Southey, to ask his evaluation of her work. In this example, one can see the ways in which the carefully crafted handwritten text, miniature or otherwise, could still serve as a gift but also as preparation for entering into a commercial print environment.

Both reading and writing, however, were part of daily life in seventeenth-century England onward. We know about much of this activity through the posthumous publication of men's and women's poetry, books of devotions and autobiographical writings, but obviously this was only a small proportion of books created and preserved in literate households. Many of these manuscript books were designed for everyday use: early modern readers often compiled large handwritten volumes of excerpts from printed texts they read, arranged and annotated on the page to suit their own needs. This practice, of course, has continued unabated through time into the electronic and digital age of note-taking and record-keeping. Such personalized handwritten volumes range from simple schoolchild exercises to complex commonplace books with extensive indexes to aid in finding information quickly, to highly personalized collections which resemble private anthologies.[20]

Perhaps one of the most extreme examples of this conversion of multiple print texts into a personal volume is Thomas Trevelyon's *Miscellany*, a 654-page manuscript volume which he finished in 1608, and his 'Great Book' done in 1616.[21] Trevelyon's compilations of 'fragments and broken sentences' were done, he informs us in his epistle 'to the reader' of the Great Book, 'to accomplysh my minde, to pleasure my fryndes'. Designed for the author's and the readers' education and entertainment, the miscellany as well as his Great Book include 'prologues', page numbers, time lines, calendars, as well as biblical and historical genealogies, cautionary tales and proverbs; the miscellany also has two hundred pages of hand-drawn images of patterns, for mazes, floral borders, alphabets, garden design and abstract motifs and decorations, uniting the utilitarian with the decorative.[22]

On a more modest scale, we find numerous examples of early modern readers interested in compiling anthologies of verses by themselves and by others, long after print was established as a medium for the publication of collections of poems. Throughout the sixteenth and seventeenth centuries, lyric poetry in particular continued to circulate widely and to be collected in manuscript volumes prior to reaching print; manuscript miscellanies also frequently include poems copied from print sources. Arthur Marotti has pointed to the importance of manuscript poetry anthologies and courtly miscellanies as 'the meeting ground of literary production and social practices'.[23] The 'Devonshire MS', for example, contains 194 pieces from the early Tudor period, including verses by Sir Thomas Wyatt, as well as an exchange of love poems between Lady Mary Douglas and Lord Thomas Howard, most likely compiled by several women members of the court.[24] Often the contents of such manuscript anthologies were collected over several years, sometimes as items sent to the compiler as part of a letter resulting in a long-term, ongoing process. Other volumes were the result of making a fair copy by either the author or a family member. The well-connected seventeenth-century English Catholic family, the Astons, created both types. In the 'Tixall Miscellany', Constance Aston Fowler (d. 1664) collected poems by her friends, neighbours and brother Herbert as well as his acquaintances, including the diplomat Sir Richard Fanshawe, and inserted published poems by Donne and others sent to her; Herbert compiled his own miscellany which was copied by his wife.[25] The nineteenth-century poet and critic Samuel Taylor Coleridge is an example of a later writer practising this social circulation of handwritten texts and compilation volumes. Prior to venturing into print, he first collected his poems and those of his friends in manuscript volumes to share with family members; he also transcribed and circulated poems by others, recording in *Biographia Literaria*, doing some forty transcriptions of the poems of William Bowles, 'as the best presents he could offer to his friends'.[26]

Other manuscript books evolved over time as they were passed from generation to generation. Among the most common of these were recipe books, kept by both men and women, and the line was very fine between recipes for creating medicines and household remedies for humans and animals and those for the creation of confectionary and cosmetics.[27] Manuscript recipe books followed conventions for recording information, including who was compiling the book, where the recipe had come from and, in some cases, whether or not it was any good.[28] Very often writers who kept one form of manuscript book often created others. Ann Fanshawe (1625–80) wrote her *Memoirs* in 1676 for her son Richard, a text which has become an important source for historians of the English Civil War as Ann followed her diplomat husband and poet Sir Richard on his journeys; she also compiled a household book containing recipes acquired on the continent as well as traditional English ones, carefully preserved side by side with medical recipes.[29] Another woman writing during the English Civil War and Restoration years but speaking from the other side of the conflict, Lucy Hutchinson (1620–81), likewise composed a biography of her husband for their children and left behind voluminous autobiographical writings, as well as a translation of Lucretius, which she presented in a fair copy to the Earl of Angelesey.[30] Such texts might well be preserved by the family or friends, and some such as alchemistical writings of the natural philosopher Sir Kenelm Digby (1603–65) ultimately would appear in print; almost twenty years after his death, Digby's servant George Hartman published, 'for the good and benefit of the Publick', *A Choice Collection of Rare Secrets* (1682), a 272-page book from a manuscript volume entrusted to him by Digby before travelling to France.

The manuscript books of a seventeenth-century English scientist and man of letters who was also involved in print publication, Richard Waller (c. 1650–1715), also provide insight into the reciprocal nature of handwriting and the book, manuscript and print. Waller, who served for many years as the secretary to the Royal Society of London, edited the scientist Robert Hooke's writings for a posthumous edition, published accounts of his experiments and translated several Continental scientific treatises for print publication, but he also left behind two manuscript volumes. He was, notably, the son of a highly educated mother, Mary More (who was a painter and essayist and circulated her own texts in manuscript copies).[31] Waller's first known manuscript volume, the translation of Mapheus Vegius's (1407–58) addition to Book XII of the *Aeneid*, was prepared between 1674 and 1675 and is a splendid, lavishly decorated folio volume that contains only that text. Waller's 'The Poems of Albius Tibullus', in contrast, is a smaller octavo volume with gilt-edged pages, a fair copy text, whose contents are dated as ranging from 1679 to 1715, the year of Waller's death, and include much more than the title suggests.[32] The second book appears to be the same hand throughout, with only the poems appearing at the end showing any signs of emendation or correction.

Although the second volume was begun shortly after the first, the two volumes offer different concepts of the manuscript book and its relation to print. The translation of Mapheus does contain the paratextual elements that mark it as a seventeenth-century book, including an oval portrait of a young Richard Waller (unsigned but perhaps drawn by his mother) and an elaborate title page designed and signed by Waller. Its contents are organized with full-page illustrations of the text facing the verses, which are themselves ornamented in the margins with whimsical pen drawings using coloured inks and gold. This volume was clearly designed not only to showcase the young Waller's skills as a translator of Latin into English verse, but also his accomplishments as an artist and a calligrapher. The handwritten book was the final, finished product, a magnificent rich text celebrating and preserving its youthful creator's accomplishments.

In contrast, the 1679 'Tibullus' volume occupies a more complicated position with respect to printed books. The first 105 folios are devoted to Waller's translation of the Latin poet Tibullus and the poets associated with him (including the only known woman Latin poet Sulpicia), but the rest of the volume, also in fair copy, contains dated sections of miscellaneous English verse. The translation of Tibullus features all the paratextual apparatus of a printed book, including an elaborate allegorical frontispiece with facing poem 'The Mind of Ye Frontispiece', a separate title page stating that 'The Works of Albius Tibullus' are 'Englished' by 'R. W.' in 1681. The frontispiece drawing is dated as being by 'R. W. 1679' so this project clearly was several years in the making. The 'Tibullus' section concludes with 'Finis Date Ap. 30 1681'. The pages are carefully laid out, with facing Latin/English parallel columns in some places, and uses marginal glosses to give sources. It uses catch words at the bottom and a running header along the top, thus mimicking a printed text in appearance.

This carefully crafted manuscript text only takes up the first half of the volume. It could have been designed as a gift or presentation copy, except that instead of addressing a specific person or patron, Waller includes a two-page epistle 'To the Reader', thus again following the template of a printed volume. However, rather than addressing an imaginary audience asking for their approval and acceptance, Waller instead comments on the convention of having a prefatory epistle: 'It is so customary to enlarge books with a Preface, or an epistle', he begins, 'that is seems almost as preposterous to neglect it, as to forget the Portico, or Gate, in erecting a stately Fabrick: Therefore something by way of a Preface'. He continues in a seemingly ironic tone, 'I shall forbeare to trouble the "Reader" with the causes, that induced me to this translation, perchance a happy command, perchance my own satisfaction'. As he notes, Waller's presentation of the poems is done in a highly personal style which may not suit all readers: 'it may seem strange that I have divided some of the Elegies into three or more Parts which I did to render them more takeing and agreeable to the Genius of the Age; their length being tedious to a light airie, & volatile witte'.

The poems in the other gatherings in the volume likewise suggest that this was not a manuscript being prepared for the printer, but instead a handcrafted repository for Waller's final polished versions of his occasional verse, gathered together and inscribed at various points over the course of his life, and that the book travelled with him to several different residences. There is an elegy on the death of his friend and fellow scientist Robert Boyle dated 1710; there is a recurring figure in the later poems 'Urania', described as being Waller's muse for the long poem on the creation of the visible world, a retelling of Genesis that entirely omits any reference to the divine and focuses instead on atoms and optics. This Urania was most likely his daughter Mary, who also is the subject of two other poems in the later section of the volume: she was celebrated by an admirer in a poem inscribed on the wall of the dancing room at the nearby Sun Inn in Northaw, Hertfordshire, which her father transcribed into this volume and then turned into Latin, and, on her death, in a poem entitled simply 'An Elegy'.

Waller had translated the texts and engraved the frontispieces for several Royal Society publications; had he wished to publish this volume, certainly he had the means and abilities to do so. The paratextual elements signal his awareness of the presence and the needs of an external readership, but he leaves his 'Reader' a generalized, ironic blank, even though the contents are clearly directed towards friends and family members. Given the fair presentation of the materials stretching over a nearly 40-year span, it does not appear he valued the contents of his manuscript book less than his printed works. This is a handwritten book that makes full use of what by that time had become the conventions of a printed book, but one which apparently had no designs or desire ever to become one.

Handwritten books as the alternative to print

Handwritten books designed for an outside readership have thus existed alongside printing presses throughout the centuries in numerous countries, functioning for their writers and readers as personal textual creations exchanged as gifts or circulated in social authorship practices. Sometimes, however, handwriting was the technology of choice because access to a press was either limited by the number of presses or controlled by political or religious restrictions on what could be printed. For most of the seventeenth century in England, the number of presses was strictly limited; unless one resided in London, Edinburgh or one of the University cities, it could be difficult to have access to printers. Well into the eighteenth century, even if one did have access, the majority of published texts produced by booksellers were not literary ones. Even in the nineteenth and early twentieth centuries, access to a printing press could be more challenging than the circulation of handwritten copies, even though the desire for a large readership was there. And, of course, until the internet age, handwriting remained the safest technology to circulate clandestine satires against the state, religious parodies and critiques of the status quo.

Writings mocking important figures in England from the Elizabethan period through the eighteenth century most frequently took the form of handwritten lampoons or libels that were copied, circulated, surreptitiously posted and frequently collected into manuscript volumes. During the reign of James I, the printing of satires and epigrams was banned by Archbishop Whitgift; however, during his funeral an unknown hand pinned a manuscript satirizing him to the cloth on his hearse.[33] Handwritten satires proliferated over the course of the seventeenth century, serving almost as news reports; most manuscript miscellany volumes compiled during the seventeenth century contain copies of poems about various political scandals ranging from the execution for treason of the Earl of Essex, the various royal mistresses of Charles II, the mismanaged Anglo–Dutch Wars and the Exclusion Crisis attempting to bar the Catholic James II from the throne. The 1662 Printing Act against the publication of seditious texts remained in effect until 1692, and the official licenser Sir Roger L'Estrange (1616–1704) zealously pursued manuscript texts as well, urging that the legal term 'libel' be expanded to include handwritten texts since 'not one in 40 libels ever comes to Presse, though by the help of MS, they are well nigh as public'.[34] Individuals such as Sir William Haward of Tandridge created a 721-page collection of such satires.[35] Professional scribes such as Captain Robert Julian assembled manuscript collections in bound volumes for paying clients; although as Peter Beal has pointed out, unlike medieval scribes, seventeenth-century ones rarely signed their works, some by Julian have been identified, such as the collection of satires against Charles II from around 1682 owned by Lord Derby and hidden in his chimney for safekeeping.[36]

In addition to being the preferred mode of publication for early modern political and religious satires, handwritten texts could provide an alternative to print when access to presses was limited by geography. In this respect, Iceland offers a case study of the importance of the handwritten book after the introduction of print to a population. Although the first printing press was established in Iceland in 1530 by the last Catholic bishop Jon Arason and a complete translation of the bible into Icelandic was printed there in 1584, only one press existed in Iceland until the middle of the nineteenth century and that was subsequently controlled by the Lutheran church. No secular literature was even published in Iceland until the 1760s.[37]

Iceland, like Europe, had had a rich tradition of medieval manuscript literary production, notably its *Eddas* written in Old Norse which were first recorded in manuscripts that began appearing in the thirteenth century, such as the *Prose Edda* of Snorri Sturluson (1179–1241), Skaldic poetry and the heroic sagas, such as *Njáls saga*. Iceland historically also enjoyed a relatively high literacy rate, even though a largely rural society, and its language remained stable. Viðar Hreinsson, in his study of the literary career of the late nineteenth century working-class poet Stephan G. Stephansson, discusses the ways in which Iceland had a long tradition of both manuscript copying and original literature created by mostly self-educated farm dwellers from the seventeenth century onward.[38] Historians of popular Icelandic literature likewise have observed that while in Europe medieval chivalric stories 'formed the basis for a booming book trade from the sixteenth century onwards, in Iceland such materials circulated almost entirely in manuscript'. Looking in particular at the circulation of romances in manuscript, Driscoll notes that while several important medieval vellum manuscript collections exist, the vast majority of the surviving copies exist in paper manuscript books created after the Reformation and the majority of those were written after 1800.[39]

One Icelandic cultural critic has gone so far as to declare that with the increasing literacy rates in Iceland in the later part of the eighteenth century, 'the nineteenth century became the age of handwritten books'.[40] Although there was no longer as strict control of the press by the church, the majority of

Iceland's population were farmers or fishermen unable to afford expensive printed books. Sighvatur Grimsson (b. 1840) was a servant and a fisherman but he was also a highly prolific lay scholar, leaving behind over 160 manuscript volumes, including eight anthologies of poetry, collections of chivalric romances and autobiographical writings. He was paid to copy sagas for others and he also collected them for himself: the title page of one such collection of thirty stories announces 'Icelandic sagas: Based on the best manuscripts, which are not widely available, from ancient times. Written in a cold fishing camp while all were ashore but finished on the island of Flatey in Breidafjordur in 1867, by Sighvatur Grimsson of Borgarfjordur, October 1, 1861–December 13, 1867'.[41]

There are further contemporary examples of the ways in which the older practice of producing hand-done books during periods in which printed texts were also in circulation could be taken up by new groups for subversive purposes as well as overcoming geographical obstacles. We see this, for example, in the circulation of handwritten newspapers in Finland in the first part of the twentieth century and the *Samizdat* literary culture that flourished underground during the Soviet era. Like the writers of satires and lampoons of earlier periods, working-class university students in early twentieth century Finland in the context of the Civil War fought between the Red and the White Guards in 1918 produced their own newspaper, ironically called *The Enlightener* (1914–25), offering parodies of both sides of the conflict and revealing the hypocrisy of the church.[42] Later in the century starting in 1967, we find the Soviet Russian *Samizdat*, meaning 'self-published', an archive of hand-typed texts including the writings of Alexander Solzhenitsyn and the poetry of Boris Pasternak circulated in the post-Stalin era, sustaining an underground intellectual and literary culture.[43]

In each of these examples, handwriting or hand reproduction was the only way in which the messages of the writers could be circulated among a wider readership. *Samizdat* is one step away from the handwritten manuscript miscellany, but like handwritten books in the age of print throughout the centuries, it, too, shaped the culture of its creators and readers, sometimes directly opposing the dominant print culture, while sometimes simultaneously mimicking and echoing it.

NOTES

1. M. Barrett and P. Stallybrass, 'Printing, Writing and a Family Archive: Recording the First World War', *History Workshop Journal* 75 (2013), 1–32.
2. C. de Hamel, *A History of Illuminated Manuscripts* (Boston: David R. Goode, 1986), 7; 113–16.

3. R. G. Calkins, 'Stages of Execution: Procedures of Illumination as Revealed in an Unfinished Book of Hours', *International Center of Medieval Art* 17 (1978), 61–70; de Hamel, *The British Library Guide to Manuscript Illumination: History and Techniques* (University of Toronto Press, 2001), 45–60.
4. C. de Hamel, *Medieval Craftsmen: Scribes and Illuminators* (University of Toronto Press, 1992), 43. For nuns known to have been scribes and illuminators, see J. J. G. Alexander, *Medieval Illuminators and Their Methods* (New Haven, CT: Yale University Press, 1992), 18–19.
5. de Hamel, *History of Illuminated Manuscripts*, 164, 159.
6. J. Dagenais, *The Ethics of Reading in Manuscript Culture: Glossing the Libro de Buen Amor* (Princeton University Press, 1994), 17, 16.
7. M. M. Smith, 'The Design Relationship Between the Manuscript and the Incunable', in R. Myers and M. Harris (eds.), *A Millennium of the Book: Production, Design and Illustration in Manuscript and Print 900–1900* (Winchester: St. Paul's Bibliographies, 1994), 23; N. Barker, 'The Aldine Italic', in *A Millennium of the Book*, 56–7.
8. M. Davies, *Aldus Manutius: Printer and Publisher of Renaissance Venice* (London: British Library, 1995); N. Barker, *Aldus Manutius and the Development of Greek Script and Type in the Fifteenth Century*, 2nd edn (New York: Fordham University Press, 1992), 114; S. Hindman and J. Farquhar, *Pen to Press: Illustrated Manuscripts and Printed Books in the First Century of Printing* (College Park, MD: University of Maryland Press, 1977), 53; N. F. Blake, 'Aftermath: Manuscripts to Print', in J. Griffiths and D. Pearsall (eds.), *Book Production and Publishing in Britain 1375–1475*, (Cambridge University Press, 1989), 406.
9. M. M. Smith, 'The Design Relationship between the Manuscript and the Incunable', 36–7, 38–9.
10. J. Briggs, *A Woman of Passion: The Life of E. Nesbit 1858–1924* (New York: New Amsterdam Books, 1987), 274–6. My thanks to Claudia Nelson for bringing this to my attention.
11. H. R. Woudhuysen, *Sir Philip Sidney and the Circulation of Manuscripts 1558–1640* (Oxford: Clarendon Press, 1996), 49–51.
12. G. D. Smith, *A Catalogue of Rare Books, Original Drawings, Extra Illustrated Works... from the Library of the Late Augustin Daly* (New York: Geo. D. Smith, 1900), 7, 12.
13. J. T. Knight, *Bound to Read: Compilations, Collections, and the Making of Renaissance Literature* (Philadelphia: University of Pennsylvania Press, 2013), 2–4.
14. Folger Shakespeare Library MS 266712; I am indebted to Heather Wolfe for bringing this volume to my attention.
15. Bodleian Library, MS Cherry 36; British Library, MS Royal 7 D. X.
16. E. Yeo, 'Inglis, Esther (1570/71–1624)', *Oxford Dictionary of National Biography* (Oxford University Press, 2004): www.oxforddnb.com/view/article/15292, accessed 9 Dec. 2012.
17. H. Smith, *'Grossly Material Things': Women and Book Production in Early Modern England* (Oxford University Press, 2012), 24–6.
18. The Royal Collection, Queen Mary's Doll House, RCIN 1171529, 1171559.

19. C. Alexander, *The Early Writings of Charlotte Brontë* (New York: Prometheus, 1983), 74. University of Missouri Ellis Special Collections MS 'The Secret and Lily Hart', Rare Vault, PR 4167.S43 1833.
20. L. Daston, 'Taking Note(s)', *Isis* 95 (2004), 443–8; L. Dacome, 'Noting the Mind: Commonplace Books and the Pursuit of the Self in Eighteenth-Century Britain', *Journal of the History of Ideas* (2005), 603–25.
21. Folger Shakespeare Library MS V.b.232; Wormsley Library, Buckinghamshire, 'The Great Book of Thomas Trevilian'.
22. H. Wolfe, 'Introduction: A User's Guide to the Trevelyon Miscellany of 1608', *The Trevelyon Miscellany of 1608: An Introduction to Folger Shakespeare Library MS V.B.232* (New Castle, DE: Oak Knoll Press, 2007), 7–8.
23. A. F. Marotti, 'Manuscript, Print, and the English Renaissance Lyric', in W. Speed Hill (ed.), *New Ways of Looking at Old Texts: Papers of the Renaissance English Text Society, 1958–1991* (Binghamton: Center for Medieval and Early Renaissance Studies, 1993), 212.
24. E. Heale, 'Introduction', *The Devonshire Manuscript: A Woman's Book of Courtly Poetry* (Toronto: Centre for Reformation and Renaissance Studies and Iter, 2012).
25. Huntington Library MS HM 904; Yale University, Beinecke MS Osborn b.4; BL, Add. MS 36452.
26. Quoted in M. Levy, *Family Authorship and Romantic Print Culture* (Basingstoke: Palgrave MacMillan, 2008), 52.
27. A. Wear, *Knowledge and Practice in English Medicine, 1550–1680* (Cambridge University Press, 2002), 49–52.
28. E. Spiller, 'Introduction', *Seventeenth-Century Women's Recipe Books: Cooking, Physic and Chirurgery in the Works of Elizabeth Talbot Grey and Aletheia Talbot Howard* (Burlington, VT: Ashgate Publishing, 2008); Sara Pennell, 'Perfecting Practice? Women, Manuscript Recipes, and Knowledge in Early Modern England', in V. E. Burke and J. Gibson (eds.), *Early Modern Women's Manuscript Writing* (Aldershot: Ashgate Publishing, 2004), 237–58.
29. British Library, Add MS 41161; 'medical recipe book', Wellcome Library, MS 7133.
30. British Library, Add. MS 17018.
31. M. J. M. Ezell, 'More, Mary (d. c.1713)', *Oxford Dictionary of National Biography* (Oxford University Press, 2004): www.oxforddnb.com/view/article/68257, accessed 11 January 2013.
32. British Library MS Add 27,347; King's College Library, Cambridge MS 'Albius Tibullus'.
33. Cited in H. Love, *English Clandestine Satire 1660–1702* (Oxford University Press, 2004), 15.
34. Quoted in G. Kitchin, *Sir Roger L'Estrange* (London: Kegan Paul, 1913), 198.
35. Love, *Clandestine Satire*, chapter 8 and Love, *Scribal Publication in Seventeenth-Century England* (Oxford University Press, 1993), 211–17.
36. P. Beal, *In Praise of Scribes: Manuscripts and their Makers in Seventeenth-Century England* (Oxford: The Clarendon Press, 1998), chapter 1.
37. M. Eggertsdóttir, 'From Reformation to Enlightenment', in D. Neijmann (ed.), *A History of Icelandic Literature* (Lincoln, NE: University of Nebraska Press, 2006), 174–250 (244).

38. V. Hreinsson, *Wakefull Nights: Stephan G. Stephansson: Icelandic-Canadian Poet* (Calgary: Benson Ranch Inc., 2012), 22; see also D. Ólafsson, 'Vernacular Literacy Practices in Nineteenth-Century Iceland', in A. Edlund (ed.), *Att läsa och att skriva* (Umeå: Umeå Universitet, 2012), 65–86.
39. M. J. Driscoll, *The Unwashed Children of Eve: The Production, Dissemination and Reception of Popular Literature in Post-Reformation Iceland* (Enfield Lock: Hisarlik Press, 1997), 1, 4.
40. D. Ólafsson, 'Handwritten Books in 19th Century Iceland', *Ennen and Nyt: The Papers of the Nordic Conference on the History of Ideas Helsinki* 1 (2001), 3.
41. National Library of Iceland MS Lbs 2328 4 to 'Collection of Icelandic Sagas copies by Sighvatur Grimsson 1861–1867', quoted in Ólafsson, 'Handwritten Books', 10.
42. K. Salmi-Niklander, 'Bitter Memories and Burst Soap Bubbles: Irony, Parody, and Satire in the Oral-Literary Tradition of Finnish Working-class Youth at the Beginning of the Twentieth Century', *International Review of Social History* 52 (2007), 189–207 and 'Manuscript and Broadsheets. Narrative Genres and the Communication Circuit among Working-Class Youth in Early 20th-Century Finland', *Folklore: Electronic Journal of Folklore* 33 (2006), 109–26.
43. H. G. Skilling, *Samizdat and an Independent Society in Central and Eastern Europe* (Columbus, OH: Ohio State University Press, 1989).

7

ADRIAN JOHNS

The coming of print to Europe

The introduction of printing into western Europe has counted as the signature event of the history of the book ever since Lucien Febvre and Henri-Jean Martin's *l'Apparition du Livre* launched the modern discipline in 1958. The purpose of *l'Apparition* was to demonstrate that Johann Gutenberg's innovation was the most important turning point in human history, separating modernity from everything that had gone before.[1] That conviction is still broadly held today. By its lights, Herbert Butterfield's famous line about the scientific revolution – that it 'outshines everything since the rise of Christianity and reduces the Renaissance and Reformation to the rank of mere episodes' – might be more aptly applied to what we have become used to calling the *printing* revolution.[2]

There are really two aspects to this idea of a printing revolution. One has to do with the development of the book itself. Clearly, the adoption of printing made possible major changes in the manufacture, character and commerce of books. The quantitative potential alone was stark, and seems to have been evident in the 1450s, even before printing itself had a stable existence. With a press, a printer could produce far more books than scribes and other copyists could ever hope to manage, and those books could be sold at much lower prices to more people. The second aspect concerns the cultural consequences – and also, although this has been more rarely noticed, the cultural *constituents* – of this transformation in the book. Printed books emerged from a new and complex place, the printing house, and their forms reflected its elaborate internal customs. Produced in quantity, books became familiar to many more people, and many more kinds of people, than ever before. Those people put them to new and unpredictable uses. Not all were immediately or intentionally transformative. But in the early modern period the most radical changes generally came from ambitions to restore the past. So readers devised new knowledge even as they revived ancient learning; they transformed the practices of everyday life by stabilizing them; and they advanced new kinds of faith in seeking to confirm the traditions of Christendom. To call this a revolution is legitimate, as long as we remember that it was a paradoxical one.

However, identifying a revolution need not, and in this case should not, involve stipulating a transformation into modernity. This is critically important if the concept of a printing revolution is to pass muster, not least because modern experiences of print reflect changes that happened long after the fifteenth century. (The development of mechanized printing and systems of copyright are two examples.) More fundamentally, it ought to be possible to conceive of a revolution as a radical change without preconceptions about the direction of that change.[3] It is a simple point, to be sure, but its implications have been neglected. They include resisting the temptation to assign significance disproportionately to phenomena that happen to look significant in retrospect while neglecting phenomena more representative of the period and place in question. This is all the more important if we *do* want to appeal to the printing revolution to help explain the modern world, because otherwise the risk of circularity is very real.

The other thing to remember is the practical character of this transformation. The efforts of Gutenberg's contemporaries and successors to adopt and adapt to the new device were all-important in shaping not only how fast the printing revolution proceeded, but what the revolution itself would be. Dealing with print required the forging of new places and habits of work, and the development of new kinds of governance. Our subject needs to be these processes that bound together machine, object and culture. Novel as they were, they were not created out of nothing. To use the language of 'impact' that is common in this field, we must ask about the impact *on* print as well as the impact *of* print – and about how the one shaped the other.

For the most part, modern attempts to survey the introduction of print in western Europe have fallen short in both these respects. This was partly a result of the conventional separation of bibliographical research – history of the book proper, as it were – from the discipline of History itself. The one has focused on particularity, at the cost of antiquarianism; the other has focused on a large-scale 'shift', at the cost of teleology.[4] For the latter, especially, aspects of Renaissance printing that seemed to align with progress toward modernity – modernity, that is, as viewed from the late twentieth century – were singled out for attention, and treated as caused by the press itself: they manifested the 'impact of print'. Those that did not were relegated from view as accidental, unrepresentative or insignificant. A simple but poignant example is the spread of printing houses from the German town of Mainz across western Europe. Until recently this was represented as a rapid and triumphal expansion, such that by 1500 many European cities possessed printing houses and the impact of print could be said to have definitively registered itself. But as Andrew Pettegree has noted in what is by far the best account of the whole subject, the impression was artificial. In reality, printing houses often proved extremely transient. Collapse followed rapidly on founding. If printers' failures had been mapped alongside their beginnings, then the expansion of the craft would have appeared both more fragile and less inevitable. Moreover, even where it did take hold, far from imposing its own 'logic', print rested upon much older trade routes and credit practices. And, finally, choosing the date of 1500 skewed perspectives too, because that proved a peak year. A sharp and prolonged crash hit the book trade at that time. Many even of the more substantial operations folded, in a crisis that not only stemmed expansion but also caused a major change in the geography of European printing. Venice – the primary centre of the late fifteenth century – was supplanted by Lyon, Paris, Basel and Antwerp. As Pettegree insists, an adequate history of the advent of printing in western Europe must integrate, and account for, these setbacks and these dependencies. We cannot understand how the successful printers survived to shape the identity and effects of print unless we appreciate the real contemporary possibility – more, the *probability* – that they would not.[5]

Printing was not a modern practice, in short, but an early-modern one. It emerged through experiments both mechanical and social, took on a role defined in terms of Renaissance concepts of mixed sciences and mechanic arts, and had to be accommodated to the political and providential perceptions of that Machiavellian era. And it was precisely *because* print was a creature of its time that it could give rise to far-reaching changes.

Experimenting with print

If the origins of European printing are obscure, that is just as its originator wished. In this respect, as in others, Johannes Gutenberg was typical of the ambitious artisans of the time. Trained, apparently, as a goldsmith, Gutenberg's first innovative venture was a plan to make and sell metal brooches to pilgrims, the idea being to profit from a forthcoming religious festival at the old Carolingian capital of Aachen. He intended to make tens of thousands – a number large enough to imply some kind of stamping technique. But he mistook the date of the pilgrimage, and found himself stuck with a warehouseful of unsellable brooches. Faced with disaster, Gutenberg resorted to making tantalizing promises to his anxious partners about another, newer, 'art and adventure' that might make good their losses. He insisted upon secrecy about this project, to the extent of sending agents to dismantle the equipment when the partnership foundered. But it involved a press, 'forms' and other tools. It is tempting to assume that these words had something like the meanings that they would acquire over the next decades – that they referred to experiments in printing.[6]

The importance of printing is obvious in retrospect, and was recognized quickly by contemporaries. So it is striking to realize that Gutenberg's early experimental efforts were in fact typical of what was a period of artisanal ambition. From the late fourteenth century, ambitious master-craftsmen in several European centres sought with considerable success to lay claim to the status of artists and knowledge-makers, as displayed in a proliferating genre of books they produced about their crafts. Goldsmiths are generally recognized to have been the exemplary case of these ambitious master-craftsmen. They not only produced elaborate, intricate models of natural and artificial processes in their workshops, but also masterminded collaborations between different crafts. Pamela Smith points out that goldsmiths experimented with cannon-making, dyeing, locksmithing, horology and engraving as well as printing. They also pioneered the Vitruvian rhetoric that printers would later use to argue for their elevated status with respect to the mechanic arts.[7] Gutenberg's brooches, the mirrored surfaces of which supposedly captured virtues emanating from relics, were typical products of this 'artisanal epistemology'. And their role as machines of natural magic – also typical – casts an intriguing light on the more famous machine that followed. Moreover, many of the artisanal experiments of the age involved casting or impressing: coiners produced currency and medals, binders used presses to stamp designs on the panels encasing manuscript books and carvers created woodblocks to make repeated copies of playing-cards and books like the *Ars Moriendi*. All were being pursued at the same time, giving rise to objects that were often amalgams of different tools and techniques. Blockbooks, for example, incorporated manuscript writing and illumination. The first generation of 'true' printed books would likewise be amalgams, and Gutenberg himself should be regarded as exemplary rather than unique.

The experiments of goldsmiths and other artisans often involved long periods away from prying eyes. Gutenberg was again typical. With the end of his Strasbourg venture he disappeared for a few years, until in the late 1440s he turned up again in Mainz with a project to print books. In 1455, a cleric and diplomat named Aeneas Sylvius Piccolomini wrote to tell a Cardinal friend just how ambitious his scheme was. 'All that has been written to me about that marvelous man seen at Frankfurt is true', he reported. He had seen pages filled with characters so clear that 'your grace would be able to read it without effort, and indeed without glasses'. Somehow Gutenberg had almost finished printing not only *a* book, but *the* book: the Bible. Piccolomini promised to try to buy a copy. But he was not optimistic – 'buyers were said to be lined up even before the books were finished'.[8]

By this time Gutenberg had seemingly solved the technical problems of printing. The success had not been immediate or easy. It turns out that in his earlier labours Gutenberg did not use punches and matrices to generate many identical copies of a single character – the kind of technique that many would regard as definitive of printing itself. He instead made many versions of each letter substantially by hand, using moulds of sand in a technique similar to that employed by metalworkers to model fragile objects. The practice resembled a translation of late-medieval handwriting into metal. Only a little later would type-founders move to more uniform punch-and-matrix production, and with it the adoption of the coherent styles – fonts – that would set printed books apart from the products of scriptoria.[9] For decades, what we conventionally call 'printed' books would be better thought of as amalgams of print and manuscript. Printed letters originated as metallic extensions of handwriting, and printed sheets would often be sent on to an illuminator's workshop for finishing by hand.

It is significant that Piccolomini believed that the whole impression (roughly 180 copies) was already spoken for. If he was correct, this implies that Gutenberg, perhaps remembering the debacle over brooches, had taken care to minimize what would become the bugbear of printers in the future: the locking-up of capital during printing itself. At the very origin of European printing lies a cautionary tale about the fragility of the whole enterprise. With a printed book, the entire impression must be produced before any one copy could be sold, and that might mean a delay of months (or years, for very large projects). This was a major problem, as printing houses typically did not have large financial reserves, and credit was at best hard to secure. Gutenberg was experimenting not only with novel techniques, but also with novel means of funding those techniques. And his experiment failed. At this very moment his backer, Johann Fust, sued Gutenberg for unpaid debt. It seems that he won and seized the entire printing operation. Fust then put it to use himself, in partnership with his adopted son, the cleric and scribe Peter Schöffer. The most spectacular result was their 1457 Mainz Psalter – the first book ever to contain a statement identifying its printer.

Gutenberg largely vanishes from the record after this. But it does seem that, his initial secrecy notwithstanding, he was involved in the initial spread of printing beyond Mainz. A different bible was soon being printed in Bamberg, with type modelled on his earlier characters and presumably with his consent. When presses began to be set up in other cities, moreover, it was generally at the instigation of erstwhile workers in Gutenberg's original house or its successors. Heinrich Keffer went to Bamberg; Johann Sensenschmidt became the first printer in Nuremburg; Ulrich Han went to Rome; and Heinrich Eggestein went to Strasbourg, where he started printing in partnership with

Johann Mentelin, one of the several men who would later be credited with inventing printing itself. From Bamberg, Johann Nicolai and Georg Herolt ended up in Perugia and Rome respectively.[10] The art that provided for communication at a distance was dispersed, not through the circulation of texts, but by the movements of skilled, experienced craftsmen.

The printing house at work

The printing houses that these early craftsmen established soon became complex operations. Printing required the labours of many different kinds of people: the master-printer himself, pressmen – two per press, compositors, correctors, apprentices and the general dogsbodies known as 'devils'. The movements of all these people and things had to be coordinated over long periods – a tricky task for a small house, with only two presses, but much more complex for the largest, with nine or ten. Sustained collaboration was thus all-important. It had to depend on customs and rules. Yet no single model for this new kind of place had existed in 1450. So early printers had to decide for themselves what arrangements would govern the workers in their relationships to each other, their masters and the outside world. The first half-century of print was a time of experiment not only in machinery but also in these social systems.

Conventionally, in early modern crafts the virtues and vices of a master-craftsman extended to the reputation of his workshop and its products. Perceptions of the character of the printer and of the books he produced were thus inseparable. So who were these men? It is not always easy to tell. The first generation, connected directly with Gutenberg, Fust and Schöffer, often have obscure backgrounds. But Nicholas Jenson may have worked in a mint, Anton Koberger was a goldsmith and Mentelin had been a scribe – all trades from which print borrowed customs and techniques. Succeeding generations saw practitioners marry into the craft or move into it from cognate enterprises like binding (as both Louis Elsevier and Plantin did) or bookselling (as did Henri Estienne).

The model of the master-printer that such figures pioneered was partly shaped by the conjunction of the invention of printing with the climax of humanism. A generation of renowned scholar-printers – Johann Amerbach, Johannes Frobenius and Johannes Oporinus in Basel, Sweynheym and Pannartz in Rome, Manutius in Venice, Henri and Robert Estienne in Paris, Koberger in Nuremberg – established the ideals to which a master should aspire. These balanced the figure at a kind of Lagrangian point, as it were, between the attractions offered by the roles of craftsman, artist and scholar. The prime exemplar in the German lands was perhaps Amerbach, who started out as a Parisian student of humanism before becoming the master of a printing house in Basel and devoting it largely to the production of patristic works. His counterpart in the south was surely Manutius, who had been a scholar before launching his printing house, and remained one while a master-printer. Each of these figures also became something of a patron in his own right, forming a household in which humanist scholars (Erasmus, for example) would live and work on the production of editions alongside the family of the paterfamilias.

Scholars venturing into the printer's domain found themselves in an alien and intricate cultural space. By the second or third generation, major houses had annual, seasonal and daily time disciplines, expressed in a panoply of customs and ceremonies. The best documented was the *officina plantiniana* which Christophe Plantin established in the 1570s, and its records give us a good sense of what it was like to work in the trade. Journeymen were expected to be present by 5am, in order to start working at 6am (late enough to allow them to attend mass); they would work until 8pm, by candlelight if necessary during the winter months. They were paid by how much they produced, which meant that they tended to agitate to be allowed to work even longer. But for pressmen in particular it was a long, arduous day, and journeymen could take drinks, including beer, to sustain themselves, either singly or, at set times, in groups. Because coordination was crucial, the house imposed penalties if one worker should fail to keep up with the others. During the 1560s Plantin also banned disputes over religion for the disruption they were liable to cause, on pain of almost a day's wage – double the fine for brawling.

The workers in printing houses organized themselves into what they called *chapels*. In Plantin's house the chapel started early and became remarkably sophisticated, with a finely graduated structure of ordinances upheld by fines and other punishments (including a spanking with the official chapel slipper). Such penalties could be levied on the master, or even on visitors. A formal procedure existed for making and addressing accusations, which ordained that they be entered into a 'complaints book' and brought before an internal court for adjudication. The court had an elaborate hierarchy of offices, numerous enough that every member of the house served in some capacity at frequent intervals. The results seem to have been harmonious enough, by and large, although there were moments of internal conflict. In 1572 Plantin even told a Spanish contact that he had threatened to shut down altogether out of frustration at one such clash, but it seems that this was exaggerated for effect.[11]

One became a member of this chapel, ideally, by graduating (being 'freed') from an apprenticeship. Master-printers liked to use apprentices as cheap labour, however, and at first few seem to have acknowledged any obligation to teach them the craft beyond what was needed for the task at hand. Moreover, because printing was not initially integrated into guilds, it was possible for a worker to leave an apprenticeship in one town after a brief period and take up work as a journeyman in another region – hence the itinerant lives of many self-proclaimed journeymen. By the early sixteenth century, printing communities in various towns were starting to form rules similar to those long operative in other crafts, limiting apprentices' numbers, mandating their training and requiring that they live with their masters.[12] From about this point the end of an apprenticeship began to be an occasion for elaborate ceremony. A German ritual known as the *Depositio Cornuti Typographici* survives to indicate what this involved. The festivities formed a sequence in which the apprentice, dressed up as a smelly, red-nosed, horned beast, was roundly abused in knockabout fashion before confessing his sins, figuratively dying and being reborn and baptized into his new identity.[13] This kind of thing seems to have been quite common, and it underlined the conjunction of skill, rationality and morality that defined the printers as a well-ordered community.

The rules of the book

Most of what these workers printed were not books at all, but proclamations, administrative documents and the millions of indulgences that enterprising churchmen commissioned. Not only did these not require the locking-up of capital in an impression, but they could also be paid for in advance, effectively removing all risk.[14] But to the extent that it was a book industry, printing depended on existing networks of communication, credit and commerce. The houses that lasted were in places linked to long-established city fairs (Frankfurt, Leipzig), those with sophisticated trade and financial systems (Venice, Antwerp) or, to a lesser extent, those with secure cultures of patronage and political power (Rome, Paris). A good counterexample is the thriving town of Albi. In 1475 Albi became the third French town with a printing house. But the place was simply too remote from trade routes. The printer responsible – another veteran of Mainz – soon departed for the mercantile centre of Lyon, leaving Albi without a printing house for the next 200 years.[15] Spain, then the most powerful nation in Europe, was Albi writ large: because it was not a nodal point for trade, most printers there remained small-scale, itinerant artisans.[16] Even a university, it is worth noting, was not necessarily sufficient to provide enough of a book market to sustain a publishing printer. Academic publishing is a more recent and fragile creation than it is comforting to remember.[17]

The coming of print to Europe

Even so, before the end of the fifteenth century several major cities hosted a dozen or more printing houses working simultaneously. And a number of the larger houses addressed a continent-wide marketplace. The question therefore arose of how houses should interact with each other when they targeted the same readers. Consider, in particular, what should happen if one printer tried to issue an impression of the same work as another for the same market – a problem that had never previously existed in any consistent way. Hans Amerbach in Basel and Anton Koberger in Nuremberg faced it in 1499, and the result was a complex, intricate correspondence making explicit the ways in which such issues were seen in terms of Renaissance conceptions of honour, virtue and obligation.[18] Civility might not dictate a particular outcome, but it certainly defined the range of positions open to a responsible printer or bookseller. Still, in general it was unclear where the moral right lay, what conventions should govern the conduct of the clash, and who had the authority to decide an equitable outcome.

As the trade and its markets expanded, the question thus became that of developing protocols for managing these kinds of disputes in general. How to shape a responsible craft of the printed book, in harmony with itself and the commonwealth? The urgency of this question was accentuated by anxieties about the power of an ill-ordered book trade to destroy the peace of the realm itself – as, in the view of many contemporaries, happened during the more violent episodes of the Reformation. Over the course of the sixteenth and early seventeenth centuries, a number of cities created legal, institutional and customary structures to address this problem of order. Four characteristic institutions emerged: the privilege, the register, the guild and the licence.

The earliest city to develop a complex, interlaced kind of administration seems to have been Venice. It is worth pausing there, as many other cities would tread a similar path. In the fifteenth century, the principal way in which the Republic's authorities engaged with the new craft was by the issuing of privileges. A privilege granted its beneficiary the exclusive power to print and sell a certain work for a defined period, ranging from one to about twenty years. Although privileges were instruments of long standing and wide application in every European jurisdiction, their use with respect to printed books was new and it took decades to be standardized. It is important to realize that a privilege was not a *right*: one could not expect one simply by virtue of having a new book to print. Privileges were entirely in the gift of the authorities, and they had to be requested, giving reasons. In Venice, early requesters often specified a need to secure the *quality* of books – which meant bemoaning the intrinsic disorder of the trade, 'by which', as one applicant put it, 'the texts of editions become every day more corrupt, which thing is a dishonour and a public injury to this glorious city'. Soon they would add unscrupulous reprinting, as detailed in a bid by Bernardino Rasma in 1496. Rasma complained of reprinting as a 'pernicious and hurtful corruption' that had apparently become endemic: anyone undertaking a substantial book should expect other printers to 'steal the proofs of the new work from the hands of the pressmen, and set to, with many men and many presses, to print the book before the original designer can finish his edition, which, when it is ready for issue, finds the market spoiled'.[19]

Privileges were awarded in large numbers. But it seems that evasion or avoidance – or, given that no archive existed to show what privileges had already been awarded, sheer ignorance – was fairly routine. By the early sixteenth century the situation was becoming unworkable. Printers would apply for them willy-nilly, blocking rivals while not actually publishing the works themselves. In 1517 Venice responded by passing the city's first law to standardize privileges. It abruptly cancelled every existing patent, at a stroke rendering all books common. From then on, privileges could only be granted for unprinted works, and they would require a two-thirds vote of the Senate. At almost the same time, *imprimaturs* (licences) were standardized too, again in a bid to protect the value of the trade from a reputation for textual corruption. Later measures added that a privileged, licensed book must be printed in Venice itself, published in good time and sold at a price the state deemed reasonable.

In 1549 a guild (or 'University') was established for Venice's book trade, centred on the grand church of SS Giovanni e Paolo. The idea seems to have been to provide a focal point for the Republic to oversee the trade by these measures, and at the same time to make printers and booksellers police themselves. The new body was responsible for upholding the general quality of printed work produced in the Republic, and specifically for tracking down clandestine books. It had a 'prior', two 'councillors' and six 'assessors', elected annually, along with a secretary and a beadle. A register was also created, to record all books published in the city. Evasion remained commonplace, of course, but by the mid-seventeenth century the combination of guild, register, licence and privilege seems to have become a stable, moderately well-functioning system.

Many cities where printing and bookselling endured seem to have developed similar systems to that of Venice. Not all cities adopted every element – Spanish towns, for example, often left printing unincorporated – and in those that did the details varied. But the general trend was clear. So, for example, in Antwerp the Guild of St Luke, previously devoted to artists, became the corporate home of bookmen in 1557. The same year, the Stationers' Company was chartered in London to oversee the English trade. The Paris guild dates from 1608. Each country also adopted privilege and licence regimes. One of the most notable outcomes of this increasingly baroque regulatory culture was the emergence of rules favouring authors. In 1545 Venice, again ahead of the pack, decreed that in order to get an *imprimatur* a book's printer must possess a written statement by its author consenting to the publication. This seems to have been the first regulation expressly recognizing something akin to an authorial right, and it is significant that its origins lie in the convergence of systems dedicated to producing an orderly trade in a well-ordered commonwealth.

It is important to recognize, however, that the four ordering institutions of print generated conflict as well as consensus. One cause was the emergent distinction between printer and publisher. For much of the early modern period, 'publisher' was not a consistent trade role. But the printed book increasingly became an object of speculative financing. Wealth gravitated away from the 'mechanick' practitioners of the press and towards those who dealt in 'copies', as these speculative entities were called. Copies were constituted as property by the register and privilege systems. Eventually copyright laws would entrench them, although at the time copyright seemed the very antithesis of property. The shift was acutely felt by printers, who regularly complained that the virtues of the master-craftsman were being subordinated to an unprincipled rapacity. Such complaints of course were widespread in the economy of the late seventeenth and eighteenth centuries, as the commercial and industrial transformations of the age gathered steam. The book trade was as riven by them as any other economic community.

More fundamentally, the protocols of order were fundamentally incompatible with each other. Whereas privileges expressed the authority of the prince, guilds and registers recorded the authority of a craft, based not in royal legitimacy but in trade customs. In many jurisdictions, for example, it was possible to practise as a printer outside guild control by royal privilege.[20] In England the King's Printer and the University Presses of Oxford and Cambridge operated under privileges, and thus under different legal and political principles from the Stationers. The Stationers' Company saw them as interlopers, and by its own lights it was right to do so; but by the same token they could represent its resentments as *lèse-majesté*. The longest-running sequence of such clashes was probably that in France, which extended from the early seventeenth century right through to the Revolution, and drew in prominent *philosophes* on both sides of what was eventually reconstrued as a clash over the concept of authorial property.[21] Here, as elsewhere, this intractable conflict inspired the first sustained reflections on the nature and implications of print itself.

But of course, privilege or guild regimes were specific to particular jurisdictions (with the somewhat theoretical exception that the Papacy and the

Empire issued privileges for much wider areas), and printed books circulated far beyond any such realm. International book merchants needed rules too, or at least shared customs that could be relied upon. Continental distribution came to centre on a few major hubs that long predated print: the merchant fairs of Germany, with Frankfurt and later Leipzig to the fore. The Frankfurt fairs in particular were lavish mercantile events held twice annually. While the fair lasted, free and fair trade reigned, with well-developed credit conventions extending from one fair to the next. For a new craft, short of ready cash and needing to reach a dispersed population, the opportunity was obvious. So book dealers from south and east of the city took the opportunity of the second of the annual fairs to rendezvous. Dealers soon started coming from further away: the Netherlands and Italy (especially Venice), then France, England, Austria and beyond. They began printing catalogues of the books they were bringing to sell and exchange, and by the later sixteenth century the city itself had taken on the task of publishing a collective list. It became the closest thing early modern Europe had to a catalogue of 'books in print'.

By this time, the Frankfurt fair had become Europe's biggest venue for the commerce of books. The town outlawed the unauthorized reprinting of titles offered there, and a custom of bartering sheets permitted dealers to distribute books across the continent without lugging around large amounts of cash. Moreover, Frankfurt was also the venue for conversations out of which books emerged. Scholars and other authors flocked there to make contacts and to discover the latest intellectual currents. As the bookseller Henri Estienne put it in his 1574 encomium to the fair, which he termed a great university (*academia*), such encounters made the event unique. 'Right in the shops of the booksellers', he reported, one could hear scholars from across Europe 'discussing philosophy no less seriously than once the Socrateses and the Platos discussed it in the Lyceum'. The Frankfurt fair realized the ancient ideal of the *encyclopedia*: it encompassed 'the whole circle of knowledge'.[22] This civic-mercantile-scholarly confluence had become *the* central node of European intellectual culture.

So print did allow for influence to extend across large distances, but mainly by exploiting long-standing trade prerogatives that were peculiar to specific towns. It could not simply transcend locale altogether. Nor did its practitioners necessarily want to, because boundaries could be put to use. By the mid-sixteenth century several Swiss towns, Calvinist Geneva in the van, were taking advantage of them to export Protestant books to Catholic France and Spain with impunity. By the eighteenth, as Robert Darnton has famously shown, the 'Typographical Society of Neuchâtel' would be making a fine trade of reprinting French works and sending them surreptitiously back into Louis XV's realm.[23] The Scots and Irish did the same to the English, while complex webs of exchange and competition obtained across the hundreds of German states and statelets, imperial privileges notwithstanding. Print's apparent power to overcome space and time depended partly on these ventures – ventures that only existed because of bounded jurisdictions.

The powers of print

Wherever the distinctiveness of print ultimately lay – in the ability to multiply copies, the potential to act at a distance or the power to stabilize texts – the key to understanding it lies in these measures and the anxieties that provoked them. The nature of the printed book emerged from social machinery as much as from technological. But what did it then *do*?

In the first place, there are several qualities that Gutenberg's contemporaries and successors identified in printed books, and which they believed to be significantly different from the qualities of earlier, hand-copied volumes. There were a lot more of them. They could be acquired at cheaper prices. They circulated more widely and became familiar to poorer and more distant parts of society. Copies from a given impression existed in large numbers and were functionally identical. And they were generally products of speculative commerce: printing an impression meant venturing capital on the uncertain prospect of future profit. All of these perceptions took hold early, and all attained the status of truisms.

But contemporary writers, readers and printers found that in each of these cases the simple formula had to be substantially qualified when it came to using real printed books. There were many books that were *not* popular, widely distributed, identical within an impression and so on. Indeed, a rational fifteenth- or sixteenth-century reader might well doubt that any one book combined all these traits. Printing-house practice made this reasonable, because, as modern investigations of authors like Shakespeare have made clear, impressions would often be corrected 'on the fly', producing variations across superficially identical copies. Nor was this necessarily a mark of failure – of mistakes, incompetence, corruption and the like. Amalgams of print, woodcut and manuscript might be regarded as *exceeding* the standards of print alone. This was certainly the case, for example, with a humanist book like Florentine poet Francesco Berlinghieri's *Seven Days of Geography*, printed by Niccolò Tedesco in Florence in the 1480s. Berlinghieri's volume combined letterpress with engravings; and it merged print and manuscript too, with presentation copies being illuminated and hand-coloured, rendering each an individuated object. It also combined commercial production and distribution with circulation through diplomatic channels, including to the Sultan in Constantinople. The book could be counted as exemplary of the powers of print, but largely because it departed from simple models of print in every way.[24]

Sometimes print implied the familiar truisms, then, but not always. When it did not, it was nonetheless print for all that. Being a good reader of printed books might well involve maintaining a delicate balance between faith in the virtues of print in general and caution about the extent to which any given book would display those virtues – and being a good historian of print requires a similar balance. This is really the obverse of the point made above, that the powers of print emerged from the careful management of complex artisanal and scholarly interactions. The first point to be made about the advent of print is therefore simply this: that it multiplied these interactions, and thereby the amalgams – books – that they generated. The defining character of the printing revolution was initially not order or regularity, but disruptive proliferation.

From the outset, a few scholars experimented with making the new craft into a tool for learning. It was not necessarily predestined to play such a role, and accommodating the worlds of art and scholarship proved a difficult and lengthy enterprise. For example, Johannes Müller of Königsberg, better known as Regiomontanus, hoped to print the entire corpus of ancient mathematical sciences at his own press in Nuremberg. Conrad Sweynheym and Arnold Pannartz projected Pliny's *Natural History* in Rome, the philosopher Marsilio Ficino oversaw Plato's works at a press in a Dominican convent, and Aldus Manutius took on Thucydides, Herodotus, Virgil and Cicero in Venice. These are the high-profile ventures that have often been taken to define the printed Renaissance, and they were probably the most important instance of the much-celebrated alignment of 'scholar' and 'craftsman'. But many were not commercially successful (where they were commercial at all), and even Manutius flirted with disaster. Still, these early projects defined roles for both the scholar-printer, to which publishers would later lay claim, and the learned editor. They led to the formation of new genres (the scientific journal, the portable classics pioneered by Manutius, and more), and the adoption of protocols and customs of reading in institutions old (schools and universities) and new (Jesuit colleges, experimental academies). And they encouraged a critical engagement with antiquity that had implications across learned culture.

This proliferation had wider implications because the domain of the printed book – the domain that both scholars and printers complained was falling under the sway of unprincipled speculators – had by this time become a persistent arena for political and other debate. This happened at different rates and in different ways, depending on local conditions. But in many places – Venice being one early example – political crises repeatedly generated moments when restricted, inner-circle political machinations broached a broader print realm of discussion. At first these moments were distinct from one another. They were opportunistic and, in Filippo de Vivo's word, 'engineered'. But over time – and it took perhaps a century or more – these repeated moves coalesced into an ongoing public political realm. Protagonists noted what was happening and were ambivalent about it. 'Things have changed shape', noted the Spanish ambassador during Venice's dispute with Rome in the 1600s, as the exchange of diplomatic letters gave way to pamphleteering: what had once been comprehensible was now liable to flare uncontrollably (the problem lying in the lack of control, not the flaring).[25] By the late seventeenth century print was associated with a permanent realm of this kind, extending across legal boundaries and appealing to readers for allegiance to its ostensibly cosmopolitan values. Its claim to authority encouraged the emergence of consistent opposition to licensing and privileges.

An especially important element here was the development and entrenchment of communities around shared protocols for reading, and for ways of recording and transmitting their readings. Often, but not always, these centred on particular titles, the Bible being the best known. There was nothing new about this in itself: one could point to the readers of Virgil in antiquity or to groups such as the Lollards before printing. But the relationship of reader to page now changed. So, because of its engagement with the international circulation of print, did a group's 'reach'. As readers annotated printed pages, recording their interpretations and reactions, they accentuated the already hybrid character of books. So normal and essential was this practice that in Venice it became illegal for any book to be printed on paper unsuitable for readers' notes; offending volumes were burned and their privileges withdrawn.[26]

There were conventions governing such annotation, and the notes themselves could be transferred from reader to reader, taking with them accepted modes of use and interpretation. Owen Gingerich's exhaustive census of Copernicus's *De Revolutionibus* shows the importance of this practice. Successive readers incorporated previous astronomers' annotations into their own copies of the book, so that when a mathematical reader of around 1620 encountered a copy, that volume could include the accumulated record of decades of readings. 'Families' of annotations can be identified, making manifest intellectual and practical traditions that we would otherwise miss. Through these families of notes (and sometimes more than notes: a few readers added their own cut-out paper models to the book), we can discern Copernicanism itself taking shape.[27]

Finally, starting in the sixteenth century authors tried to come to terms expressly with the extent and nature of print itself. They did so in two ways: by attempting to produce a taxonomy and typology of all printed works, and by writing histories of the adoption of printing. In both ways they contributed to the development of the first systematic institutions of bibliography and the history of the book.

Where printed books ended up – the lucky few, at least – was in libraries. Collections both expanded and proliferated, and their organization became a recognized problem. By extension, writers like Konrad Gesner sought to define the contours of a new *bibliotheca universalis* formed by the entire output of the press. Through such ventures the world of knowledge itself became conceivable in novel ways. It could be atomized, sifted, sorted and mapped, producing new systems of knowledge. The readers who were true adepts at these tasks came to be highly valued. The best of all were those who could master both the literary microcosm and macrocosm, as it were, using simple practices such as the stringing of notecards onto cords (*fila*, the root of today's 'files') to index collections, and employing such devices as tools to advance abstract conceptual visions about the universal library. Probably the greatest of them all was Gottfried Wilhelm Leibniz, who pursued extraordinarily elaborate reflections on the implications of an endless amassing of print. Leibniz would yield nothing to Borges in his fantasies of a universal library.[28]

Conceptualizations of print's relation, not just to particular cultures, but to human civilization *tout court*, originated partly in such ventures. But they also derived from a new genre of histories of print that emerged in earnest in the seventeenth century. At first, this genre appropriated a Vitruvian rhetoric that had been used to elevate the status of the mathematical sciences. The implied consilience was interesting: in Aristotelian terms the mathematical sciences had been regarded as deficient because 'mixed', treating physical reality by mathematical techniques. Printing too was mixed, combining as it did mechanics with the liberal arts.[29] Beginning in the early- to mid-seventeenth century, however, more detailed accounts appeared of printing's origin and consequences. Many of them focused in the first instance on the identity of the press's inventor, or on its introducer into a particular country. Several realms promoted their own candidates in competition with the already mysterious Gutenberg: Laurens Coster in the Netherlands, Mentelin in Strasbourg and so on. Scholars and practitioners competed to identify and appraise what might be construed as evidence – and they found that that evidence pointed in different directions. In trying to divine a single origin out of what had been a period of diversity and mixing (Coster's Haarlem, for example, had in fact been a centre for the production of blockbooks), they extended beyond crediting individuals to defining print itself. And they involved characterizing the moral nature of printers and printing houses too.[30] Beginning with Joseph Moxon's *Mechanick Exercises* in 1683–4, manuals about printing fleshed out these claims. Polemics on the proper regulation and public role of print also appeared, with Milton and Locke being succeeded by Condorcet and Diderot and, later still, by Immanuel Kant.

Such works were the relatively formal tip of a broad and popular tradition, which saw print celebrated not only on pages, but also through processions, dinners, images and statuary. By the time of Leibniz's death in 1716, to deny that the advent of print constituted a new historical epoch would have meant challenging common sense. The Enlightenment's vision of itself as a manifestation of the powers of print was rooted here, in both scholarly understandings and popular commemorations. Ultimately, it would coalesce into the conviction so widely shared today that modern rationality resulted from a communications revolution. It was fitting, then, for the leaders of the French Revolution to consider moving Gutenberg's ashes to the Panthéon in Paris, as they did in 1792. By this time they could have no doubt that he was the first modern revolutionary of all.[31]

NOTES

1. L. Febvre and H.-J. Martin, *l'Apparition du Livre* (1958 repr. Paris: Albin Michel, 1999).
2. E. L. Eisenstein, *The Printing Revolution in Early Modern Europe* (Cambridge University Press, 1983).
3. Compare S. Pincus, *1688: The First Modern Revolution* (New Haven, CT: Yale University Press, 2009), 30–44.
4. Compare D. J. McKitterick, *Print, Manuscript, and the Search for Order, 1450–1830* (Cambridge University Press, 2003) with Eisenstein, *Printing Revolution*.
5. A. Pettegree, *The Book in the Renaissance* (New Haven: Yale University Press, 2010), 53–5, 62, 65.
6. A. Kapr (trans. D. Martin), *Johann Gutenberg: The Man and His Invention* (Aldershot: Scolar Press, 1996), 71–89.
7. P. Smith, 'In a Sixteenth-Century Goldsmith's Workshop', in L. Roberts, S. Schaffer and P. Dear (eds.), *The Mindful Hand* (Amsterdam: KNAW, 2007), 33–57.
8. M. Davies, *The Gutenberg Bible* (San Francisco: Pomegranate Books/British Library, 1997), 18–20.
9. Blaise Agüera y Arcas, 'Temporary Matrices and Elemental Punches in Gutenberg's DK Type', in Kristian Jensen (ed.), *Incunabula and Their Readers: Printing, Selling, and Using Books in the Fifteenth Century* (London: The British Library, 2003), 1–12, esp. 11; 'Computational History in Action: Discovering Gutenberg's Printing Process', http://research.microsoft.com/apps/video/dl.aspx?id=104803 (8 October, 2004).
10. Kapr, *Johann Gutenberg*, 224.
11. L. Voet, *The Golden Compasses: A History and Evaluation of the Printing and Publishing Activities of the Officina Plantiniana at Antwerp*, 2 vols. (New York: A. Schram, 1969–72), Vol. II, 359–60.

12. Voet, *Golden Compasses*, Vol. II, 355.
13. W. Blades, *An Account of the German Morality-Play, entitled* Depositio Cornuti Typographici (London: Trübner and Co., 1885).
14. P. Stallybrass, 'Printing and the Manuscript Revolution', in B. Zelizer (ed.), *Explorations in Communication and History* (London: Routledge, 2008), 93–101.
15. M. Desachy, *Incunables Albigeois* (Rodez, France: Éditions du Rouergne, 2005), 11, 43–5.
16. C. Griffin, *The Crombergers of Seville: The History of a Printing and Merchant Dynasty* (Oxford: Clarendon Press, 1988), 1–7.
17. I. MacLean, *Scholarship, Commerce, Religion: The Learned Book in the Age of Confessions, 1560–1630* (Cambridge, MA: Harvard University Press, 2012), 3–4.
18. B. C. Halporn, *The Correspondence of Johann Amerbach: Early Printing in its Social Context* (Ann Arbor, MI: University of Michigan Press, 2000), 234–8.
19. R. Fulin, 'Documenti per Servire alla Storia della Tipografia Veneziana', *Archivio Veneto* 23 (1882), 84–212, esp. 121; H. F. Brown, *The Venetian Printing Press* (London: J. C. Nimmo, 1891), 55–6.
20. A. Johns, *The Nature of the Book: Print and Knowledge in the Making* (Chicago, IL: University of Chicago Press, 1998), 527, n172.
21. D. T. Pottinger, *The French Book Trade in the Ancien Regime, 1500–1791* (Cambridge, MA: Harvard University Press, 1958), 210–37.
22. J. W. Thompson, *The Frankfort Book Fair* (Amsterdam: G. T. Van Heusden, 1969 [1911]), 169–71.
23. R. Darnton, *The Literary Underground of the Old Regime* (Cambridge, MA: Harvard University Press,1982).
24. S. Roberts, *Printing a Mediterranean World: Florence, Constantinople, and the Renaissance of Geography* (Cambridge, MA: Harvard University Press, 2013).
25. F. De Vivo, *Information and Communication in Venice: Rethinking Early Modern Politics* (Oxford University Press, 2007), 202, 210–11; P. Lake and S. Pincus, 'Rethinking the Public Sphere in Early Modern England', *Journal of British Studies* 45 (2006), 270–92.
26. Brown, *Venetian Printing Press*, 76–7.
27. O. Gingerich, *An Annotated Census of Copernicus'* De Revolutionibus (Leiden: Brill, 2002).
28. D. Selcer, *Philosophy and the Book: Early Modern Figures of Material Inscription* (London: Continuum, 2010).
29. Johns, *Nature of the Book*, 79–82.
30. M. Lowry, *Nicholas Jenson and the Rise of Venetian Publishing in Renaissance Europe* (Oxford: Blackwell, 1991), 49–50.
31. M. Lyons, *Reading Culture and Writing Practices in Nineteenth-Century France* (University of Toronto Press, 2008), 96.

8

CYNDIA SUSAN CLEGG

The authority and subversiveness of print in early-modern Europe

Observations in the work of two leading historians of the book, each of them considering the influence of the printed word on the French Revolution, clearly illustrate the different models of authority and subversion that have informed histories of the book in early-modern Europe. In his 1989 essay, 'Philosophy under the Cloak', Robert Darnton observed that:

> the problem of demarcating forbidden literature appears at first as a question of language. When the police interrogated one of their prisoners in the Bastille, a bookseller named Hubert Cazin who had been caught with all kinds of forbidden books and compromising papers in his shops in Reims, they asked him to explain a puzzling term that cropped up often in his correspondence: 'philosophical articles'. Cazin defined it as a 'conventional expression in the book trade to characterize everything that is forbidden'. The police had heard other terms ... they had a favourite expression of their own: 'bad books'.[1]

A few years later, in *Cultural Origins of the French Revolution*, Roger Chartier told his readers: 'With the tripling or quadrupling of book production between the beginning of the century and the 1780s, the multiplication of institutions that enabled clients to read without having to buy, and the increasing flood of ephemeral print pieces (the periodical, the libel, the topical pamphlet), a new way of reading, which no longer took the book as authoritative, became widespread'.[2]

Darnton's conception of authority is traditionally political – the ordering and policing powers of the state. Subversion in this model is engaging with that which authority forbids, whereas Chartier relies less on notions of legality than on features of print and their intersections with a reading public. The concepts of both institutional and textual authorities – and their subversions – help to explain the ways in which books impacted culture in early-modern Europe. From printing's earliest years the multiple institutions that controlled and patronized printing acknowledged the printed word's authority – but they also saw it as subversive. The interrelationship between authority and subversion was surprisingly complex and requires understanding how printing was patronized and controlled both within and across national boundaries. No matter how seamless institutional intentions were, however, the real story of authority and subversion is told by books – individual books that embodied authority and individual books that subverted it. Individual books' stories appear here throughout a narrative that centres on institutions but ends with a consideration of the interplay of authorities and subversions in the case of one English book, Holinshed's *Chronicles of England, Scotland, and Ireland* (1587). This story told by institutions and books argues the interrelationship between authority and subversion: authority emerged as a response to anxieties about subversion, and, conversely, without authority (institutional and textual), subversion would not have accounted for much.

Understanding how official authorities impacted printing in early-modern Europe is complicated by national and local differences. Even so, certain practices, like monarchs and magistrates issuing privileges, were widespread. Except for Papal printing privileges, authority over print did not extend beyond principalities. Papal privileges claimed validity throughout western Christendom and threatened excommunication to printers who violated their protections.[3] In the Italian city states the heads of state or their agents conferred privileges to publishers, printers and authors applying for them. Privileges assured their holders the exclusive right to print and sell the book in question for a limited time period (the average being ten years). Each privilege required a separate application and, in most cases, payment to the issuing authority. While an author might seek privileges from multiple authorities, printers and publishers usually operated within a single jurisdiction. The renowned Venetian printer, Aldus Manutius, obtained a ten-year privilege for Pietro Bembo's writings from the Venetian Collegio, which managed the Senate's business. Aldus's petition to the Collegio required Bembo's permission since in Venice, uncharacteristically, a printing privilege was contingent upon an author's prior consent. Aldus also obtained a Venetian privilege to protect works printed in his own italic typeface – a privilege that was difficult to enforce.[4] In some countries, royal privileges to select printers developed into an elaborate system of royal authority over printing, often with a printing overseer who appointed censors and assured that privileges were granted only upon the censor's recommendation.

Akin to privileges for specific books and classes of books were monopolies. Most monopolies were enjoyed by a single printing establishment within a geographical locale, a diocese or a university, but in England a single London guild enjoyed a monopoly that gave its members the exclusive right to exercise their craft of printing. For all practical purposes this constituted a national monopoly, although the Crown recognized the right of the universities of

Cambridge and Oxford to operate presses. The London Company of Stationers received its monopoly in its 1557 charter. Issued by Queen Mary I, the charter conferred on the Stationers' Company prerogatives common among English trade guilds, which included the rights to own property, keep apprentices and engage in searches to protect the trade from 'foreigners' (non-members) and poor workmanship. It allowed the Stationers to petition the City of London for a livery (granted in 1560), which assured the Company voting rights in London and parliamentary elections, participation in London governance and status among London livery companies. Further, the charter provided for the company's government by a master and two wardens, who shared their authority with the company's elected court of assistants. In principle, this monopoly, like those created by individual printing privileges, provided a means by which the right to print a text or have it printed could be construed as a property right, although one to be conferred and administered by the company rather than the Crown.

The London Company of Stationers' principal task, besides admitting new members and administering routine company business, lay in acknowledging and protecting the integrity of its members' textual property rights. This was accomplished through a system of registration. The company's clerk entered into the Company's Register Book: a book's title, the stationer's name who 'owned' the title, the entry date and, rarely, the author's name (but only for identification purposes). The entry constituted a licence to print the entered title and guaranteed the exclusive right in the copy to the licensee, his heirs or his assignees. The register also noted before 1639 the ecclesiastical licenser and, after 1639, the government's censor who approved the book for publication. The company's officers (usually the junior or senior warden) could issue the company's licence without ecclesiastical or state authorization if they felt the book did not violate the law. Company members who transgressed against another stationer's right in a copy were subject to the jurisdiction of the court of assistants, which issued fines, seized illegal copy and destroyed offending presses. The government supported the stationers' printing monopoly by prosecuting non-company printers in the state and church courts, a protection that disappeared when the courts of High Commission and Star Chamber were abolished at the outbreak of the English Civil War. In 1662, shortly after the monarchy's Restoration, Parliament passed a printing act that reinstated licensing and gave the Secretary of State authority over licensing, printing and news. This act effectively placed printing and press control under parliamentary jurisdiction, a precedent that led to subsequent licensing acts and ultimately to ending licensing in 1710, when the 'Act for the Encouragement of Learning' replaced licensing with copyright and recognized authors' rights to their intellectual property.

The Stationers' Company often has been misunderstood as a creature of royal authority, formed to administer state surveillance of print. Although the language Queen Mary employed in the 1557 patent for the charter reveals that she intended the company to serve as a 'suitable remedy' to the Protestant press, when Elizabeth I confirmed the charter in 1558, she had little interest in protecting the Roman Catholic church. This is not to say, however, that the Stationers' Company did not participate in print control. Explicit in the Stationers' Company's Charter was the notion that the exercise of their privilege could not be 'repugnant or contrary to the laws or statutes of this our kingdom of England, or to the prejudice of the commonwealth of the same'.[5] To protect their monopoly, the Company's best interest lay in preventing printing against English statutory law – law that protected the monarch from treason, the aristocracy from scandal and whatever church settlement that currently existed from opposition.

While the English Crown privileged a printers' guild, throughout Europe monarchs, mayors and religious officials, and later parliaments and councils, appointed printers to attend to the increasingly prolific printed business of state, local or church government. Official printers were usually paid a subsidy since proclamations, edicts, ordinances, statutes and other such works had little commercial value. Sometimes an official printer's title was honorific. Philip II, for example, recognized Christopher Plantin of Antwerp as 'Arch-Typographer of the King' in the Low Countries. This position held so little authority that when Philip II extended his patronage to Plantin for the *Biblia Regia* (1568–72, the polyglot Bible in Latin, Greek, Hebrew and Aramaic) Plantin's press faced financial ruin. Not only did the King neglect payments and charge the press for costly vellum copies he commissioned and later returned, but it took twelve years for the Inquisition in Spain to approve the book for sale.[6] Neither the King of Spain's patronage nor a papal imprimatur, however, was sufficient to protect Plantin's rights in the polyglot Bible: Plantin still obtained privileges for the eight-volume work in the Low Countries, Germany, France, Castile, Aragon, Naples, the Papal States and Venice.[7] In England the position of printer to the king or queen was a lucrative office both because anything printed was privileged and because official printing included bibles and liturgies (both with considerable commercial value since each parish church had to purchase copies).

As this discussion of printing privileges and monopolies suggests, in early-modern Europe the means by which authors, printers and publishers retained authority over the books they produced also made the books' contents subject to official control. Like the privilege granted to the stationers by their royal charter, most privileges operated on at least the implicit assumption that the books printed would not be 'repugnant or contrary' to religious and civil authority. The problem of subverting these authorities, however, was enormously complicated both by the religious and political differences that spread across Europe in the sixteenth and seventeenth centuries, and by the multiple authorities that exerted control.

From ancient times the Christian Church exercised an authority over the written word derived from its authority over doctrine and its power to root out heresy, so it is not surprising that the Church took an early interest in controlling the new printing technology. In 1501 Pope Alexander VI issued the bull, *Inter Multiplice*, which called upon archbishops to assure that no books contrary to the orthodox faith were printed in their provinces without their imprimatur, although they could delegate the jurisdiction for censorship to local authorities. The inundation of heretical books spawned by the Reformation led the Pope to intensify censorship: and in 1542 Pope Paul III instituted the Congregation of the Roman Inquisition, and in 1559 the Congregation published its first index of prohibited books (although similar indexes had been previously published by some universities' theology faculties and by several local inquisitions, including Spain's). The 1559 Roman Index contained more than 1,000 prohibitions and was divided into three classes: the names of authors all of whose works were prohibited, the names of authors and specific works, and the titles of anonymous books. It also listed sixty-one printers and prohibited anything they printed. The Roman Index imposed penalties for possessing prohibited texts and required bookstores to display lists of books for sale. Not surprisingly, the first Roman Index named prominent Protestant reformers, but it also included the humanists, Erasmus and Valla, and editions of the bible. Besides the Roman Index, several expurgatory indexes appeared. One of these, issued in 1571 under the authority of Philip II of Spain, specified passages of offending texts, along with portraits of and dedications to offending authors, that should be inked out.[8]

The Roman Index may have envisioned a rigorous censorship applicable throughout western Christendom, but it was embraced only in the Iberian peninsula, the Spanish Low Countries, Poland and Bavaria. In Venice, which for a time cooperated with the Inquisition, the government saw itself as sufficiently Catholic to oversee all pre-print approbation. Although France did not embrace the Inquisition, books printed in cities associated with heresy, like Geneva, were banned, and the authorities in Paris, Lyon and other printing centres issued their own catalogues of condemned books. The Holy Roman Empire's political patchwork of Imperial cities, free cities and principalities vastly complicated the administration of censorship, even though Imperial ordinances banned books that were erotic, defamatory or subversive to Church or state authority. After the 1555 Peace of Augsburg (which had established the principle of *cuius regio, eius religio*: whose region, his religion) some local authorities controlled printing, with the result that what was promoted in one city might be banned in another. Even in Protestant principalities, the writings of all reformers were not treated equally. In the Imperial city of Frankfurt, which housed Europe's most important book fair, the established Book Commission required merchants who attended the fair to obtain and display Imperial privileges on their bookstalls, publish a catalogue of their offerings and deposit copies with the Commission. While the Frankfurt Book Commission could not be described as lenient, both Catholic and Lutheran theological works received Imperial privileges, clearly contrary to the Roman Index's intent.

Catalogues and indexes seem to indicate that after Luther enlisted the powerful tool of printing to reform religion, subversion was clear cut, but matters were more convoluted. Sometimes books were revised to comply with the letter but not the spirit of the law. In Protestant England, somewhat perversely, the index was employed to identify desirable books for Bodley's library at Oxford.[9] Two examples, one of a single book, Jacques-Auguste de Thou's *Historiae sui temporis*, and the other of a whole class of books, Calvinist devotional and instructional literature in seventeenth-century England, demonstrate the complicated nature of subversion in a confessional age. The Oxford Renaissance scholar Ian Maclean describes de Thou's book as a 'frank account of recent history written in very elegant Latin by a distinguished Gallican magistrate with impeccable Catholic credentials'. Before the book's publication in France, the authorities had forced de Thou to remove some passages on the Council of Trent. Despite this alteration, the book was seen as anti-Tridentine, and in 1609 *Historiae sui temporis* was placed on the Roman Index. Despite the interdiction, Melchior Goldast, a scholar and literary agent in Frankfurt, joined bookseller Peter Kopf to publish a German edition, which they had printed in Offenbach to escape Frankfurt's censorship. Their German edition restored material on the Council of Trent that had been cut and added marginalia that emphasized the anti-papal content.[10] This illustrates how a single book might fare in different confessional locales.

By the time Charles I came to the English throne in 1625 confessional differences had escalated into political crisis. The outbreak of the Thirty Years War provoked deep anti-Catholic sentiment among the majority of English Protestants, who, like archbishop George Abbot, leaned towards Calvinism. The King surrounded himself with court clerics, William Laud among them, who generously might be described as irenic – a wise policy, perhaps, since Charles's queen, Henrietta Maria, and most of her household were Catholic. Shortly after Charles came to the throne, he issued a proclamation with far-reaching implications for subversion by prohibiting 'Writing,

The authority and subversiveness of print

Preaching, Printing, Conferences, or otherwise' on 'opinions concerning Religion' that differed from the doctrine and discipline of the Church of England.[11] The Calvinist majority, however, had a very different view from the Laudians at court about what constituted the English church's doctrine and discipline. Where Laudians emphasized the common grounds between the English Church and Rome and adopted a liturgical style which resembled Roman Catholic worship, Calvinists declaimed against vestiges of Catholicism (such as venerating saints or bowing at Jesus's name) and emphasized the necessity of 'the Word truly preached'. The pre-print approval of books, entrusted to the chaplains of both the Bishop of London and the Archbishop of Canterbury, reflected these differences – and problematized print licensing since Laud, as Bishop of London, denied publication to Calvinist writers while Archbishop Abbot allowed it. When Laud became Archbishop, he refused licences for Calvinist books, but their printing continued. Enterprising publishers simply avoided the ecclesiastical authorizers by reprinting previously licensed books. A 1627 edition of Calvinist preacher William Gouge's sermons, for example, was printed without being submitted to the ecclesiastical authorizers because the individual sermons had been formerly printed and the printer/publisher thereby 'owned' the copy. Once a title had been entered in the Stationers' Register, that title remained the printer's property to be printed and reprinted at will. This had enormous implications since at the same time that Laudians were emphasizing liturgical beauty, restricting Calvinist preaching and refusing licences for Calvinist books, a cohesive godly Calvinist community's spiritual identity was being nurtured by printing that was entirely legal – and yet subversive.

Confessional identity was not the only ground on which authority and subversion were exercised. Every state and principality had regulations and laws that prohibited politically seditious writing and printing – although how this might be defined resided in special circumstances and changed from one local authority to the next. In Elizabethan England, for example, the Queen's unmarried status and her refusal to designate an heir provoked considerable anxiety about the succession, which in turn led parliament to include writing, printing or publishing words about the succession in a statutory definition of sedition. In a world where politics was defined by monarchical (or even magisterial or civic) power, the matter of authority and subversion was fairly clear. Authority resided in the ruling power and subversion appeared in anything that denied or challenged that power. Only a few conflicts over books extended beyond state boundaries – but in those that did, their widespread dissemination demonstrates the difficulty in containing subversion. In 1595 Robert Person's *A Conference about the Next Succession to the Crowne of England* (under the pseudonym R. Doleman) was printed in Antwerp. It advanced the Spanish Infanta's claim to the English succession by denying Tudor legitimacy and by advancing elaborate legal and theological justifications for depriving a ruler. Lord Burghley, Elizabeth I's chief minister, knew in advance of the book's publication but was unsuccessful at preventing its circulation both in England and abroad. While the *Conference*'s interest in the English succession might be seen as subversive only to Elizabeth's authority, it was part of a wider conversation about political resistance going on throughout Europe.

In 1579 *Vindiciae, contra tyrannos*, purportedly by Stephano Junio (actually by the French Huguenot, Philippe de Plessis Mornay), was printed in Basel. Almost immediately it was reprinted and republished in French and Dutch, as well as its original Latin. The same year a Latin edition appeared in England with the imprint 'Edinburgi', and a year later another Latin edition appeared in England imprinted simply 'printed abroad'. Born of the French wars of religion and grounded in both Roman Law and Judeo-Christian scripture, the *Vindiciae* contended that in response to natural law's dictates and in order to preserve common humanity, anyone must be willing to use force to combat political tyranny. Although authorities across Europe sought the text's suppression (James I had copies burned in 1622), this became a foundational text of resistance theory with other books adopting its arguments, including George Buchanan's *De jure regni apud Scotos*, printed in Edinburgh with royal privilege in 1579, and Juan de Mariana's *De rege et regis institutione libre* (Toledo, 1599).[12] A 1580 edition of Buchanan's *De jure*, surreptitiously printed in Antwerp by G. van den Rade, had on its title page: 'Ad exemplar Ioannis Rossei. Edinburgi, cum priuilegio Scotorum Regis'. The next year two London printers, Thomas Dawson and Edward Aggas, issued a surreptitious edition with the same title-page imprint. Besides their monarchomach views, these books reveal multiple subversive strategies. Their Latin editions were accessible to readers across national boundaries, which allowed widespread dissemination. They cleverly used patronage and privilege. Mariana's book was written as a counsel book for Philip III of Spain; even though it lacked a royal printing privilege it had the King's support. In 1605 Andre Wechel printed editions in Mainz and Frankfurt, with privileges. In 1611 Wechel editions appeared in both Mainz and Paris, and the French edition, published in association with the privileged press at the seminary at St Sulpice, carried the King's privilege (an interesting afterlife for a book the Parlement of Paris had burned on 8 June 1610). Buchanan was tutor to James VI of Scotland (later James I of England), so the royal privilege for the Scottish publication is unexceptional. Clearly, however, the book was perceived to be dangerous enough in both Antwerp and London to require surreptitious printing. The title page's advertisement of the Scottish King's privilege served as a strategy to deflect attention from the book's subversive argument. Even though the *Vindiciae* was printed in centres sympathetic to its Huguenot origins – Basel, Strasbourg, Geneva, possibly London ('printed abroad') – the absence of publishers' names (or Basel's false 'Edinburgi') on their title pages defied authorities. *Conference about the Next Succession*'s title page does the same by claiming to have been 'licensed' but offering only 'N' as its place of publication.

These immensely popular books that openly advocated resistance theory highlight the principal problem for controlling subversive books. Notoriety could increase demand, and sufficient demand offered a motive for publishers, printers and booksellers (perhaps also smugglers) to risk evading the highly complicated and often contradictory regulatory systems that were in place across Europe. Subversion, it seems, was uncontrollable and, indeed, inescapable beyond very narrow local boundaries – even for a monarch, as James I's effort to control books printed outside of England attests. In 1610 when the English ambassador, Henry Wooton, discussed with the Venetian Cabinet a printed libel that had referred to Venice as a 'corpse' and James as 'a crow that settled on it', he told them that he did not wish the book suppressed 'so as not to give it importance or cause it to be sought'.[13] In another case, James unsuccessfully sought the suppression of *Corona Regia* (1615), a book offering a stinging mock encomium of his pretensions. James's agents' search for the book's author and printer was relentless, and when found, James asked the Belgian Archduke to punish the book's makers. The Archduke refused, and subsequently an English ship seized one of the Archduke's. One observer noted that some were 'inclined to suspect that this is His Majesty's way of showing his resentment at the Archduke's reluctance to punish the authors and printers of *Corona Regia*'.[14]

The example of James's putative act of retaliatory piracy for his own failed effort to exert control over another authority who refused to exert control over a printed book, epitomizes the complex interplay of authorities and subversions being considered here. It also raises the question of another kind of authority – that of the book itself. Adrian Johns argues that in the sixteenth and seventeenth centuries, print had a problem of credit with readers. 'If an early modern reader picked up a printed book', Johns imagines, 'then he or she could not be immediately certain that it was what it claimed to be'. One reason for this, he says, was piracy; the other that 'illicit uses of the press threatened the credibility of all printed books'. Johns here maintains that the very conditions of subversive texts and subversive printing practices that have been considered here led to a second order of subversion – that of the authority of the printed text. In *The Nature of the Book* Johns considers printing's implications for creating and transmitting knowledge, particularly scientific knowledge. He argues that it was not until the Royal Society established a means to protect authorship and establish authorial control over printed texts that the 'advent of fixity' arrived.[15] Once this happened, printing could repair the problem of credit and only then could printing be seen as possessing authority. Johns is countering Elizabeth Eisenstein's contention that the printed text's essential nature – its fixity (uniformity and synchronization) – produced the enormous cultural shift that took place in sixteenth- and seventeenth-century Europe, which included the Renaissance, the Reformation, the Copernican Revolution and the birth of science. Since 1979, when Eisenstein's *The Printing Press as an Agent of Change* responded to a perceived historiographical problem (that 'the effects produced by printing have aroused little controversy, not because views on the topic coincide, but because almost none have been set forth in an explicit and systematic form') historians of the book have expanded, mediated and qualified Eisenstein's sweeping arguments.[16]

Besides Johns, who moved the fixity of printing – or at least scientific printing – forward nearly two hundred years, scholars have reconsidered the impact of printing on scholarly communities, politics, the arts and even the Reformation. Many of Eisenstein's assessments of printing's significant cultural implications have stood, albeit sometimes modified. Andrew Pettegree and Matthew Hall, for example, have demonstrated that in Germany where printing was dispersed across a wide area, inexpensive and easy to produce religious tracts and vernacular books made economic sense, and their production impacted the Reformation. However, in countries where printing was concentrated in one or two large cities and in well-capitalized, established printing houses, printing had little influence on religious reform.[17] With regard to printing's impact on learning, Ian Maclean agrees with Eisenstein that printing led to an increase in new areas of learning, including natural philosophy and the literature of discovery, and that 'this increase allowed for a broader range of views to achieve dissemination'. Maclean, however, goes beyond the early sixteenth-century humanist-publishers to consider the challenges posed by confessionalism and an increasingly saturated market for learned books. Even so, he observes that the new merchant/publishers still supported scholarship and sought 'to ensure that the texts they produced were of the best quality possible'. Like Pettegree and Hall, Maclean attends to the economic realities printers and publishers faced, and also in facing these realities, the resort of some to piracy, but, unlike Johns, he does not see this as undermining the authority of the book. Instead, Maclean sees printers enhancing the book's authority and marketability through features of the text, since a book's physical features mattered to authors and editors, '[w]ho demanded good-quality paper, decent-size typeface, a pleasant mise en

The authority and subversiveness of print

page, and (in most cases) a generous format size, for their works. These act homologically as visual guarantors of the quality of the content.'[18]

Texts, then, could exert considerable authority – or, conversely, they could employ strategies to disguise their authority, as when *Vindiciae, contra tyrannos* appeared in octavo, a format, Anne McLaren reminds us, contemporaries associated with cheap and insignificant texts.[19]

McLaren's attention to formal properties speaks to Roger Chartier's observations about print which began this chapter – that the proliferation in print of ephemeral texts diminished the authority of the book, and, implicitly, diminished all authority. What is telling about Chartier's remarks is that the authoritative nature of the printed word is taken for granted. Both McLaren and Mclean remind us that by the end of the sixteenth century printers and publishers were sufficiently sophisticated to adapt the paratextual elements of their products to specific ends. In the case of some texts, rapid, cheap and careless printing either mattered little or made no pretense to textual authority. One example illustrates this, the English Martin Marprelate tracts. The seven pamphlets, containing witty and satiric diatribes against the English bishops and the established church, appeared between 1588 and 1589 from a secret printing press that was moved from place to place in the English countryside to escape the authorities. Everything about them flouted printing conventions. Their author (or authors) repudiated his own authority by taking the pseudonym of Marprelate. The title pages joked about the requisite naming of printer and place of publication, as when that of *Hay any work for Cooper* read, 'Penned and compiled by Martin the Metropolitan: Printed in Europe, not farre from some of the Bounsing Priests'. The first three tracts were in quarto format, the rest octavo, and all were badly printed on poor quality paper. Everything about these tracts – the material books and their contents – was subversive.

By the late sixteenth century, as the Marprelate example suggests, notions of textual authority resided in something more than the idea of 'fixity' so central to the arguments of Eisenstein and Johns: books could be imperfect yet invoke authority. Aldus Manutius sought a reputation for being an accurate and informed editor of Roman and Greek authors. Indeed, as Malcolm Lowry points out, 'he made something of a fetish of the precision and accuracy of his texts'.[20] The authority Aldus's scholarly publications possessed among contemporary humanists is confirmed by Erasmus, who in an early letter to Aldus wrote, 'I should think my studies had received the gift of immortality, if they saw the light of day printed in your types'.[21] Even so, Aldus had to append correction lists to some of his books. Erasmus's *Novum Instrumentum*, a text that reflected humanism's scholarly search for original authority, gained for Erasmus considerable respect as a humanist editor.[22] The *Novum*

Instrumentum, which quickly became an authoritative exemplar for Biblical scholarship and translation, served as a textual foundation for the burgeoning industry of bible translation and publication. Even so, the *Novum Instrumentum* had errors that its hurried printing at John Froben's press left uncorrected. And Froben was not a careless publisher. A contemporary reported that Froben favoured the costly option of repeating a day's work rather than allow a single error in a book he was printing.[23] Such concern for accuracy extended across the world of scholarly publication in the sixteenth and seventeenth centuries, with the well-respected publishing houses employing 'as many as three, four, or even more correctors', all of whom were the highest paid workers in the print shop.[24] Yet, piracy did exist; Lyon printers notoriously reprinted Aldine classical quartos. Such books, though, may not have had flawed texts, but if they did, their purchasers should have known. After all, as Froben asserted, 'a man who buys a good book at a high price gets a bargain, while someone who buys a bad book cheaply makes a loss'.[25]

Humanist interest in accurately transmitting, first, classical texts and later, books of humanist scholarship points to their faith in print's authority well before the time Johns allowed. The issue here concerns what constituted knowledge. If, as Johns defines it, knowledge is knowledge only when it is verifiable and replicable (science), then, yes, Johns is right. The problem lies in what sixteenth- and seventeenth-century readers regarded as knowledge. Besides their interest in classical literature, theology and religion represented an important category of knowledge, and from early in the sixteenth century, scholars submitted religious texts, including scripture and the writings of the early Church fathers to the same kind of critical textual scrutiny that humanists applied to the classics. Major publishing houses, including Froben, Estienne in Paris and Plantin in Antwerp published the early church fathers – not the least of which was Erasmus's edition of St Jerome. Eisenstein was correct in noting the interest in natural history and the care that was given to preparing these texts for the press. The latter half of the sixteenth century saw the beginning of a similar interest in national history, which produced books like de Thou's *Historiae sui temporis* (Paris: Drouart, 1609) and William Camden's *Britannia* (London: Ralph Newbery, 1587), both printed with great care. George Bishop's 1590 Camden edition bore the royal arms on its title page, an even greater mark of authority than the notice of privilege, '*cum gratia and privilegio regiae maiestatis*', which appeared in both the 1587 and 1590 editions. While modern historians may dismiss the historiographical methods of the sixteenth and seventeenth centuries, these early historians saw themselves as striving for historical accuracy, and their books possessed considerable authority. Authors in many areas of learning sought such respect, but not everything printed (even well printed) was respectable. As Andrew Pettegree and

Matthew Hall remind us, while print was instrumental in the growth of science, it 'also disseminated much nonsense, particularly in the realm of medicine and astronomy. Print can disseminate error as much as truth.'[26]

In matters of print authority, then, the challenge in studies of the history of the book has been to find a comfortable middle ground between sweeping historical generalizations about print culture and narrow but valuable close bibliographical analysis. Printing, for example, may not have caused the Reformation – but in some places certain printed books did advance it. Likewise, printing may have given greater fixity than manuscripts – and with some kinds of books a high degree of fixity may be found – but anyone who has wrestled with textual problems inherent in early-modern books (Shakespeare's plays, for example) recognizes the complicated relationship between authoritative meaning and the printed text. Did Hamlet desire that his too 'sullied' or too 'solid' flesh would melt? Or did Othello liken himself to the 'base Indian' or 'base Judean' who 'threw a pearl away richer than all his tribe'? Do these differences necessarily subvert textual authority? The relationship between subversion and authority needs to be seen not as antithetical but as interdependent. To illustrate what this might mean in relationship to early-modern books, the remainder of this chapter focuses on a sixteenth-century English book: the second edition of Rafael Holinshed's *Chronicles of England Scotland and Ireland* (1587).

Until recently Holinshed's *Chronicles* enjoyed little credit from scholars interested in either early English printing or early English historiography. One of the problems is the variability among extant editions – the lack of fixity. Although it has long been known that censorship of the three-volume work (usually bound in two volumes) led to the presence of cancel leaves in both volumes, variations in cancels and the irregularity of their actually replacing censored text has often led to the view that the book reflected shoddy printing practices. The mere fact of censorship has also been seen as an assault on the book's authority. In *Reading Holinshed's Chronicles*, Annabel Patterson sees anxiety about censorship as central both to evasive publication strategies and to the project's larger protocols. According to Patterson 'the publication of both editions of the *Chronicles* suggests, if not scofflawry, at least a degree of circumvention of the regulation': the publishers evaded the requirement for preprint licensing and for entering the licence in the Stationers' Registers immediately following that review.[27] Furthermore, the *Chronicles*' principal interests lay in telling stories of freedom of speech denied and punished and in doing so was inherently subversive. Actually, the licensing, printing and censorship tell a quite different story.

Holinshed's *Chronicles*, first published in 1577, was conceived by Reyner Wolfe, the Queen's printer for Latin and Greek texts, as part of a vast

'Polychronicon', which he and Holinshed worked on for twenty-five years. The project was incomplete in 1573 when Wolfe died. A year later when his wife Joan followed him, her will provided the means for Holinshed to receive the 'benefit proffit and commoditie' of the *Chronicle*. Her executor, together with members of her family and of Wolfe's printing house, published the first edition. They employed as printer Henry Bynneman, a recognized craftsman with experience printing histories. In 1580 the earl of Leicester and Sir Christopher Hatton would secure for Bynneman a royal privilege to print 'all Dictionaries in all tongues, all Chronicles and histories whatsoever'. Ralph Newbery and Henry Denham, who acquired Bynneman's patent after his death in 1583, planned a second edition of the *Chronicles*, and on 6 October 1584, together with the surviving publishers of the 1577 edition (or their assignees), entered in the Stationers' Register their licence 'to print Holinshed's Cronicle in folio'. This entry reflected and recorded the change in partnership shares that had occurred after the 1577 edition and was not, as Patterson suggests, an attempt to obtain a licence before the troublesome additions to the 1577 text were completed. On 30 December 1584 Henry Denham and Ralph Newbery entered their 'license and allowance... by the queene maiesties graunte' to print dictionaries and histories. This notice of royal privilege contained a list of eight titles, headed by Holinshed's *Chronicles*.[28] When the second edition appeared in 1587, its colophon indicated that Henry Denham printed it 'cum privilegio'.

Besides appearing under the authority of royal privilege, the 1587 *Chronicles* conveyed textual authority, printed in three volumes in large-folio format gathered in six. Denham, approaching the printing with considerable seriousness and care, placed the project in the hands of Abraham Fleming (BA Cambridge 1580), a poet, translator and 'learned corrector' often employed in his printing house.[29] Fleming worked on the Holinshed revision between 1585 and 1587. One of his most important tasks was extending to the present the 1577 *Chronicles*' account of Elizabeth's reign; the other was editing the entire text. He imposed a more discerning paragraph structure; created an episodic structure by inserting responsive editorial comments, Latin epigrams and transitions; extended and improved the 1577 edition's printed marginalia; and created detailed indexes. Perhaps one of Fleming's most remarkable tasks was proofreading the entire 1587 edition. As a complete set of bound proof sheets at the Huntington Library attests, this was clearly directed at producing a typographically excellent text. The combination of the royal privilege and the printed text's quality lends considerable authority to the 1587 *Chronicles*.

Even with this authority (or perhaps because of it) on 1 February 1587 the Privy Council sent a letter to the Archbishop of Canterbury requesting 'the staye of furder sale and uttering' of a 'new booke of the Chronicles of England ... until they shall be reviewed and reformyd'. The concern was not with the *Chronicles* themselves but with the recent additions made 'as an augmentation to Hollingsheades Chronicle' that contained 'sondry thinges which we wish had bene better considered, forasmuch as the same booke doth allso conteyne reporte of matters of later yeeres that concern the State, and are not therfore meete to be published in such sorte as they are delyvered'.[30] The order appointed reviewers experienced in those State matters that warranted 'reformation'. The text was censored in three stages, the first of which called for deletions and revisions in the Scottish history, and in the English history's accounts of Campion's trial and Leicester's campaign in the Low Countries. At the second stage a history of all the archbishops of Canterbury was cut, probably by the current archbishop. The final stage shows careful editing designed to influence international and domestic opinions about English justice. This was probably as an effort to contain negative reactions to Mary Queen of Scots' execution and to address concerns about a shift from a military to a diplomatic solution in the Low Countries.[31]

The cancel sheets for the *Chronicles* are extraordinary in that Fleming composed them to maintain the narrative's integrity. Where it was feasible to eliminate long passages inessential to the history, they were cut, most likely to ensure a timely revision and to save labour and paper costs. To this end, long antiquarian lineages of the Cobham and Leicester families and of the lords chancellor and wardens of the Cinque Ports were removed. Most of the time, however, Fleming left the sequence of events intact, even as he condensed some accounts or removed offending material in others. For example, he kept the government trial of Edmund Campion for treason, but eliminated reports that Campion's supporters 'bruited about' that he was tried for religion and not for politics. He condensed the adjacent description of the duc d'Alençon's departure from England to avoid offending the Dutch. Fleming also changed the tone of some passages, as, for example, when he softened the fiercely anti-Catholic language used for the trial and execution of the Babington conspirators who had plotted against Queen Elizabeth. Fleming created such textual continuity between the uncensored printed page and the cancels that censorship would be undetectable were it not for the interruptions in pagination and signatures.

Holinshed's *Chronicles* reveals the complex relationship between authority and subversion. A book whose folio format, royally privileged printing and meticulous care in production accrued to it considerable authority became subversive because of political vagaries. Had Leicester's campaign in the Low Countries been successful and had Mary Queen of Scots not been executed, the *Chronicles* may not have been regarded as subversive. Furthermore, had the book not possessed authority, it might have been ignored. The *Chronicles* also testify to a printed text's potential for textual instability. Although this instability derived from censorship and revision, it was also created by practices in the printing house where offending leaves were irregularly removed (or not removed at all) and where three sets of cancel leaves were produced and irregularly introduced. Even with all this, the 1587 edition of Holinshed's *Chronicles* has exerted considerable cultural authority since it served as the historical basis for more than a generation of poets and playwrights, including, of course, Shakespeare.[32]

The instances of authority and subversion considered here suggest that in early-modern Europe printed books acquired so much authority that they became instrumental to the exercise of political, religious and even cultural power at the same time as they became subject to that power. Traditionally the language of authority and subversion belongs to the realm of these kinds of power, but in studies of the history of the book, the language of authority and subversion accrues to the texts themselves, both in their material properties and in their contents. The habit of mind that juxtaposes authority and subversion in the political, religious and cultural realms causes us to envision the antitheses to textual fixity, stability and continuity as some form of subversion. This, however, is not entirely the case with books – that is, not with individual books. So many of the examples of individual books considered here (not the least of which being Holinshed's 1587 *Chronicles*) call upon us to refine our understanding of authorities and subversions and to see them not as antithetical but as coexistent and interdependent. Subversion depends on some form of authority – textual, paratextual or magisterial. This applies even to libel, the kind of writing that since Roman times was seen as inherently subversive. It is hard to imagine that libelling a common murderer or thief would matter at all; libel becomes subversive only when directed at those with religious, political or economic power. Similarly, in the early modern period, authorities would not have cared much about what was printed if they had not regarded the printed book as possessing authority. What is telling about the examples of authority and subversion considered here is that it was the printed text's authority that led princes and principalities to both promote and restrict printing – often simultaneously. Ironically the means taken by institutions to impose their authority became so fixed that entrepreneurial printers easily developed strategies of subversion.

The challenge of book history is to make sense of this complex interplay of authorities and subversions, and this is a challenge that perhaps cannot be fully met. The problem lies in the fact that, as we have seen here, so much of the evidence comes from copies of individual books and, as Joseph Dane reminds us, imagining a narrative of book history based on book copies is difficult: 'The singularity of the individual book and the singularity of the problems any book or group of books poses will always challenge such narratives'.[33] In terms, then, of a narrative of authority and subversion in early-modern Europe perhaps the best that can be done is to account for the multiple authorities which printed texts might claim (or that might claim them) and to recognize the inevitable intrusion upon these authorities by the subversions of individual books.

NOTES

1. R. Darnton, 'Philosophy Under the Cloak', in R. Darnton and D. Roche (eds.), *Revolution in Print: The Press in France 1775–1800* (Berkeley: University of California Press, 1989), 29.
2. R. Chartier, *The Cultural Origins of the French Revolution*, Lydia G. Cochrane (trans.) (Durham, NC: Duke University Press, 1991), 90.
3. I. Maclean, *Scholarship, Commerce, Religion: The Learned Book in the Age of Confessions, 1560–1630* (Cambridge, MA: Harvard University Press, 2012), 153.
4. B. Richardson, *Printing, Writing and Reading in Renaissance Italy* (Cambridge University Press, 1995), 40, 41, 39.
5. E. Arber, *A Transcript of the Registers of the Company of Stationers of London*, Vol. I (London and Birmingham: [privately published], 1875–94), xxx.
6. J. J. Murray, *Antwerp in the Age of Plantin and Brueghel* (Newton Abbot: David and Charles, 1972), 68–78.
7. L. Voet, 'The Making of Books in the Renaissance as told by the Archives of the Plantin-Moretus Museum', *Printing and Graphic Arts* 10 (1965), 35, 41.
8. Maclean, *Scholarship, Commerce and Religion*, 156.
9. Maclean, *Scholarship, Commerce and Religion*, 156.
10. Maclean, *Scholarship, Commerce and Religion*, 33, 37.
11. J. F. Larkin, c.s.v., *Stuart Royal Proclamations*, Vol. II (Oxford: Clarendon Press, 1983), 92.
12. See A. McLaren, 'Rethinking Republicanism: *Vindiciae, contra tyrannos* in Context', *Historical Journal* 49 (2006), 23–52; George Garrett '*Vindiciae, contra tyrannos*: A Vindication', *Historical Journal* 49 (2006), 877–89.
13. *Calendar of State Papers, Venice*, Vol. XI (London, 1864), no. 909, pp. 489–90.
14. Quoted in W. Schliener, '"A Plott to have his Nose and Ears cutt of": Schoppe as Seen by the Archbishop of Canterbury', *Renaissance and Reformation*, 19 (1995), 183.
15. A. Johns, *The Nature of the Book* (University of Chicago Press, 1995), 5, 628.
16. E. Eisenstein, *The Printing Press as an Agent of Change: Communications and Cultural Transformations in Early Modern Europe*, 2 vols. (Cambridge University Press, 1979), I: 6.
17. A. Pettegree and M. Hall, 'The Reformation and the Book: A Reconsideration', *Historical Journal* 47 (2004), 785–808.
18. McLaren, 'Rethinking Republicanism', 878.
19. McLean, *Scholarship, Commerce, and Religion*, 236, 237, 239.
20. M. Lowry, *The World of Aldus Manutius: Business and Scholarship in Renaissance Venice* (Ithaca: Cornell University Press, 1979), 224.

21. P. S. Allen, 'Erasmus' Relations with his Printers', *The Library*, 13 (1916), 297–31; quoted in Malcolm Lowry, *The World of Aldus Manutius*, 220.
22. See L. Jardine, *Erasmus, Man of Letters: The Construction of Charisma in Print* (Princeton, NJ: Yale University Press, 1993).
23. Maclean, *Scholarship, Commerce, and Religion*, 121.
24. Maclean, *Scholarship, Commerce and Religion*, 121–2.
25. From the preface of Janus Cornarus's *Opus medicum practicum of 1537*, quoted in Maclean, *Scholarship, Commerce and Religion*, 122.
26. Pettegree and Hall, 'The Reformation and the Book', 805.
27. Annabel Patterson, *Reading Holinshed's Chronicles* (University of Chicago Press, 1997), 11.
28. Arber, *Transcript of the Registers of the Company of Stationers of London, 1554–1640*, II: 331–2.
29. Elizabeth Story Donno, 'Abraham Fleming: A Learned Corrector in 1586–87', *Studies in Bibliography* 42 (1989), 205.
30. *Acts of the Privy Council*, J. R. Dasent (ed.) (London, 1897), XIV: 311.
31. For a detailed account of the censorship see Clegg, *The Peaceable and Prosperous Regiment of Blessed Queene Elisabeth* (San Marino, CA: The Huntington Library, 2005), which reproduces the Huntington Library copy containing the proof sheets, a discussion of the proof marks and facsimiles of original leaves replaced by the cancels.
32. See I. Djordjevic, *Holinshed's Nation: Ideals, Memory and Practical Policy in the Chronicles* (Burlington, VT: Ashgate, 2010).
33. J. A. Dane, *The Myth of Print Culture: Essays on Evidence, Textuality, and Bibliographic Method* (University of Toronto Press, 2003), 192.

9

JAMES RAVEN

The industrial revolution of the book

Until the early nineteenth century, all book and print production processes in all parts of the world succeeded or failed as a result of manual labour. Hands, not powered machines, engraved wood blocks and plates, cut punches and cast, composed and inked type. Hands worked paper mills and different kinds of xylography and letter-press, using many different sorts of material. Hands hung drying paper and silk, and bound the products. Across Europe, men and women lived and often suffered from the making of lead-based type and rag-based paper and from the exertions of pulling the letter- and rolling presses. Many operatives worked in small, hot and unpleasant printing rooms. In all parts of the world, eyes as well as hands suffered from the demands of microscopic cutting and refining of wood blocks and copper and other metal plates.

Unlike the coming of print (wood blocks in second-century East Asia and thirteenth-century Europe; moveable type in eleventh-century China and fifteenth-century Europe), the second mechanized, industrial revolution in book production was experienced worldwide in one century. It was, nonetheless, hugely variable in its regional adoption and impact. This nineteenth-century transformation has been identified with publishing capitalism, and yet its history is many-faceted, with complicated antecedents. Technological bravura led the revolution, its products sometimes dismissed as industrial literature. Thomas Carlyle (and cultural pessimists around the globe) denounced the new machinery as mechanizing minds, devaluing literature and learning, and replacing craftsmanship (in writing as well as in publishing) by the robotic and the mass-produced. The unprecedented cheapness of industrially printed materials encouraged more people to read but also developed a greater sense of the indeterminacy and anonymity of the reading public.

Periodization of this transformation remains problematic. Many historians have pointed to the increase in the number of printing presses in particular European workshops in the age of Aufklärung or Enlightenment. In Venice, the Bassano Remondini firm undercut the publishing establishment from about 1750 by reproducing popular works whose protected printing privileges had expired. The Société Typographique de Neuchâtel undertook vast reprinting activities, and (among others) the London printing firms of Samuel Richardson and of William and Andrew Strahan introduced a greater industrial process to the expanding book trades. Such firms typify the broad commercialisation and development of a consumer culture associated with eighteenth-century Britain and western Europe and the enterprise of new manufacturers such as Josiah Wedgwood the potter and Matthew Boulton and James Watt, the makers of popular metal goods. Certainly, the increased output and building expansion of several London, then Paris and Leipzig, and later New York and Boston printing houses was remarkable, far outstripping the overall capacity of their forebears where one printing press had been the norm and two unusual. Nevertheless the achievements of the eighteenth century must be measured against the concentrated activity of early centres of printing such as those of the Aldine press of Aldus Manutius in Venice, of the *Officina Plantiniana* of the Plantin-Moretus family in Antwerp and the Kobergers in Seville. These, and many others, commanded numerous presses. The Plantin printing house comprised, at its peak, sixteen presses in 1574 and up to a dozen between the 1620s and 1730s.[1] The limitations of the manual printing press remained, however. Concurrent printing enabled a certain efficiency of scale, but the productivity of each printing press remained much the same.

Just as critical as the technologies of printing and engraving were the changing productive relationships between printers, publishers and the broader structure of the book trades. This was especially so in Europe and its colonies. By the eighteenth century, most stationers were viewed as paper suppliers and most printers as the clients (and in their own despairing words 'mere mechanicks') of publishing booksellers. The originating finance remained fundamental to the manufacturing chain from writer to reader, its links maintained by financiers, whether printers, self-publishing authors, merchants or wholesale and literary-property owning booksellers. Publishers assisted in the development of advertising, the creation of demand and the exploitation of expanding distributive and transport methods, from travelling carriers, postal services, coaches, wagons and marine and (eventually) rail networks. Even in publishing, however, bookselling careers operated under constraints imposed by broader resource limitations.

Across all trades in the early-modern world from Asia to Europe, most fixed capital had been invested in ways that produced only indirect gain. In western Europe, with the development of fixed-site production and selling, the property of the shop and dwelling-house (where almost all booksellers were tenants and many were sub-tenants) offered no long-term investment. Raw materials and goods comprised the essentials of long-term business investment. By modern standards, productivity rates stayed low. Excessive reliance on (manual) labour and a vast reservoir of under-employment created little inducement for cost-reducing innovations in all trades and industries. With so much capital tied up in a specific item of production (an edition) before any of it could be sold to realize returns, the publishing sector was especially handicapped. The book trades further suffered from the relatively inefficient deployment of resources that economists now term 'path dependency', that is, the continuation of working practices that were technically flexible but hidebound by cultural inertia. As a result, the bringing of new money into the trades, and its more versatile exploitation, are all the more striking. The transformation of the book trades in the nineteenth century can be found here: the breaking of an earlier economic regime that allowed only low productivity rates, with particularly high labour-intensity.

The expansion of printing and book production did not occur evenly worldwide, or even within Europe. Different countries and regions responded to what have been called their own book trade rhythms.[2] Centralization affected some states more than others. In France, Lyon provided short-lived independence as an early publishing and distributive centre, but the traditionally dominant Paris supported most publishing during the eighteenth century and its supremacy was even more concentrated during the next two hundred years. Mechanization served to enhance the centrality of Madrid in the Spanish publishing industry, but also created a powerful new urban printing centre in Barcelona by the end of the nineteenth century. By contrast, the states of Germany, the Low Countries and Italy boasted a number of important, interconnected distributive centres, including Venice, Frankfurt and Antwerp. In Germany Frankfurt and Leipzig were rivalled by Stuttgart, Munich and Berlin. England and later Ireland (but not Scotland) bore more resemblance to the single metropolitan model of France. This model differed again to that of early-modern China where Jiagnan, the region immediately south of the lower reaches of the Yangtze, became the central clearing-house in the empire. Jiagnan published more books than any other area and despatched them to Beijing and other far-flung cities. Even so, nothing like the national dominance of London (or indeed Paris) existed in China until, with the development of mechanized printing, Shanghai gained unquestionable ascendancy.[3]

In France and England, the economic publishing and distributive dominance of the capital ensured that rivals struggled to compete; such supremacy was capped by periods of prohibitions to printing outside named towns. London became a magnet, attracting ambitious would-be booksellers and publishers from all over England and – especially during the eighteenth century – a remarkable injection of Scottish flair and audacity that transformed the trade. Edinburgh, Dublin (at least before 1800) and Glasgow developed important book export businesses, but London remained the main publishing source for the books, magazines and other print sent out to the British provinces and then to the colonies in North America, the Caribbean, India, the US, Africa, Australasia and the Far East. In almost all of these places, local feeder networks distributed the centrally produced publications but also added their own local (usually jobbing) productions. In addition, second-hand and antiquarian book distribution greatly increased in volume and complexity, as did access to books and print. Libraries – private, institutional and commercial – all had celebrated pedigrees, but all came of age in the nineteenth century (even though the definition of what a 'library' was varied hugely around the world).

Technological revolution

In the eighteenth century, technological progress had been a limited force in the book trades, restricted to typefounding and design, and to a lesser extent to paper manufacture and experiments with intaglio techniques and the rolling press. The first successful lithography, using paper laid upon a drawing made in lithographic chalk on a damp stone, dates from the work of the Czech Alois Senefelder in Germany in 1798.[4] Thin India paper arrived in Europe in about 1750; coated paper and transparent paper were patented in 1827. From the early nineteenth century, technical and mechanical improvements made printing, papermaking, bookbinding and transportation cheaper and faster in Europe and North America. By contrast, Japanese interest in letterpress printing declined in favour of traditional wood-block xylography, although greater efficiencies were also introduced. In China, by the end of the nineteenth century, a revolution in production processes akin to those in Europe had transformed the productive capacity and commercial market of its much older book and printing trades.

Steam-driven machinery, following Watt's British patent for a steam engine in 1781, shattered technological constraints in weaving, spinning and the production of machine tools (among other applications), but the book trades were not similarly transformed until after 1814. Nicholas-Louis Robert patented a papermaking machine at the paper mill of Didot Saint Leger in Essonnes, France. Mechanized papermaking first became commercially viable in 1807 with machines made by Henry and Sealy Fourdrinier in London, but throughout the century local stationers commonly complained about shortages of inexpensive paper. Criticism led to the introduction of new sources for papermaking: first esparto grass and straw and then wood pulp. By 1825 half of all paper in England was manufactured by machine, with total output increasing thirty-fold between 1820 and 1900. In the final third of the nineteenth century, papermaking costs were reduced by about two-thirds.[5]

For the publishers of Europe and the Americas, the nineteenth century might be said to begin in 1814, the year in which a steam-driven press first printed *The Times* in London. The replacement of the manual printing press shattered the principal technological shackles of three and a half centuries of printed publication by moveable type in Europe and of the far more ancient printing activities of East Asia. The long quest to improve the wooden printing press, to reduce manual effort and to increase productivity, culminated in successful experiments with an all-metal lever press at the very end of the eighteenth century, but it took a further decade to produce an effective alternative to the hand-operated press. Following Earl Stanhope's experiments with an iron press in 1800 (and various successful initiatives in using stereotyped plates), George Clymer (an American of Swiss origins) patented the Columbia iron press in 1817. Soon after Clymer's arrival in England his press was rivalled by the British Albion press. The key development, however, was mechanization, now enabled by the greater stability of the iron press. Frederick Koenig first patented a power-driven platen screw-press in 1810, but his further patent of 1814 featured a machine with an inking roller, cast-iron platen and, crucially, an impression cylinder. Koenig adapted the cylinder from a patent of 1790 by William Nicholson, until it could print up to 1,100 sheets an hour compared to 300 under the iron hand press.[6] Colour printing also became more widespread after 1800 with various experiments in oil-based ink application and diverse methods, including the advance of chromolithography at mid-century. By that time, publishers also commissioned the first experiments in photographic insertions.

Stereotyping of composed type gradually increased from the late 1820s (led by notable exponents such as the French printer Firmin Didot of Essonnes who is credited with naming the process). The process, using plaster moulds, reduced the wear on type and enabled the keeping of the stereotyped plates instead of huge quantities of expensive and cumbersome standing type. In about 1820, London supported twelve establishments for the casting of stereotype plates. In 1848, type was fixed on a cylinder instead of a flat bed, enabling the number of impressions per hour to increase to as many as 12,000. From the 1850s *papier mâché* and then plate-metal moulds further transformed stereotyping techniques. The first industrial binding machines operated from 1827, with major developments in mechanical binding proliferating in the final quarter of the nineteenth century.[7] Engraving techniques and materials also changed. In 1834, John Murray II of London, to take just one example, reissued Thomas Macklin's lavishly illustrated bible with steel-engraved plates, a process that reduced costs and offered striking new design possibilities.

The automation of punch-cutting, typecasting and composition produced a further technological leap in the nineteenth century. Typecasting machines invented in the US in 1838 proved capable of casting 6,000 pieces of type an hour. This rose to over 50,000 pieces an hour by the end of the century. Rotary printing presses developed from about 1865 and linotype and monotype systems in the 1890s. In 1885, the American Linn Boyd Benton mechanized punch cutting by the pantographic machine, and in the same year Ottmar Merganthaler, a German-American, introduced Linotype, combining the casting and composing of type in a single line. A rival Monotype machine cast and composed individual pieces of type. Industrial binding and packaging similarly advanced, with great economies of scale in such factories as Reclam in Leipzig and Mame in Tours. In some states normally sidelined in general book trade histories, new establishments gained international status. In Hungary for example, the Pallas Literary and Printing Company was founded in 1884 with a typefoundry, lithographic press, bindery and rotary and intaglio printing presses on the same site. Hakubunkan Shinsha, founded in 1887 in Yumi, now part of Tokyo, spearheaded the redevelopment of printing by metal moveable type in Japan, and from one integrated and mechanized publishing site.

We need, nonetheless, to be cautious about dividing a modern from an ancient book trade at the point that power-driven machinery first printed a newspaper in London. The take-off in publication volume in western Europe from the 1740s reflected the entrepreneurial initiatives of publishing booksellers, most of whom now left the printing to dedicated printers. The take-off resulted from the expansion of capital resources and increased middle-class, provincial and institutional demand. Publishers and booksellers promoted significant change in the decades immediately before 1814. Many ancient firms continued and adapted, but many others struggled to survive. Across Europe, and especially in Britain, greater productivity resulted from financial and organizational innovation, within a trading structure fractured by newcomer booksellers with their cheap reprints and other innovations in salesmanship and product design. Large, powerful publishers invested in literary properties (with variable protection in different countries). In France a new legal interpretation of copyright protection in 1778 was strengthened after the Revolution in 1793. Although such directives proved fitful, leading Austrian publishers benefited from further protection in 1832, as did their German counterparts in 1835. The changing mechanics of distribution continued to be a pivotal feature of this publishing history, while control, by the agents of local and national government, remained both a restraint and a stimulus.

Political and financial control must not be underplayed: the legal constraints of many European governments continued to maintain barriers to the social extension of knowledge and education. Social reaction ranged from elite criticism in France and England to popular condemnation of *die Lesewut* (or reading craze) in Germany. Suspicion of machinery had accounted for the revival of xylography in Japan, and created resistance to change in China in the late nineteenth century. Governments adapted such reaction to fiscal advantage, as governments are prone to do. The Riancey amendment in France represented a form of taxation on fiction from 1850, and censorship measures followed in Portugal, Austria and some Italian states. By contrast, two generations or so after challenges to copyright legislation in Britain, punitive taxation on paper and advertisements was successively lifted and state censorship relaxed in France after the 1830 July Revolution.

In such ways, the 1814 divide is undermined by the continuation of many structural features of the early-modern and eighteenth-century trade through the 1820s and beyond. Printers did not speedily adopt Koenig's new steam press. Not until the 1820s did many publications issue from what *The Times* itself called 'the greatest improvement connected with printing since the discovery of the art itself'. Country book and newspaper printers often retained the old wooden or Stanhope iron presses.

In many respects, the 1840s marked a clearer transition from one age of bookselling to the next. The industrial, mass production of books accelerated after the mid-nineteenth century, and few of the older practices remained visible. The modifications to the Koenig press promoted by Edward Cowper and Augustus Applegarth streamlined production still further. One of their later eight-cylinder presses attracted large crowds at the London Great Exhibition of 1851.[8] More tellingly, the mid-nineteenth-century British tussles over taxation on books, paper and advertising fuelled passionate argument about the future of publishing and bookselling. Similar resistance to copyright, patent and grants of privilege extended to negotiation (and transgression) of international, cross-border agreements in the next fifty years. The law and the assertiveness of guilds and privilege- and property-owning groups seemed to steer transitional moments in the book industry. In the Netherlands, for example, a new institute was founded in 1815 to succeed the guilds, regulate the trade and combat piracy. A further central distribution office opened in Amsterdam in 1871.

Edicts and legislation assumed a certain finality, but the realities of their interpretation (or of compliance with them) were often quite different matters, and highlight the crucial agency of individual entrepreneurs and lobbyists. William Hutton, founder of the first circulating library in Birmingham, is typical of those who tested boundaries and helped define moments of change in the nineteenth century. In his prime the richest English stationer, bookseller and papermaker outside London, Hutton epitomised the age in which the book merchant (according to the puff for his 1841 autobiography) 'had risen to opulence and eminence by force of his merits alone'.[9] In 1826 Louis Hachette established his Paris publishing house, principally issuing educational manuals and journals, dictionaries of modern and ancient languages, and modestly priced but exactingly edited versions of French, Latin and Greek classics. Hachette's 'railway library', publications for reading on the train, paralleled that of W. H. Smith in Britain. Railway extension boosted all levels of distribution, developing for books and journals what amounted to a new stage of opportunity in book and print production, marketing, distribution and reception. Railways created new markets as well as supplying existing ones, progressing steadily during the 1840s. Hachette's publications and W. H. Smith's bookstalls supplied long-distance passengers and those travelling regularly to work. Both firms helped to popularize reading in trains, where it was much easier than in horse-drawn coaches.

Circulations were impressive. Hachette's *Le Journal pour tous*, founded in 1855, gained a weekly circulation of 150,000 copies. Just as national circulation increased in Britain, leading firms such as Longmans and Macmillan, together with the university presses of Oxford and Cambridge, hugely extended their international dealings, requiring extensive investment and high-risk credit development. Henry S. King, brother-in-law of the 'prince of publishers', George Smith, developed the firm that was to become Kegan Paul by means of his international banking interests and work as India agent. For King, publishing primarily offered new opportunities for financial diversification and innovative entrepreneurship. Nevertheless, the publishing world remained dominated by aversion to risk and liable, in John Sutherland's memorable phrase, to 'toe-dipping caution'.[10] Credit and insurance availability did lower book trades transaction costs, but development was uneven. Banking operations continued to be based primarily on the relative respectability and credit reputation of the operators. As Charles Kegan Paul was to remind readers of his memoirs at the end of the nineteenth century, ready access to capital remained indispensable to the successful publishing business.[11]

In 1891, Samuel Smiles offered a mixed account of the changes in his biography of one of the greatest nineteenth-century publishers, John Murray II, who had died in 1843. Smiles wrote that 'the old association of booksellers, with its accompaniment of trade-books, dwindled with the growth of the spirit of competition and the greater facility of communication ... Speculation [for retail booksellers to buy on special terms] has now almost ceased in consequence of the enormous number of books published.' Smiles concluded that 'the country booksellers' were dying out because 'profits on books being cut down to a minimum, these tradesmen find it almost impossible to live by the sale of books alone. Cheap bookselling, the characteristic of the age, has been promoted by the removal of the tax on paper'. His next point echoed Carlyle: 'This cheapness has been accompanied by a distinct deterioration in the taste and industry of the general reader. The multiplication of Reviews, Magazines, manuals, and abstracts, has impaired the love of, and perhaps the capacity for study, research, and scholarship on which the general quality of literature must depend.'[12]

Cheaper books

Obituaries of the sensational London bookseller James Lackington in 1815 recalled the foundation of modern cheap book retailing and the success of his book emporium for which, in the words of his trade motto, 'small profits do great things'. Beginning in the 1820s, the transformation in printing capacity ensured the advance of further developments in publishing and bookselling. The production of very cheap books in large quantities and in slighter formats replaced the earlier, economically necessary publication of editions in small numbers, often in cumbersome multivolumes, at relatively high prices.

Ultimately, it was the reduction in printing, typesetting and paper costs that enabled new economies of scale and the satisfaction by publishers of new levels of demand. The early-nineteenth-century publishing industry was propelled by cheap popular literature and notably by reprint series and the new 'book series' such as John Murray's *Family Library*, first issued in 1829, and Gervais Charpentier's *Bibliothèque Charpentier*, launched in Paris in 1838. Lower prices were exemplified by Michel Lévy's one-franc literary series, but increasingly cheap print (once the preserve of chapbooks and ballads) extended to a great range of manuals, guide books, dictionaries and religious books. British railway books and 'yellowbacks' of the 1840s and 1850s retailed at between 1s and 2s 6d, with cheaper paper-covered novels, travel books and the like selling at 1s or below. George Routledge's *Railway Library* of more than 1,000 titles began in 1848, the year of W. H. Smith's first station bookstall. Louis Hachette's *Bibliothèque des chemins de fer* commenced in 1853.

The risks of high capital expenditure and storage had long made it unwise to print large editions, but there were increasing exceptions. The gigantic editions of popular titles reprinted over and over again included school books, hymn books and cheap morality periodicals. During the nineteenth century, the greatly expanding number of titles and hugely increased volume of print (as well as its increasing secularization and specialization) clearly resulted in more extensive distribution and a wider readership. Production runs for the most successful titles were now immense. In an industry of unprecedented publishing capacity, Chapman and Hall in London published and sold more than half a million volumes of Dickens in the last three years of the author's life.[13] Routledge's *British Poets*, begun in the 1850s, included several editions of well over 110,000 copies. Yet these, again, paled before the cheap editions of the poets and the colossal paperback series of 6d novels, commonly manufactured by newspaper machines in runs of 25,000 and more. Hachette's *Journal pour tous*, Cassell's 'National Library' and 'Masterpiece Library', and many others, were to effect a mechanization of literature beyond even the anticipation of Carlyle.[14]

By the mid-nineteenth century, therefore, the extension of cheap print supported the development of a new working-class market, quite distinct from the older chapbook and ballad readership of the previous two centuries. In the Low Countries, the hugely popular *Nederlandsche Muzenalmanak* was offered in five differently priced versions between 1819 and 1847. Many publishers extended their ethical and commercial mission to bring knowledge to the working classes, with a further and immense development of the European colonial and overseas market. Domestic publishers were infuriated by the contrast between success at home and the increased piracy abroad of successful literary titles. Linguistic divisions played a part: in Belgium, French publishing benefited from the wider francophone industry while Flemish publications were modest at the beginning of the nineteenth century. Norwegian publishing continued to be dominated by Danish interests and, among many examples, publishing in Polish, Slovak, Balkan and Baltic languages championed minority revivalist movements.

Newspaper publication requires special mention. By 1850, ten times more newspapers were published than in 1750, and nearly three times more than in 1830. In many parts of the world, mechanized printing of newspapers transformed print supply. Spanish-American presses, for example, produced relatively few books but a huge and escalating volume of periodical and newspaper publication through the nineteenth century. In regions where printing had long been established, the newspaper revolution was just as marked. In 1821, 267 different newspapers and periodicals were published in England and Wales; by 1851, this total reached 563.[15] The increase in the size of newspaper editions was even more remarkable, a transformation boosted in the 1850s by experiments in the manufacture of paper using straw and wood as cheap alternatives to rag. By 1821, each of the leading

British Sunday newspapers sold between 10,000 and 14,000 copies weekly. By 1843, these sales amounted to between 20,000 and 55,000 each, and by 1854, some 110,000.[16] The British government finally removed stamp duty on newspapers in 1855, although the one remaining 'tax on knowledge', that levied on paper (reduced from 3d to 1½d in every pound weight in 1836), was not abolished until 1861.[17] In Britain, some 125,000 separate newspaper and periodical titles were published during the nineteenth century.[18] By 1907, newspaper production was to account for 28 per cent of the total net value of all British publications.[19]

The new reprinting regime was marked by the changing size of average print runs, based on the reduced unit cost of the book. The critical development occurred in the 1840s. The size of the average print run in Britain doubled between 1836 and 1916, but with an average print run of 500 copies in the 1830s, this increased by half again to 750 in the 1840s (increasing by a further third to 1,000 between 1860 and 1920).[20] Large print runs and low prices, personified by the profile of American firms like Ticknor and Fields (of Boston, founded 1854), contributed to a business model in advance of most European publishers. Structured, mass and centralized popular publishing responded to growing consumer demand, advanced by the continued expansion of part-issues, periodicals and newspapers, circulating libraries, public libraries and, especially in the late nineteenth century, by new demand for educational literature and school books. Publishing (however much directed by strong-minded entrepreneurs) remained in thrall to capital requirements, legal frameworks, technological constraints and the efficiency of distribution networks. Increased divisions between publishers and booksellers transformed onward-selling, discount and remaindering systems. The mechanized production of cheap books opened up markets, even though contradictory principles were also at issue. Campaigns on behalf of authors' rights proved inimical to the campaign for cheap books. Older cooperative methods changed, especially in the US, as publishers superseded booksellers, selling books wholesale to merchants and other outlets. Despite the longer print runs enabled by mechanization and efficiencies of scale, profit margins tightened in an increasingly competitive market. Publishers needed to sell a greater proportion of an edition to cover costs, accentuating the need for more accurate forecasting of demand and the printing of low-risk quantities.

In the final decades of the nineteenth century, the surging demand for educational books across the globe was never homogeneous but it did broaden, as prestige titles led to a multitude of cheap, small format books for elementary schools. Greater stratification of the market resulted from expansion in the literate population and particular professional, intellectual and leisure communities. The broad literary market depended upon greater 'churn', requiring fresh titles to maintain its strength. By contrast, the increasing specialization of knowledge supported the extension and division of periodical publications. As publishers sold more books but received less per volume, market-building was sustained by a transformation in distribution systems and greater competitiveness in foreign markets.

Domestic supporting agencies notably included commercial libraries, while demand was further boosted by subscription book-clubs, private and town debating and literary societies, advancing working-men's clubs (founded either by or for labouring men) and the solemn recommendations of the periodical reviews and magazines. In most European and American countries, serialization advanced still further as a dependable form of lowering publication risks and attracting new custom; various hybrid and mutant forms of the periodical and serial sustained, in particular, the market for fiction. It has generally been claimed that the publication of the infamous three-decker novel supported the circulating libraries; more certainly, railway stalls were supplied by cheap fiction in single volumes, part-issues and so-called 'library series'.

The London bookseller G. R. Porter confidently welcomed the cheapening of literature: 'books can no longer be considered, as they were in bygone times, a luxury, to be provided for the opulent, who alone as a class, could read and enjoy them. From year to year the circle is widening in which literature becomes almost a necessity of life'.[21] Nevertheless, the material cost of many books also limited the social extension of book buying, borrowing and reading. A new Balzac novel in the 1830s cost more than the weekly income of most French working-class families. New, not reprinted, 'literature' remained the most expensive category of publication throughout the century. In times of financial restraint the market withered. As John Murray III wrote to Gladstone in 1851, 'it must be borne in mind that books are a *luxury*; when a time of distress comes, the first expense to be curtailed is the purchase of books. That is done (without any outward display of economy) rather than laying down a carriage or dismissing servants.'[22] Despite all the cheap weekly part-issues, the popular reprint series and the increased production of small publications, booksellers maintained the relatively high price of many types of book. Only the second-hand trade and the market stall sustained working-class readers at times when new editions proved beyond their purse. Many of the writers experienced by working-class readers were dead and unfashionable. It is also the case that inequalities in terms of access to print increased across Europe. The publication of almanacs, ABCs and religious primers hugely increased in Italy in the nineteenth century, for example, yet 75 per cent of the population as a whole remained illiterate in 1870 (90 per cent in the rural south).

Printing and publishing houses

In Europe and in the Americas, distinctions among publishers, printers and booksellers also took on modern appearances by the mid-nineteenth century, even though the combination and acquisition of the separate businesses occurred regularly. In Britain, the printing firm Bradbury and Evans expanded and advanced as publishers; Smith Elder began as a trading company, then added publishing and finally took on a printery.[23] In the same way, many press products acquired greater distinctiveness in terms of their type or firm of origin, yet some publishers were able to develop many types, each contributing to the definition of the brand.

The transformation of the British trade and of the range of printed literature in the first half of the nineteenth century was led by the so-called 'list' publishers including Blackwood, Longman, Murray and Bentley, where 10,000 or more copies of an edition were published. Throughout western Europe the maintenance, and in many cases the advance, of books as luxury items in the eighteenth century underscores the significance of the steep rise in publication tallies from the 1820s and the lowering of publication costs. At the same time, publishers widened their market by offering variously priced editions, appealing to a range of incomes, and serving increased demand for educational texts, travel books and science literature.

Publication costs lowered in accordance with available capital, labour and new technological capabilities, but the pricing of many books reflected a fresh evaluation of the market in which price cutting and onward-sales discounting introduced new perils for the wholesale publisher. Retailing and allied services (as well as the amount and length of credit offered) expanded to match the changing commercial potential of the audience. The customized packaging of books, part-issues and magazines, so competitively practised in the late eighteenth century, advanced to new levels in the mass market of the mid-nineteenth century. Coloured wrappers, extravagant advertising and new technical accomplishment in illustration, indexes and title pages all served to lure new custom. Clashes were inevitable. Publishers of some new books had for decades inflated rather than discounted prices. Subscription collection and, increasingly, more adept market profiling had also continued to nurture specialist publication. Most readers now benefited from a discount on the cover price of a book, but the division between wholesale publishers and retail booksellers widened further. Nevertheless, the ever-larger editions of cheap books risked on the market forced tighter and tighter profit margins on the booksellers. The solution was not to come until 1890 and the net book agreement, proposed by Frederick Macmillan. The net book agreement fixed retail prices and provided a basis upon which royalties could be paid.

In the 1840s and 1850s, however, in a period of unrestricted competition, many booksellers were forced increasingly to work in concert to combat variable trade and retail pricing.

By the mid-nineteenth century, unprecedented industrial plant sustained and enhanced productive capacity. In 1853 Harper and Brothers in New York erected a celebrated seven-storey factory to replace a burned-out and much more modest establishment. In 1866, Clowes printing factory employed 568 men working at more than fifty presses in London. Spottiswoode and Co., also of London, boasted 450 men, and the government printing office of Eyre and Spottiswoode, 388.[24] Thereafter, employment mushroomed. The Paris firm of Paul Dupont and the Brockhaus family in Leipzig each employed more than a thousand workers by the final decade of the nineteenth century.

A freer, more competitive, and expanding market, together with more efficient technologies and distributive systems, provided enterprising publishers with unprecedented opportunities. In France, about 6,000 titles were printed in 1828, 10,000 in 1855, about 20,000 in 1880 and over 28,000 in 1900. German publishing (more than just in German states proper) expanded from about 3,900 titles in 1800 to 14,000 in 1843 and over 30,000 by 1900. In the Netherlands, annual book production increased from a few hundred titles in 1800 to some 3,000 by 1900. In some countries the rise was sharpest at the end of the nineteenth century: Spain produced about 500 titles each year in the 1870s but this had risen to 2,000 by 1905; the increase in Italy was from about 2,000 titles in 1820 to 8,000 in 1890. In Britain, according to the crude title counts offered by Peddie's *English Catalogue of Books* during the nineteenth century, 25,000 book titles were published between 1800 and 1835 and 64,000 between 1835 and 1862. Many traditional producers continued, adapted and expanded. The English Stock of the Stationers' Company, providing dividends to its members from the publication of almanacs, still served as the mainstay of cheap publishing even by the early Victorian years. The use of cheaper raw materials and new industrial processes (notably in papermaking) lowered unit costs and hugely improved the return on invested capital. Between 1846 and 1916, the volume of publication was to quadruple while the average price of literature halved.[25] The machine age had indeed arrived. In 1841 some 50,000 men and women were employed in the paper, printing, book and stationery trades in Britain; by 1871 the total was some 125,000.[26]

Advances in printing technology also reshaped textual appearance and authors achieved new control over spelling, punctuation and other accidentals. With the increased speed of production, publishers, in contrast to their predecessors, used printing and composing developments and the easier production of multiple proofs to encourage authors to make changes during

The industrial revolution of the book

the publication process.[27] In Britain, modified commission agreements gradually challenged outright sale of copyright as the most popular form of publishing contract. The new commission contracts specified the fees charged for organizing the printing, binding and distribution of the books, as well as securing a percentage of all sales. Less popular contract types included simple royalties, royalties reserved until the sale of a specified number of books (a system open to accounting abuse), fixed-term shared profits (after the publisher undertook all production costs) and series contracts, used for sets by several authors.

Nineteenth-century publishing houses throughout Europe continued to work largely in the image of their businessmen publishers and their preferences. Powerful reputations also supported the extension of publishing and business ventures. The humblest operators struggled to cope with credit and risk management, while the superior resources of the grandest publishers allowed them to invest more diversely in property, annuities and a broader range of commercial and banking activities including investments overseas and the colonial trades. Large printing firms such as those of Paul Dupont in Paris and the family Brockhaus in Leipzig epitomized the changes in the nineteenth century where such book trade leviathans resembled contemporary captains of industry rather than workshop master-printers. In France and its colonies, Hachette enthusiastically founded mutual friendly societies and benevolent institutions for workers, while writing pamphlets about assistance for the poor. At the same time, he proved an active campaigner in the settlement of international literary copyright questions. William Darton, the most important British publisher of juvenile literature of the first half of the nineteenth century, built upon the specialist marketing to parents and children pioneered by the Newberys.[28] George Smith, whose entrepreneurship secured Thackeray's success after *Vanity Fair*, combined munificence with hardnosed management.[29]

Building on export initiatives of the eighteenth century, publishers took full advantage of empire and overseas. Between 1828 and 1898 the decadal value of publications exported to the British colonies and the US increased nearly thirty-fold, from about £35,800 to about £1,089,000 (or more than £1,336,500 including further foreign trade).[30] London publishers and London newspapers dominated an imperial communications network. The firm founded in 1843 by the Scots Daniel Macmillan and his brother, Alexander typified the increasing reliance of publishers on overseas trade in the second half of the century.[31] Hachette led numerous firms in France serving a diaspora from the French Caribbean and West Africa to Indochina.

Globalization was thus led by firms such as Hachette in France, Samuel Fischer and Bernhard Tauchnitz in Germany, George Putnam, Houghton

Mifflin and Harpers and Co. in the US, Gyldendals in Denmark, Norstedts and Albert Bonnier in Sweden and Macmillan in Britain. Supply across the Atlantic was not straightforward. Until the end of the nineteenth century, for example, France remained the greatest supplier to the Spanish American world of translated classics into Spanish. A campaign led by the British and Foreign Bible Society improved the overseas dispatch of cheap bibles. Millions of copies of religious texts were exported by the Religious Tract Society, the Bible Society and the London Missionary Society with similar organizations elsewhere in Europe. The first British Act concerning international copyright passed in 1838. Foreign authors were protected by the same copyright in Britain as British-born authors, provided that their country of birth offered reciprocal arrangements. The 1838 Act brought certain success, with agreements between Britain, France and Prussia in advance of the more formalized International Copyright Act of 1844. Booksellers and authors suffered even more by cheap reprints entering the colonies (American reprints in Canada were a particular difficulty). This was addressed by the 1842 Copyright Act, but its clause protecting the imperial trade by forbidding colonial reprinting of books copyrighted in Britain could not be effectively policed. Restrictions against the import of foreign books into overseas British dominions similarly often remained unenforceable.[32]

The importation of cheap books into different countries often encountered resistance. The successful reprinting and then importation of English books by foreign publishers such as Galignani in the first half of the nineteenth century enraged the London trade.[33] As a result, a series of customs acts attempted to tighten control, with the 1842 Customs Act requiring proprietors of copyright to supply customs officers with the particulars of publications thought to be infringed by imported piracies. The Leipzig publisher, Christian Bernhard Tauchnitz, visited Britain in 1843, enthused by Continental market possibilities for books by English authors. Tauchnitz offered to pay authors for his right to reprint publications abroad (while making it clear that he did not actually need to ask authors for their permission to do so). The agreement effectively excluded British publishers from the European market, while the protection of home interests depended upon customs officers remaining vigilant and well-informed. Tauchnitz did offer authors and publishers assistance in confronting the much more difficult American market, and a British–American governmental agreement was signed in 1853. Nevertheless, the new agreement remained unratified by the US Senate and unauthorized reprinting of British books continued in America until an 1891 Act of Congress (and even that offered only limited protection).

The expanding market in the West was paralleled by the transformation of publishing in East Asia where speculative publication now more confidently eclipsed traditional production for the civil service, universities and other private and institutional clients. In China, more than three-quarters of all publications (by title at least) might be termed commercial even by the 1630s. As court and local government sponsorship of printing proportionately fell away during the Ming dynasty in particular, and was replaced by non-commercial family publishing, the further and continuing shift towards commercial publishing placed new reliance upon the commercial distribution of texts. Differences in what was meant by 'commercial' and 'private' are critical to comparative global histories of the book, while recognition of the continuing importance of non-commercial publishing in China, India, South and East Asia and parts of Africa offers reassessment of the circulation of private and non-commercial texts in Europe, the Americas and Australasia. The production of printed books and pamphlets paid for by authors or institutions and designed for private or closed institutional circulation can be obscured by attention to the remarkable surge in commercial publication where more writers advanced manuscripts for publication and entrepreneurial publishers identified new and reduced-risk opportunities. In China and Japan commercial printing developed more according to the genre of writing than to broad market demand, but sales networks had advanced since the seventeenth century.

The industrial revolution of the book brought cheaper print to new readers, as well as fresh criticism of literary production. We might question the extent to which increased book production in the century before steam-driven presses and papermaking machines, lithography and photography significantly increased the number of book readers, given that demand from institutions (and from those already acquiring books) was more obvious than that from working men and women. By contrast, the extension of cheap print and newspaper circulation, especially from the 1840s, represents the most pointed evidence for expanded literacy and for a broader audience for print, even though literacy remained very low even in parts of the world where printing had been established for some centuries. These changes also brought alterations to the physical appearance of books, print and newspapers, enabled by advances in font design, engraving and other typographical techniques. Newly efficient distribution systems, the circumvention of restrictive practices and the employment of labour in the publishing industry on an entirely new scale underpinned the transformation in the production, dissemination and impact of print.[34] A technologically led economic regime replaced the relatively high labour-intensity and low productivity rates of the early-modern book trade. For printers and operatives many of the unpleasant working practices of confined printing houses were abandoned, but it is worth remembering that the glories of quality books and of cheap and mass publishing still rested upon hard and difficult labour conditions. In the mechanized age, people still made books as much as they wrote and read them.

NOTES

1. L. Voet, *The Golden Compasses: The History of the House of Plantin-Moretus*, 2 vols. (Amsterdam: Vangendt and Co., 1969–72).
2. J-Y. Mollier and M-F. Cachin, 'A Continent of Texts: Europe 1800–1890', in S. Eliot and J. Rose (eds.), *A Companion to the History of the Book* (Oxford: Blackwell, 2007), ch. 22, 303.
3. C. Brokaw and K. Chow (eds.), *Printing and Book Culture in Late Imperial China* (Berkeley, CA: University of California Press, 2005), chs. 1 and 2; C. A. Reed, *Gutenberg in Shanghai: Chinese Print Capitalism, 1876–1937* (Vancouver: University of British Columbia Press, 2004).
4. M. Twyman, *Lithography 1800–1850: The Techniques of Drawing on Stone in England and France and their Application in Works of Topography* (Oxford University Press, 1970), esp. chs. 3, 9.
5. A. Weedon, *Victorian Publishing: The Economics of Book Production for a Mass Market 1836–1916* (Aldershot: Ashgate, 2003), 64.
6. C. Clair, *A History of Printing in Britain* (London: Academic Press, 1965), 210–24.
7. L. S. Darley, *An Introduction to Bookbinding* (London: Faber and Faber, 1965), 111.
8. M. Plant, *The English Book Trade*, 2nd edn (London: Allen and Unwin, 1965), 275–6.
9. *The Life of William Hutton, Stationer of Birmingham and the History of his Family: Written by Himself, With Some Extracts from his other Works* (London: Charles Knight and Co., 1841), vi.
10. J. Sutherland, *Victorian Novelists and Publishers* (London: Athlone Press, 1976), 10.
11. C. K. Paul, *Memories* (London: Kegan Paul, Trench, Trübner and Co., 1899), 277.
12. S. Smiles, *A Publisher and his Friends: Memoir and Correspondence of John Murray, with an Account of the Origin and Progress of the House, 1768–1843*, 2 vols. (London: John Murray, 1891) 2: 516–17.
13. R. L. Patten, *Charles Dickens and his Publishers* (Oxford University Press, 1978), 310–14.
14. A. Rauch, *Useful Knowledge: The Victorians, Morality, and the March of Intellect* (Durham, NC: Duke University Press, 2001), esp. ch. 1.
15. M. Harris and A. Lee (eds.), *Press in English Society from the Seventeenth to the Nineteenth Centuries* (Rutherford, NJ: Fairleigh Dickinson University Press, 1986).
16. I. Asquith, 'The Structure, Ownership and Control of the Press, 1780–1855', in G. Boyce et al. (eds.), *Newspaper History – from the Seventeenth Century to the Present Day* (London: Constable, 1978), 100.

17. K. Gilmartin, *Print Politics: The Press and Radical Opposition in Early Nineteenth-Century England* (Cambridge University Press, 1996), ch. 2.
18. J. S. North (ed.), *The Waterloo Directory of English Newspapers and Periodicals 1800–1900*, 2nd ser., 20 vols. (Waterloo, ON: North Waterloo Academic Press, 2003); also available at www.victorianperiodicals.com.
19. S. Eliot, *Some Patterns and Trends in British Publishing, 1800–1919*, Occasional Papers of the Bibliographical Society, 8 (London: The Bibliographical Society, 1994), 105.
20. Weedon, *Victorian Publishing*, 28, 49, 67.
21. Cited in J. J. Barnes, *Free Trade in Books: A Study of the London Book Trade since 1800* (Oxford University Press, 1964), 96.
22. Murray to Gladstone, 3 September 1851, cited in Barnes, *Free Trade in Books*, 79.
23. P. L. Shillingsburg, *Pegasus in Harness: Victorian Publishing and W. M. Thackeray* (Charlottesville: University Press of Virginia, 1992), 147.
24. Plant, *English Book Trade*, 358.
25. Weedon, *Victorian Publishing*, 158.
26. Eliot, *Some Patterns and Trends*, 93–96, 104–5.
27. A. C. Dooley, *Author and Printer in Victorian England* (Charlottesville: University Press of Virginia, 1992).
28. L. Darton, *The Dartons: An Annotated Check-List of Children's Books Issued by Two Publishing Houses 1787–1976* (London: The British Library, 2004).
29. P. Shillingsburg, *William Makepeace Thackeray: A Literary Life* (Houndmills: Palgrave Macmillan, 2001), 54.
30. Weedon, *Victorian Publishing*, 39 (table 12.3); G. Johanson, *A Study of Colonial Editions in Australia, 1843–1972* (Wellington, NZ: Ellbank Press, 2000).
31. S. J. Potter, *News and the British World: The Emergence of an Imperial Press System, 1876–1922* (Oxford University Press, 2003); E. James (ed.), *Macmillan: A Publishing Tradition* (Houndmills: Palgrave, 2002), 11–51.
32. Relevant clauses reproduced in C. Seville, *Literary Copyright Reform in Early Victorian England: The Framing of the 1842 Copyright Act* (Cambridge University Press, 1999), 266–8.
33. G. Barber, 'Galignani and the Publication of English Books in France from 1800 to 1852', *The Library*, 5th ser., 6 (1961), 267–86.
34. R. J. Taraporevala, *Competition and its Control in the British Book Trade 1850–1939* (Bombay: D. B. Taporevala Sons and Co., 1969).

10

ALISTAIR McCLEERY

The book in the long twentieth century

The history of publishing in the twentieth century can be seen as a palimpsest, where the traces of earlier patterns have been effaced by change, but nevertheless can be discerned through the intervening layers of business and cultural practice. The earliest trace inscribed on it is of the localized growth of printing and publishing from the fifteenth to the nineteenth century. The development of a multifunctional industry – choosing titles, making books, selling books – was constrained by rudimentary communication systems, confined largely to waterways and sea roads, and resulted in a large number of independent, family-based enterprises. The advance in more efficient communication systems in the nineteenth century, particularly of railway networks and shipping companies, sustained national concentrations of publishers in the largest commercial or most politically important cities where sources of capital – financial, cultural, educational and social – were more plentiful. The companies remained by and large family-owned but, because of the increased investment needed in rapidly changing technologies and in stock-holding, they became more specialized, focusing as publishers on the selection, organization and promotion of titles.

This second level of the palimpsest was overwritten in the twentieth century by a breaking out of national boundaries and the creation of transnational publishing corporations that provide the major theme of this chapter. However, in looking at the publishing industry from the perspective of the early twenty-first century, all three levels of the palimpsest are still evident: relatively small to medium independent companies, often structured as sole traders or partnerships, serving local or regional needs; medium to large publishers at national level, sometimes imprints that have survived since the nineteenth century, whose success often brings with it the risk of takeover by the uppermost level of enterprise operating transnationally; and that final level of conglomerate, evidence of both the concentration of ownership that accelerated in the late twentieth century and the self-definition of publishing as a form of content management regardless of material form.

The existence of the palimpsest ensures that neither a simplistic chronological narrative nor a newsreel-like country-by-country synopsis will provide a sufficient explanation of the historical movement towards that uppermost contemporary level. A nomothetic, rather than an idiographic approach is needed. Book historians have tried to understand the meaning of events by analysing unique events and experiences, and have avoided the nomothetic challenge to develop a generalized understanding of patterns and principles based on the analysis of large bodies of evidence. Indeed, the failure of book history to date has been to provide a synoptic and nomothetic account of the transition towards the contemporary in moving on from the well-tilled fields of nineteenth- and early twentieth-century publishing. Three reasons for this failure are suggested here: first, the predominance of the Anglo-American and the literary sectors of publishing in current scholarship and a reciprocal lacuna in understanding the development of non-English language publishing;[1] second, the lack of examination of the growth of global trading systems and regulators which performed an enabling function in the movement from national to transnational;[2] and third, a reluctance on the part of many book historians to move beyond the idiographic to seek pattern and principle, a reluctance that has perpetuated a mapping, rather than a broader analytical, mission within book history.

The structure of the global book publishing industry has now polarized, comprising a small number of global publishing/media conglomerates and a large number of small specialist niche publishers. At the time of writing, there are ten major conglomerates that, in addition to being vertically integrated, also operate globally across media platforms to facilitate the exploitation of common intellectual property rights. These dominant companies, in terms of revenues derived from publishing, are: Pearson; Reed Elsevier; Thomson Reuters; Wolters Kluwer; Bertelsmann; Hachette Livre; McGraw-Hill Education; Grupo Planeta; Cengage Learning; and Scholastic. (Bertelsmann has taken over Penguin from Pearson and is currently merging it with Random House, already the largest trade publisher in the world.) What is striking perhaps about this list is the geographical concentration of ownership in Europe and the diversity of output represented, with educational, professional and academic publishing as the preeminent sectors. Yet neither of these features – the geographical and the taxonomic – has particularly attracted the attention of book historians. At the other end of the spectrum, national industries include a larger number of smaller, independent publishing companies, where the domestic market represents their primary focus and the source of their titles and revenue. They serve that local market in terms of specific cultural, and linguistic, needs. These companies may not necessarily have survived from the second level of the palimpsest but they share its distinctive characteristics. Histories of the book organized within the borders of the nation state give them undue prominence: partly through a misleading sense of historical survival and continuity from the nineteenth to the twenty-first century; and partly because of their undoubted contribution to the nation state's sense of itself.[3]

The description of the third, the contemporary, level of the palimpsest contains two implicit views of publishing: as a function in which value is added to textual (and graphic) content in the transmission from author to reader; and as a transnational industry with distinct but changing structures operating, by and large, within a liberal capitalist economy in pursuit of profit – if only to sustain itself. The former perspective defines the publisher as managing a process across all platforms in which there is a progressive accretion of value; while the latter acknowledges, despite perceptions to the contrary, including self-perceptions, that the publisher is market-focused but not necessarily market-led. Transnational operations increase market access through the transmission of content through other publishing businesses, all under common ownership (and possibly sister companies in TV, film and other media). The importance of transnational operations lies less in the achievement of economies of scale and other synergies, though these can be significant, than in dominance, to the point of control, of national markets. That dominance, as the case of Harlequin discussed below shows, need not imply the distribution of 'transnational content', that is, material derived from Anglo-American culture and sold through, unmediated, into national markets as is the practice of the film and TV industries. Rather than agents of homogeneity, translations from English seem to be a form of recognition of and acquiescence in cultural difference. The continuing power in the label of 'cultural industry' that is applied to publishing should not be underestimated. It implies acting in support of a national, or on occasion linguistic, culture in a manner distinct from the other mass media. Indeed, the move in the course of the twentieth century away from the hardback to the paperback as the major format for print publishing has typically been viewed as a key component in the democratization of knowledge; it reflects that trend, of course, but it also arises from the need to expand markets by lowering price through longer print runs in an attempt to create a virtuous circle of supply and demand.

At the beginning of the twentieth century, the Germans were using the label *Kulturverlag* to designate a publishing business of the kind that underpinned the new (since 1870) country's growing sense of nationalism and of pride in its scientific, industrial and cultural advances.[4] A number of these *Kulturverlage* from the end of the nineteenth century onwards promoted a form of German cultural nationalism through mass distribution of books regarded as culturally significant. In the period before the First World War, national publishing in Germany, rather than in the UK or US, represented the then peaks of achievement both in book production and in innovative marketing.[5] Yet this predominance, while evident to contemporaries who flocked to the Leipzig and Frankfurt Book Fairs each year, fails to register in most current Anglophone studies of twentieth-century publishing which focus on the UK and US as if that was all that mattered.

German publishing and printing companies had made large investments in printing technology and maintained, even for popular markets, high standards of quality in production. German institutions were graduating highly skilled graphic designers who were encouraged in their innovation and creativity. Even in the period after the Second World War, German-trained designers, such as Giovanni Mardersteig, Jan Tschichold and Hans Schmoller, continued to exercise a strong influence on the quality and appearance of the printed book throughout Europe. Covers and format were often seen as crucial in the branding necessary for marketing and promotion. Germany had book-distribution machines at railway stations, mainline and branch, from before the First World War and, in the period after it, pioneered the marketing integration of books and films. The paperback first appeared in Germany as a publication in its own right, seeking out fresh markets, and not just as the hardback without a board cover. The *Kulturverlage* produced, as paperbacks, good books at low prices. In doing this, they were addressing the democratization of German society by coopting working-class intellectuals into mainstream German culture. They also provided a visual contrast to the garish covers of the trash literature that was thought to be a major corrupting factor in the decline of traditional German values.

Although the defining characteristics of the paperback can be traced back to the nineteenth century and before (the binding and cover material, the convenient size and the long print run), in Germany at the beginning of the twentieth century the format gained in importance as the major vehicle for print publishing. The development of the format had always been closely linked to function. If books were to be rebound by their owners to create a more permanent and uniform library, then the publishers need only issue them in inexpensive covers. If books were regarded by their owners as relatively disposable upon reading, after whiling away the time on a railway journey or on holiday, for example, then the publishers need only issue them in inexpensive covers. If books were to be carried around a great deal, on a train or to the salon of a spa hotel, then publishers needed to produce them in conveniently portable sizes and weights. However, in the first half of the twentieth century, publishers like Reclam and Albatross found that they could pursue the commercial goal of expanding national markets, while maintaining this mission of the democratization of knowledge through provision of good books at low prices. They found that they could reduce costs by reprinting, in long runs and in uniform formats, titles that had already proven themselves in either the cockpit of the marketplace or that of criticism. The pre-existing reputation (of title or author) would be the selling-point, rather than the visual appeal of the cover. Mass-market consumption did not demand self-advertisement of the individual title, but it did require recognition of, and confidence in, the publisher as brand. Advertising the brand rather than the individual titles promoted confidence among both bourgeois and working-class readers alike. The 'Universal-Bibliothek' of Reclam, for example, comprised (and comprises) a large series of reprints of well-known authors at low prices that began with a liberalization of German copyright law in 1867. The standardization of the Universal-Bibliothek lent itself in 1912 to the introduction of its own book-vending slot machines of which there were 2,000 by 1917, as Reclam exploited both a hunger for self-education and a renewed cultural nationalism.[6]

Yet this German precedent, while again evident to contemporaries, receives little recognition within a book history that remains stubbornly focused on London and New York. In particular, the advances achieved by German publishing houses such as Reclam, from branding through standardization of size to creating a popular market, are credited to Anglo-American publishers such as Allen Lane. The latter's establishment of Penguin Books in 1935 can rightly be perceived as a transformative moment in the history of British publishing but not in a wider global context. Lane did bring a dynamism and energy to the adoption of the German precedent. He had learnt the lesson that to sell the Penguin brand entailed convincing the public of the rightness and reliability of its badged titles. The initial ten Penguins were a judicious mix of detective fiction, of the 'naughty but nice' autobiography of Beverly Nichols, of the light, deft humour of Eric Linklater and of the accessible seriousness of *Ariel*, the biography of Shelley by André Maurois. This blend brought commercial success even in the first year of operation: three million books were sold, using 600 tons of paper, and creating a turnover of £75,000; the bestsellers were Dorothy L. Sayers, *The Unpleasantness at the Bellona Club*; Margot Asquith, *Autobiography*; Beverly Nichol, *Twenty-Five*; Liam O'Flaherty, *The Informer*; and Mary Webb, *Gone to Earth*, and from his share of the profits Allen Lane bought a nine-ton cutter, christened 'Penguin'.[7]

The first major US paperback house, Pocket Books, was founded in 1939 based on the German-originated Penguin model (eschewing the class of birds and choosing a kangaroo as its logo) after several ventures, including that of the Boni brothers, had failed in the preceding two decades. Its first ten titles were as conservative as those of Penguin four years earlier: a judicious mix of detective fiction, including Agatha Christie's *The Murder of Roger*

Ackroyd, the classic, Shakespeare and Emily Brontë, the contemporary, Dorothy Parker and Thornton Wilder and the title that defies categorization, Felix Salten's *Bambi*. Nevertheless, in order to compete for readers, each title had its own distinctive cover, ranging from the semi-surrealist to the semi-photographic. Avon Books, its major competitor, was founded in 1941 and was almost immediately sued by Pocket Books for plagiarism of the format. Pocket Books lost – little wonder given its own debt to Penguin and the latter's to German precedent set by publishers such as Reclam and Albatross in the development of the paperback.[8] Avon's covers were even more striking than those of its rival; they ranged from the semi-photographic to the semi-pornographic. Title competed with title, lacking the emphasis on both brand and decorum characteristic of their German (and British) predecessors.[9]

Some German paperback publishers, such as Tauchnitz, had realized, however, even in the mid-nineteenth century, that the market for German books was limited by the size of the German-language-speaking community itself. So they sought to extend that market by also publishing in English, both for English-as-a-second-language speakers and for the primary English markets around the world including the US. In this, they anticipated the late twentieth-century move by Bertelsmann (Germany), Hachette (France) and Planeta (Spain) into English-language publishing. They also anticipated the growth of an international marketplace regulated by copyright legislation. Tauchnitz itself had established by the mid-nineteenth century a confident reputation for its reprints of British and American authors in an English-language paperback series not for sale in the UK for copyright reasons. From 1841 to 1937 it issued some 5,000 titles, selling some 60 million copies in total. All the great figures of English literature, particularly the Victorian novelists, were to be found in its easily recognizable format. The strengthening of intellectual property conventions, including significantly the International Copyright Act (Berne Convention) of 1886, to regulate increasingly globalized commerce and communication in a manner that would protect, in the case of copyright, the interests of its creators, owners and licensees, only served to provide Tauchnitz with something of a monopoly as far as its copyright titles of these prominent and popular authors were concerned. The company 'conquered' the US, dominating retail and library sales of English popular fiction there for the second half of the nineteenth century. (Tauchnitz did produce American authors such as Washington Irving, Hawthorne and Longfellow but in editions for sale outside the US.) Tauchnitz also exploited the European railway network both to distribute books across national borders and to extend the number of readers and retail outlets for them. European competitors such as Asher or Heinemann and

Balestier were seen off; but the US market was effectively closed to Tauchnitz imports on the introduction of the Chace Act in 1891 as part of a programme of increasing American protectionism.[10]

German publishing before 1918 was, in sum, less of a profession for gentlemen and more of a business demanding the highest standards of professionalism. It produced books for its own internal markets, driven by a sense of cultural mission as well as profit, and it sought to enter other, particularly English-language, markets in an embryonic attempt to obviate the lack of a large population (as the US had) or a large Empire (as the UK had). Its decline after 1918 was due to the economic hardships of the postwar period and, after 1933, to the effects of Nazi policy upon the book trade and its readers and upon Jewish members of both groups. Yet both the US and the UK were to benefit as these high standards of German practice, and its qualities of innovation and creativity, were to be transmitted in the 1930s and beyond to both countries by Jewish immigrants such as Kurt Enoch, Kurt Wolff, George Weidenfeld and Paul Hamlyn. As Germany entered into almost two decades of self-destruction through two world wars and a subsequent territorial and ideological division, the contribution of its émigrés ensured the transfer of such excellence to Anglo-American publishing.[11]

Excellence survived in Germany itself to reemerge in the second half of the century. Bertelsmann, founded in 1835, weathered these storms and stresses of twentieth-century German history to undertake an expansion in the 1950s through another form of the democratization of knowledge, the book club. It successfully used its model of operating book clubs to enter national markets in France, Italy, the Netherlands and Spain.[12] By the 1970s the company had also moved, through strategic acquisitions, into magazine and music publishing and later into broadcasting. Bertelsmann, through its ownership of Random House and now Penguin (some irony surely), has become the largest trade (consumer) publisher in the world. Springer Verlag, founded in 1842, undertook an international expansion from the 1960s onwards, including the setting up of branches in Japan, India and Hong Kong. A flirtation with Bertelsmann ended in 2003 but a series of further mergers and acquisitions created Springer Science and Business Media, one of the world's largest publishers of scientific, technical and medical (STM) journals and books, as well as online services. Holtzbrinck, although younger than either Bertelsmann or Springer (it was founded in 1948), adopted the former's model of the book club to fuel its rapid growth in the 1960s through acquisitions of other publishers in Germany. By the 1980s, the company felt secure enough to begin a series of takeovers of publishing houses in the US and the UK, including established names such as Farrar, Straus and Giroux, Holt and in 1999 Macmillan with its strong interests in both trade and academic publishing. That these three companies now stand among the world's most important publishers (in English) can be ascribed both to the reassertion of Germany's leading position in publishing and to the vulnerability of US and UK publishing houses when exposed to a newly dominant free-market ideology after a long period of protectionism. This in turn brought about a paradoxical situation by the end of the twentieth century of the dominance of Anglo-American published content but the increase in non-US or UK ownership of these globalized publishers through companies such as Bertelsmann, Springer and Holtzbrinck.

The competition to German publishing in the US and the UK before 1914 and until the 1970s had been largely complacent. The US possessed a large and growing internal market that it tried to protect assiduously, for example, through the earlier noted 1891 Chace Act, misleadingly termed the International Copyright Act. The latter contained a clause requiring that foreign works be manufactured in the US to achieve copyright protection there. The Chace Act was superseded by the Copyright Code of 1909 but the manufacturing clause survived. It remained in place until 1978 when American manufacturing began to move overseas, as it had done in the UK and Europe from the 1960s, in a move to reduce production costs and, in some cases such as Singapore, to take advantage of investment there in new printing technologies. This protectionism by the US at the beginning of the twentieth century could be justified by its continuing need to nation-build after its Civil War and the continuing settlement of new territories coupled with continuing immigration from Europe. Publishers, of newspapers as well as of books, provided a common currency for the nation. Yet the US did not join the Berne Convention of 1886 until 1989. The imperative to protect its home market, long after the need to nation-build, outweighed any sense of a new need to participate in international trading. This imbalance may have weakened US-based companies' ability to resist takeover in the last quarter of the twentieth century. That home market had been boosted in 1945–6 by the GI Bill and consequent expansion in higher education and then perpetuated by that other consequence of war, the baby boom. Not that war was over: cold succeeded hot. The perceived competition with the Soviet Bloc in science and technology, as well as the need to demonstrate the superiority of western culture, led to the National Defense Education Act of 1958 with increased support for universities and libraries. The United States Information Agency (USIA), later the United States Information Service (USIS), was created with a brief to fight the cultural battle, particularly in non-aligned countries, through the weapons of American books and American authors, to the benefit of the industrial-publishing complex. From a 1947 profile of 648 publishers producing 487 million books, the US publishing industry had grown by 2005 to

81,000 publishers responsible for 3.1 billion books – albeit that, as discussed above, the largest of these were now in 'foreign' ownership.

After the Second World War, US publishers were driven by the same need to grow beyond this large home market as fuelled the transnational ventures of German companies. The War itself, and the subsequent Marshall Plan for Europe, had lifted American eyes to the prospects of international sales. However, just as clear was the need to reach an accommodation with fellow Anglophone publishers in the UK, itself worried about the transition to national independence within its Empire (with India the first to negotiate its autonomy in 1947). Particularly in the period from 1948 to 1975, both UK and US businesses tried to perpetuate a transatlantic protectionism through two measures: through strategic alliances and mergers between companies or the opening of branches in one another's countries (Cambridge University Press set up in the US in 1949; Oxford University Press limped behind in 1950); and through the mutually beneficial Traditional Markets Agreement (TMA). Until its termination in 1975 after an anti-trust suit brought in the US in 1974, the TMA divided the markets for English-language books into those that were exclusive to one or other of the UK or US editions and those that were 'open' where both editions competed against one another. UK publishers tended to exercise their monopoly in those territories (with the occasional exception of Canada) which had constituted part of the former Empire, now Commonwealth. Australia, and to a lesser extent New Zealand and South Africa, were key protected markets for UK publishers. No British publisher would buy or sell rights in a particular title unless a monopoly was ceded over sales in the traditional market. Contracts for the publication of specific titles would condense this list of markets as 'British Commonwealth and Empire as constituted in 1947'. By the early 1960s they specified 'British Commonwealth and Empire as constituted at the date of this agreement together with the Republic of South Africa, the Irish Republic, Burma, Egypt, Iraq, Israel, Jordan and the British Trusteeships with the rest of the world an open market except the US, its dependencies and the Philippine Islands'. From the mid-1960s some UK contracts omitted Israel; while others, in the face of aggressive US competition, clarified the position of Canada by specifying 'UK and Commonwealth including Canada'.

The TMA was significant because of the dependence of the UK on its overseas markets. Exports accounted for 40 per cent of the total British books manufactured in 1961; 25 per cent of these were destined for Australia alone. The UK domestic market remained small and publishers there had always relied on strong export sales, except for those obviously committed to a niche market. For the best part of thirty years, the TMA protected those sales from US encroachment. For some time, moreover, UK publishers could depend on a common legal framework within most of the territories specified within the TMA, in terms of both a foundation of English legal principles and practices and a tendency, even after independence, to look to precedents set in the courts of London.

The UK had therefore guarded closely the imperial markets within which its home-based companies could prosper, in books as much as in sugar or textiles. Such an international trading network demanded not only regulation by the imperial centre but also a process of international legal standardization and control reflecting (and contributing to) a globalizing commercial imperative in which national jurisdictions had to be brought into harmony one by one. The creation of the International Telegraph Union in 1865 was an early example of this process, followed among others by the Berne Convention of 1886 noted above. Yet this also represented the beginning of a gradual secession of national legal sovereignty to organizations such as the General Agreement on Tariffs and Trades (GATT) and the World Trade Organization/World Intellectual Property Organization (WTO/WIPO) in the pursuit of and resulting from a dominant (from the 1980s) ideological belief in free trade. By the 1990s, international copyright regulation enabled US and UK authors and publishers to trade everywhere in intangible rights, rather than material books, in order to optimize revenues. That general commitment to open markets, on the other hand, would leave national publishers in the UK and US open to takeover by competitors elsewhere (as opposed to the deterrents to foreign ownership found at this period, for example, in a Canada constantly threatened by the economic and cultural muscle of its southern neighbour). The legacy of Reaganism in the US and of Thatcherism in the UK would be for their publishing industries an increased foreign ownership. By 2003, five out of the eight largest publishing houses in the US were part of transnational conglomerates: Pearson (UK), Thomson (Canada), Reed Elsevier (UK and Netherlands), Bertelsmann (Germany) and Wolters Kluwer (Netherlands).

Throughout the twentieth century, Anglo-American complacency would also be challenged and slowly dispelled by the growth of indigenous publishing in the British Dominions, such as Australia and Canada. Behind its own form of statutory protectionism, Canadian publishing sought to assert its independence both from the 'mother country' and from the US. In the case of Harlequin this resulted not in stagnation but in a secure base from which a programme of international expansion could be undertaken to the point where the company now publishes its romance novels in twenty-nine languages in 107 countries. After a fragile beginning in 1949 as a paperback reprint publisher, Harlequin found its market niche from the early 1950s in the issuing of medical romances, a market that it consolidated on obtaining the North American publication rights to the novels of Mills and Boon. The latter had been specializing in this genre of fiction since the 1930s and had built up a very efficient editorial operation, a large backlist and a stable market in the UK. By 1964, Harlequin had dropped its own list and was focusing solely on reprinting Mills and Boon titles. These it sold into the much larger North American market through supermarkets and other retail outlets where buying one of its books could become a regular part of general shopping. In 1971, Harlequin bought Mills and Boon. When it was itself taken over in 1981 by another Canadian company, Torstar, owner of the *Toronto Star*, this signalled the beginning of a period of further North American expansion. Silhouette, based in the US, was taken over in 1984, giving Harlequin by 1992 85 per cent of the total North American market for genre romance. In 1974, it had entered the German market; by 1981 it had branches in Scandinavia and Finland; after 1989, it opened subsidiaries in Hungary, Poland and the then Czechoslovakia; and in 1995 it penetrated the largest single market in the world, China, publishing in both Mandarin and English.[13] At the time of writing, the incumbent Canadian government is dismantling many of the barriers to foreign ownership of Canadian companies. It takes little imagination to envisage a cash-rich Chinese company buying Harlequin in the same reverse manoeuvre as Harlequin effected on Mills and Boon in 1971.

Eva Hemmungs Wirtén argues cogently that Harlequin went beyond just the basic act of translation, undertaking a more sophisticated form of transnational editing to acculturate Anglo-American books for overseas markets. The English-language originals are not only translated into Swedish, for example, but their cultural references and values are adjusted for the sensibilities of the Swedish reader.[14] This would seem to support the concept of 'glocalization', a term coined by the sociologist Roland Robertson to denote a form of syncretism or hybridity in which the local borrows and adapts the global. While glocalization might seem to have validity only where an indigenous language and culture thrive, and are not suffering linguistic competition from English, such a form of customization supports the argument suggested above, that the transnational trade publishing industry may appear less guilty of propagating a homogeneous form of content than the film, TV and games industries.

The collapse of the TMA after 1975 hastened the creation of further cross-Atlantic conglomerates, such as HarperCollins (1987), and the concentration of ownership noted above. The complacency of the British industry had been bolstered not only by the TMA but also by the net book agreement (NBA), a form of internal price-fixing. Publishers' attitudes reflected the smug insularity of the UK itself, basking not only in victories in the two world wars but also in the 'special relationship' with the US that the TMA itself characterized. The collapse of the latter also prefigured the UK's hesitant, and often recalcitrant, membership of the then European Economic Community, now European Union. This has had to date little effect upon conditions for readers as publishing has been regarded, due in the main to French influence, as a cultural industry. It is therefore part of the cultural exception that allows individual member countries to regulate publishing at the national level through, for example, the level of VAT (sales tax) or statutory fixed retail prices. However, those EU countries that were originally part of the Soviet Bloc in the period roughly 1946–89 have moved away from a command economy (producing approved publications serving the interests of state and party) to the liberal capitalist model of western Europe and North America. Not that there were not shades of grey in this transition: Poland under communism demonstrated great innovation in graphic design and in the production particularly of children's books while most Soviet Bloc countries encouraged and supported cultural (but not nationalist) publishing within limits; and in the immediate period after 1989, many of these countries experienced a brutal form of capitalism with local enterprises taken over by western companies, for example most of Hungarian publishing by German firms, and others resorting to pornography to ensure their survival. Within the EU, the only boundaries to the sale of books are linguistic and even these are being eroded through the steady adoption of English as the language of sectors of higher education and business. Transnational trading in e-books, driven by the consumer need to have the latest bestseller instantly and by companies such as Amazon that recognize no national borders, for taxation as well as for trading, may eventually lead to some harmonization between and within all states of the EU (and there is precedent for this in the European Union's Database Directive). Further integration of the regulation of publishing globally under the auspices of the WTO may be a further consequence of the growth of the e-book (and of English as a common language).

Yet, if there is to be one nation's publishing industry that would surely run counter to this move to the global and to the growth of Anglo-American (and English-language) content, then France would be prime candidate. Certainly for the first seventy years of the twentieth century, French publishing had reflected the linguistic nationalism and insularity of the nation, partly explained by its access to those imperial territories in north and west Africa that it was resolutely turning francophone. Political polarization within metropolitan France both stimulated a growth in publications and also accentuated the inward-looking nature of much that was being produced. It was not really until the shock of German occupation during the Second World War, and the humiliation of collaboration, had dissipated that

French publishing began to look outwards. During the war, the degree of accommodation within publishing with the Nazis generally reflected the nation as a whole, both in the occupied zone and in Vichy. Many companies continued but under the control of the occupation forces or of Pétainist ministers and, in both cases, limited in the material resources, particularly paper, available to them. Clandestine publishing took place in support of the resistance, whether the Free French or the Communists; the Free French also smuggled in material produced in exile.[15] However, in the immediate aftermath of the war, a state of literal and metaphorical exhaustion was apparent: stocks were almost non-existent and reprints seemed easier undertakings than new works. These conditions, coupled with continuing economic austerity and rising labour and material costs, produced by the 1960s consolidation within the industry in the form of two dominant groups, Hachette and Presses de la Cité.

This environment of austerity was largely true of postwar Europe as a whole (including the UK). Paper shortages continued to limit production not only of trade books but also of school textbooks and other materials vital to reconstruction and recovery. To the west of the newly established Iron Curtain, purges took place of publishers and writers linked with prewar fascist movements or guilty of collaboration with the Nazi occupation administrations. To the east of the Iron Curtain, within the new sphere of Soviet influence, purges took place of those who might hold views subversive of the newly imposed Communist regimes and publishing was controlled, just as strictly as under the Nazis, as a key tool of party policy. The resulting shortages of human capital throughout continental Europe slowed down the development of its publishing industry and its ability to reach prewar levels of national attainment (or in the case of Germany pre-1918 levels). In France the postwar recriminations and investigations did not formally close until 1955 and, by then, the new international divisions had hardened. In western Europe, publishing was viewed by many as a key instrument of anti-Communism, even if only as a demonstration of freedom of expression; while in the Soviet Bloc, the publishing industry, firmly embedded within the command economy, could only ever be a vehicle for party propaganda.

However, that freedom of expression in western Europe, coupled with the low costs of entry in setting up a publishing company to those with energy, insight and creativity, led to the establishment of many new publishers in the late 1950s and early 1960s. In France, the development of the paperback as an agent in the democratization of knowledge came late: Livre de Poche (an imprint of Hachette) was founded in 1953 and its success in stimulating volume sales was swiftly emulated by others. French publishers also belatedly realized the need to serve that volume market through retail outlets other than the traditional bookshop and, as did publishers elsewhere, seized the opportunities presented by the growth of supermarkets in the 1960s (followed eventually by hypermarkets) to widen the range of consumers. However, the process of consolidation also continued, increasing the dominance of Hachette and Presses de la Cité who were more able than their smaller competitors to take advantage of new opportunities. As in Germany and the US, the drive to growth characteristic of the twentieth-century company eventually led both Hachette and Presses de la Cité to seek new markets outside the limited ecumene of *la francophonie*. The former became part of the Lagardère media group in 1981, merged with the smaller Hatier group in 1996 and took over Larousse in 2004.

It also expanded into the rest of Europe through the acquisition of Salvat in Spain in 1988, the Orion group in the UK in 1998 and Hodder Headline in 2004 before crossing the Atlantic with the takeover of the Time Warner Book Group (principally Little, Brown and Company) in 2006. Larousse had originally been part of the Presses de la Cité group after a merger in 1988 to form the second-largest publishing company in France (after Hachette) and the tenth largest by turnover globally. However, Presses de la Cité was in turn taken over by the hyper-ambitious Vivendi, formerly a water company that had used its under-exploited assets to invest heavily in broadcast media and film, particularly after the deregulation of the telecommunications industry in France in 1998 following the Anglo-American precedent. Vivendi overextended itself with acquisitions in the US, including Houghton Mifflin (2001), and in the early twenty-first century held a fire sale of its companies. Lagardère bought 40 per cent of its publishing interests (Larousse) in 2004 and the balance, including overseas companies, enjoyed four years of independence as the newly minted Editis before being taken over by the Spanish Planeta group. Editis remains the second-largest publishing company in France while Planeta, having moved decisively into Anglophone as well as Francophone publishing, stands in eighth position in the global league table of publishers.

The development of this uppermost level of the palimpsest contains little that is exclusive to the publishing business. Models of the acquisitive corporation existed, and exist, in other sectors of the economy. So too models of the movement from national to postcolonial to globalized can be found in other sectors such as the car or pharmaceutical industry. It bears some resemblance to the organizational theorist Kenichi Ohmae's five-stage model of globalization: the export-orientated company in stage one opens up overseas branches in stage two before in stage three relocating production to key markets, where in stage four they create copies of the parent company to provide a full service to those markets but these copies are then consolidated with the centre in stage five to create the globalized, transnational corporation. However, publishers do not necessarily manufacture standardized products such as cars or pharmaceuticals. They are *Kulturverlage*: supporters of a culture while remaining commercial in outlook. The case of Harlequin demonstrates a respect for the distinctiveness of markets in cultural as well as linguistic terms.

Yet the pressure to produce content that can be sold globally remains. The culture, created and contributed to by publishers without determining whether the chicken or egg comes first, can be a global culture as much as a national one: a global culture of English boy wizards, Catalan Gothic and Scandinavian noir. It has also to be recognized that linguistic distinctiveness is not a necessary condition for the sustenance and maintenance of cultural distinctiveness. The lack of a separate language may handicap the evolution of a distinct culture, including literature, but it does not prevent it as the examples of Austria, Ireland and the Hispanophone countries of South America demonstrate in their various ways. The notion that language was essential to the growth of national consciousness stems from the work of Benedict Anderson. Anderson posits that the coming of print in the late fifteenth century created an 'imagined community' that was linguistic. Print established a uniform, fixed written language shared by all within that community but that was based on the language practices of the secular centres of power. The linguistic communities, cohering around and ruled by those centres, formed nation states.[16] Contrary to Anderson, however, the gradual decline of Latin as a transnational written language was fuelled more by the Reformation and Enlightenment than any sense of nationalism. And no such obstacles in the path of the onward march of the English language have yet appeared on the horizon. As its use expands, English can become the channel to this global culture – in books as much as in films or television programmes.

Non-Anglophone publishers work within a marketplace that is self-restricted by their language. This has been an advantage in at least two ways. First, the established language or languages protected key areas of culture and education from the invasion of material produced in English and offered at relatively lower prices (through economies of scale and in particular lower unit costs only partially offset by transportation charges). Second, local publishers could profit from the international success of books by Dan Brown or J. K. Rowling by buying up the particular language rights and seizing a monopoly in, say, the Bulgarian or Turkish markets. Local imprints of transnationals could benefit in a similar manner in translating and selling content already owned by their parent company. The defence of language, in other words, both protected the internal market and allowed these local publishers to boost their income through the introduction of external products translated for those markets.

This linguistic defence is breaking down; the use of English has seeped from international trade and business into Higher Education with its own international aspirations and now explicit purpose in preparing graduates for work often in transnational businesses. It is spreading into other levels of education – how otherwise could students be prepared intensively enough before entering Higher Education to benefit from its English-medium teaching? Its use in textbooks at all levels (except perhaps kindergarten) is constantly reinforced in many countries through music, film and television. Over 80 per cent of the material available online is in English, a further factor consolidating the hegemony of the English language. Companies like Hachette and Bertelsmann and Planeta, arising from national bases, might seem, then, to be farsighted in their strategic acquisitions of companies that give them strong positions within this transnational market for English-language trade publications, whether print or e-book. In fact, the growth of the latter will simply accelerate the consolidation of transnational publishing as described above.

The twin processes of technical and linguistic change are mutually reinforcing. They are creating not only digital natives but also near-native users, and therefore readers, of English. This generation need not restrict itself to English-language textbooks: it represents a market for English-language trade publishing as well. The market for translation rights in new, English-language science fiction novels has now disappeared. Readers of this genre of fiction in France, Germany and Spain prefer to read the original than wait for a translation; and the print book or e-book can be quickly or instantly theirs through an online retailer such as Amazon. The time-lag between English-language publication and French translation of *Harry Potter and the Order of the Phoenix* led to the English version becoming the number one children's bestseller in France in the interval. The same thing happened in Germany on the publication of *Harry Potter and the Deathly Hallows*. These may be particular instances and, indeed, examination of the sheer quantity of English-language titles on the shelves of bookshops in many European cities might be regarded as anecdotal and unsystematic. However, it should give pause for thought while we wait for more comprehensive evidence for reading in English substituting for reading in the native tongue. What can be stressed here is the huge potential for such substitution, as opposed to additionality, as a rational outcome of the development of transnational publishing since the beginning of the twentieth century.

Governments can counterbalance external forces, linguistic and commercial, by privileging national and regional companies and products without infringing statutory commitments to a free market. The chief defence of this form of intervention is a cultural one, the so-called 'cultural exception'. A commonality of transnational culture, including media integration of product development and marketing, threatens small-nation linguistic and cultural diversity. International organizations recognise that this would be to our global detriment. However, they also acknowledge globalization as actually an impediment to choice within the marketplace and therefore licence intervention. Increased transnational flows of books are a challenge to an open marketplace, particularly in the sense that economies of scale will nearly always enable larger publishers, with the cooperation of larger booksellers, to supplant the smaller. Government, directly or through its agencies, must then take up the responsibility for maintaining the open marketplace by preventing the development of cartels, both those that seek to dominate the entire cycle and those that operate across media; and by ensuring freedom of expression for writers and a concomitant freedom of choice for readers. There is a nexus here of economic, social and cultural responsibility through which national and regional governments must ensure diversity by applying mechanisms to fill the gap between social and cultural benefits and market viability.

Even those countries that have strengthened their cultural defences at a national level, through exploitation of the 'cultural exception' from free trade agreements, in setting up content quota or other systems of control, find it difficult to maintain these because of the lack of borders online. The movement away from centralized (and limited) broadcasting services, for example, to the decentralized (and seemingly unlimited) availability of material on the internet has made a mockery of such protectionist systems. The growth of English reading as substitution rather than addition will be hastened by the existing dominance in the global market of English-language e-books; and the present state systems of protection and support for non-English writing and publishing are based on print and on national borders, both of which represent a situation that is passing. Transnational publishers seek even now, not just the big book, in terms of its bestselling status, like J. K. Rowling or Dan Brown, but the transnational bestseller so that profits can be optimized across the globe. That bestseller need not originate in English, as the example of Stieg Larsson's Millennium Trilogy illustrates; but it must be marketable in English. The transnational groups seek material that is marketable in English across national and regional borders, in print or as e-book, because either it is not too culturally specific or, on the contrary, it is sufficiently specific to satisfy the literary, chair-bound tourist. The nomothetic gain from the publishing history of the twentieth century may lie, not so much in developing a robustly theorized account of the development of the transnationals themselves, their growth and changing patterns of ownership, but in the definition of such publishers as *Kulturverlage* contributing to a global rather than a national culture.

NOTES

1. J. Thompson, *Merchants of Culture: The Publishing Business in the Twenty-First Century*, 2nd edn (New York: Plume, 2012).
2. The notable exception to this criticism is to be found in the work on international copyright by E. Hemmungs Wirtén: *Terms of Use: Negotiating the Jungle of the Intellectual Commons* (University of Toronto Press, 2008) and *No Trespassing: Authorship, Intellectual Property Rights, and the Boundaries of Globalization* (University of Toronto Press, 2004).
3. S. Shep, 'Imagining Post-national Book History', *Papers of the Bibliographical Society of America*, 104 (20) (2010), 253–68.
4. The first recorded use of the term *Kulturverlag*, which is often also used to describe the publisher (*Kulturverleger*) was in 1912 in H. von den Steinen's dissertation at Heidelberg University, titled *Das moderne Buch* (Berlin: Gebr. Unger, 1912). On *Kulturverlag* and *Kulturverleger* as concepts, see also Ute Schneider, 'Profilierung auf dem Markt – der Kulturverleger um 1900', in R. Berbig, M. Lauster and R. Parr (eds.), *Zeitdiskurse. Reflexionen zum 19. und 20. Jahrhundert als Festschrift für Wulf Wülfing* (Heidelberg: Synchron, 2004), 349–62.
5. For a complete overview of the German book market in the period, see G. Jäger (ed.), *Geschichte des Deutschen Buchhandels im 19. und 20. Jahrhundert. Das Kaiserreich 1870–1918* (Frankfurt: Buchhändler-Vereinigung/MVB/de Gruyter, 2001–10); and E. Fischer and S. Füssel (eds.), *Geschichte des Deutschen Buchhandels im 19. und 20. Jahrhundert. Weimarer Republik* (K. G. Saur/de Gruyter, 2007–12). The series will also include handbooks on the book market of the Third Reich, exile publishing and postwar publishing, as well as the German Democratic Republic 1949–89 and the Federated Republic of Germany 1949–89 (in preparation).
6. D. Bode (ed.), *125 Jahre Universal-Bibliothek: 1867–1992. Verlags- und kulturgeschichtliche Aufsätze* (Leipzig: Reclam, 1992); and D. Bode: *Reclam, Daten, Bilder und Dokumente zur Verlagsgeschichte, 1828–2003* (Leipzig: Reclam, 2003).
7. See Thompson, *Merchants of Culture*; J. Feather, *A History of British Publishing*, 2nd edn (London: Routledge, 2005); and E. de Bellaigue, *British Book Publishing as a Business since the 1960s* (London: British Library, 2004).
8. M. K. Troy, 'Behind the Scenes at the Albatross Press: A Modern Press for Modern Times', in J. Spiers (ed.), *The Culture of the Publisher's Series, Volume One: Authors, Publishers and the Shaping of Taste* (Houndmills, Basingstoke: Palgrave Macmillan, 2011), 202–18 and 'Books, Swords, and Readers: The Albatross Press and the Third Reich', in *Angles on the English-Speaking World* (2010), 10 (Special issue: 'Moveable Type, Mobile Nations: Interactions in Transnational Book History'), 55–72.
9. A. McCleery, 'The Paperback Evolution: Tauchnitz, Albatross and Penguin,' in N. Matthews and N. Moody (eds.), *Judging a Book by Its Cover: Fans, Publishers, Designers, and the Marketing of Fiction* (Farnham, Surrey: Ashgate, 2007), 3–17.
10. A. McCleery, 'The Paperback Evolution: Tauchnitz, Albatross and Penguin' and 'Tauchnitz and Albatross: A "Community of Interests" in English-Language Paperback Publishing, 1934–51', in *The Library: The Transactions of the Bibliographical Society* Sept 7 (3) (2006), 297–316.

11. See also the meticulously researched encyclopedia of publishers, booksellers and rare book dealers who emigrated from Germany after 1933: E. Fischer, *Verleger, Buchhändler und Antiquare aus Deutschland und Österreich in der Emigration nach 1933. Ein biographisches Handbuch* (Erlbingen: Verband Deutscher Antiquare, 2011).
12. S. Lokatis, 'A Concept Circles the Globe: From the Lesering to the Internationalization of the Club Business', in *175 Years of Bertelsmann – The Legacy for Our Future* (Gütersloh: Bertelsmann, 2010), 130–71.
13. P. Grescoe, *The Merchants of Venus: Inside Harlequin and the Empire of Romance* (Vancouver: Raincoast Books, 1996); C. Gerson and J. Michon (eds.), *History of the Book in Canada. Volume Three 1918–1980* (University of Toronto Press, 2007), 185–8; 405–8.
14. E. Hemmungs Wirtén, *Global Infatuation: Explorations in Transnational Publishing and Texts: the Case of Harlequin Enterprises and Sweden* (Uppsala University, 1998).
15. V. Holman, 'Air-borne Culture: Propaganda Leaflets over Occupied France in the Second World War', in J. Raven (ed.), *Free Print and Non-Commercial Publishing since 1700* (Aldershot: Ashgate Publishing, 2000), 194–221.
16. B. Anderson, *Imagined Communities: Reflections on the Origin and Spread of Nationalism*, rev. edn (London: Verso, 1991).

11

JON BATH AND SCOTT SCHOFIELD

The digital book

In 1995 the entrepreneur Jeff Bezos launched Amazon.com, an online bookstore. By the end of the year it had sold approximately half-a-million dollars' worth of books. That same year Apple Computers was struggling to stay afloat in the wake of the expensive development, and commercial failure, of the Newton, a hand-held computing device. At the time it would have been difficult to see the two events as connected, but from the vantage point of nearly two decades later we can recognize them as pivotal moments in the history of the electronic book. In 2014, Apple and Amazon are two of the key competitors not just in the sale of electronic books, but also in the design and manufacturing of hardware used to read those books, and in the greater network infrastructure that underlies our digital lives. What happened between 1995 and now?

To help understand the rise of the e-book, this chapter will begin by examining the tangled relationships between authors, publishers, electronic content retailers, hardware and software developers, legal systems and others that have all played a part in the development of the digital book. In this regard the study of the history of e-books is no different from other fields of study that fit within the rubric of book history, crossing as it does boundaries between literary, historical, economic and material branches of research. However, to see book historians as mere commentators on electronic textuality would be to miss the many important contributions that scholars are making in the creation and use of new electronic reading technologies. This chapter is devoted primarily to scholarly reactions to the electronic book and the resultant explosion in studies of both the past and future of the book.

In the same year that Bezos was launching Amazon, the literary scholar Jerome McGann published 'The Rationale of Hypertext', a powerful case for the advantages of harnessing computing technologies for the study of paper books and other non-digital media: 'the electronic environment of hyperediting frees one to a considerable extent from these codex-based limits'.[1] McGann, in particular, was excited about the electronic text's capability to contain multimedia objects, and in subsequent work, such as his *Complete Writings and Pictures of Dante Gabriel Rossetti*, he has shown just how useful electronic scholarly resources can be.

Within McGann's statement, however, there are also traces of another discourse that surrounded the electronic text as it emerged in the 1990s, that of liberation and constraint ('frees' and 'limits'). To its proponents, the electronic text was going to usher in a new age of democracy, an age where information would no longer be imprisoned within books and libraries. These proclamations of the 'death of the book' were met from the other side by passionate pleas for the beauty of printed books and the romance of reading as opposed to the cold embrace of the computer.

Balance has been introduced into the argument by book historians and others who, while acknowledging the individual strengths of both the electronic and the paper book, refused to divide them into separate, opposing, objects. The rise of the electronic book must be studied in the light of the emergence of other media types, such as the printed book and the newspaper. These scholars show that the codex does not automatically imprison information in a fixed form, nor is the electronic text by default flexible and open to all. Most importantly, they are demonstrating that the electronic text still has much to 'learn' from the paper book when it comes to organizing information. And, rather than commenting on the electronic book from the margins, many of these scholars are following McGann's model and becoming actively engaged in the creation of new reading environments. Like the scholar-printers of previous generations who studied the history of printing in order to make better books, these scholar-coders are helping to shape the future of the book by looking at its past.[2]

A short history of the e-book

As with most significant inventions, determining 'the' first appearance of the electronic book is difficult and not without controversy. Vannevar Bush's concept of a memex, which he proposed in 'As We May Think' in the July 1945 issue of *Atlantic Monthly*, is generally considered the foundation of the electronic text as we have come to know it: 'A memex is a device in which an individual stores all his books, records, and communications, and which is mechanized so that it may be consulted with exceeding speed and flexibility'.[3] Bush imagined a machine that not only contained books, but that allowed the user to link items into a trail of related content. This idea of linking inspired Ted Nelson and Douglas Englebart, independently, to develop the notion of the computerized hypertext link, which is the basis of internet navigation.[4]

The digital book

While electronic, the memex as Bush imagined it was not digital – it was based on microfilm and other photographic technologies. The first truly digital texts were the result of the collaboration of Father Roberto Busa, a Jesuit priest, and Thomas Watson, the founder of IBM. Busa was interested in linguistically analysing the complete works of Thomas Aquinas, and approached Watson to see if computers could be used for this purpose. Up until this point computers had been strictly designed and used for mathematical calculations. Watson initially balked at the idea, but Busa convinced him to become a partner in the project, and together they made digital text possible.[5]

With text-based computing becoming reality, the next several decades saw the development of numerous systems for the creation and manipulation of electronic texts. At the same time various groups were working towards building communications networks for computer sites (one must remember that at the time computers were both extremely large and expensive, and therefore generally owned and operated by institutions and not individuals). These two strands of development came together in 1971 when Michael Hart, a student at the University of Illinois, used his institutional mainframe, which was part of the ARPANET research network, to create Project Gutenberg, a repository for electronic texts, and to post as its first text an electronic version of the United States Declaration of Independence.

In the mid- to late 1970s affordable personal computers, such as the Commodore PET, Apple II and Radio Shack TRS-80, came on the market, and electronic text became available to the general public. Not only could users of these machines create and save electronic documents using word processing programs, much of the entertainment value of the machines was derived from text-based games, such as *Adventureland* and *Colossal Cave Adventure*, that users could either buy or program for themselves by typing in the source code printed in computer magazines. Despite the extraordinary popularity of these games, which showed that people were willing to spend significant time reading from a screen, and the fact that authors were increasingly using computers to write their manuscripts, the personal computer was not seen by publishers as a viable reading device.[6] There were works of literature released on disc – most notably, Eastgate System's 1987 release of Michael Joyce's *Afternoon*, a work which used hypertext links, and William Gibson's 1992 *Agrippa (a Book of the Dead)*, which was on a disc that erased itself after being read – but outside of these literary experiments no major publisher committed to publishing electronic texts.[7]

As the CD-ROM became established as the replacement for the floppy disc in the early 1990s, publishers began to experiment with it as a means of distributing e-text. In particular electronic reference books, dictionaries and encyclopedias such as Microsoft's *Encarta* achieved a degree of success. This period also saw the release of the first dedicated e-reader, the Sony BookMan in 1992, but few titles for it were ever made available and it was soon discontinued.

This same period saw the emergence of the world wide web, a network of linked documents on the internet, and with it an explosion of readily accessible electronic text. In 1991 Tim Berners-Lee launched the first website, and in 1993 the first graphical browser, Mosaic, made it possible for websites to contain both images and text. Scholars like Jerome McGann seized upon the new technology to start making literary hypertext editions on the web. The web also enabled e-commerce, and with it the means for publishers to sell and distribute electronic texts without requiring customers to purchase discs from bookstores. The Softbook, the Rocket eBook and other e-reading devices came on the market in the late 1990s, and major publishers Barnes and Noble, Time Warner and Random House opened electronic book divisions. In 2000 Stephen King released *Riding the Bullet*, the first mass-market novel published exclusively electronically and, despite the servers crashing because of demand, it sold over 400,000 copies in the first day. The day of the e-book seemed to have arrived.

Not even a year later those same publishers closed their electronic text divisions, citing a lack of sales. When asked to explain the failure of e-publishing, Time Warner's Larry Kirshbaum believed it was because of the inadequacy of reading devices: 'The real problem is a technology issue. No reading device comes close to reproducing the experience of reading a book.'[8] While commercial publishers waited for a solution to their hardware problems, in 2004 Google announced plans to digitize millions of books starting with the collections housed in the Harvard, Stanford, Oxford, University of Michigan and New York Public libraries. Public outcry and lawsuits quickly followed, as claims of copyright infringement were made and concerns over Google building a monopoly on information were raised. Legal settlements have been made and overturned, but Google (and other agencies such as the Internet Archive) continue to digitize books. As of 2013 they had scanned 30 million books.

The major technological hurdles facing the development of a viable e-reader were cleared up by the middle of the 2000s. Electronic paper, sometimes called e-ink, allowed for a screen that closely resembled the printed page and required little energy, thereby extending battery life. Rechargeable batteries were becoming smaller, lighter and more powerful. Solid-state memory eliminated the need for a hard drive or disc. And cellular data networks and wireless internet meant that the device did not need to be connected to a computer for the user to purchase books. In 2007 Amazon launched the

Kindle and it sold out within five hours. By controlling both the hardware and the distribution of content, Amazon was able to avoid the problems that had doomed the previous generation of e-readers, and their model was soon copied by others, such as Barnes and Noble and Apple. Within three years Amazon was selling more e-books than paper books, and the greatest challenge to the e-reader became tablet computers and smart phones, devices that could provide additional functionality. The e-book publishing business is still evolving, as evident in the 2012 United States Department of Justice's accusations that Apple colluded with publishers to fix e-book prices, but it is safe to say that electronic books have become a part of the mainstream reading experience.

The death of the book?

As we have just seen, the development and eventual commercial success of the electronic book can be discussed in terms of technological innovation, publishing economics and legal challenges. But to more fully understand the impact of the digital book on society we must also look at the reactions of readers and writers to this change, for it is they who, in the end, choose to use the screen or the paper page. That they have not been unanimous in welcoming the new technology is evident from E. Annie Proulx's proclamation in the *New York Times* on 26 May 1994 that '[n]obody is going to sit down and read a novel on a twitchy little screen. Ever.'

The rise of the personal computer in the 1980s and the creation of the world wide web in the early 1990s led some to forecast that the 'death of the book' was at hand. This was not the first time that the book's primacy as the carrier for knowledge was seen as under threat – it having previously been threatened by the newspaper, motion picture and television, to name just a few. In *The Gutenberg Galaxy* (1962) and other works, Marshall McLuhan postulated that just as ancient and medieval modes of thinking had been radically altered by the inventions of writing and printing, the effects of new electronic modes of communication such as the creation of a 'global village' needed to be studied in order to avoid their negative consequences: 'Instead of tending towards a vast Alexandrian library the world has become a computer, an electronic brain ... And as our senses have gone outside us, Big Brother goes inside. So, unless aware of this dynamic, we shall at once move into a phase of panic terrors, exactly befitting of a small world of tribal drums, total interdependence, and super-imposed co-existence.'[9] Central to McLuhan's argument was a belief that changes in technology, especially communications technologies, must profoundly alter the way people, and thus societies, think and interact.

This technological determinism was echoed by later critics seeking to explain how the forms of media influence their reception and use. Most notably, in her landmark 1979 study *The Printing Press as an Agent of Change*, Elizabeth Eisenstein argued that the shift from manuscript to print had been fundamental to, among other things, the scientific revolution, the Renaissance and the Protestant Reformation. As will be seen later, Eisenstein's theories are not universally accepted, but they have been tremendously influential; a clear example of this influence was seen at the end of the 1990s when Johannes Gutenberg, the man generally considered the inventor of the printing press, was named by numerous sources including *Time* as the most influential person of the second millennium.

This belief that one communications technology can completely supersede another, and in the process radically change society, is at the heart of all discussions (both for and against) that claim that the computer is a threat to the book. As this discourse emerged in the 1990s, proponents of electronic text cast 'the book' as a restriction on both authors and readers, and proposed that the computer and electronic text would liberate both those who create and use texts and the texts themselves. George Landow, one of the first literary scholars to widely publicize hypertext as a medium for scholarship and education, argued that because hypertext systems allow readers to choose their own path through a text, and to become authors in their own right, they 'intrinsically promote a new kind of academic freedom and empowerment'. Jay David Bolter compared the permanence of the physical book with the seeming ephemerality of the electronic text, which exists only on the screen, and concluded that '[a]ll information, all data, in the computer world is a kind of controlled movement, and so the natural inclination of computer writing is to change'. Similarly, in *The Electronic Word: Democracy, Technology, and the Arts*, Richard Lanham wrote of the transition to electronic text as 'a movement from the fixed and silent signal of the printed book to a richer but more volatile signal, writing + voice + image, of digital display'.[10] For these scholars the fixed nature of the printed book, which Eisenstein credited for enabling so many of the intellectual advances in the centuries following the invention of printing, was now a prison for information. Electronic texts, which exist ephemerally on screens and on networks, promised to free readers, authors and even information from the book's shackles and to create a new era of democratic knowledge creation and sharing.

This techno-utopianism elicited outrage from bibliophiles who worried about the material book, and what it represented to them, disappearing. The best-known of these responses is *The Gutenberg Elegies: The Fate of Reading in an Electronic Age*, by Sven Birkerts. As evident from the title, Birkerts considered the battle lost: 'The stable hierarchies of the printed page – one of the defining norms of the world – are being superseded by the rush of impulses through freshly minted circuits'. For Birkerts, and many others, the printed book is not a prison but a means of escape, and reading is as much about the contemplative act as it is about navigating to the correct snippet of information. Along with the loss of the 'joy' of reading, Birkerts feared that, by exchanging the traditional close reading of specific texts for a broad reading practice based on foraging through a wide swath of networked texts, society is moving from a search for wisdom to just placing 'faith in the web'.[11] Rather than resulting in freedom, the death of the book will result in a loss of individuality.

The attitude of the staunch electronic text supporters to book lovers such as Birkerts was perhaps best summed up by William J. Mitchell's description of them as 'addicted to the look and feel of tree flakes encased in dead cow'.[12] However it is interesting to note that both sides of the argument are based strongly upon the materiality, or supposed lack thereof, of the textual object. To their detractors physical books are seen as limiting because their pages are sequential and their content finite. Electronic books, by comparison, are boundless and multilinear. But for those concerned about the potential death of the book, the physical form of the book acts as a valuable carrier of information and can be tremendously important to the reading experience, while the impermanence of the electronic text lessens its long-term cultural impact and ease of use. E-book detractors like E. Annie Proulx have also been quick to point out that e-texts do have a material form – the hardware used to create and read them – and this hardware is not without its problems.[13] With this emphasis on materiality it is not surprising that bibliographers and book historians, whose core idea according to Leslie Howsam is 'that the material form of a text affects (and to some extent effects) the meaning attached to it by the recipient', began to examine the electronic text and to change the debate from whether the end of the book was at hand to a more nuanced discussion of how various forms of text, including electronic, change over time and influence each other.[14]

Book history and the electronic book

Early in the first of his Panizzi lectures, D. F. McKenzie asserts that 'it would now be more useful to describe bibliography as the study of the sociology of texts'. One paragraph later, he begins to unpack the larger implications of this proposed definition by focusing acutely on what he means by texts: 'I define "texts" to include verbal, visual, oral, and numeric data, in the form of maps, prints, and music, of archives of recorded sound, of films, videos, and any computer-stored information, everything in fact from epigraphy to the latest forms of discography. There is no evading the challenge which those new forms have created.'[15]

That McKenzie included such a diverse range of media under the rubric of text should not come as a surprise, especially given the panoptic nature of his argument, but that he considered computer-stored information and other electronic media as subjects fit for bibliographical analysis seems especially prescient for the time. Nearly twenty-five years later, when Matthew Kirschenbaum explained in the introduction to his *Mechanisms: New Media and the Forensic Imagination*, that 'the methodology for the book draws heavily from bibliography and textual criticism ... scholarly fields dedicated to the study of books as physical objects and the reconstruction and representation of texts from multiple versions and witnesses (sometimes collectively called "textual studies")', he was responding, whether consciously or not, to McKenzie's call from decades earlier.[16] That Kirschenbaum offered a methodological statement for his specialized study of digital media was unremarkable, but that he insisted repeatedly on the centrality of bibliography and textual criticism to his research suggests that, in 2009, such approaches required explanation. In this section, we show that *Mechanisms* represented less of an epiphany and more a fuller realization of what a number of scholars had been suggesting (if not always acting upon) for two decades or more since McKenzie included electronic media under the purview of the sociology of texts.

Disciplinary reconciliation is often less the result of scholars coming together than it is the consequence of scholarly gesturing, and in this case the rethinking of the relationship between the digital and predigital textual forms. In book history, humanities computing and information studies there have been, and still are, voices who argue that new technologies like the e-book need to be seen as an important stage in a long, interconnected continuum of textual forms and that new technologies will likely coexist with, rather than replace, earlier media. Such assessments often derive from an historical analysis of reactions to technological change, particularly how societies have worked with different media during periods of transition and how they responded to these moments. What follows is a sampling of those scholars who insist that we look to the history of the book, or to the methods of bibliography and textual studies, to better understand the structures and processes of digital media. There has been significant work conducted in this field, and that work continues as we write. Therefore, this discussion should be regarded as representative rather than comprehensive.

Paul Duguid's oft-cited essay 'Material Matters: The Past and Futurology of the Book' is a response to the supersessionist arguments of his day.[17] Writing in the mid-nineties, Duguid argued that the then recent predictions signalling the death of the book formed the latest example in a familiar, centuries-old belief in the inevitable obsolescence of older technologies. To illustrate his point, Duguid showed how prognosticators of the early twentieth century believed the typewriter would replace the pencil, and that the sliding door would signal the end of the hinged door. These predictions proved wrong as each of the older technologies continued to function. As for the source of the prediction, Duguid pointed to a series of misconceptions: that older technologies are simpler, and newer ones complex; that new technologies naturally supersede rather than coexist with older ones; and that new technologies offer a form of liberty that the older ones fail to provide. This last point is particularly powerful, for it is tied to a larger binary that sees the new as synonymous with innovation and human progress, and the old with backwardness and stagnation. In place of a rhetoric of alternatives, Duguid suggested that any study of technology should not be treated in isolation, but rather be seen as part of the larger social and historical contexts from which it emerged. Similar gesturing is present in the work of John Lavagnino when he writes: 'Electronic texts aren't the free-for-all that we are often led to imagine: just like printed texts, they are created, read, and transmitted within systems we didn't create, that influence us and that we can fully break out of only through the exertion of extraordinary effort'.[18] The lesson offered by both writers, which was often ignored in the 1990s, was that the new electronic media shared much with earlier textual forms, and that studying the past was thus crucial to understanding the present.

While writers like Duguid and Lavagnino would call for a more contextualized and nuanced understanding of electronic texts, others such as Paul Erickson and Adrian van der Weel would focus specifically on the absence of book history in treatments of electronic media. Writing in 2003, Paul Erickson argued that 'book historians, along with other scholars, had paid virtually no attention to how the physical means of transmitting electronic texts influences their meaning', and that such an analysis was essential since the 'familiar models used for text production, circulation and consumption in both manuscript and print, as the channels of transmission are very different in electronic media'.[19] Two years later, Adrian van der Weel would make a similar case by arguing for a closer study of the book's 'digital transformation' within a book history framework. Unlike Erickson, however, van der Weel's focus was on the continuities existing between predigital and digital forms. He noted, for example, that e-media formed the latest chapter in a continuum of textual transmission dating back to manuscript and other early forms of inscription. He further contended that since bibliography already had an established set of theoretical models and established vocabulary for describing different aspects of textual transmission, it made more sense to borrow from and augment these existing templates than to theorize digital media from scratch.[20] While Duguid,

Lavagnino, Erickson and van der Weel all provided important cases for how the established methodologies of bibliography and book history might be used and adapted to discuss digital media, they also emphasized the larger social contexts in which media change occurs. Significantly, they all cited McKenzie and his theory of the sociology of texts in their works.

For the last decade, some of the most innovative scholarship emerging in the digital humanities community has come from individuals championing the history of the book, seeing this complex interdiscipline not only as a precursor to our current technologies, but as an essential touchstone for understanding how those technologies work. By foregrounding materiality as an essential hermeneutic for thinking about electronic media, Matthew Kirschenbaum, for example, has reminded us of the 'embodied inscriptions' found in 'digital data'. 'Phenomena we call virtual', writes Kirschenbaum, 'are in fact *physical* phenomena lacking the appropriate mediation to supplement wave-length optics; that is, the naked eye'.[21] While the computer and printed codex are very different things, nevertheless they are both physical materials shaped by processes and are thus subject to similar forms of investigation. What makes Kirschenbaum different from the earlier critics discussed above is the way he conceives of materiality. For example, while Lavagnino anticipated Kirschenbaum by noting that 'Electronic texts do preserve significant traces of their transmission, and we can learn to recognize those indications and make deductions from them about the history of texts', his ultimate conclusion was that 'these indications are not "physical"'. Erickson too suggested that, 'if we are to understand anything about how people read electronic media in the future, it is crucial that we try and understand it now, since almost all forms of evidence that historians of the book rely on to learn about reading in the past – marginalia, borrowing records from libraries, diary entries – do not and will not exist for most electronic media'.[22] While Erickson's concerns are valid, they fail to grasp the extent to which electronic storage can capture instantiations of a writer's work, a point Kirschenbaum explores in detail through a central and unavoidable lesson of his book: it is difficult to erase in digital environments.

Delete, trash or burn a file, and still a trace remains. The problem is not so much ensuring that files survive, but rather having the knowledge of where to search for them when they seem to have disappeared. By applying (rather than just gesturing towards) the methodological tools traditionally reserved for the study of books to electronic media, Kirschenbaum draws attention to the continuities and discontinuities between the two forms. In place of the familiar narrative that envisions how new digital forms eclipse old paper ones, Kirschenbaum reminds us how materiality can serve as a common denominator for measuring media of all kinds.

The digital book

The informing principle guiding Kirshenbaum's study is similarly pronounced in the work of Johanna Drucker, as she also looks to the humanities for a theoretical framework while testing, building and prototyping digital tools in a laboratory environment. In her book *Speclab: Digital Aesthetics and Projects in Speculative Computing*, Drucker offers a counterpoint to the objectivity of early humanities computing, arguing for the importance of aesthetics and subjectivity in the digital work that leads to knowledge production. Much of that argument is documented through Drucker's experiences as an established art practitioner and art historian working at the University of Virginia's Speculative Computing Lab in the late 1990s and early 2000s. Virginia's laboratory was essential to the formation of what we now call the digital humanities as figures such as Jerome McGann, Bethany Nowviskie and John Unsworth oversaw and collaborated with others on groundbreaking projects such as the Rossetti and Blake Archives, while supervising the work of second-generation digital humanists. At Virginia, and now at the University of California, Los Angeles, Drucker continues to make practitioners rethink the methods they bring to bear in the digital humanities, while critiquing the design and function of the tools they rely upon. When discussing e-books, for instance, she notes:

> Their limitations have stemmed in part from a flawed understanding of what traditional books are. There has been too much emphasis on formal replication of layout, graphic and physical features and too little analysis of how those features affect the book's function. Rather than thinking about simulating the way a book *looks*, then, designers might do well to consider extending the ways a book *works*.

And one way they might extend such thinking, Drucker continues, is by turning away from iconic metaphors associated with the codex (turning the page etc.) to focus on the functions unique to electronic environments (real-time refresh, live links etc.). In other words, e-books are ideal when they are customized to take advantage of the technological potential of electronic environments and designed to account for the practices and activities of users.[23]

Like Drucker, Katherine N. Hayles has also emphasized the importance of functionality as a signifier in digital reading environments, and like Kirschenbaum, she has noted the importance of materiality in such discussions. In an important article of 2003, Hayles argues adamantly that a remediation from print to digital amounts to a complete translation, one where even the most familiar terms, such as 'text', take on new meaning. Moreover, transferring a literary work from print to digital allows for completely different kinds of navigation; but remediation from print into digital also amounts to the loss of certain physical and sensory features including the texture of paper and smell of binding.[24] The effects of media translation have been a central focus of much of the recent scholarship that bridges the gap between book history and digital humanities.

Many of the studies described above have coincided with more nuanced understandings of traditional media. Indeed, another important influence on the rethinking of digital text comes from studies of the early printed codex, and particularly those that reassess the relationship between manuscript and print in the first centuries of print. In *Print, Manuscript and the Search for Order 1450–1830*, David McKitterick describes the introduction of print as 'a period in which we frequently find less a revolution than an accommodation', one where 'the boundary between manuscript and print is as untidy chronologically, as it is commercially, materially and socially'. This demonstrates that 'in practice, each new technology does not replace the previous one. Rather it augments it and offers alternatives.' Similar to McKitterick, Adrian Johns offered an important reassessment of print culture, one that not only took account of the coexistence of different media, including manuscript, but one that also showed print production as a messier, more unstable and iterative process than earlier studies allowed. Just as later scholars of digital media had reassessed the work of early hypertext theorists, Johns and others offered new readings of earlier seminal studies on print, including most notably the work of Elizabeth Eisenstein.[25] It is no coincidence that the e-book is now conceived as more material, while the print-book is being defined as less stable.

The most recent revolutions in the biblio-materiality of digital books and related media have often involved a kind of balancing act. As some scholars scrutinize the most granular aspects of digital storage, and others focus on the logic and function of the digital page, both sets of scholars are often attuned to the importance of predigital forms in their thinking about digital media. For example, Kirschenbaum puts his training in bibliography and book history to use, while Drucker's expertise in graphic design and artist books informs her thinking of the graphics of digital texts. It is in this context that new digitally informed, team-based book history projects such as Implementing New Knowledge Environments (INKE) have emerged. In a recent article entitled 'Beyond Remediation: The Role of Textual Studies in New Knowledge Environments', members of INKE look at predigital forms as templates for the modelling of future reading environments, while also insisting that scholars make the most of digital innovations instead of simply creating electronic simulacra of the codex. For example, there are numerous instances in the early-modern period, such as the printing of George Herbert's 'Easter Wings', where books were either printed in landscape orientation or designed to be rotated in the hand in order to better meet the needs of their content and its readers. However, computer screens have, until very recently, been designed to be used in only the landscape orientation, and even tablet devices, with their ability to be rotated from horizontal to vertical orientations, have thus far had few applications that take advantage of this feature in any meaningful way.[26]

The open-access, peer-reviewed resource, *Architectures of the Book*, or *ArchBook* (www.archbook.ca), one of INKE's original initiatives, similarly argues for the importance of the past as a vital resource for current digital thinking. In a typical *ArchBook* essay, an author will survey the history of a specific textual feature (e.g. manicules, table of contents, variorum commentaries) 'but with an eye to the continuities and discontinuities that feature might have with current digital environments'. Part journal, part blog, part repository, *ArchBook* is itself a composite of traditional and emerging approaches to scholarly publication. Evidence of the influence of textual studies on the creation of digital interfaces is INKE's work towards creating the 'Social Edition', an editing platform that encourages collaboration and community engagement in the scholarly edition.[27] Members of the group working towards this new interface have also spent several years studying the Devonshire Manuscript, a collection of verse written and compiled by a community of women and men living in sixteenth-century England, and have published a collaborative scholarly edition of the manuscript.[28] As a community of textual editors working on a text created by a literary community, they are in a good position to begin to model future editing environments that will both enable historical modes of collaboration and create new means for scholarly engagement.

INKE is not the only group working in this area; the Open Annotation Collaboration and the Institute for the Future of the Book, to mention two currently active groups, also bring book history into their work to varying degrees, and a quick perusal of the programme for any recent textual studies conference will reveal numerous individuals similarly engaged. With one foot in the past and one in the future, one eye on new media and one on older forms, these scholars gesture towards a future where digital humanists and historians of the book combine forces to study and build new reading environments. Such cooperation is not only healthy: it is necessary.

NOTES

1. J. J. McGann, 'The Rationale of Hypertext', *Text* 9 (1996), 15.
2. Aldus Manutius and D. F. McKenzie are just two of the most famous of such scholar-printers.
3. V. Bush, 'As We May Think', *Atlantic Monthly* 176:1 (July 1945), 106.
4. See T. Nelson, *Literary Machines* (Sausalito, CA: Mindful Press, 1981).

5. S. Hockey, 'The History of Humanities Computing', in S. Schreibman, R. Siemens and J. Unsworth (eds.), *A Companion to the Digital Humanities* (Malden: Blackwell Publishing, 2004), 4.
6. For authors' use of the word processor, see M. Kirschenbaum's *Track Changes: A Literary History of Word Processing*, (Harvard University Press, forthcoming 2015).
7. For discussion of *Agrippa* and *Afternoon* see M. Kirschenbaum, *Mechanisms: New Media and the Forensic Imagination* (Cambridge, MA and London: MIT Press, 2009), ix–xiv.
8. Quoted in Paul D. Colford, 'Time Warner Closing Book on E-publishing', *New York Daily News* (5 December 2001).
9. M. McLuhan, *The Gutenberg Galaxy* (University of Toronto Press, 2011), 32.
10. G. P. Landow, *Hypertext, The Convergence of Contemporary Critical Theory and Technology* (Baltimore: Johns Hopkins University Press, 1992), 177; J. D. Bolter, *Writing Space: The Computer in the History of Literacy* (Hillsdale, NJ: Lawrence Erlbaum, 1990), 31; R. A. Lanham, *The Electronic Word: Democracy, Technology, and the Arts* (University of Chicago Press, 1993), 227.
11. S. Birkerts, *The Gutenberg Elegies: The Fate of Reading in an Electronic Age* (New York: Fawcett Columbine, 1994), 3, 228.
12. W. J. Mitchell, *City of Bits: Space, Place, and the Infobahn* (Cambridge, MA: MIT Press, 1995), 56.
13. E. A. Proulx, 'Books on Top', *New York Times* (26 May 1994), A13.
14. L. Howsam, *Old Books and New Histories* (University of Toronto Press, 2006), 56.
15. D. F. McKenzie, *Bibliography and the Sociology of Texts* (Cambridge University Press, 1985; 1999), 13. For a similar, later gesture on the importance of a bibliographical approach to electronic documents, see McKenzie's '"What's Past Is Prologue": The Bibliographical Society and the History of the Book', in P. D. McDonald and M. F. Suarez (eds.), *Making Meaning: 'Printers of the Mind' and Other Essays* (Amherst: University of Massachusetts Press, 2002), 259–75.
16. Kirschenbaum, *Mechanisms*, 15.
17. P. Duguid, 'Material Matters: The Past and Futurology of the Book', in G. Nunberg (ed.), *The Future of the Book* (Berkeley: University of California Press, 1996), 64–6, 78, 89. For more on the above themes, see also J. S. Brown and P. Duguid, *The Social Life of Information* (Boston: Harvard Business School Press, 2000).
18. J. Lavagnino, 'The Analytical Bibliography of Electronic Texts', paper presented at the conference of the Association for Literary and Linguistic Computing and the Association for Computing in the Humanities, University of Bergen, 1996 (www.hit.uib.no/allc/lavagnin.pdf, 182).
19. P. Erickson, 'Help or Hindrance? The History of the Book and Electronic Media', in D. Thorburn and H. Jenkins (eds.), *Rethinking Media Change: The Aesthetics of Transition* (Cambridge, MA: MIT Press, 2003), 95–116.
20. A. van der Weel, 'Bibliography for the New Media', *Quarendo* 3: 1–2 (2005), 97, 101–5.
21. Kirschenbaum, *Mechanisms*, 6, 19.
22. Lavagnino, 'The Analytical Bibliography', 180. Erickson, 'Help or Hindrance?', 110.

23. J. Drucker, *Speclab: Digital Aesthetics and Projects in Speculative Computing* (University of Chicago Press, 2009), 1–10, 166, 165–74.
24. N. K. Hayles, 'Translating Media: Why We Should Rethink Textuality', *Yale Journal of Criticism* 16:2 (2003), 270.
25. D. McKitterick, *Print, Manuscript and the Search for Order 1450–1830* (Cambridge University Press, 2003), 3, 12, 20. A. Johns, *The Nature of the Book: Print and Knowledge in the Making* (University of Chicago Press, 1998).
26. A. Galey et al., 'Beyond Remediation: The Role of Textual Studies in New Knowledge Environments', in Brent Nelson and Melissa Terras (eds.), *Digitising Medieval and Early Modern Material Culture* (Toronto/Tempe: ITER and the Arizona Center for Medieval and Renaissance Studies, 2012) 21–48, 38.
27. R. Siemens et al., 'Toward modeling the social edition: An approach to understanding the electronic scholarly edition in the context of new and emerging social media', *Literary and Linguistic Computing* 27(4) (2012), 445–61.
28. R. Siemens et al., *A Social Edition of the Devonshire MS (BL Add 17,492)* (Toronto and Tempe: Iter and Medieval and Renaissance Texts and Studies, forthcoming). Current social texts at http://en.wikibooks.org/wiki/The_Devonshire_Manuscript.

PART III
Methods, sources and approaches to the history of the book

12

MICHAEL F. SUAREZ, S.J.

Book history from descriptive bibliographies

Every bibliography tells a book-historical story. The trick is learning how to *read* a volume that at first glance appears to belong among the most off-putting of genres, the most boring material in the library. For a start, bibliographies seem to be little more than lists – and repetitious lists at that. To make matters worse, here in the pages of a humanities book, a learned tome shelved in familiar precincts of the library, is print that definitely looks as if it belongs in the mathematics or engineering section: 4°: π^2 A–3C^4 3D^2; [\$2 (+P3) signed]; 200 leaves, pp. [4] 1–395 [1]. This may seem distinctly unfair, because many of us book historians went into the humanities in part because we found algebra uncongenial and calculus unkind. A collation formula (which is what that string of signs is) is a slightly weird, short-hand way of describing the structure and completeness of a book. We won't discuss collation formulas in this chapter, however.

My aim in these pages is to alert the reader to the usefulness, even indispensability at times, of reading – not just dipping into – descriptive bibliographies. My purpose is to show how such reading will quicken book-historical understandings. By discussing a few examples, I aim to rouse in the reader a sense of the genuine pleasures of poring over descriptive bibliographies to recognize and identify the latent book-historical narratives waiting to be discovered in their pages. I also want to explain in the clearest possible terms a few essential concepts that will go a long way toward helping book historians get the most out of descriptive bibliographies.

More than the sum of its parts: what a good bibliography can do for you

'I have no biography. I have only a bibliography', observed Milorad Pavić, author of the international bestseller *Dictionary of the Khazars*.[1] A well-executed author bibliography is far more than a mere enumeration of titles with accompanying descriptions of first editions; rather, author bibliographies are no-nonsense writerly biographies revealing the shape and lineaments of a literary career. Dan H. Laurence, the bibliographer of Bernard Shaw, professed his conviction that the most significant contribution made by those who created modern author bibliographies is 'the graphic recreation of the subjects' lives in the context of their professional business involvement and experience; of their struggles and frustrations and yearnings reflected through commercial intercourse'.[2]

The astute student of book history who dares to read them will readily discern in the bibliographies of Samuel Johnson, Marianne Moore, Tom Stoppard or Virginia Woolf the business relationships and publishing choices that chiefly defined the author's employment over a lifetime of writing.[3] In such pages may be found not only a tally of the number and variety of books produced, but also information about the sale and ongoing reception of those works as they are reprinted over time. We may learn, for example, from Edwin T. Bowden's excellent *Washington Irving Bibliography* that Irving's *The Sketch Book* was published in at least seventy-six editions and subsequent impressions – not including the publication of excerpts or translations – beginning with the appearance of the first edition in 1819 until Irving's death in 1859, a remarkable indication of the author's popular reception.[4] Reading through the many entries for translations of Irving's writings, one can begin to garner valuable particulars about early markets and readerships for US authors in Europe and Latin America.

Well-prepared descriptive bibliographies may provide the book historian with essential details about what the author was originally paid, or how much income he or she made from sales, and even financial data about the publishing house's costs and profits (or losses) for particular works. Bibliographies commonly furnish information about original-language editions, authorial emendations, reviews, censorship history, serializations, abridgements, translations for foreign markets, appearances in anthologies, prizes and awards and the like. Not infrequently, matters of intellectual property come into play. When available, descriptive bibliographies can supply otherwise difficult-to-find information on matters such as print runs, wholesale and retail prices, marketing plans or advertising patterns and other useful data from publisher's archives, printer's ledgers, contracts, correspondence and related documents. There is no substitute for having the facts. Because the bibliographer spends years travelling to libraries and archives, combing through such records and painstakingly examining multiple copies of books with an analytic eye, the data that he or she marshals can save the book historian a tremendous amount of time and trouble.

Bibliography thus becomes the foundation of publishing history. As practised by such skilful scholars, bibliography proves itself immensely fruitful for the history of reading and reception. Because book forms both effect and affect meanings, information about format, paper, type, edition bindings, dust jackets and the like can valuably lead book-historical researchers to form significant historical inferences from painstakingly gathered and systematically arrayed bibliographical evidence. Such particulars can also help when historians of book production, distribution and/or reading and reception need to examine an individual copy and identify it as belonging to a particular edition, impression or issue (see below). Recognizing the importance of bibliographical inquiry for textual criticism and scholarly editing, some bibliographies helpfully record any significant textual alterations. Alan Tyson's *Bibliography of Beethoven* (1963), for example, pays scrupulous attention to recording textual variants, while Edwin Bowden has taken great care in his Washington Irving bibliography to highlight 'textual variants in superficially similar states of impressions, and revisions – particularly revisions by the author – in new editions'.[5]

In the early days of serious Anglo-American bibliographical scholarship, Anthony Trollope's bibliographer, Michael Sadleir, rightly maintained that descriptive '[b]ibliography can be extended beyond a mere descriptive analysis of any one writer or period; it can be made to illustrate, not only the evolution of book-building [i.e. production], but also the history of book-handling [i.e. the book trade] and the effect [of the publishing industry] on the aims and achievements of authorship'. Hence, Sadleir's bibliography is best employed not only as 'a reference work for collectors', but also as 'a commentary on the book and publishing crafts of mid-Victorian England'.[6] Sadleir was himself in the business of making and selling books; as the director of the publishing firm Constable and Robinson, he well knew that studying the history of a writer's publications in detail over time could shed considerable light on the conditions of authorship and on the publishing practices of the age.

'The annals of a literary career'

An excellent example of what descriptive bibliography can do for book historians is David Fleeman's *Bibliography of the Works of Samuel Johnson*, a massive work that traces the publication histories of Johnson's writings, not only throughout the course of the author's life, but for 200 years following his death as well. Fleeman's achievement led David Vander Meulen to suggest that the *Bibliography* 'may be the most important work of Johnsonian scholarship ever written'. Robert DeMaria was no less fulsome in his praise when taking the measure of what the *Bibliography* had accomplished, 'Fleeman has made Johnson more intelligible than he was before, and he has delineated in remarkable fashion his material imprint on the world.... It is unlikely that any work on Johnson will ever achieve more'.[7]

For Fleeman, the narratives that come to light through the practice of descriptive bibliography are part and parcel of the author's biography. As he explains, his bibliography is not merely a piling up of bibliographical and book-historical details: 'I have not arranged this compilation as if it were itself an enormous index, but rather as the annals of a literary career.' Accordingly, Fleeman painstakingly delineates every instantiation of Johnson's known writings over the course of more than 200 years. The entry for *Rasselas*, for example, provides the reader with a chronicle of nearly 530 significant appearances of this novella. Among the highlights in its production history are publications in eighteen foreign languages across the nineteenth and twentieth centuries. In this instance, as in many others, Fleeman's remarkable bibliography provides the foundation for constructing a detailed reception history of each of Johnson's principal works. Because '[t]he popularity of *Rasselas* can be measured only when we have reliable information about the number of editions published, the kinds of markets they were aimed at, the adventitious inducements they offered to readers in the form of illustrations, the places they were published, and the languages into which they were translated', what Fleeman calls 'the business of this bibliography' is absolutely indispensable for book-historical scholarship. Fleeman's close attention to physical books themselves helps us to understand 'not merely the mind of the author of the text, but also the activities of the producers of its materials, the aims of its manufacturers, and the commercial estimates of the requirements of its readers'. As Vander Meulen insightfully reminds us, it is 'the human context that ultimately is the object of this historical delving'.[8]

It is of cardinal importance for book historians and bibliographers alike to understand that transmission history is an essential aspect of reception history. The most reliable and tractable means for scholars to comprehend the publication histories that embody the public presences of an author (or, indeed, of a publishing house) is to read and carefully analyse a well-wrought descriptive bibliography. The author of a bibliography, then, by focusing on the history of material production through the close examination of physical objects that constitute the surviving historical record, provides the reader not merely with a history of the career and reputation of his or her chosen subject, but also with detailed understandings both of the intended reading audiences for particular works and of the critical fortunes of those works.

Thus, in a remarkable way for the book historian who pays careful attention, we are able to discern not only Johnson's works in history, but also the long lives of their literary and cultural agency over two centuries. Fleeman's desire to put on display the history of Johnson's popular reception is perhaps most evident in his decision to include more than 300 miniature dictionaries that quite dubiously claim some connection with Johnson's great folios. 'These dictionaries find their place here as illustrating Johnson's popular reputation as a lexicographer', Fleeman explains, 'rather than for their uncertain debts to his work'.[9] Because of the bibliographical and book-historical industriousness of Fleeman and others who are intellectually courageous enough to dedicate their mental energies to the unglamorous but foundational labour of producing descriptive bibliographies, book historians are thus enabled to undertake the systematic study of their chosen subjects with a comprehensiveness and attention to revealing historical detail that was simply not possible before such works became part of the scholarly record.

Fleeman's 'map of Johnson's career' also contains a wealth of information on paper, watermarks, composition, typography, presswork, production costs, retail prices (and, sometimes, trade discounts) and the operations of the book trade itself.[10] Johnson's *Dictionary* is exhaustively treated over the course of some 250 pages; entries for the principal lifetime editions include a catalogue of hundreds of press figures and of catchwords, both of which are especially useful for understanding the progress of the sheets through the press. (An adept bibliographer may also employ such information to discover last-minute textual revisions.) Throughout Fleeman's work, we encounter evidence of a remarkable bibliographical intelligence shining light upon examples of shared printing, books in parts, unusual formats, duplicate setting and a variety of similar issues treated in concrete terms. In addition, there is frequently information about the bindings and provenances of the copies he has consulted. In many ways, then, Fleeman's bibliography is not only enormously valuable in itself, constituting a kind of master-class in bibliography and book-trade history during the hand-press period, but also is sure to serve as the basis for subsequent bibliographical and book-historical research for many years to come.

Bibliography becomes the foundation of publishing history

Descriptive bibliographies are by no means limited to chronicling an individual author's career; other, typical subjects include the productions of an individual printing firm or publishing house, a specific genre within a given time period (e.g. separately published English poems from the first half of the eighteenth century), or a collection of books having a particular provenance.[11] A surprisingly compelling example of a genre bibliography is Carol Fitzgerald's *The Rivers of America: A Descriptive Bibliography* (2 vols., 2001), which chronicles the sixty-five titles published in The Rivers of America series between 1937 and 1974. Tracing some 350 different printings of these books on the major rivers (and river systems) of the US, Fitzgerald's bibliography offers an absorbing prospect of the publishing business in the US over the course of some forty years.

Perhaps remembering D. F. McKenzie's declaration that the task of bibliography is to reveal the human presences in recorded texts, Fitzgerald provides more than 120 brief biographies of individuals who contributed to the series as illustrators, authors or editors. For each title (e.g. *The Brandywine*, *The Charles*, *The Hudson*), there immediately follows a section providing information – judiciously harvested from interviews, correspondence and publishers' archives – about such matters as: how the author and illustrator were chosen, the details of contracts, missed delivery deadlines, notable moments in the editorial process and how the book was received. Fitzgerald's bibliography then provides a list of reviews, a catalogue of other works by the same author and a bibliography of the sources used to produce the entry. I cannot profess any particular interest in American geography, nor had I ever read any of the books in the series Fitzgerald describes, but her treatment of the subject, both thoroughgoing and humane, made it engrossing for this student of publishing history.

'What was a novel in the late 18th and early 19th centuries? ... Who wrote them? Who published and sold them? How expensive were they? What was their appeal and popularity? How were they reviewed?'[12] *The English Novel 1770–1829: A Bibliographical Survey* begins with this series of questions; all the answers are found in the bibliography. This remarkable work of scholarship convincingly demonstrates just how productive bibliographical inquiry can be for literary and book history. The introductory essays for each volume, by James Raven and Peter Garside respectively, together comprise some 200 pages of analysis concerning such matters as the publication of Gothic novels, the most productive authors of novels, the authorship of new novels by gender, the place of publication of new novels, Dublin reprints, the principal publishers of novels by decade, the volume structure of novels, the publication of epistolary fiction, the place and frequency of publication of further editions of novels and so on. In these pages, then, we find bibliographical information turned into book-historical knowledge.

The 'bibliographical survey' of Garside, Raven and Schöwerling, when subjected to rigorous analysis, yields insights into the history of authorship, publishing and reading that would be otherwise unobtainable. Although these volumes do not claim to belong to the category of descriptive bibliography, as they neither provide collation formulas nor attempt to describe ideal copies of particular editions and distinguish them from various issues and impressions, they do nonetheless constitute a groundbreaking work of bibliographical scholarship. Without the meticulous labour of gathering bibliographical facts about the publication of 3,677 works of fiction produced over the course of sixty years, we would simply have no basis for the many important book-historical understandings that we find in the editors' introductions. No wonder, then, that these volumes provide a more comprehensive and accurate description and analysis of fiction publishing in England in the late eighteenth and early nineteenth centuries than any other study.

Four bibliographical concepts every book historian will profit from knowing

Just as physicians need to know anatomy and chemistry in order to practise their craft, so too do book historians benefit from understanding bibliography, even when their work is not strictly bibliographical. Four key concepts will help such historians get the most out of the descriptive bibliographies they consult. First, the term 'edition' denotes all the printings made at any time from a single setting of type, whether from standing type or from plates (stereotype, electrotype, etc.) made from that type. Thus, the key to understanding the concept of edition is *type*; no matter how far separated in the time of their production, two books printed from substantially the same type belong to the same edition.

How then to distinguish books printed at different times from the same type? 'Impression' denotes all the copies of a book (or other printed artefact, such as a broadside) printed from the same setting of type (that is, the same edition) at a given time. Thus, an impression is a subset of an edition. A later printing from the same type is not a new edition, but is a new impression. Thus, the key to understanding the concept of impression is *time*. When printing is done from stereotype plates, what are often casually called new editions are, bibliographically speaking, new impressions of the same edition, because the type is substantially the same. Because one setting of type (i.e. one edition) can be the parent of multiple impressions, it is sometimes difficult to distinguish one impression from another, especially for books printed from plates. Nonetheless, the identification of different impressions is often highly useful in understanding the production history of a work.

How ought we to classify the books produced when the printer uses the same setting of type, producing a number of copies on ordinary paper and a smaller number on large paper to sell at a higher price? These books all belong to the same edition and the same impression, but they are not the same. Similarly, how are we to deal with the case of a printer producing a very large press run from plates and then over time selling them with title pages distinguishing some as 'The Seventh Edition', others as 'The Eighth Edition', and still others as the 'Colonial Edition'? Clearly, these books too all belong to the same edition and constitute a single impression, but they also differ in ways that it would be useful for the book historian to recognize and document. When a work printed at one time from the same setting of type (that is, the same impression) appears for sale in two or more forms intended to distinguish them as units of sale, we classify those varying forms as different issues. In the case of the 'Colonial Edition', for example, we might say that a number of sheets from the impression were 'separately issued' for sale in India. The key to understanding the concept of 'issue', then, is *unit of sale*. In much the same vein, imagine a bookseller who publishes a novel, but after some years has only sold half of his print run. He tries to reinvigorate sales by tearing off the old title pages and substituting instead a new title leaf, perhaps with a more sensational title, certainly with a new publication date, and with the false claim that this book is the 'Second Edition, enlarged'. The book is now properly described as a 're-issue'.

Finally, there is a fourth category, 'state', used to describe variants within an edition not intended to create a distinctive unit of sale. Such changes typically include corrections or alterations made during printing (e.g. stop-press correction; resetting a forme, wholly or partially because of an accident during printing), or after the first copies have been sold (e.g. the insertion of an errata slip or of advertisements; the addition or deletion of matter from the preliminaries, such as a dedication). The key to understanding the concept of 'state', then, is *variation*, which the publisher does not intend to call to the attention of the consumer. More generally, 'state' is typically used to recognize differences between or among copies when those differences are insufficiently consequential to suggest that the copies belong to different editions or issues.[13]

James Bond, Tom Stoppard and Raymond Chandler

Jon Gilbert's *Ian Fleming. The Bibliography* (2012) provides a good example of how bibliography can inform and enliven the scholarship of the book historian, and the cultural historian as well. Gilbert's book is packed with information and insights about the history of the James Bond novels throughout the process of their production: typescripts, uncorrected and corrected proofs, publication in hard covers (often in multiple impressions), paperback editions and later editions and impressions as well. Fleming, an accomplished book collector, publisher and noteworthy patron of book-historical scholarship, well understood the historical value of such materials, and he seems to have saved them whenever possible. As thoroughly as the ample surviving documentation will allow, then, Gilbert sheds light on the life histories of these popular works of fiction from the author's early notes through the publisher's editorial process and subsequent book production. Here too is a careful chronicle of Fleming's non-fiction writings, his short stories and his well-known children's novel, the posthumously published *Chitty Chitty Bang Bang* (3 vols., 1964, 1965).

Gilbert's bibliography reproduces all the principal book jackets, with illuminating discussions about Fleming's close engagement with their production. This study also sheds light on the reception history of the Bond novels, supplying information about print runs in Britain and the US. (Sadly, Gilbert's bibliography does not include translations.) We learn, for example, that Fleming's inaugural volume, *Casino Royale* (1953), had an initial production of fewer than 4,750 copies, whereas *You Only Live Twice* (1964) was first produced in more than 80,000. Book historians poring over Gilbert's bibliographical account will readily recognize the central importance of book club editions in the mass consumption of Fleming's fiction. There is still a great deal of work to be done by some enterprising book historian, however, on the relationships among the appearances of Bond films and the distribution and sales of the novels, as these are essential connections for understanding the Bond phenomenon. Similarly, the failure of Gilbert's bibliography to document the Bond novels as a global brand cries out for redress. Though neither as ambitious nor as demanding a work of scholarship as, say, Fleeman's *Samuel Johnson* or David Supino's *Henry James* (see below), *Ian Fleming. The Bibliography* is well worth studying for what it can teach us about the Anglo-American publishing of popular fiction in the 1950s and 1960s.

One of the most creative and engaging bibliographies I have had the pleasure of reading is *Tom Stoppard: A Bibliographical History*, which chronicles the multifaceted career of a truly great contemporary dramatist, perhaps best known to popular audiences as the coauthor (with Marc Norman) of the screenplay for *Shakespeare in Love*. This fascinating scholarly work is the product of close collaboration between William Baker, a professor recognized for his bibliography of Harold Pinter (2005), and Gerald Wachs, who is almost certainly the world's foremost private collector of Stoppard materials. Their study is by no means a mere catalogue of an individual's collection, however; the British National Sound Archive and the Harry Ransom Center at the University of Texas at Austin are among the other principal repositories of the Stoppard materials delineated in this remarkable bibliography.

Seeking to document Stoppard's entire creative output as it survives, not only in print, but also on stage and screen, Baker and Wachs's 'bibliographical history' is organized neither by individual works, nor chronologically by phases of Stoppard's career, but rather according to the various genres of Stoppard's productions. There are fourteen in all, including: Plays and Sketches for the Stage, Radio and Television; Screenplays; Adaptations and Translations for the Stage; Fiction; Published Letters to Newspapers, Magazines, etc.; Editions of Collected or Selected Works; Articles; Radio and Television Interviews and Broadcasts; and so on. The most revealing aspects of this bibliography are found in the sensitive ways that the 'formatting and description conventions employed differ for each section as appropriate to the generic areas and modes of publication'.[14] It is in this respect above all others that the authors of *Tom Stoppard* prove themselves most bibliographically adroit.

Baker and Wachs stretch the limits of conventional bibliography to excellent effect, very appropriately expanding its mission to include multiple kinds of recorded texts, just as D. F. McKenzie envisioned in his Panizzi lectures, *Bibliography and the Sociology of Texts* (1986). We should remark, however, that the system of generic organization employed by Baker and Wachs frequently requires that the reader seeking all the citations for a given work will have to search across more than one genre. Stoppard's early stage play *Jumpers* (1972) is thus found not only under Plays and Sketches, but also under Editions of Collected Works, and is further referenced in multiple categories such as Published Letters to Newspapers, Magazines, etc.; Interviews Collected in Books; and Radio and Television Interviews and Broadcasts.

The entries in this descriptive bibliography are extraordinarily extensive and as highly detailed as any book historian might wish, including, for example, information about a particular edition's (or impression's, or issue's) binding, retail price, press run and how much the author made from its publication. Copy-specific annotations are also given for books consulted. Where relevant, we learn about the locations of any related documents, such as drafts and typescripts, as well as about the first dramatic production of any given work. Also helpful in this regard is the accompanying CD-ROM, containing eighty-nine images chiefly of book covers and dust jackets. This book, a comprehensive bibliographical catalogue of the creative output of a living person, successfully traces the cultural imprint of one of the most important dramatists in the English-speaking world. Yet, the significance of this 'bibliographical history' goes far beyond documenting Stoppard's cultural impact, because it pushes the bounds of descriptive bibliography into sound recordings, videos and other electronic media. By powerful example, Baker and Wachs teach their readers how the institutional stewardship of contemporary culture, private collections and the rigor of bibliographical description may productively coalesce to produce new kinds of studies that are especially appropriate for students of cultural production, transmission and reception in the twenty-first century. Bibliographers, book historians, and students of communication and media studies will all be better at what they do for having encountered this volume.

Raymond Chandler: A Descriptive Bibliography (1979) by Matthew Bruccoli, one of the finest textual and literary scholars of American modernism, highlights the impact that such scholarly works can have on the world of books. Bruccoli's bibliography both reflected and contributed to an important book-historical phenomenon: the growing marketplace in the late 1960s and 1970s for collecting popular American literature and culture. Bruccoli's volume was not only a response to this burgeoning interest; it also promoted a growing vogue for editions of Chandler, Dashiel Hammett and other authors of detective fiction. As almost any book dealer will attest: the existence of a descriptive bibliography fosters collecting by institutions and, especially, individuals.

This bibliography by a scholar of Bruccoli's great reputation also had a pronounced legitimating effect on the writings of Chandler, a mass-market author who was until then little regarded by the academy, and on the work of his close colleagues as well. Bruccoli's book makes extensive use of photographs to document his bibliographical descriptions and analytic insights. (Dust jackets are reproduced, as are both rectos and versos of title pages for the first American and English editions of each of Chandler's works.) Accordingly, Bruccoli's volume might usefully serve as an instruction manual to help the historian of twentieth-century publishing understand descriptive bibliography as an investigative practice that can yield historical insights unobtainable by other forms of scholarly research.

What about illustrations?

There is still much work to be done on the bibliography of illustrated books, a highly promising area for scholars wishing to undertake genuinely exciting new research that could have a great impact on our understanding of artists and author-artist collaborations, of publishing and marketing and of reading and reception. Ruth Mortimer's bibliographies of sixteenth-century French and Italian illustrated books do much to point the way forward. The aim of these volumes is neither to enumerate and characterize all the surviving works by a single author, nor to establish the known output of any given press, artist or publishing house. Rather, Mortimer's catalogues describe two particular collections of books in a single department of the Harvard College Library.[15] Her seemingly unremarkable remit notwithstanding, these bibliographies constitute a noteworthy achievement in the history of descriptive bibliography.

Because bibliographical scholarship has been primarily concerned with the uses of bibliographical analysis in service of scholarly editing – and because intaglio illustrations (*viz.*, engravings and etchings) are not produced alongside letterpress text on a common press (as are the relief illustrations made by woodcuts and wood engravings), but instead are made separately on a rolling press and subsequently added to the letterpress sheets – descriptive bibliographies have been consistently poor in describing illustrations with sufficient care. Reading Mortimer's bibliographies, however, one comes away with a compelling history of sixteenth-century book illustration and of visual culture more generally. Although the reader wishing to construct a coherent narrative must do so from the alphabetically presented, individual entries, the chronological listing at the end of each catalogue makes such a task surprisingly tractable. All book historians will readily perceive that illustration is an index of reception and that it can have a marked effect on book production, price (both wholesale and retail), reputation and reader response. The entries in Mortimer's descriptive bibliographies are marvellous opportunities for immersing oneself in the particularities of such matters.

The one predecessor of Mortimer who must be mentioned is Allan Stevenson, who produced the second volume of the catalogue of the Hunt Botanical Collection in Pittsburgh. Stevenson's groundbreaking essay in that volume, 'A Bibliographical Method for the Description of Botanical Books', as well as his actual practice, set a standard for bibliographical description of illustrations with a scholarly thoroughness and accessibility that, to my knowledge, had never been achieved before – and perhaps has never been equalled since.[16] Every book historian interested in the history of illustration could learn a great deal from reading Stevenson's scholarship, which deserves to be far better known outside the world of botanical bibliography and collecting.

A digression on degression, or what's the matter?

Most descriptive bibliographies make use of 'the degressive principle', a common system for succinctly deploying bibliographical information based on a hierarchy of entries. At its best, degressive bibliography works like this: once the earliest books appropriately classed under a particular heading (e.g. those belonging to the same edition, whether subsequent impressions, varying issues or textually significant states) have been fully described, later entries categorized under the same 'family' do not repeat information that has already been given, but explain only how subsequent works differ from the parent work that has earlier been described in full. Degressive bibliographies are most often characterized by a numbering system that enables the reader easily to understand the publication history of a text and to locate individual instances of that text. In the Baker and Wachs bibliography of Tom Stoppard, for example, 'A' signifies the general category 'plays, and sketches for the stage, radio and television'. A23 is the heading for Stoppard's play *Arcadia*, so A23a is the first edition (Faber and Faber 1993); A23b the 'revised edition with corrections'; A23c the 'Fireside edition'; A23d the first American edition, and so on.

Such a system is bibliographically trustworthy, however, if and only if all 'descendant works' are examined with the same degree of thoroughness as the parent work. Otherwise, potentially significant differences will be overlooked, thus compromising the intellectual value of the bibliographical project and its book-historical reliability and use. Responsibly practised, the degressive display of bibliographical information saves space and, hence, makes printed bibliographies more affordable. Ideally, delineating how a given volume is dissimilar from earlier publications brings new, identifying features into sharp relief and helps the reader more readily understand what changes have occurred that make a given printing distinctive and distinguishable.[17]

When later editions are comprehensively included and fully described, then the practical exigencies that conduce toward characterizing variant issues and states – and subsequent impressions too – in lesser detail for the sake of economy are understandable, even if they perhaps inevitably have some regrettable consequences. (Sometimes, for example, it becomes difficult to piece together the full complement of bibliographical information the reader requires.)[18] When, however, later editions are given short shrift – through more cursory description, or, as is too commonly the case, omission – then the degressive principle in practice becomes the enemy of the comprehensiveness that is of central value to bibliographical scholarship.

For all its practical viability – particularly when enumerating multiple iterations of works produced in the machine-press period – the principle of degression all too frequently results in a practice that is at odds with the central tenets of many leading book historians. Roger Chartier, Jerome McGann and D. F. McKenzie all emphasize that every iteration of a work in its published texts is important because it instantiates an historically valuable theory of that work, its author and its most likely market (or reading public). Yet, as a central organizing principle of most bibliographies published since the second half of the twentieth century, degression typically (but not inevitably) means that, although the bibliographical details provided for the early printings of a work are as complete as possible, less bibliographical information is included for subsequent printings. The result, whether intended or not, is that later iterations of a work seem to be less important. The Oxford scholar Falconer Madan, who first adumbrated the degressive principle in 1903 and committed it to print in 1906, certainly believed that the oldest printings were far and away of greatest interest, and that the bibliographical and historical significance of texts declined in proportion to their distance in time from the first edition. The American textual editor Fredson Bowers also shared this belief.[19]

The idea that earlier instances of publication are more bibliographically valuable and more culturally revelatory than later publications may be generally attributable to the esteem we accord to what is old, but it is also a consequence of two particular cultural practices that may be of limited usefulness for understanding the life of a work as it circulates over time. The first of these is the conduct of the commercial market in antiquarian books, which typically prizes first editions far above subsequent printings of a text. Generally speaking, in the antiquarian market and the world of bibliophily and collecting, the higher the edition number, the lower the book's monetary value. Thus, in the absence of copies with special bindings or especially significant provenances ('association copies'), the second edition almost invariably fetches a higher price than the fourth; the fourth is accounted of greater worth than the seventh, and the seventh greater than the tenth. Hence, the degressive principle as it is commonly practised – while perfectly suited for antiquarian book dealers and the collectors of early editions who need to learn about bibliographical 'points' in order to identify and ascertain the value of their early editions – may be less congenial to the book historian who seeks to understand the life of a given work over its whole history of publication and reception.

The second cultural practice that has conditioned the hierarchies of information contained in bibliographies – particularly the degressive principle – is the use of bibliographical studies in service of textual criticism. We should not forget that, even in the twenty-first century, many bibliographical protocols, intellectual attitudes and habits of mind have their origins in a (now outdated) conception of bibliography as primarily the servant of scholarly editing and textual criticism which, in turn, was perceived to be the servant of literary studies. It is fair to say that the foundations of bibliography as practised throughout most of the twentieth century (the 'New Bibliography' of W. W. Greg, A. W. Pollard, R. B. McKerrow and their successors) were rooted in attempts to establish the 'true' text of the plays of Shakespeare and his contemporaries and, hence, became inextricably linked with the vexing business of describing and analysing Elizabethan and early-Jacobean play texts. By and large, the texts published after the death of the author (with the exception of author-directed posthumous publication) are generally considered of lesser value for scholarly editors. In contrast, for the book historian later instantiations of a work are also of considerable importance because they can reveal a great deal about the life-history of the work.

A fifth (and final) bibliographical concept: format

Descriptive bibliographies can be of great help to book historians for tracking changes in a work's format over time. Few technical terms used by bibliographers are more easily misunderstood by non-specialists than 'format'.[20] Most people quite reasonably think of 'format' as meaning 'layout', or textual presentation (sometimes called 'mise-en-page'), especially because 'format' in this sense is one of the headings for the pull-down menus in Microsoft® Word. There is also a second, bookish sense for format: the term is often predicated generically to describe a book's size and shape – think of the 'large format' shelves in our libraries. Yet, in descriptive bibliographies (and in bibliographical writing more generally) 'format' most often refers to one of four kinds of book form: folio (Fo, or 2°, where the printed sheet is folded once to form two leaves), quarto (4to, or 4°, folded twice for four leaves), octavo (8vo, or 8°, folded three times giving eight leaves) and duodecimo (12mo, or 12°, folded to form a gathering of twelve leaves). Less frequently, the reader might also encounter three other formats: sixteenmo (16mo, 16°, sometimes called sextodecimo), twentyfourmo (24mo, 24°, sometimes called vicesimo-quarto) and thirtytwomo (32mo, 32°, sometimes called tricesimo-secundo). Generally speaking, most works go down format – say, from quarto to octavo to duodecimo – as they are reprinted over time.

A book's format is a useful index of its intended audience, use and, often, price. Format, a central dimension of a book's expressive form, signals something of its contents and hospitality to its readers. In his diary for January 1790, James Boswell recorded a conversation with Edmond Malone in which Boswell revealed his ambition to publish *The Life of Johnson* in folio. Malone, who was attuned to the ways of the London trade and the predilections of contemporary readers, explained that his friend 'might as well throw it into the Thames' because 'a folio would not now be read'.[21] Writing to her sister, Jane Austen remarked with mock scornfulness on 'those enormous great stupid thick quarto volumes', further confiding, 'I detest a Quarto'. She castigated those who would 'not understand a man who condenses his thoughts into an octavo', a format that betokened greater accessibility, portability (and, hence, sociability), authorial restraint and unpretentiousness. Her jocular observations, made in 1813, reflect a shift in sensibility more than a century in the making.[22]

In the era before the widespread use of steam-driven machine presses and machine-made paper (also called 'wove paper') for book making (c. 1455–c. 1830 and beyond), a book's format is usually defined by the number of times the original printed sheet of paper, hand-made at the vat (called 'laid paper') has been folded to create its component leaves. When a sheet is folded once to make a folio, consisting of two leaves, the chain lines are vertical, the vergures (thin parallel lines, alternating light and dark) are horizontal, and the watermark generally falls in the centre of the leaf. When the sheet is folded twice to make a quarto, consisting of four leaves, the chain lines are horizontal, the vergures vertical, and the watermark shifts into the centre of the inner margin. When the sheet is folded three times to make an octavo, consisting of eight leaves, the chain lines return to vertical, the vergures to horizontal and the watermark migrates to the top, inner corner.

Despite the convention of defining format by the way the sheet is folded, it is more accurate to define it as the way that pages of type are imposed in the forme for printing; how the sheet is folded after printing is a consequence of imposition. (Two matching formes – called the 'inner forme' and the 'outer forme' – were made for each sheet; the typeset pages were arranged according to established patterns to create the correct sequence of pages when the sheet, having been printed on both sides, was folded.) Format, then, is best thought of as a classification of a book's structure as a consequence of its production.

With the growing use in the nineteenth century of machine-made paper, in which sheets were cut from a continuous roll, formats become more difficult to identify. Because the iron hand press (e.g. the Stanhope, Albion and Columbian) remained in widespread use for book work throughout much of the century, however, the concept of format remains useful for classifying the pattern of typographical imposition used to make a book. When books are made on machine presses from machine-made paper, however, 'format' is typically associated with leaf dimensions, or with book-trade descriptions, and thus is more an expression of a book's size and shape, rather than a classification of the volume's structure resulting from its method of production.

A model for bibliographers and book historians: the exemplary *Henry James*

There is perhaps no better picture of the Anglo-American publishing world from the mid-1870s to the early 1920s in a single volume than David Supino's *Henry James: A Bibliographical Catalogue*.[23] Supino traces in unprecedented detail the lineaments of James's authorial career and the fortunes (and misfortunes) of the publishing houses on both sides of the Atlantic that produced and sold his writings. Supino's exemplary work is a model of integrative scholarly method, powerfully combining close bibliographical scrutiny of particular textual artefacts with the archival recovery of book-historical information in as much detail as the surviving documents allow.

Using the Houghton Mifflin Archive, for example, Supino chronicles the US printing history of *The American* in its original stereotype edition, providing the production dates, press-runs and binding times for the twenty-seven impressions made from 1887 to 1919. He also registers evidence that copies of an early impression of this edition were imported into England (and sold for 10s 6d). The bibliography further provides details of an undated English 'piracy' and gives reasons for establishing the likelihood that it preceded the yellowback unauthorized edition, also undated, printed from the same plates.

Crucially, Supino is always testing his sources against one another, as when he discovers, for example, a divergence between the documentary evidence in the Houghton Mifflin Archive about the binding of the first two impressions of *The American* and the evidence produced by scrutinizing the actual publications in their several forms (4.4.0). With characteristic restraint, Supino posits a likely explanation for this conflict, but then is quick to point out that the available evidence neither confirms nor disproves the account he proposes. Reading further in the same entry, we learn that the Houghton Mifflin 'trade editions' of *The American* (1922ff), marketed as part of its Riverside Literature Series ('Riverside College Classics'), were made from a duplicate set of plates of the New York Edition (which was owned by the James estate and Scribner's). These and other comparable editions and issues of his novels from the extensively revised New York Edition did more to establish James's posthumous reputation in America than anything else.

Supino's transatlantic scholarship enables us to compare the reception of *Daisy Miller* (1879 [1878]) in the US and UK. The first American edition was published as part of Harper's Half-Hour Series and priced at $.35 in cloth and $.20 in wrappers; in only a few weeks 20,000 copies were sold. The story of the first English edition is just the opposite. Sold in two volumes and priced at 21s, it sold just 285 copies in its first nine months on the market. Tellingly, the American editions quickly became progressively more expensive: the second American edition (issued as part of the Franklin Square Library) cost $.75; the third (1892ff) was priced at $3.50 for the trade issue and $15.00 for the deluxe (limited to 250 copies). Featuring 101 illustrations, expensive paper, a richly decorated binding and an accompanying box, both issues were obviously marketed as a gift book.

Antiquarian booksellers and collectors of modern first editions have long accepted the notion that the first impression of the first edition of *The Portrait of a Lady* (1881) may be recognized by the unique appearance of a full stop immediately following the copyright statement on the title-page verso. The market value of early impressions of the *Portrait* has depended on this key to identifying the novel's earliest printing, and there are large sums of money and much cultural prestige at stake based on its truth. Yet, Supino's careful study of the first seven impressions has enabled him to establish definitively that this bibliographical shibboleth is a false custom – and to produce a reliable test for making a true identification. Now, libraries and private collectors who paid handsomely for what they 'knew' to be a first impression are discovering that what they have is actually something else of rather less monetary value than they had imagined. Others, presumably holding a later impression, are finding themselves pleasantly surprised. 'Expert' antiquarian booksellers and scholars have learned yet again that there is no substitute for sustained engagement with the printed artefacts themselves and immersive attention to a bibliographical or book-historical problem.

It is the artful combining of evidence from publishers' archives – e.g. from Macmillan (British Library), Charles Scribner's (Firestone Library, Princeton), Harper and Brothers (Butler Library, Columbia) and Houghton Mifflin (Houghton Library, Harvard), from private papers and correspondence and from the meticulous examination of the books themselves, that makes Supino's bibliography such a wide-ranging and reliable resource.

The pages of *Henry James: A Bibliographical Catalogue* are rich with ore that book historians can and should profitably mine. A good case in point is the index delineating the publication history of each of James's stories and tales, recording the first magazine publication and all subsequent book publications of those narratives from 1875 to 1923. This conspectus of James's career as a writer of short stories and novellas, some 100 in all, appearing in twenty-seven different newspapers and serials (not including piracies) is highly revealing and could easily serve as the foundation for an important book-historical scholarly publication. I feel morally obligated to warn young and old alike that Supino's elegant bibliography is highly addictive; as a great artist's career unfolds, the details are fascinating in themselves, even as they beautifully coalesce to establish a narrative that adds up to far more than the sum of its parts.

Supino's study is a fitting place at which to conclude this discussion, because it amply demonstrates what bibliography can do for book history – and what book history can, in turn, accomplish for bibliography. Generally speaking, bibliographical studies benefit from the social reach of book history, even as book-historical research becomes stronger when it incorporates insights from bibliography's attention to textual artefacts, which in the best descriptive bibliographies is both close and comprehensive. These related and, often, overlapping areas of historical inquiry should be practised in ways that are mutually informing. Read with care, the descriptive bibliography is a powerful instrument for the book historian's success.

NOTES

1. See www.khazars.com/en/biografija-milorad-pavic-2/autobiografija-milorad-pavic.
2. D. H. Laurence, *A Portrait of the Author as a Bibliography*, an Engelhard Lecture on the Book, at the Library of Congress; Center for the Book viewpoint series no. 9 (Washington, DC: Library of Congress, 1983), 17.
3. J. D. Fleeman, *A Bibliography of the Works of Samuel Johnson: Treating his Published Works from the Beginnings to 1984*, Prepared for publication by J. McLaverty with the assistance of C. Ferdinand, 2 vols. (Oxford: Clarendon Press, 2000); C. S. Abbott, *Marianne Moore: A Descriptive Bibliography* (University of Pittsburgh Press, 1977); W. Baker and G. N. Wachs, *Tom Stoppard: A Bibliographical History* (London and New Castle, DE: The British Library and Oak Knoll Press, 2010); and B. J. Kirkpatrick and S. N. Clarke, *A Bibliography of Virginia Woolf*, 4th edn (New York: Oxford University Press, 1998).
4. E. T. Bowden, *Washington Irving Bibliography*, The Complete Works of Washington Irving, Vol. XXX (Boston: Twayne Publishers, 1989), x.
5. Bowden, *Washington Irving Bibliography*, xii.
6. M. Sadleir, *Trollope: a Bibliography* (Folkstone: W. M. Dawson and Sons, 1928), ix.
7. D. L. Vander Meulen, 'An Essay towards Perfection: J. D. Fleeman's *A Bibliography of the Works of Samuel Johnson*', in *The Age of Johnson: A Scholarly Annual* 13 (2002): 389–435 (389); R. DeMaria, Jr, Review in *The Journal of English and Germanic Philology* 101.1 (Jan. 2002), 142–5 (144–5).
8. Fleeman, *A Bibliography of the Works of Samuel Johnson*, xxi, xxiv–xxv; Vander Meulen, 'An Essay', 395.
9. Fleeman, *A Bibliography of the Works of Samuel Johnson*, 556.
10. Fleeman, *A Bibliography of the Works of Samuel Johnson*, xxiii.
11. See, for example, D. F. McKenzie, *The Cambridge University Press, 1696–1712: A Bibliographical Study*, 2 vols. (Cambridge University Press, 1966); W. S. Peterson's *A Bibliography of the Kelmscott Press* (New York: Oxford University Press, 1984); and D. Foxon, *English Verse, 1701–1750: A Catalogue of Separately Published Poems with Notes on Early Collected Editions*, 2 vols. (Cambridge University Press, 1975).
12. *The English Novel 1770–1829: a Bibliographical Survey of Prose Fiction Published in the British Isles*, 2 vols., General Editors: P. Garside, J. Raven and R. Schöwerling (Oxford University Press, 2000), I:[1].
13. An excellent guide to these and other bibliographical terms is John Carter's *ABC for Book Collectors*, originally published in 1952 and available at: www.ilab.org/eng/documentation/30-john_carters_abc_for_book_collectors.html. See also, G. T. Tanselle, 'The Bibliographical Concepts of Issue and State', *Papers of the Bibliographical Society of America* 69 (1975), 17–66.
14. W. Baker and G. N. Wachs, *Tom Stoppard: A Bibliographical History* (London and New Castle, DT: The British Library and Oak Knoll Press, 2010), xx.
15. Harvard College Library Department of Printing and Graphic Arts, *Catalogue of Books and Manuscripts. Part I: French 16th-Century Books*. 2 vols. Compiled by

R. Mortimer (Cambridge, MA: Belknap Press of Harvard University Press, 1964) and *Part II: Italian 16th-Century Books*. 2 vols. Compiled by R. Mortimer (Cambridge, MA: Belknap Press of Harvard University Press, 1974).
16. See *Catalogue of Botanical Books in the Collection of Rachel McMasters Miller Hunt*, Vol. II, comp. by A. Stevenson (Pittsburgh: The Hunt Botanical Library, 1961), cxli–ccxliv, esp. clxvi–clxxvi.
17. See G. T. Tanselle, 'The Arrangement of Descriptive Bibliographies', *SB* 37 (1984), 1–38.
18. For a discussion of this problem see Vander Meulen, 'An Essay', 402–4.
19. Madan, 'Degressive Bibliography: A Memorandum', *Transactions of the Bibliographical Society* 9 (1906–8), 53–65; Bowers, 'Purposes of Descriptive Bibliography, with Some Remarks on Methods', *Library* 5th ser. 8 (1953), 1–22. See also D. W. Krummel, 'On Degressive Music Bibliography', *Notes* 56, 4 (June 2000), 867–78: www.questia.com/library/journal/1G1-63859282/on-degressive-music-bibliography.
20. G. T. Tanselle, 'The Concept of Format', *Studies in Bibliography* 53 (2000), 67–115.
21. J. Boswell, *Boswell: The Great Biographer, 1789–1795*, M. K. Danziger and F. Brady (eds.) (New Haven and London: Yale University Press, 1989), 32–3 (13 January 1790). For changes in taste and paper-size as the eighteenth century progressed, see G. Pollard, 'Notes on the size of the sheet', *Library*, 4th ser., 22 (1941), 105–37.
22. J. Austen, *Jane Austen's Letters*, 3rd edn, D. Le Faye (ed.) (Oxford University Press, 1995), 206 (To Cassandra Austen, 9 February 1813).
23. D. J. Supino, *Henry James: A Bibliographical Catalogue of a Collection of Editions to 1921* (Liverpool University Press; University of Chicago Press, 2006; 2nd edn, revised, 2014).

13

KATHERINE BODE AND ROGER OSBORNE

Book history from the archival record

The *OED* defines the archive simply as 'A place in which public records or other important historic documents are kept'. Whether in a library or museum, an online database or a dusty box in an attic, archives are the basis for all humanities scholarship. In book history, they hold a particularly special place, because scholars in this field are concerned with not only what is ostensibly recorded in the archive, but the material evidence of print culture that archives contain. Quite simply, archival research provides the principal way for book historians to explore and understand the history and nature of authorship, publication, distribution and reception of print culture. Since the early twenty-first century, there has been significant growth in interest in the concept of the archive, in the context of, and arguably motivated by, the processes and implications of digitizing our cultural heritage. This extensive body of critical scholarship spans a range of fields, including literary studies, history, philosophy, sociology, anthropology and political science. Much of this research builds upon important analyses of the archive by philosopher Jacques Derrida and historian Michel Foucault. These scholars' conceptions of the archive are complex and challenging, but broadly speaking, both emphasize its contingent nature – the way in which an institution tends to respond to changing values – and its relationship to history and memory, as well as to social, political and technological power.

We accept the broad argument of recent critical scholarship on the archive: that these are not passive and innocent collections of documents and reflections of our collective past. Scholars now regard archival collections as representations of history, as cultural texts in their own right. The meaning of any given archive is constructed at several levels – first by the values held by the men and women who originally created the records it preserves, and later by those of subsequent owners and of the archivists whose task it is to order and preserve the records. Archives perforce change with shifting cultural values. However, we do not survey these arguments in detail.[1] Our focus is more practical, and considers how book historians can approach – and read – the archive in all its complexity. We explore the two main ways of reading the archive in book history: first, analysing individual documents within the archive (a qualitative approach); second, using what the archive contains as the basis for bibliometric studies (a quantitative approach). More briefly, we consider the emergence of new, digital archives, and the opportunities and challenges these present for book history. For each approach to the archive – qualitative and quantitative – and for material as well as digital collections, we consider, in turn, the main sources for book history and highlight some of the scholarship that makes the best use of those sources, as well as discussing the practical and methodological issues raised by archival research.

Reading the qualitative archive: sources

Archives contain books but, as D. F. McKenzie reminds us, 'no book was ever bound by its covers'.[2] The many other archival records associated with print culture – of authors, publishers, printers, booksellers, policy-makers and readers – are part of the 'bound'-less history of the book. Having served their original purposes, these records can be put to use again in the hands of book historians, as vital sources of information about the history and operations of print culture. The three main categories of archival records most used in book history are correspondence, publishers' records and booksellers' and library records.

Correspondence from and to people involved in the production and reception of books provides some of the most direct evidence of relationships between individuals in print culture and of the broader operations of the communications circuit. An author's correspondence might include letters to friends, literary agents, publishers and readers, and provide insight into the way a book was written, edited, printed, distributed and read. The correspondence collected in the archive of a literary agent might provide access to direct communications with an author, or opinions about the work that the author was not privy to. Further removed from the author, the correspondence of a library or bookseller might provide specific reasons why a book was or was not purchased for a particular group of readers. Scholars can be greatly assisted by editions of an author's correspondence, bringing together material from archives across the world. Despite their value, such collections are often one-sided, so a trip to the archive – or consultation of related, but tangential correspondence between other people – can be necessary to fill in the other side of the correspondence.

Scholarly editions, particularly those that are accompanied by editorial projects devoted to an author's correspondence – such as the Cambridge editions of Joseph Conrad and D. H. Lawrence – provide some of the best examples of how correspondence is used in archival research. The temporal specificity of correspondence has been of particular value to scholarly editors, who use such sources to track the composition, publication, distribution and reception of books. Correspondence can draw attention to the involvement of a range of actors in print culture, including scribes, printers, publishers, booksellers and readers. In this respect, the use of correspondence provides a good example of the ways in which authority is attributed to items within the archive. In cases where the primary objective of a scholarly edition is to capture the author's final intentions, the authority of readers' and booksellers' correspondence about the work is attributed little value. However, the value of such correspondence increases in editions that aim to represent the work as it was delivered to specific audiences. Scholarly editions also provide some of the best examples of the ways in which previously undiscovered correspondence can destabilize established arguments by directing attention to new information. The Mark Twain Project, for instance, identifies this potential of correspondence as one of the main reasons it delivers online versions of Twain's works that are amenable to revision.

In addition to correspondence with authors, publishers' archives contain numerous records relating to all aspects of book production and distribution. These records can include evidence of the calculation of pre-publication costs, content acquisition, editing, design and illustration, preparation and manufacturing, marketing and selling, post-publication costs, author royalties, distribution and general and administrative costs. With such a multitude of variables to include in the decisions about whether or not to accept an author's manuscript, some have likened the business of books to gambling.[3] The participants in this gamble include author and publisher, but in a busy publishing house, this activity will also include editors, outside readers, salespeople, accountants, printers and others, all of whom may leave records of their involvement. The production files, readers' reports, estimates, contracts, sales reports and statements all provide evidence of how books were transformed from authors' manuscripts to printed form. Publisher records are not only found in the business records of a company. Sometimes, the production of a book can be pieced together by consulting the records of an author or literary agent. Contracts, statements, rejection letters and other such records could be scattered across several collections, requiring the researcher to connect fragments, retained separately and under different circumstances.

Instances of exemplary use of publishers' records abound, but it is worth noting a few to show the range of evidence available in such archives. An early but notable example is Robert L. Patten's *Charles Dickens and His Publishers* (1978). Patten augments the main narrative with a series of appendices – constructed from publishers' archives – that detail the sales, profits, income and circulation of Dickens's books, and the printing history of his monthly serials, including circulation figures. More recently, Ben Yagoda was able to offer a detailed account of the business and culture of *The New Yorker* because of the extensive records held at the New York Public Library. In *About Town*: The New Yorker *and the World It Made* (2000) Yagoda draws on eighty years' of correspondence, manuscripts, readers' reports, photographs, cartoons and other records related to the publishing activities of *The New Yorker* to describe the material and cultural conditions under which many of the most significant American writers saw their work delivered to readers. Similarly, in *A Feeling for Books: The Book-of-the-Month Club, Literary Taste, and Middle-class Desire* (1997), Janice Radway draws on the personal archives, including oral history recordings, of judges of the American Book-of-the-Month Club to describe the culture of the book that evolved through the engagement of the judges with publishers and readers since the club's establishment in 1926.

Collections of bookseller or library records are rarer than authors' or publishers' archives, and those that do exist often supply only a fragment of the historical record that these institutions would have produced. Such records found in research on library usage in nineteenth-century America have been used, however, to demonstrate that male library patrons 'commodified their reading into categorizations like "useful knowledge" and "rational amusements"', in order to adopt specific acts of reading in the definition of character.[4] Such civic activities occurred across the world, and so the minute books and annual reports of both small and large libraries often indicate the types of reading to be pursued under the watchful eye of committees. The range of studies of library records suggests the rich sources of information potentially held in the archives of libraries around the world. The records of booksellers can be read in a similar way to library and publisher's records. The bookseller frequently takes a gamble with the books stocked on the shelves and serves the community in a similar way to libraries by providing a meeting place for book talk and a collection of books that reflect the taste of the community served. As institutions, libraries and booksellers provided a space for communities to procure the books they used for entertainment or edification, leaving records that can be analysed to explore how individuals and cultural groups perceived their position in the community, nation and the world.

Researchers have regularly drawn on the records of libraries and booksellers to describe the readers and reading of particular times. The most notable of recent studies is William St Clair's *The Reading Nation in the Romantic Period* (2004). In his revisionary literary history, St Clair draws on around fifty separate archives, including those of a number of booksellers and lenders. This research contributes significantly to the development of quantitative methods, as discussed in the second part of this chapter, but this occurs in conjunction with consistent reference to the evidence of individual and collective reading found in correspondence, journals and other commentaries housed in the archives of book clubs, authors and libraries. James Raven draws on a similar number of archives in *The Business of Books: Booksellers and the English Book Trade, 1450–1850* (2007), demonstrating how booksellers were central to the evolution of books from a luxury to a commodity. Using archives rich in documents relating to the everyday lives of African-Americans, Elizabeth McHenry expanded the conception of nineteenth-century literary societies in *Forgotten Readers: Recovering the Lost History of African American Literary Societies* (2002). Such studies as these draw attention to the content of archives by compiling rich and compelling narratives that make the archives 'talk'.[5]

Reading the qualitative archive: issues and methods

While serendipitous discovery on-site can be thrilling, advance planning when visiting an archive will enable more effective use of the researcher's time. The contents of archives can be considered from afar through a range of printed and online guides, providing opportunities to prioritize visits according to the descriptions provided. The website of the Society for the History of Authorship, Publishing and Reading (SHARP) is a good source of information about the location of publishers' and printers' archives and other resources. Such guides often identify institutions or individuals that can provide more detailed finding aids, in some cases down to the collection level. This sort of information is useful to novice and experienced researchers alike, and can provide invaluable assistance to those who have to travel great distances to conduct their research. No two archives are the same, but all have protocols that dictate entry and use, including in some cases the need for official introductions or permission to visit. Seasoned researchers will always advise novices to make contact ahead of time and become familiar with the archive's policies. This applies particularly to retrieval times. Some archives store material off-site and may take more than twenty-four hours to deliver requested material. Ordering such material ahead of time will save time and money.

It is a good idea to communicate with the archivist in advance of a visit. Archivists have specialized knowledge of the material that researchers come to see, knowledge that can be useful in formulating and expanding the researcher's questions. Most collections do not have comprehensive finding aids – and some are uncatalogued – and a good archivist will increase the productivity of your visit, providing links and clues that are not evident in the guides or published material. The archivist will also be an important guide to the provenance of the records, enabling the researcher to better understand the original accession, the collection policies that preserved the records and the effect of these on any collection's ability to represent the past.

In addition to these practical considerations, a range of methodological issues are important when accessing and interpreting the archival record. These issues highlight how the researcher does not simply read history off the archive, but takes account of the construction and nature of each collection. Perhaps the most important issue to bear in mind is that, whether it relates to an individual, business, institution or state, no archival record is either complete or fully revealing. Rather, there are various levels of construction and mediation of the archive. Most records have already undergone a process of 'archiving'. Individuals make decisions about what documents they want to keep or discard. For instance, Vance and Nettie Palmer (two prominent twentieth-century Australian authors) destroyed their business records – presumably believing them not worthy of preservation – removing from their personal papers information regarding earnings, contractual arrangements and other financial dealings. This same principle, on a larger scale, applies to an institution's records. For instance, the Doubleday Records at the Library of Congress are heavily weighted to the valuation of the editor Ken McCormick, who selected and annotated groups of records that he thought were important or interesting.

All archives are formed in relation to the methods, rules and spatial limitations of their managers, whether the archivist is professional or amateur. The creation, organization and storage of business or personal records influence decisions about which records to retain, and which to dispose of. Consequently, the records we find in the archive come with contexts that exhibit changing attitudes to value and historical knowledge. An impulse to collect the 'best' records or the most 'memorable' or 'important' is shared by the archivist and the author or business in question. The records that are retained or donated might reflect a hagiographic impulse or the sentimental feelings of an individual. When records are donated and transferred to a formal archive – whether a library, museum, public record office or university – another process will further shape the archive through selection and disposal of records, according to the archivist's methods of valuation. Finding aids may also reflect value judgments, for example by cataloguing folders containing the records of famous writers, but relegating more obscure authors to general folders filed alphabetically or otherwise.

Book history from the archival record

Archival records are not only incomplete and mediated by various levels of archival intervention; they are also subjective. The records of individuals and institutions are strongly influenced by the beliefs, perspectives, values, interests and aims of those that produce them. For instance, in terms of correspondence records, authors have been known to provide competing accounts of an event to different correspondents, depending on the stake each recipient has in a book. All of these issues point to the careful sifting and interpretation required of archival research. James L. W. West III's account of preparing a scholarly edition expresses these requirements well:

> The editor must examine the surviving notes, manuscripts, typescripts, proofs, and other evidence. The editor must also read the relevant letters and journals and study the publishers' records and account books. From these materials an account of the composition of the work can be fashioned. The narrative will be assembled from the evidence that is otherwise inert. One does not 'allow' the archives to talk; one 'makes' them talk, crafting stories in the same way that biographers and historians do, by selecting and arranging the evidence and writing a story that ties the whole together.[6]

In other words, reading the archive involves not only exploring a wide range of sources, but producing a narrative out of this sorting and sifting, one that further shapes – or manipulates – the contents of the archives used. As with the organization of the archive, the historical narrative is selective and subjective. When researchers enter the archive and sit down to receive the documents they hope will inform their narratives, it is important to remember this selection and subjectivity in order to appreciate the complexity and contingency of the field.

Reading the quantitative archive: sources

The subject of book history is, as Simon Eliot writes, 'rooted in the material world'; and while this material world incorporates elements that cannot be quantified – such as the tone of an editor's correspondence with an author or an individual's reading experience – it is also 'characterized in part, and therefore is to be understood in part, by countable quantities: reams of paper, tons of type, print runs, and percentage returns on capital'.[7] The three main categories of archival resources used in quantitative book history are the records of publishers and allied trades; bibliographies and library catalogues; and information created by legislative and governing bodies in managing the book trade.

The archives of individual publishers, booksellers and printers provide rich sources for quantitative book history. Many such records take the form of lists: for instance, of print runs, wages, shipments and sales. Features of the archive can also be transformed into data for quantitative analysis. For instance, in *Edging Women Out* (1989), Gaye Tuchman and Nina Fortin analyse gender trends in Victorian novel publishing in part by sampling the number of novel manuscripts – by men and women – accepted and refused by London publisher, Macmillan. Where this and other studies – such as Darnton's *The Business of the Enlightenment* (1987) – analyse quantitative information from a single publisher's archives, other studies survey multiple archives. From the fifty publishing and printing archives he surveys for *The Reading Nation in the Romantic Period* (2004), St Clair draws data on prices, print runs, intellectual property and readership to explore the movement of, and access to, literature in the eighteenth and nineteenth centuries.

The archives of organizations related to the book trade – including the many (usually national) associations, societies and guilds of publishers, authors, booksellers and libraries – also represent a key source of historical data, especially regarding members and business and legal processes. A particularly important archive of this type is that of the Stationers' Company, a guild of printers, typesetters, bookbinders and booksellers based in London and operating from the fifteenth to the twentieth century. This company supervised entry into the publishing trade, controlled working conditions and wages, set the retail price on books and regulated copyright. Its archives represent a unique and important source of quantitative information on British print culture. Other sources of bibliometric information arising from the book trade include listings of publications and publication statistics in trade journals such as *Publishers' Weekly*, *Publishers' Circular* or *The Bookseller*; the catalogues of book fairs, including those of Frankfurt, London and New York; and sales data (while collected differently in different countries and regions, the global sales database, Nielsen BookScan is an increasingly prominent – though expensive to access – source of information on sales).

The lists and descriptions of books compiled by bibliographers and librarians sit at the heart of quantitative book history. Union catalogues – which describe the collections in a number of libraries and include the Library of Congress Catalogue and the WorldCat Database published by Online Computer Library Center Inc. (OCLC) – provide valuable bibliographical information. So too do the many national and other bibliographies, which incorporate information about printed material ranging from the basic (titles, authors, publishers, dates and places of publication) to the detailed (specifics of printing, illustration, binding, size, price and editions). All this can be rendered as metadata for quantitative studies, and is particularly suitable for such analysis: devised with reference to established standards and fields, the data have a high degree of consistency across the record. Significantly, these sources frequently collate many of the records of the book trade discussed above, as well as multiple other sources (including previous bibliographies). For instance, *The English Novel 1770–1829: A Bibliographical Survey of Prose Fiction Published in the British Isles* (2000) is compiled from 'eighteenth- and nineteenth-century review notices, booksellers' and printers' records, advertisements and term catalogues, followed by extensive searches of ESTC [English Short-Title Catalogue], OCLC, and hands-on stack work in many hundreds of libraries worldwide'.[8]

Quantitative analysis of library catalogues and borrowers' records has contributed significantly to reading history. In *A Measure of Popularity: Public Library Holdings of Twenty-Four Popular Authors, 1883–1912* (1992), Eliot surveys over eighty library catalogues from England and Scotland to explore the relative popularity of authors such as Walter Besant, Charles Dickens and Margaret Oliphant. Jonathan Rose's *The Intellectual Life of the British Working Class* (2001) incorporates quantitative analysis of library records and survey results – in addition to analysis of autobiographies and memoirs – to explore the autodidact tradition in Britain. In a different national context, Tim Dolin's recent quantitative studies of the holdings and borrowings of subscription libraries have significantly expanded understandings of reading practices in Australia in the nineteenth and early twentieth centuries. Bibliographies likewise provide the source for quantitative research in a number of studies, underpinning, for instance, analyses of trends in national histories of the book for Britain, Canada and Australia.[9]

A final, major archival source of information for quantitative archival research in book history comes from the records of legislative bodies managing and monitoring the various aspects of the book trade, including copyright, taxes, trade and legislation. Alexis Weedon's *Victorian Publishing: The Economics of Book Production for a Mass Market, 1836–1916* (2003) incorporates data from a range of government records. For instance, she uses the Annual Statement of Trade published in Parliamentary Papers to explore the international expansion of the British publishing industry. In a pair of essays discussing the use of publishing statistics, Robert Darnton and Priya Joshi both employ quantitative information from the Indian Civil Service (ICS) archives. Joshi's 'Quantitative Method, Literary History' focuses on the quarterly 'catalogues' registering and describing new publications in India, while Darnton's 'Book Production in British India, 1850–1900' uses the annual 'reports' quantifying and analysing book publication in each province. Both highlight salient features of Indian print culture in the colonial period, from the slow emergence of the novel in India to some surprising similarities in book production in India and England.[10]

Reading the quantitative archive: issues and methods

Darnton's and Joshi's essays also provide a useful introduction to some common challenges in bibliometric research. The chief – indeed, overarching – difficulty for such research is data quality. As with archival records generally, historical data is often 'patchy ... much more has been lost than survives'.[11] However, this inevitable incompleteness – while obviously decreasing coverage and consistency – is not the only issue affecting the quality of historical data, as the case of the ICS archives shows. Although Darnton and Joshi work on ostensibly the same archive, as both acknowledge, their statistics and results differ significantly; as Joshi puts it, they are 'mutually inconsistent ... incompatible in significant points of content and abstraction'.[12] Their justifications for the historical data they study highlight two further issues affecting data quality.

The first arises from record keeping and reporting procedures. Darnton argues that the annual reports 'cover data that were not included in the catalogues', while Joshi describes reporting procedures for these same documents as so lackadaisical as to render them 'abstract at best, and at worst simply misleading'. Inconsistent record keeping and reporting procedures – which can create gaps, inconsistencies and errors in the historical record – affect even the most well-known and utilized resources in quantitative book history. For instance, although registration with the Stationers' Company provided the normal means of securing copyright in Britain for much of the last five centuries, Michael Robertson estimates that only two-thirds of British titles are included in the company's entry books. Likewise, Michael Suarez proposes that approximately 10 per cent of titles and editions published in the eighteenth century no longer exist, and are thus not recorded in the *English Short Title Catalogue* for that period.[13] It is significant that, even for these major records, the quality and completeness of historical data can only be estimated.

A second issue affecting the quality of historical data is perspective. As with individual archival records, historical data are not created in a vacuum but are inflected by the perspectives and intentions of the individuals and institutions that create and curate them. In the case of the ICS archives, both Darnton and Joshi agree that the reports and catalogues often reveal more about British perceptions of Indian culture than about the publishing industry in that country. While historians frequently read against the grain created by such perspectives – as Joshi does, in highlighting the presence of both British and Indian interests in the quarterly catalogues – such an approach is only possible if one first identifies the perspectives shaping the historical data at hand. As with archival records generally, perspective also affects preservation of historical data, with documents archived because of particular understandings of significance, rather than at random or because they represent the range of activities in which particular individuals, companies or institutions engaged. Whether book historians read archival records qualitatively or quantitatively, they face similar challenges, and these require analysis of the archive itself as well as examination of its contents.

Closely related to perspective is the common problem for bibliometric studies of categorization or terminology. Darnton raises this issue with respect to the categorization of religious texts in the ICS annual reports. Noting that, '[i]n India, unlike England, religion was so broad as to be nearly coextensive with culture', Darnton describes the difficulty – for contemporary scholars as well as British officials of the period – of 'deciding whether a particular book should be categorised under religion or philosophy or poetry'. Such difficulties, which obviously influence the results of analysis, are not particular to data from other cultures. Rather, they are endemic to all quantitative representations of culture specifically because this approach requires that a range of qualities, experiences or artefacts be collected under a limited number of headings or categories. As Weedon writes, '[c]ategorization is a useful tool to group together similarities whether through the putting together of books by genre, authors by social background, or publishers by turnover', and this process 'aids the analysis of broader historical trends which could not be understood otherwise'.[14] However, the creation of categories also inevitably occludes variations and differences within the historical record.

A number of methods – ranging from detailed knowledge of the data to sophisticated statistical approaches to gauge probability and error – exist to counteract these common challenges in bibliometric studies. In Eliot's words, all aim to use quantitative resources 'to the full without asking them to bear a weight of interpretation that they are not strong enough to carry'. Detailed knowledge of one's data – a 'biography of a data source' – is a key first step.[15] Producing such a 'biography' requires asking and answering as many questions as possible about the data: Who compiled it? When was it created? What selection criteria were used in its construction? What was the purpose of the information and who was it intended for? Why has it been kept and by whom, and what physical, social or material circumstances have affected its curation? If the data has been managed or created by a professional archivist, librarian or bibliographer, that person should be consulted in answering these questions. Although not all answers may be forthcoming, addressing as many as possible will provide a vital basis for ascertaining data quality, including coverage and accuracy, the perspectives involved and the terminology used. Employing multiple sources also provides an important means of gauging the reliability of data as well as counteracting gaps in the record.

While the majority of quantitative studies in book history use very basic statistical methods, more sophisticated techniques have been employed by such scholars as Simon Eliot and Alexis Weedon. Even with simple statistical approaches – such as counts and proportions – an understanding of such issues as sampling, timescales, data fluctuations and data visualization are important. In terms of more sophisticated statistical methods, the most relevant for book history are those used in historical research, including measures of central tendency (mean, median and mode) and dispersion (range, variance and standard deviation), frequency distributions, linear correlation statistics and other metrics of relationships between variables (such as categorical and continuous) and linear and multiple regression. All of these measures should be presented with error statistics, and thereby assessed for their level of statistical confidence. Good reference works exist for book historians wishing to develop skills in statistical methods. These are designed for use with statistical software, including the proprietary Statistical Package for Social Sciences (SPSS) or the free-to-download 'R' Statistical Package (which includes excellent online resources and discussion boards). Weedon also provides an introduction to sophisticated statistical approaches for book historians.[16] Whatever level of statistical analysis is employed, it is imperative to select an approach that suits the data, and the questions one intends to ask.

Sophisticated statistical approaches have considerable potential in book history, but – in contrast to history and the social sciences – the field has no established tradition of using such methods. A number of scholars point to problems with this situation: Michael Suarez comments that, '[m]uch book historical work manifests a statistical innocence that impoverishes otherwise valuable research', while St Clair argues that the relative absence of statistical approaches render this field, and the history of reading in particular, 'at the stage of astronomy before telescopes', ill-equipped to 'describe, understand, and theorise complex systems'. The incorporation of such methods into book history will take time. Where Saurez complains that book historians are unable to understand and learn from relevant statistical research in other disciplines (intended for audiences familiar with statistics), book historians who incorporate sophisticated statistical methods – or collaborate with statistical experts – will obviously be faced with a different problem of audience: namely, that the predominant readers of their work (other book historians) may have difficulty interpreting the meaning and significance of their findings.[17]

Book history from the archival record

All these methods for working with historical data – from knowing your source well to the careful application of statistical methods – are designed to assist in counteracting common problems relating to the quality and composition of historical data. But no matter how well one applies these methods, it is impossible to discover, create or claim a perfect data set. In an important way, book historians will always be left – as in Darnton and Joshi's discussion of the ICS archives – arguing for the value and reliability or, more accurately, the extent of the value and reliability, of the historical data they employ (whether those arguments are made primarily with reference to the personalities and institutions involved in creating and curating the data, or through statistical analyses of error and confidence). This awareness of the inevitable limitations of historical data has motivated some scholars to offer metaphors or analogies to describe the type of knowledge achievable using quantitative methods, and Darnton is surely the most inventive in this respect. For instance, he argues that, in struggling with statistics, 'the historian works like a diagnostician who searches for patterns in symptoms rather than a physicist who turns hard data into firm conclusions'. Elsewhere, he compares the 'general picture of literary culture' offered by historical statistics to 'the early maps of the New World, which showed the contours of the continents, even though they did not correspond very well to the actual landscape'.[18] These metaphors emphasize the importance of quantitative methods in book history, in particular their capacity to enable analysis of and insight into aspects of the field that would not otherwise be possible. At the same time, they highlight the importance of established methods (akin to those used by the diagnostician or map maker) for understanding the nature and composition of the sources used, and warn against an interpretation of those results as the truth or final word on historical phenomena.

Reading the digital archive

Digital technology is challenging the definition of, and how we use, archives. The term 'digital archive' can be used to refer to almost anything existing in digital form from discrete collections of related electronic documents (such as the Rossetti Archive or Emily Dickinson Electronic Archives); to digitized versions of existing material archives (for example, the Nineteenth Century British Library Newspaper Database or the National Library of Australia's Trove Newspaper database); commercial databases (including academic search and citation engines such as JSTOR and Web of Knowledge); and emerging digital libraries (most prominently, Google Books, but also non-profit initiatives such as the Internet Archive and HathiTrust).[19] Darnton has described the e-book as a new form of digital archive for book historians, and the term has even been ascribed to the internet itself.[20] Multiple archival resources relevant to book history have now been digitized, including many of the sources already discussed in this chapter. To give just a small selection of possible examples, projects such as the *Australian Common Reader* and *What Middletown Read* provide access to rich databases of library records, while the Stationers' Company archives as well as many national bibliographical records – including *AustLit*, for Australia, and *Canadiana*, for Canada – are now available in digital form.

The benefits of digitizing archives have been widely acknowledged. Chief among them are increased access and decreased cost. While archival material can be widely dispersed in the physical world, digitized archives can be accessed from a computer terminal, reducing the need for researchers to find the money and time to travel to archives. This additional time potentially allows research into a greater number and range of archives, encouraging expansion of the parameters by which scholars currently conceive of book history projects. Digitization of archival material also increases search options. While search possibilities differ between digital archives, many provide facilities to search by words or even concepts, and thus enable researchers to identify references and records they would only otherwise find serendipitously. Increasingly, book history projects generate their own digital archives. This output will enhance sharing of resources and the likelihood that existing projects will be expanded, including through collaboration between researchers in different places.

The increased access to archival records provided by digitization benefits both qualitative and quantitative approaches to reading the archive. In respect to the former, researchers can view documents before visiting the archive, the better to formulate research questions and approaches, or compare individual records held at different locations. For quantitative approaches, many digital archives provide access to large amounts of data. For instance, one can search an online bibliography for information about particular authors, texts, publishers and so on; but this information can also be extracted or 'mined' as quantitative lists or metadata (whether using inbuilt searches and facilitated extraction, or by creating automated searches and data harvesting programs). The access to data provided by digital archives greatly increases the potential speed and viability of bibliometric studies. For such studies, digital humanities initiatives also provide increasingly sophisticated and user-friendly tools for managing, analysing and visualizing historical data, including Zotero, TAPOR, Mallett and Gephi. Even Excel – software that might now be considered 'old-fashioned' – offers a useful platform, and array of tools, for simple statistical analysis of book historical data.

Arguably, it is in the visualization of data – including geospatial data – that new technology holds the most exciting possibilities for book history. The 'Mapping the World Republic of Letters' project, for instance, visualizes the trajectories of over 55,000 letters between 6,400 correspondents in the Electronic Enlightenment database to represent intellectual networks in this period and provoke new insights into how ideas circulated. Among other projects that demonstrate the new possibilities for book history of geospatial analysis, the Innerpeffray Library Project uses geographical information systems (GIS) technology to visualize borrowing distances and patterns for Scotland's first public lending library. While GIS is not without potential difficulties – particularly, identifying suitable data and analysing trends over time – computer technologies promise to expand significantly the presence and impact of geographical research for book history. More broadly, digital humanities researchers are proposing new ways of conceptualizing the visualization of data that could be usefully incorporated into book history. As computers enable data to be manipulated and represented in multiple ways, computer visualizations can provide a form of hypothesis testing, as described in Willard McCarty's *Humanities Computing* (2005). Alternatively, data visualization can be understood as a speculative and intuitive process that provokes researchers to new questions, thus functioning as a problem-generating rather than problem-solving strategy.[21]

While digital archives and methods for reading them have enormous potential for book history, this trend presents its own challenges for reading the archival record. The emphasis that is sometimes placed on the 'seemingly infinite' potential of digital archives – including 'unprecedented access to rare or inaccessible materials; comprehensiveness ... [and] consolidation' – downplays the many aspects of our cultural heritage that are not being, or cannot be, translated to digital form.[22] Issues preventing digitization include funding, copyright and storage space. Digitizing documents to appropriate scholarly standards is often very time-consuming and, hence, expensive, so even when archives are digitized, they may not be in forms useful to researchers. Although the situation is improving as book historians become involved in digitization initiatives, some existing projects do not incorporate aspects of the archive important for book history, such as the covers and title pages of books, the size of pages and the nature of bindings. Other aspects of print culture – including the weight, smell and feel of the material record – are difficult or impossible to represent digitally. The danger also exists that a single digitized record will be considered sufficient to represent all versions of a work (regardless of the manifestation and physical characteristics, such as marginalia and other page markings). If these other versions are neglected or destroyed, we could witness a reduction in, rather than expansion of, our access to the cultural record. Some commentators also point to a canonical focus in digitization projects, with records of well-known authors and institutions translated into digital form, while others are overlooked.

Conclusion

This chapter has not presented one mode of reading the archive – qualitative or quantitative – or one type of archive – material or digital – as inherently preferable. Rather, different approaches are necessary for different questions, and different archives are useful for different purposes. As Eliot writes, without qualitative case studies, we would lack the 'texture and taste of bookmaking humanity'; without quantitative studies we would lack 'the context to confer ... a proper significance' on the details of the case studies.[23] Likewise, despite some recent portrayals of digital archives as superior to the 'analogue' version, these new archives bring their own challenges, as well as possibilities, for book history. Ultimately, where a particular project might necessitate a particular method or mode of access, only a combination of approaches and resources is sufficient to provide adequate insights for book history more broadly.

Jared Gardner provides a good example of this need for multiple methods of reading archives in describing his work on the rise of newspaper comics at the turn of the twentieth century. After researching this aspect of print culture using online archives – including the 'underground electronic archive[s]' of individual collectors – he went to the material archive to find an illustration, only to discover that, 'In the "flesh", these early comics supplements were different than anything I could imagine', including in their size, colours and intertextual references to other parts of the paper.[24] Where the digital archives provided him with access to a breadth of materials – including materials that would otherwise have remained within non-institutional collections – researching the individual documents in the material archive offered him a different, and no less important, understanding of this feature of print culture.

NOTES

1. M. Foucault, *The Archaeology of Knowledge*. Trans. A. M. Sheridan Smith (New York: Pantheon, 1972); J. Derrida, *Archive Fever: A Freudian Impression*. Trans. E. Prenowitz (University of Chicago Press, 1996). For excellent summaries of these theoretical and critical debates see M. Manoff, 'Theories of the Archive from Across the Disciplines', *Portal: Libraries and the Academy* 4.1 (2004), 9–25 and F. Blouin and W. G. Rosenberg, *Processing the Past: Contesting Authority in History and the Archives* (Oxford University Press, 2011).

2. D. F. McKenzie, *Oral Culture, Literacy and Print in Early New Zealand: The Treaty of Waitangi* (Wellington: Victoria University Press, 1985), 45.
3. See, for example, J. L. W. West, *American Authors and the Literary Marketplace since 1900* (Philadelphia: University of Pennsylvania Press, 1988).
4. W. Wiegand, 'Libraries and the Invention of Information', in S. Eliot and J. Rose (eds.), *A Companion to the History of the Book* (Malden: Blackwell Publishing, 2007), 541.
5. J. L. W. West, *Making the Archives Talk: New and Selected Essays in Bibliography, Editing, and Book History* (Philadelphia: University of Pennsylvania Press, 2011).
6. West, *Making*, 2.
7. S. Eliot, 'Very Necessary but Not Quite Sufficient', *Book History* 5 (2002), 283.
8. James Raven, 'Britain, 1750–1850', in Franco Moretti (ed.), *The Novel*, Vol. 1: *History, Geography and Culture* (Princeton University Press, 2006), 430.
9. T. Dolin, 'First Steps Toward a History of the Mid-Victorian Novel in Colonial Australia', *Australian Literary Studies* 22.3 (2006), 273–93 and 'The Secret Reading Life of Us', in B. Matthews (ed.), *Readers, Writers, Publishers: Essays and Poems* (Canberra: Australian Academy of the Humanities, 2004), 115–33; S. Alston and J. Bowslaugh, 'A Statistical Analysis of Early Canadian Imprints', in P. L. Fleming, G. Gaillichan and Y. Lamonde (eds.), *History of the Book in Canada Volume One: Beginnings to 1840* (University of Toronto Press, 2004), 88–92; M. F. Suarez, 'Towards a Bibliometric Analysis of the Surviving Record, 1701–1800', in M. F. Suarez and M. L. Turner (eds.), *The Cambridge History of the Book in Britain*: Vol. V, *1695–1830* (Cambridge University Press, 2009), 39–65; K. Bode, *Reading by Numbers: Recalibrating the Literary Field* (London: Anthem Press, 2012).
10. P. Joshi, 'Quantitative Method, Literary History', *Book History* 5 (2002), 272; R. Darnton. 'Book Production in British India, 1850–1900', *Book History* 5 (2002), 256.
11. A. Weedon, 'The Uses of Quantification', in S. Eliot and J. Rose (eds.), *A Companion to the History of the Book* (Chichester: Wiley Blackwell, 2009), 33.
12. Joshi, 'Quantitative Method', 268.
13. Darnton, 'Book Production', 259; Joshi, 'Quantitative Method', 268. M. Robertson, 'The Archives of the Worshipful Company of Stationers', *The Indexer* 17.4 (October 1991), 269; Suarez, 'Towards', 40.
14. Darnton, 'Book Production', 250, 240; Weedon, 'The Uses', 39.
15. Eliot, 'Very Necessary', 289.
16. Weedon, 'The Uses'. For statistical skills see K. H. Jarausch and K. A. Hardy, *Quantitative Methods for Historians: A Guide to Research, Data, and Statistics* (Chapel Hill: The University of North Carolina Press, 1991); C. H. Feinstein and M. Thomas, *Making History Count: A Primer in Quantitative Methods for Historians* (Cambridge University Press, 2002); and G. R. Hawke, *Economics for Historians* (Cambridge University Press, 1980).
17. Suarez, 'Historiographical Problems', 165; St Clair, *Reading Nation*, 9.
18. R. Darnton, *The Forbidden Best-Sellers of Pre-Revolutionary France* (New York: W. W. Norton, 1995), 169; 'Book Production', 240.
19. Manoff, 'Theories', 10.

20. R. Darnton, *The Case for Books: Past, Present, and Future* (New York: Public Affairs, 2009), 75–7.
21. F. A. Black, B. H. MacDonald and J. M. W. Black, 'Geographic Information Systems: A New Research Method for Book History', *Book History* 1 (1998), 11–31; J. Drucker and B. Nowviskie, 'Speculative Computing: Aesthetic Provocations in Humanities Computing', in S. Schreibman, R. Siemens and J. Unsworth (eds.), *A Companion to Digital Humanities* (Oxford: Blackwell, 2004), available at: www.digitalhumanities.org/companion.
22. M. L. McGill, 'Remediating Whitman', *Publications of the Modern Language Association* 122.5 (2007), 1592.
23. Eliot 'Very Necessary', 284.
24. J. Gardner, 'A Technophile's Doubt', *American Periodicals: A Journal of History, Criticism, and Bibliography* 17.1 (2007), 123–5

14

MARY HAMMOND

Book history in the reading experience

Argentinian-born critic Alberto Manguel's optimistic view of reading as a universal practice, and of readers as all-powerful, addresses a set of questions which has informed a growing strand in book history research over the past two decades: the history of readers and reading:

> [I]n every case, it is the reader who reads the sense; it is the reader who grants or recognises in an object, place or event a certain possible readability; it is the reader who must attribute meaning to a system of signs, and then decipher it. We all read ourselves and the world around us in order to glimpse what and where we are. We read to understand, or to begin to understand. We cannot do but read. Reading, almost as much as breathing, is our essential function.[1]

Ever since Robert Darnton, one of the founders of book history, first argued in 1986 that 'Reading has a history', increasing numbers of scholars have been wrestling with the questions that writing such a history inevitably pose.[2] What do we actually mean by 'reading'? Is 'reading' a book the same thing as 'reading' a film, a play, a painting or a social situation, as Manguel implies? If we decide to take 'reading' in its most literal sense to mean active engagement with a text, then who during the act of reading is actually creating the meaning: the author, the reader or a combination of both? Does a book, a magazine, a manuscript or a document on a computer screen have any meaning (beyond its materiality as a bundle of paper and ink or an arrangement of pixels) *before* it has been scanned by a human eye (or a human finger) and processed by a human brain? What contribution does the editor, printer, publisher, illustrator, paper-maker, binder or software designer make? Is meaning the same in every case, for every reader? How does meaning – and the specific conditions which help to create it – change over time and space and across different media? And how can historians capture traces of reading experiences which may be – and usually are – ephemeral and unrecorded? This chapter aims to show some of the ways in which these important questions have been addressed.

The politics of reading

For Manguel the reader is in charge of meaning, and conceptually the act of reading extends beyond the trained deciphering of marks on a surface (or pixels on a screen) to the 'reading' of one's place in the world. Indeed, in Manguel's view these things are essentially codependent: the reading of a text draws on and grows out of this other, more basic part of human social behaviour, becoming almost as natural a function as breathing. But for most book historians, this is a problematic formulation. Book historians might continue to argue over whether the history of reading ought to encompass other 'reading'-related activities such as listening or viewing (which Manguel embraces quite easily), but most agree that reading in the book historical sense is not natural, but rather cultural. It implies an act of interpretation connected to a system of signs (writing, or other visual or physical mode of coding), which is in turn dependent on a set of learned behaviours and skills (reading). Learning to read, and being able to read competently, comfortably and openly, requires the presence of certain basic conditions such as access to education and to reading material, free time, good light, good eyesight or access to visual aids, and often the permission of whichever authority controls these things (whether a parent, a teacher, a priest or a set of laws.) The availability of these essential prerequisites for reading changes according to context and across time and space, and is often the site of considerable struggle; there have in fact been many moments in history when for some people the act of reading – far from being natural – is difficult, impossible, or even downright dangerous.

The nature of what reading potentially enables – primarily *knowledge*, whether political, religious, imaginative, scientific or sexual – is one common reason for this struggle. For example, a fourteenth-century person living in England and not versed in Latin was usually unable to read the Bible for him/herself. Indeed, the ecclesiastical reformer John Wycliffe's 1382–95 translations of parts of the Bible into vernacular Middle English, designed to enable ordinary readers to study scripture for themselves, were considered heretical by the Roman Catholic authorities then in power in the country. But ideas about appropriate access to knowledge change over time. A hundred years later religious power had shifted and with it notions about the function of reading: late fifteenth-century Protestant church-goers were positively encouraged through a number of contemporary works to read and interpret the bible for themselves as part of their devotional practice.[3] Similar examples of reading being controlled or prohibited continue throughout history. In the antebellum southern states of America it was against the law for slaves to learn to read, and those who were caught reading faced harsh punishments.

But we know from first-hand accounts that many African Americans in antebellum America (both North and South) did read, and that during and after the American Civil War of 1861–5 freed or runaway slaves still living in the South clubbed together to form secret impromptu schools and self-help literacy groups in the face of these threats.[4] The courage and determination which readers often demonstrate only serves to highlight the difficult – and clearly historically specific – conditions under which they are sometimes forced to operate.

The power that comes from knowledge is one issue. But the pleasure which reading provides has long been another bone of social contention. In many cultures, private reading was or still is a problem because it defies moral policing: no one can monitor a reader's thoughts, or control his or her emotional (or indeed physical) responses to a text. For this reason, in addition to restricting the access of certain social groups to literacy skills as a way of restricting their knowledge, reading materials have throughout history also often been controlled as a way of policing a reader's pleasure. One obvious result of this was the Obscene Publications Act of 1857 in England, which sought to control the spread of pornography. But there are other, more complex examples. Women have often been subjected to restrictions on their reading; even novels were deemed inappropriate for western women during much of the eighteenth and nineteenth centuries due to their perceived romantic (for which read sexual) content.[5] Similarly, in many developing countries there has long been and often still continues to be a marked disparity in literacy rates between men and women, and most experts acknowledge that this has as much to do with the ideology of separate spheres, which denies women access to knowledge and pleasure beyond their roles as wives and mothers, as with an economic system which finds investment in female education unsustainable.[6]

History offers many more examples of cultures whose populations are divided along ideological lines between 'readers' and 'non-readers'. Not all of these are motivated by the overt politics of race, state, gender or religion, either: many of us know people even today who deem reading a waste of time, or an effete pleasure inimical to more 'healthy' pursuits such as sport. Reading, then, is a practice which, while in many cultures it might be commonplace, is also always complicated. It can be highly political and contentious even in those same cultures where it seems to be the most natural. If we are to attempt to understand how reading and readers operate, we need to account for and try to record both the obvious and the more subtle and less visible forces exerted on different readers and their experiences, since these forces encompass issues of gender, generation, region, sexuality, class and even genre or medium as well as race, nation and faith. In return, we will find that the history of reading can tell us a lot about how we have constructed, interpreted, persuaded, informed, controlled, liberated or entertained ourselves in the past, and the means through which we have sought to do so. Investigating this history requires considerable detective work.

The problem of evidence

One of the problems facing historians of reading (something, intriguingly, that they share with historians of sexuality), is the paucity and unreliability of the evidence. Most reading acts in history remain unrecorded, unmarked or forgotten; many others have (for what should by now be obvious reasons) been deliberately hidden or falsified. There are exceptions, of course, and these tend to be recent, western and canonical: we know a lot about what famous eighteenth- and nineteenth-century figures such as William Ewart Gladstone or Charles Dickens read because we have many of their letters and records of the contents of their libraries. In fact, the nineteenth century is one of the eras for which we have a great deal of information even for less famous readers because it represents the great age of mass reading in the western world due to increasing literacy rates, technological advances in printing, and a developing curiosity about social and cultural habits which gave rise to the era of the survey. The survey method has produced some very useful data since, too: projects such as Mass Observation (UK, 1937 to the early 1950s) reveal a great deal about what ordinary people read and how and when and where they read in the first half of the twentieth century. Still more recently several scholars have carried out their own surveys of reading communities both in and beyond the West: see, for example, Jonathan Rose's book on working-class readers in the nineteenth- and twentieth-century UK, Janice Radway's work on twentieth-century American Book Clubs, the Australian Common Reader Project and Hanna Adoni and Hillel Nosek's survey of media consumption habits in twenty-first-century Israel.[7] In our own time, blogs and online purchaser reviews such as those logged by Amazon.com tell us a great deal about readers' responses to texts worldwide. But to find out what people in more ancient cultures read (and indeed what they meant by 'reading'), or what semi-literate or secret or just downright ordinary and therefore forgotten readers read in the past is a different matter altogether.

Historians of reading have used a variety of methods to capture, analyse and try to understand the reading experiences of the past, both the canonical and the quotidian. First, as readership historian Shafquat Towheed has remarked, many book historians agree that 'texts cannot be analysed outside the systems that surround them, be they social or mechanical'.[8] This means that before we approach the problem of a reader's engagement with a text, we must examine the social and cultural spaces in which the reading act is likely to have taken place. Manuscripts, scrolls, clay tablets, books, magazines, posters, cereal packets, exam papers, letters, graffiti, texts, blogs and email and everything else carrying sets of readable symbols are all defined by very different physical properties which determine the kinds of spaces and contexts in which they are likely to be encountered, and this materiality has an impact on the reading experience itself. These spaces and contexts are historically and geographically specific: an advertisement in an eighteenth-century gentleman's periodical (designed to be perused at leisure, usually while seated in a relatively quiet space such as a coffee house or library) is not at all the same thing as a neon sign in twenty-first-century Tokyo (designed to catch the eye of a hurried urban passer-by and impart its message at speed while competing for attention with myriad other appeals to the senses). Public or private libraries, places of worship, living rooms, bedrooms, cafes, classrooms, book clubs and reading groups, bathrooms, train carriages, the open streets – all these and many others offer reading venues in their own particular ways. Changes in communication practices – the advent of mobile phone technology, for example – also continually create new reading spaces and may even create new laws: texting is now ubiquitous in many countries, for example, but texting while driving is now an offence in most of them.

So what can 'reading' the spaces of reading tell us? Social historian Alistair Black's work on British Public Libraries since 1850 has been able to demonstrate that the design of public reading spaces in the modern British context created a form of social censorship, preventing readers from browsing and – through a culture of silence – trying to prevent them from discussing their reading in situ. But he also suggests that readers have always found ways around these strictures. They discuss their reading in whispers or by passing notes; where they are denied access to the shelves they discuss recommendations with colleagues, friends and family instead. And some readers – usually in groups – break the rules in the library, disrupting other readers and each other. Censorship itself may thus have created new ways of reading, and new communities of readers.[9] Similarly, Ian Desai has recently shown that while the Indian revolutionary Mahatma Gandhi was not in his youth a great reader, long years spent in British prisons exchanging books (and readers' annotations in books) with fellow prisoners changed his habits, so that 'jail sentences became opportunities for collective engagement with books and collaborative mobilization of the information and ideas within them … the colonial system itself helped circulate the very conditions, materials and people that ultimately were able to overcome its power'.[10]

Reading spaces continue to exert an influence today: the 2011 publishing phenomenon *Fifty Shades of Grey*, an erotic trilogy by E. L. James, has often been said to owe its early success to the discreet nature of e-readers, and its ongoing success to Twitter.com and internet blogs. Ever since the nineteenth century it has been acknowledged that reading in public spaces such as train carriages serves a number of social functions, from avoiding the gazes of predatory fellow-passengers to advertising one's literary taste. But the e-reader has recently enabled the hiding of a book's cover so that the passenger sitting opposite cannot judge your book – or, by extension, you – at all. There is no doubt a great deal of freedom in this (though perhaps also missed opportunities for making an impression). New social media technology has also enabled the sharing of tips, ideas and opinions about reading on an unprecedented scale. This has profoundly affected both the publishing industry and the reading experience: 'word of mouth' has gone viral. One problem for future reading historians, indeed, will be how to capture and analyse so much e-communication.

Fifty Shades of Grey's success as an e-book serves to indicate that a text's physical properties are also of prime importance in helping to determine the nature of reading experiences, and this is something else which readership historians look to as evidence. In the pre-printing-press era (prior to the seventh century in East Asia and the mid-fifteenth century in the West), manuscripts were painstakingly hand-scribed and sometimes coloured ('illuminated') and adorned with gold to indicate the devotion of a particular monastic order or the wealth and importance of a particular patron. The writers were craftsmen, the manuscripts expensive and the readers few and privileged. By the eighteenth century the price of producing many texts had come down and literacy rates were increasing, but books were still out of reach for many people and the gentleman's library in which volumes were bound identically in leather (often to match the owner's library furnishings or to illustrate his family's wealth) was still the norm. By the mid-nineteenth century efficient mass-production meant still wider reading audiences, and texts that were designed to appeal to a far more diverse range of reading tastes.[11] Publishers began to compete for these markets, and some of the key methods through which they did so were the use of advertising and the adoption of eye-catching book jackets. Books were not the only types of text to receive a material makeover either: the tabloid newspaper – which (not coincidentally) gets its name from the nineteenth-century invention of pre-measured medicine in tablet form – has since the 1880s been the archetypal traveller's medium, designed for those who want news or information quickly. The broadsheet, by contrast, always declared itself to be aimed at the more serious reader who had time to spread the paper out and digest smaller print and longer articles more slowly. It was only in 2004 that *The Times* – after more than 200 years as a broadsheet – decided to relaunch in tabloid format to reflect its readership's increasingly transient lifestyle. Advertising has undergone similar changes, with the text-heavy and image-light advertisements of the late eighteenth and early nineteenth centuries (a result of the high price of reproducing quality illustrations in this period) becoming increasingly image-based during the 1870s and afterwards. The effect of this on readers was profound: if in 1845 a reader stood at a train station and read the advertising posters he or she would have been confronted with a wall of small print which required time to process. In the twenty-first century, station advertising is increasingly a matter of deciphering clever images (sometimes entirely without text, or bearing only a brand name), or working out the relationship between an image and its associated, often cryptic, accompanying text.

We all read in different ways according to our – and our text's – physical, cultural and historical context. A text entitled *Pride and Prejudice: a Novel in Three Volumes* by The Author of *Sense and Sensibility*, first published without the author's name by T. Egerton of Whitehall in 1813 at the relatively high price of 18 shillings, is a very different thing from a modern scholarly edition of *Pride and Prejudice* by Jane Austen with an explanatory introduction, copious scholarly notes and essays in the back, at a price most students can afford. Is it the same novel? To a point. Is the experience of reading it the same in both cases? Not exactly. A reader living contemporaneously with Austen (let us call her Reader A), privileged enough to be able to read in 1813 when literacy rates were around 65 per cent for men and 50 per cent for women (with illiteracy highest among the poor), and wealthy enough to be able to afford 18 shillings for a novel (more than a week's wages for most people) or pay for a circulating library subscription, is not having the same experience as a student reader in the twenty-first century (let us call him Reader B) wading through a paperback copy while taking notes for the following day's class. Reader A is likely to have plenty of leisure time and a private comfortable place in which to read (unless she belongs to a household which discourages novel-reading, in which case she is likely to be reading in secret.) And she receives her copy in three volumes, possibly from a circulating library, which means she might have to wait a week or more for one of them.

By contrast, Reader B has a deadline, and he might never have picked up the book at all had it not been for the syllabus which insisted that he do so. It's also unlikely that he will be reading in secret (though his mates might conceivably rib him for reading an Austen novel, since – unlike in Austen's own day – she is now generally thought of as a women's author). While

Reader A is anxious to read the latest work by a talked-about anonymous novelist, Reader B is anxious to get a good grade. There might be (and those of us who teach literature hope there always is) pleasure involved for the reader in both reading experiences, but the pleasure is of a different type in each case. It is prompted by different impulses, and mediated through what (following French literary theorist Gérard Genette) have come to be known as the text's paratexts, by which we mean everything outside the text not usually constructed by the author such as a text's cover, size, font, introduction or preface, end- or footnotes, endpapers, colophon etc. All these help a reader to interpret the text in a particular way, regardless of the author's contribution. A cover illustration forms our expectations. The notes and introduction guide our interpretation of the text. The presence of the word 'Classic' on the spine or in the jacket blurb, or the knowledge that our friends will want our opinion on this new book the next time we see them, both feed in different ways into our sense of what and why we are reading. Reader A does not need footnotes to explain certain phrases or words that have lost or changed their meaning over time. Reader B probably does, but then he might also have seen a TV adaptation of the novel, or know that *Bridget Jones's Diary* is a spin-off of it. Even the presence or absence of an author's name (and reputation) helps to shape the reading experience, setting up our expectations based on what we already know, and what we hope to find out.

But how do we know that these sorts of things mattered to real historical readers, and in what ways? Sometimes readers leave us with useful records of their experiences which do mention paratextual details as significant. Perhaps unsurprisingly given his profession, Manguel is one such reader: he tells us that while he was growing up in the cities of Buenos Aires and Tel Aviv in the 1950s and 1960s, his ambassador father made a clear distinction between the leather-bound books he kept in his library and the cheap paperbacks he carelessly left outside on the patio table, from whence Manguel liked to rescue them 'as if they were stray cats'.[12] But few readers untrained in literary theory or book history would think to record such details. A text's material properties – cover, design, weight, dimensions, price and so forth – must be important, or publishers would not invest so much energy in them. Indeed, as one experienced contemporary literary agent put it, nowadays paratexts are explicitly designed to 'generate word of mouth' about a book in order to sell more copies of it.[13] But since for most readers these are unconscious influences and therefore go unrecorded, we must look for them elsewhere – namely in an educated assessment of the likely edition, provenance, condition and cultural significance of the text being read, as far as we are able to ascertain it. And that requires knowledge of book history more broadly: of print runs, genres, the specifics of publishing houses, tax and censorship laws, prices and papermaking and printing technologies, and as many other pertinent details as we can find. Analysis of the evidence of reading must always work in full partnership with other book history skill sets.

Recent sustained work on collecting the evidence of reading serves to illustrate this issue. Scholars working on the Open University's *Reading Experience Database 1450–1945* (RED) have spent several years painstakingly collecting evidence from all over the British Isles of real readers' experiences, and still more recently have helped to create sister databases in New Zealand, Australia and the Netherlands.[14] Drawn from diaries, autobiographies, letters, commonplace books and marginalia, these entries are useful in their own right. They certainly prove what a precarious process reading can be, as this entry dating from the 1850s suggests: 'After breakfast', the journeyman engineer Thomas Wright tells us, 'I had taken up the "Weekly Examiner", and was intent upon a more than usually scurrilous and illogical leading article, when the paper was suddenly snatched from my hands by my landlady, who sternly asked me if I thought reading a newspaper on a Sunday morning was proper behaviour in the house of a God-fearing couple.'[15] This is in itself an illuminating example of the politics of reading: we may with some justification ask ourselves what pleasure there was for Thomas in an article that he judged 'scurrilous and illogical', and we might also wonder what, in this period, was wrong with reading newspapers on a Sunday. Wright's memories also provide interesting evidence of the fact that not all reading experiences are sustained or complete – readers get interrupted, or they must read in chunks, or they must go back and reread to remind themselves of something.

But though RED contains over 30,000 fascinating entries like this, few of its included readers trouble to record the material properties of the works they discuss, or how they got hold of them. Readership historians need to be aware that collecting testimony is one thing, but the task of interpreting it is something else because the data are often incomplete. With this in mind, the RED team had to be conscious not only to ask the right questions, but also to fill in the blanks as necessary. RED's input forms contain fields for all sorts of data from title and genre of text through age, gender and socioeconomic group of the reader to date and place of reading experience. But in addition the data inputters have often had to make an educated guess at a text's publication date where it was not specified, to enter missing details about an individual reader where these can be ascertained from some other source and even to correct readers' sometimes erroneous memories of titles or authors' names in an historically sensitive manner as appropriate. In short, we have had to 'read' the facts behind the readers' stories, supplementing them using other types of evidence while also remaining faithful to their testimony.

There is another reason why we have to be cautious when analysing evidence drawn from real reading experiences: not only is the human memory a fallible thing, subject to error, but readers do not always tell the truth, or the same story to each listener. The politics of reading mobilizes a whole web of potential meanings which are by definition unstable, because the act of reading (and what we choose to read or to *say* we read) carries significance far beyond words on a page. For example, when asked by three different people – say, a teacher, a scientifically minded boyfriend and a best friend – to name her favourite book, a teenager might give three different answers: to the teacher she might say Dickens's *Great Expectations*, to the boyfriend she might say Stephen Hawking's *A Brief History of Time* and to her best friend she might claim Stephenie Meyer's *Twilight*. Or she might just as easily tell one or all of them that she despises reading and prefers music; readership historians also need to be sensitive to a potential reader's freedom *not* to read (or not to admit that she reads). Which of these is true of our teenager? We cannot know for sure; we must always analyse such data with one careful eye on the context in which it was provided. To give a more concrete example, when asked by the British right-wing tabloid the *Sun* to name his favourite childhood book, British Conservative Party Prime Minister David Cameron said it was *Our Island Story*, by H. E. Marshall: 'This is a children's history of Britain, from the Romans to the death of Queen Victoria', he explained, 'written in a way that captured my imagination and nurtured my interest in the history of our great nation.'[16] While acknowledging the possible truthfulness of Cameron's declared choice, a readership historian would be inclined (and wise) to consider that his explanation might reveal as much about his office and the political views of his readers as his literary taste.

Of course, readers do not always leave evidence of their reading in quite so fulsome or public a manner. They also note down mere titles of books they have read in private journals, discuss (and indeed argue about) their reading in letters to close friends and family and leave notes or scribbles in books for their own purposes. RED collects evidence from all of these sources and they have been just as illuminating as those taken from memoirs, though they bring their own problems too. Entries such as the one below come from marginal notes found in a book, and they indicate that in this case the reader (one Jon Drummond Erskine, born 1776 in Scotland and later to become a landowner in India) not only took his reading very seriously, but was able to write as well as read in more than one language. The entry describes: 'Some pencil marks and marginal MS notes throughout the text. Generally they highlight points of grammar or translation, mostly in English but at least one is in Persian (p. 132).'[17] In this case, we know who the scribbler was. But scribbles are often left anonymously, at an unspecified period, for unspecified reasons. In some situations, such as while studying texts in an archive, it is possible to date or narrow down the source of the marginalia based on the handwriting, the text's provenance (the presence of a bookplate bearing an owner's name, for example), and/or the care with which it has been policed in its current location (scribbling in books after they find their way into an archive being generally frowned upon). But in less closely monitored contexts (such as in a contemporary public library, or when purchasing from a second-hand website or store) it is usually impossible to tell when the marks were made, beyond noting that it must have been before the present moment of their discovery. These anonymous marks can be useful in themselves: they can tell us, for one thing, that a particular book was not just borrowed (or bought, or given as a present), but that it was actually quite carefully engaged with by a reader. This is something that sales figures and library borrowing records alone cannot do (useful as they are in other ways).

Readership historians usually want proof that a text has actually made it out of the seller's wrapper or off the pile of library books by the bed, that it has been scanned by a reader's eyes and processed by a reader's brain, whether in whole or in part. Marginalia provide that proof. In some cases marginalia can do more than that: sometimes readers' notes are quite comprehensive, or quite specific, and they can help us to understand how at least one person interpreted a text. But even the least specific or the most basic marginalia can also indicate patterns or trends. As Heather Jackson – an expert in eighteenth-century marginalia – has demonstrated, while many books from the Romantic period contain the owner's bookplate or other identifying marks (so we know whose marginalia we are looking at and when it is likely to have been written) even those that do not are useful since the very prevalence and extent of marginalia in them is unusual by modern standards and demonstrates how reading practices change over time. As she explains, while in many periods and cultures it is normal practice to keep a book pristine (as Manguel's father did with his leather-bound library copies in twentieth-century Buenos Aires), based on the practice's prevalence, to the eighteenth-century reader scribbling in the margins even of an expensive leather-bound book 'must have felt like a natural thing to do'.[18] Still, Jackson is careful to situate her analysis of this practice in the context of broader changes in the industrial and social landscapes. In this case, her theory is supported by the material evidence in many eighteenth-century books of blank spaces left by publishers for readers' comments, and of discussions between eighteenth-century readers themselves. Jackson's work reminds us that studying marginalia on its own, like collecting readers' testimonies, is akin to reading a book with half its pages missing. We must keep searching if we want to know the full story.

The problem of evidence is complicated still further when we want to compare reading experiences over time, since different conditions for reading and for preserving the evidence of reading prevail in different temporal and national contexts. Some climates are better than others for preservation purposes: the Middle Eastern climate is good, but that of India is not. Preservation can also be a result of the choice of materials: parchment generally survives better than papyrus, for example. Equally, sometimes preservation comes down to luck: volcanic ash in Herculaneum preserved some of the contents of one Roman library, while Second World War bombing destroyed many publishers' and booksellers' records in London. But generally speaking, scarcity of evidence is usually a result of there being comparatively few readers and texts in a given culture, and such scarcity is always compounded by age. As a result, compared with the evidence available from the eighteenth century onwards, there is relatively little available for ancient cultures, so what there is requires particularly careful analysis.

The discovery of the Rosetta Stone on the west bank of the Nile in 1799 is a good example of the uses to which writing traces may be put. Famously, because the Rosetta Stone carries roughly the same proclamation in three different types of script – Ancient Egyptian hieroglyphs, Middle Demotic script and Ancient Greek – early nineteenth-century scholars who knew Greek were able to teach themselves to decipher hieroglyphs for the first time (and what a reading experience that must have been!). But the presence of the same message in three languages also indicates a historically specific writing and reading context. The Stone was carved in about 196 BCE in a fraught bi-cultural society (the Ptolemaic Kingdom, 330–32 BCE) whose political decrees had to appeal equally to both the Greek and the Egyptian cultures coexisting uneasily under Ptolemaic rule. The Stone also demonstrates language in transition and thus a particularly skilled readership: the established Middle Demotic language was in the process of being replaced by Ancient Greek as the lingua franca of law and politics. Building on this evidence, recent scholarly work has been able to explore the ways in which the power struggle between these different languages and cultures continued to be enacted for readers through other types of text, including poetry.[19] Many reading contexts offer similar complexities and sometimes, as here, we have to build up a picture of reading experiences from very little evidence, inferring the reading act solely from the fragments accessible to us.

Theoretical approaches

Thus far we have examined historical acts of reading through traces inscribed on stones, in the margins and on the covers of books, in the spaces where reading took place and in readers' own accounts of their practices. Many book historians also set great store by economics and the material evidence of printing and distribution such as print runs, pricing, editions, book sales, library records, fan letters and educational practices. All of these can be invaluable in helping us to build up a picture of how, what, where and when readers read in the past and, as I have shown, they can often help fill in some of the blanks left by readers' own testimonies. But these sorts of empirical approaches are not the only ways in which reading has been examined and understood. They were in fact predated by theories of reading which, emerging in Europe and the US in the 1960s and 1970s and known as 'reader-response criticism', sought to address the heavily author and text-based trend in literary studies which had prevailed there throughout the first half of the twentieth century. These theories can be extremely useful to readership historians as a way of supporting an understanding of reading acts, particularly where the evidence for them is scarce.

One of the first challenges to the idea that meaning is controlled exclusively by the author came from French critic Roland Barthes, who complained that much contemporary criticism tended to privilege the author as the sole purveyor of meaning and assume that the text serves merely as a means to understand that author's mental processes. Feeling that this approach served to glorify the literary critic doing the interpreting rather than aid in an understanding of the work, he offered an alternative model in which writing, rather than occurring in a vacuum and being the product of individual genius, can be seen instead as 'a tissue of quotations drawn from the innumerable centres of culture'.[20] This new emphasis on situating a text in culture and history was to have significant impact on contemporary critics who saw it as offering a new way of thinking about the act of textual interpretation itself. If a text is not the product of individual genius but part of an exchange of memories, ideas and stories ('quotations') drawn from many different historical and geographical locations, then a reader will need a particular set of competencies in order to understand it fully. In turn, this means that every reader will read the same text differently according to his or her particular experience – and that some will understand it more fully than others. This is the argument of the German critic Wolfgang Iser, who identified for the first time the work that a reader has to do to make sense of a text.[21] For Iser, every text contains gaps which a reader must fill in. Some gaps are placed there by the author as part of the work's structural strategy: crime fiction is an obvious example of a genre in which filling in the gaps (working out 'whodunnit') is a large part of the pleasure. But other gaps might be a result of different forces not put there deliberately by the author, but constituting nonetheless a crucial part of the reading experience. These might include the limits of the reader's own vocabulary (perhaps s/he doesn't understand all the words or concepts used so must skip them, or create a substitute), or the lapse of time which renders certain words or concepts difficult for the untrained reader to grasp. The earlier example of a nineteenth-century reader of Austen's *Pride and Prejudice* having contemporary knowledge of the book's setting and language which might be lost on a twenty-first-century reader is a case in point.

Iser's radical model of every reader as an individual and every reading experience as unique has been influential, and it represented a much-needed critical move away from the tyranny of approaches which claimed that an essential, stable meaning is always located in the text. But it came to be challenged by the American critic Stanley Fish, who pointed out that while some parts of reading might indeed be unique to the individual, certain groups of readers – which he called 'interpretive communities' – might also interpret other aspects collectively as a result of their social positioning (their age, gender, class, nationality, education, income bracket, beliefs etc.).[22] Readership historians have found this concept extremely useful as a way of accounting for shared opinions among and relative reading competencies between certain groups. Readers of the bible who use it to express an affiliation to a particular denomination are a clear example of this, but there are many others; indeed, the idea of an 'interpretive community' can help to explain why some people reject or embrace certain interpretations or types of text, and even why a highly educated writer like Manguel, in whose family books were ubiquitous, might see reading as analogous to breathing.

Building on these foundational texts which turned the critical spotlight back on the reader, numerous scholars have since developed new critical and theoretical models. One such approach is provided by linguists Daniel Allington and Joan Swan, who have demonstrated that textual interpretation is best analysed as a mediated experience, always occurring as a result of consultation (however subliminal) with other readers.[23] This emphasis on readers as immutably social beings invites us to pay closer attention to the analysis of their cultural situations, and may even help us to get around the problem of the unreliability of individual reader testimony. Other researchers working outside the humanities, such as cognitive neuroscientist Stanislas Dehaene, have gone far beyond textual evidence and demonstrated the effect of reading on the human brain at the cellular level.[24] The possibilities that this work opens up are exciting indeed, though at present it is unclear whether such physical changes leave traces permanent enough for scholars to analyse retrospectively, or what they might be able to tell us if they do.

The field of reading history is still growing. New evidence is being uncovered all the time, and newer ways of interpreting it are continually being offered. What is unlikely to change, though, is the necessity to read this

Book history in the reading experience

evidence carefully, relationally and holistically. Readers are constituted in, through and by the cultures they inhabit, and the traces they leave are of a practice that is variously private and public, sacred and profane, individual and social, enjoyable and dutiful – and many other things, each according to its context. We must remain alert to the fact that the history of reading, like the history of sex, is anything but an open book.

NOTES

1. A. Manguel, *A History of Reading* (London and New York: Penguin, 1997), 7.
2. R. Darnton, 'First Steps Toward a History of Reading', in *The Kiss of Lamourette: Reflections in Cultural History* (New York: W. W. Norton and Co., 1990), 155. First published in *Australian Journal of French Studies* 23 (1986), 5–30.
3. W. R. Owens, 'Modes of Bible Reading in Early Modern England', in S. Towheed and W. R. Owens (eds.), *The History of Reading Vol. I: International Perspectives, c.1500–1990* (Basingstoke: Palgrave Macmillan, 2011), 34.
4. B. Hochman, *'Uncle Tom's Cabin' and the Reading Revolution: Race, Literacy, Childhood and Fiction, 1851–1911* (Amherst: University of Massachusetts Press, 2011); H. A. Williams, *Self-Taught: African American Education in Slavery and Freedom* (Chapel Hill: University of North Carolina Press, 2005).
5. B. Jack, *The Woman Reader* (New Haven: Yale University Press, 2012); J. Pearson, *Women's Reading in Britain 1750–1834: a Dangerous Recreation* (Cambridge University Press, 1999) and K. Flint *The Woman Reader 1837–1914* (Oxford University Press, 1995).
6. E. M. King and M. A. Hill (eds.), *Women's Education in Developing Countries: Barriers, Benefits, and Policies* (Published for The World Bank. Baltimore: The Johns Hopkins University Press, 1993), 26.
7. J. Rose, *The Intellectual Life of the British Working Classes* (New Haven: Yale University Press, 2001); J. Radway, *A Feeling for Books: the Book of the Month Club, Literary Taste, and Middle-Class Desire* (Chapel Hill: University of North Carolina Press, 1997); www.australiancommonreader.com; H. Adoni and H. Nossek, 'Between the Book and the Reader: The Uses of Reading for the Gratification of Personal Psychosocial Needs', in R. Crone and S. Towheed (eds.), *The History of Reading Vol. III: Methods, Strategies, Tactics* (Basingstoke: Palgrave Macmillan, 2011), 49–65.
8. S. Towheed, 'Introduction', in Crone and Towheed (eds.), *The History of Reading Vol. III*, 10.
9. A. Black, with S. Pepper and K. Bagshaw, *Books, Buildings and Social Engineering: Early Public Libraries in Britain from Past to Present* (Aldershot: Ashgate, 2009).
10. I. Desai, 'Books Behind Bars: Mahatma Gandhi's Community of Captive Readers', in S. Towheed and W. R. Owens (eds.), *The History of Reading Vol. I: International Perspectives, c.1500–1990* (Basingstoke: Palgrave Macmillan, 2011), 178–9.
11. S. Eliot, 'From Expensive and Few to Cheap and Many: the British Book Market 1800–1890', in S. Eliot and J. Rose (eds.), *A Companion to the History of the Book* (Oxford: Blackwell, 2007), 291–302.

12. Manguel, *A History*, 141.
13. Email exchange with agent Peter Straus of Rogers, Coleridge and White Literary Agency, UK, 14 November 2012.
14. See www.open.ac.uk/Arts/RED.
15. T. Wright, *Some Habits and Customs of the Working Classes* (London, 1867), 226–7, available at www.open.ac.uk/Arts/reading/UK/record_details.php?id=7922, accessed 7 November 2012.
16. See www.thesun.co.uk/sol/homepage/features/2349004/Celebrities-from-Gordon-Brown-to-Chris-Tarrant-on-their-favourite-book.html?pageNo=5.
17. Marginalia by J. D. Erskine, in W. Jones, *A Grammar of the Persian Language* (London: printed by W. and J. Jones, 1783), 132, available at www.open.ac.uk/Arts/reading/UK/record_details.php?id=6957, accessed 6 November 2012.
18. H. J. Jackson, *Romantic Readers: the Evidence of Marginalia* (New Haven and London: Yale University Press, 2005), 61.
19. S. Stephens, *Seeing Double: Intercultural Poetics in Ptolemaic Alexandria* (Berkeley and Los Angeles: University of California Press, 2003).
20. R. Barthes, 'The Death of the Author', first published 1967; reprinted in *Image-Music-Text*, trans. S. Heath (New York: Hill and Wang, 1977).
21. W. Iser, 'Interaction between Text and Reader', first published 1970; reprinted in D. Finkelstein and A. McCleery (eds.), *The Book History Reader*, 2nd edn (New York: Routledge, 2006), 291–6.
22. S. Fish, 'Interpreting the Variorum', first published 1976; reprinted in Finkelstein and McCleery (eds.), *The Book History Reader*, 2nd edn, 450–8.
23. D. Allington and J. Swan, 'The Mediation of Response: A Critical Approach to Individual and Group Reading Practices', in R. Crone and S. Towheed (eds.), *The History of Reading Volume 3*.
24. S. Dehaene, *Reading in the Brain* (London and New York: Penguin, 2009), and S. Dehaene, F. Pegado, L. W. Braga, P. Ventura, G. N. Filho *et al.*, 'How Learning to Read Changes the Cortical Networks for Vision and Language', *Science* 330: 6009 (3 December 2010), 1359–64.

15

LESLIE HOWSAM

Book history in the classroom

Many scholars whose research includes the history of the book have lately become committed to transferring their knowledge to a new generation of learners. This is a recent phenomenon: only since about the turn of the millennium has a topic called 'book history' been offered to undergraduates. In earlier decades, a handful of advanced students were instructed in what was then identified as bibliography – and only in large research universities in Europe and North America enjoying long traditions of literary scholarship and furnished with rich collections of rare books and manuscripts. Many of that older generation of students were reluctant learners, forced into mandatory studies construed as a standard introduction to literary scholarship. Only a few became inspired to embrace bibliographical knowledge for its own sake, whether in a literary, a library or another setting. Book-history students of the twenty-first century, however, may have little or no knowledge of literary or historical scholarship; perhaps they even lack the experience of reading for pleasure; their college and university libraries may own very few old and rare books – indeed, access to rare books may even be limited to an image on the internet. Far from being experienced as limitations, such challenges are intellectually liberating, allowing instructors and students to think in fundamental ways about what they mean by the book, its history and its place in the world where they have grown up.

Approaches vary widely according to discipline, nationality and chronological focus, and from the ambitious to the prosaic, but it is possible to identify some connecting themes, and some of the inherent challenges and opportunities. This chapter argues that the study of the history and culture of the book offers a valuable way to help students to understand some key institutions of contemporary society – the media of communication, the libraries, the literature and the journalism. So-called 'digital natives', those who were born into an internet world, may benefit especially but so will 'digital immigrants', who remember arriving there and the journey it entailed. Learners of both kinds find the history of the book attractive because it puts the digital communications and 'new media' with which they are familiar into juxtaposition with 'old' media and their development over centuries.

At its most ambitious, the history of the book has the potential to serve as framework for a global history of knowledge and culture. The book's long trajectory and dramatic turning points (marks on clay, codex, moveable type, steam and stereotype, paperback, competition with broadcast media, pixels on screen) provide a coherent narrative spine for introducing transnational history. Encompassing all aspects of the written record, but also taking the historical nature of communication as its very subject, the book embraces a chronology coterminous with the recorded history of humankind. And even though it takes the written record as its subject, the study of book history nevertheless also includes aspects of oral culture: scholarship in the long history of the book can scarcely avoid interrogating the ways in which knowledge and stories have passed between the traditions of the spoken word and those of inscription, handwriting, printing and digital media. It has a built-in point of view from which interpretations can be critically engaged: the recognition that readers, the book trade and writers share experience, and compete for authority, in overlapping networks of text and context, material form and interpretation. Hence, for example, a Eurocentric bias is difficult to sustain in the face of Asia's precedence in the art of printing with moveable types; but equally, as the historian Christopher Reed's research demonstrates, mechanized printing in nineteenth-century Shanghai functioned in a world that was proudly conscious of that long-ago primacy.[1]

Furthermore, and again at its most ambitious, the history of the book has the potential to frame a materialist approach to the study of written texts. In this teaching and learning scenario, the artistic contribution of authors is not denied, but the student learns how to engage critically with the myth of authorial genius.[2] Literary scholars who are book historians interrogate the material nature of the novels, poems and essays whose aesthetic and formal nature has been their discipline's primary concern. Students can use these scholarly studies as entry points to a sometimes daunting body of knowledge, the canon (and the counter-canons) of literary works. To engage with textual studies is to think seriously about the forensic traces that are left behind by printers, editors, designers, publishers and other collaborators in the disposition of an author's words on the pages of multiple and variant editions of a work. Because it shows how the text became entangled in its material carrier, book history provides a framework, or point of view, that can highlight a literary work's textuality. Another important contribution is the way in which the history of the book puts literary canonicity itself into perspective. They learn that the books judged to be the 'best' or 'most representative' works of a national heritage may have been published by a firm working closely with that nation's critical establishment.[3]

In studies of culture and communication, meanwhile, the history of the book has the potential to frame the contemporary media of internet, film, television and radio in a richer theoretical context. Journalism and other forms of presentation (documentaries, features, phone-in commentary and feedback) are merely the latest manifestations of news delivery, and contemporary broadcast and social media are successors to the print, manuscript and oral technologies that worked in specific past societies. Popular culture's sophisticated awareness of how film-makers adapt texts for the screen can be extrapolated to an understanding of how Victorian novels that appeared to be the single-handed creation of a literary genius were actually the result of editor–author collaboration, or hard-fought compromise, or perhaps began with an editorial commission.[4] A critical understanding of the marketing of best-sellers, book prizes and cinema tie-ins can help us understand the way in which cultural artefacts are created and manipulated.

At its most prosaic, however, the history of the book is just another module (or course of study, or programme) appearing on the curriculum of a school, college or university and presenting learners with the possibility of incorporating its subject matter into their education. Such a listing could be intriguing, but it might also be confusing. The book: what kind of history is that? What country or time period, or which national literature, does it cover? How will the materials and the assignments involved relate to my earlier experiences of studying and learning? Is this for me? Sometimes the initial response will be one of engaged curiosity. In other cases, though, students may question the relevance of studying the history of an object which has, after all, been declared dead, and one about which their own parents, friends and teachers may have strong opinions, strongly expressed.

In other words, the history of the book comes with a good deal of cultural baggage which has to be unpacked before the subject's intellectual and pedagogical potential can be fully realized in the context of classroom encounters with material books, and with the scholarship of book historians. Widespread propaganda about digitization and e-books, combined with widespread misunderstanding about the impact of print technology on western culture in earlier centuries, means that instructors have to help students unlearn what they think they already know – about 'the book' and about 'history' – in order to introduce new and compelling perspectives.

Unlearning what 'everyone knows' about the book in history

At the end of 1999, the German printer Johannes Gutenberg was named 'Man of the Millennium' by *Time Magazine*, for his contributions to European civilization. For most people around that time, however, a simpler fact prevailed: Gutenberg had invented the printing press. To many European and North American adults who had grown up in the late twentieth and early twenty-first centuries, the celebration of Gutenberg's achievement was entirely understandable. It made sense not only of the past, but of their own present day. The superstition-racked middle ages, where monks controlled knowledge and laboriously reproduced manuscripts by hand, seemed to have ended abruptly. And modern, rational enlightened thought, widely circulating among open-minded thinkers and from them to avid readers and learners, appeared to have begun. A technology that felt at least as consequential as gunpowder, the compass or the internal combustion engine seemed to have changed the world. A new communication medium, remarkably analogous to the internet, demonstrated that even old words and phrases appeared to have taken on new meanings when they were repurposed in new formats. How could it be a coincidence that geographical innovation and religious reform, in the persons of Christopher Columbus and Martin Luther, had seized on this new media technology of the fifteenth century? Literacy itself seemed to have been enabled by this new technology to facilitate reading. Around 2,000 writers, artists and thinkers were seizing upon the possibilities of a world wide web to express ideas that appeared to vibrate in unison with the technology in which they were expressed, and the millennium seemed to belong to Gutenberg. Although scholars have nuanced or disproved every aspect of this compelling story, it persists in the popular media and even in school and university textbooks. It is the task of the history of the book to displace the myth of print's transformation of European culture, in favour of a narrative which is not only more accurate, but also much more relevant for our time.

To unlearn the popular, compelling and fundamentally flawed history of the book, it is important for students to be persuaded to abandon some comfortable shibboleths:

First, the technology of printing did not substitute textual stability for the instability of manuscripts by introducing the characteristics of fixity and accuracy – and hence did not change texts in a fundamental way so as to enable modern forms of knowledge and of literary authorship in Europe. This myth has been challenged by numerous scholars, but their counter-narrative has not yet entered the popular culture. It's unlikely that a feature film or blockbuster novel will dispel the Gutenberg myth; instead, the task of doing so will remain among the chief objectives of the book-history curriculum.

Second, the book – as understood historically – does not always take the iconic material form of a set of leaves made of paper printed on both sides, bound together along one edge and protected by a hard or soft cover. Technically known as the codex, what is familiarly called 'the book' is only one of many forms in use now and in the past. Books can be made of other materials, and their texts can take other forms. As for the history of the book, a definition in terms of the codex is even less satisfactory. The academic term is even more capacious than the generic one – book history is a way of thinking about how people have given material form to knowledge and stories, in the past and in our own time. Even within the short history of printing, book history embraces the study of periodicals, newspapers and ephemera as well as the bound codex volumes we now associate with the terminology.

A third point is that the textual form of 'the book' includes more genres, literary forms and subject matters than most commentators seem to assume. Modern imaginations, shaped by European, North American or Australasian education systems, and reinforced by the experience of retail bookstores, often overlook the many other printed works on the market. One such is sacred books, whose historicity and commercial value can be overlooked because the authorship is attributed to divine and historic figures, so that to a superficial observer, the vagaries of the book trade seem to have had no place. Another is the use of the codex form for managing large amounts of information, in such genres as the telephone directory and the railway timetable.[5]

Fourthly, the computer and internet combined have not managed to bring about the death of the book, any more than literary theory has literally caused that of the author. Like earlier technologies before them, these new ways of putting words in front of the eyes and minds of readers are unsettling. We do not yet know whether or not they are transformative.

And finally, it will be necessary to unlearn the habit of characterizing one society or another's means of communication in terms of a 'print culture' without offering a deep knowledge of how printers (later publishers), and retail booksellers and their customers, actually operated and how they themselves conceptualized what they were doing. Both writers and readers were connected with, and by, the books and periodicals they read – and so, more concretely, were the men and women of the book trades. But given our knowledge that the texts people were reading, buying and selling, writing and printing were inherently variable, it is impossible to speak of a unified public sphere, any more than to use 'print' culture as a blanket term.

Resources for teaching and learning the history of the book

This chapter does not aim to prescribe how the history of the book should be taught, or to recount systematically how it is actually taught in particular classrooms.[6] Pedagogy varies too much for it to be practicable to do so, depending as it does upon the instructor's or the institution's definition of 'book' and their approach to its history. Book history is taught and studied in different ways in various nations and institutions, and differently again from the perspectives of several academic disciplines and interdisciplinary configurations. Such practical matters as the instructor's research period and specialty, or the availability of material resources, necessarily shape any given curriculum. Master classes, or concentrated, skill-dedicated workshops in a Rare Book School, will be different again. Rather, the purpose of this chapter is to acknowledge some of the challenges inherent in the enterprise, to offer some ideas about what the learning objectives of such courses, modules or workshops might include and to discuss some possible kinds of resources and approaches.

An undergraduate course, or degree, in English does not prepare the holder to work as a qualified literary critic, and nor do a few courses in history comprise the education of an archival researcher. Further, professional, training is needed, but the initial degree does prepare its holder to be a good citizen and a well-rounded person. The same is true of the history of the book. Many of the skills of book historians are specialized, and cannot possibly be taught in a period of three or four months (or six or eight months) to undergraduates in a conventional curriculum. For some bibliographical research, such skills as paleography, diplomatics and collation are indispensable, but difficult to acquire. However it is possible to gain a broad appreciation of the history of the book, and even of some of its more esoteric knowledge, without aspiring to be an expert. Despite the importance of materiality to the field of study, the intellectual skills associated with book history can be taught without recourse to any specialized materials at all. The conventional methods of reading, thinking, discussing and responding in writing are as applicable to this as to any other subject, and need not even be framed as 'book history'. A course in American literature, for example, could fruitfully draw upon numerous articles and chapters, and use Ronald J. Zboray and Mary Saracino Zboray's *Literary Dollars and Social Sense: A People's History of the Mass Market Book* (2005) for the background.

For a course in the interdisciplinary history of the book, however, a set of introductory chapters or readings (such as the ones in this volume) can sketch a useful chronology and introduce broad general concepts. A number of textbooks and readers are on the market. Using such a work as a starting point, the instructor is in a position to add more specialized readings, which can be connected to research assignments. Every instructor will have his or her own preferred books and articles, the ones that feel comfortably teachable. From a learner's point of view, selected readings should address issues that reiterate the objectives of the course in such a way that the experience makes sense as a whole. For example, an opportunity might be provided to read and review a scholarly monograph whose subject is a single powerful book. Each work of this kind offers its own narrative of production and reception, so that the general message of book history is reinforced by the specific instance. Examples include James Secord's *Victorian Sensation: The Extraordinary Publication, Reception, and Secret Authorship of Vestiges of the Natural History of Creation* (2000) and Patricia Coit Murphy's *What A Book Can Do: The Publication and Reception of Silent Spring* (2005). Such works tell a graphic story about more than the intellectual, political and social impact of a work; they also recount and analyse its authorship, publishing and reading.

In some institutional settings, there is room for creative and exploratory approaches to teaching the history of the book, even without invoking specialized techniques or inaccessible materials. An instructor who has introduced a chronological and thematic outline of the general tenets of book history could branch out by assigning students to read 'bibliofictions' – novels where the materiality and the mingled cultural and commercial nature of books are intrinsic to the plot. The students are assigned to read books about books, but this time fictions rather than histories. Geraldine Brooks's *People of the Book* (2008) is only one of dozens of examples. This approach could easily be made multimedia by incorporating excerpts from films (Jean-Jacques Annaud's 1986 *The Name of the Rose* or *84 Charing Cross Road*, directed by David Jones in 1986) and television (Dylan Moran's and Graham Linehan's *Black Books*, broadcast in Britain 2000–4). The examples offered here are intentionally popular and accessible, but the approach could be varied to draw out the bibliographical themes in canonical literature (Gissing's *New Grub Street* is but one example). Tests and assignments would demonstrate to what extent students had understood the real-life themes underlying various fictional treatments.

Paradoxically, one of the best places to study the history of books in depth may be the internet. Students accustomed to hearing some teachers' disdain for Wikipedia.org, and aware of professorial anxieties about the use of online essay banks for systematic cheating, may be surprised to find that a number of humanities academics have spent their working lives side by side with software programmers. They will learn that a number of scholars were inspired early in the life of the internet, by the possibilities inherent in systematically demonstrating the diversity of certain books – along with their beauty, their complexity and something of their history. Two of the earliest such projects, those addressing themselves to the multimedia artists William Blake and Dante Gabriel Rossetti, have designated themselves as 'hypermedia archives'. Online resources can also be used to illustrate bindings, page designs and other features of rare books in special collections around the world, as well as to demonstrate how a hand press works, or how type is set in a composing stick.

Assignments can be devised to make pedagogical use of an institutional library's subscriptions to online research databases, and also to deal with the inevitable limitations of students' knowledge. Students often find themselves thwarted when asked to take advantage of the rich range of online resources for studying the history of the book, only to discover that their particular question remains unanswered by scholars, or is too complex to tackle within the limits of an assignment. They may not know that considerable knowledge exists only in scholarly monographs and printed reference works. They may still be uncertain about what the subject entails, or lack the background knowledge necessary to identify a personal interest. One answer to this situation is for the instructor to construct a set of assignments, with print and digital materials packaged expressly to provide an experience of reading texts and images in their original form (or a digitized version of that form), but with the primary materials supported by appropriate secondary and tertiary sources.

Despite the range of materials available for learning about the history of books by reading about it, however, an education in the subject should always include some opportunity for students to get their hands on some genuinely old and rare books. Any librarian who has an interest in special collections and rarities is a natural collaborator for the instructor in a course in the history of books. In many institutions, library and information professionals are keen to become involved in the pedagogical project, and embrace the opportunity to participate in the teaching of book history classes. Their contribution will probably take place inside the library, of course, where students' encounters with their bibliographical heritage can be carefully monitored even while being kindled. The instructor can circumvent this necessary limitation, however, if he or she has a small budget for purchasing a few copies of old – but not rare or valuable – books for classroom purposes. The opportunity to dissect a book has been documented by a number of classes as among the most memorable aspects of their education.[7] The lessons that some old books are not rare, and can be ripped apart in the interests of learning (and conversely that some rare books are not old and must be preserved in the interests of future scholarship) are some of the most important outcomes of any course in the history of the book.

The librarian is not the only potential collaborator for the teacher of book history. Historians often find teaching partners in the English department, while professors of English literature have been known to discover a shared interest in the material book among their colleagues who teach French or Italian studies. Nor should instructors limit their search for colleagues to their own campus. A community where institutions of higher learning lack a bibliographical press can probably find a local craft printer, bookbinder, marbler or papermaker willing to offer a guest lecture, or to receive student visits and entertain questions. Local antiquarian and second-hand booksellers are not only a fount of knowledge, but also the purveyors of inexpensive books for student projects. A small press publisher, a freelance editor or a local bookseller might be pleased to give an occasional lecture. Book collectors are another set of extraordinarily well-informed book people, and many of them are generous and anxious to pass some of their knowledge on to a younger generation. Among visual artists, the 'Book Arts', which currently flourish among practitioners attuned to the changing role of media in their own work, offer another source of expertise which can be shared with students.

Perhaps the ideal collaborator – or indeed instructor – for the history of books is a handpress printer oriented to pedagogy and managing a bibliographical press. The lesson that the book is an object which is also a text is one that can be learned by the body, as the learner sets up a text on a typographer's composing stick and pulls the bar of the platen press or the handle of the cylinder proofing press to create an object in multiple copies. The opportunity to learn the rudiments of the printer's craft in practice is to be found in only a handful of universities and libraries. Printer and scholar Noel Waite notes that 'In the 1960s several "bibliographical" presses were established by those wishing, among other things, to teach the methods of textual transmission in the medium of print as practised in the handpress era. Although these presses were attached to institutions of learning, they were run by enthusiasts, whose productions went beyond the call of duty'. A bibliographical press has been further defined as 'a workshop or laboratory which is carried on chiefly for the purpose of demonstrating and investigating the printing techniques of the past by means of setting type by hand, and of printing from it on a simple press'.[8] This kind of press might print everything from facsimile pamphlets to wedding invitations, but its purpose is pedagogical, not commercial. The university or library where a bibliographical press is installed has a valuable experience to offer students, one well worth the necessity for employing a competent printer and making room for the equipment and supplies.

Learning the history of the book with the body as well as the mind is not confined to the printing shop. It happens in the library, too, or wherever there is an opportunity for people to touch, smell and investigate old books:

handling books leads to a sensory and emotional understanding that does not occur in many other fields of study. The rigorously scholarly instructor will, no doubt, aim to keep the study of the book and its history on an austerely academic and even scientific level. But it is impossible to deny altogether the ineffable, almost spiritual dimension that pervades the study of books and periodicals in past and present cultures. It is a routine occurrence in the classroom for a few students to feel very strongly indeed about their visit to the special collection library, or their opportunity to pull on the bar of an iron press. There is a tactile aspect to the history of the book that seems to connect directly to human emotions. The materiality of a written document surviving from the past is one element. The fact that this material object carries a written text laden with meaning is another, especially when the student can see how that meaning is molded and enhanced by the tactile and emotional responses the materiality creates. Feeling the way the ink bites into the page of an early printed book to create a three-dimensional entity; transcribing a reader's marginal notes and connecting them to a fuller knowledge of the life of that reader's mind; smelling the scent of a freshly printed book or one that has been handled for centuries. These kinds of sensory experiences and aesthetic responses can be called forth by other objects, but they are particularly powerful when evoked by the text-bearing objects we call books. It is not necessary for the student of the history of the book to experience this emotional reaction, but it is important for the teacher to anticipate it.

While the sensory experience of learning about old books is often intense, so is the intellectual engagement that comes with thinking abstractly about how they work. The history of the book has a theoretical component, and a course of study directly focused on that history will have to decide when, and how, to introduce such ideas as Robert Darnton's 'communication circuit', D. F. McKenzie's 'sociology of texts', Pierre Bourdieu's 'literary field' and Benedict Anderson's 'print capitalism'. The extent to which students are required to engage with these ideas will depend upon their disciplinary background and their level of study. Some instructors will choose to introduce these concepts at the beginning of a course, in order to frame the ideas that are to be inculcated. Others will wait until later in the semester, once a chronology or trajectory of 'the book' through history has been established, some virtual or hands-on processes experienced, and some exemplary scholarship read and analysed. Both are possible, but it might be most useful to introduce some of these ideas in two stages, initially as straightforward models, and then again midway through the course, this time as concepts which can be undermined when tested in the real world of book-historical research. The important thing to stress is that each of these concepts comes with its own panoply of critical scholarship. Whether they are introduced at the outset or later, none of the theoretical approaches should be taught as a rigid model. No model has yet been introduced that can explain everything we need to know about the book in social, economic and cultural context. Indeed the student who has learned to think in terms of one or other of these models may have to unlearn that way of thinking, in order to accommodate something more theoretically capacious. If the history of the book can make the ambitious claims discussed above, in various disciplines and interdisciplinary settings, then a vigorous debate over theoretical approaches is inevitable and necessary.

One approach to introducing students to the cut-and-thrust of debate within the history of the book is to set up assignments where scholars' work is paired with that of their critics. Two examples will suffice. The collaborators who were among the founders of the history of the book, Lucien Febvre and Henri-Jean Martin, suggested that, if other calculations were correct, 'then about 20 million books were printed *before 1500*' (that is during the fifty or so years of the incunabula period in Europe). This statistic was reproduced without qualification by Benedict Anderson, who used it as the basis for a political interpretation of the impact of print. It will be salutary for students to learn how that figure has been systematically disproved by Joseph Dane. Another such exercise is provided by Elizabeth Eisenstein's *The Printing Revolution in Early Modern Europe*, which offers an inspirational and engaging argument – until it is challenged by a reading of Adrian Johns, whose *The Nature of the Book* initiated its own equally powerful analysis by qualifying Eisenstein's.[9]

History of the book in the college or university

While there are numerous stand-alone courses in the history of the book, at schools and universities around the world, there are only a few fully fledged degree-granting programmes. Because of book history's inherent interdisciplinarity, such programmes normally draw on resources from across the institution, even though they might be located in a single faculty or department. While the approach can be strictly theoretical, in some institutions students are offered practical training in publishing studies, book science or book studies. Here the teaching programme is oriented to employment in practice-based or vocational trades, with the historical and theoretical component serving in a supporting role and instructors valued for their real-world expertise. In more academic settings, however, the study of the book presents itself as an interdisciplinary or cross-disciplinary arrangement, a formal or informal collaboration among instructors with shared interests. In such cases, a degree focusing on the history of the book, whether graduate or undergraduate, is typically a degree in English, library and information studies or another discipline, with a certificate or acknowledgement of concentration in the field. Holding a Master's degree with this kind of endorsement enhances the student's profile in applications to competitive doctoral programmes where bibliographical and book-historical knowledge are prized.

The history of the book has made significant and well-recognized contributions to studies in the history of science, as the work of Ann Blair, Adrian Johns, James Secord and others attests. A course of study for science majors, organized around the history and practice of scientific communication, can provide students with a valuable orientation to aspects of their own discipline. It could also serve as a meaningful way to fulfil the typical 'breadth' requirement for sampling the humanities or social sciences. At the teaching level, scholars in book history working within an arts, humanities or social science faculty might find unexpected collaborators among professors of science or engineering, in the shape of aficionados of the history of science and technology, willing and able to share their knowledge, expertise and book collections.

Here is another learning objective for studies in the history of the book: critical thinking and research skills. In the syllabus of most programmes in both humanities and social sciences, the study of critical reading and research methodology looms large. Students must be introduced to the concept that each secondary source they use is not only a piece of analysis and narrative but also part of an ongoing scholarly conversation, and that ideas and interpretations build upon the theory and practice of earlier scholars. At the same time, students are introduced to the methods of research, the use of printed books in the library, and (in some disciplines) of manuscript sources in the archive. Some instructors find it useful to incorporate in this module an awareness of the material form of written artefacts from the past. Students who learn how to read the outside (as well as the inside) of a book can recognize the names of publishers, identify whether a work is aimed at an academic or a popular readership, distinguish a textbook from a monograph and so forth. All these skills, essentially bibliographical, are crucial to appreciating academic writing. Similar exercises can extend to the reading of different scholarly genres, such as the website, the scholarly article or the book review.

The university administrator with a budget to consider will be interested in offering book studies because they are attractive to learners from both practical and intellectual perspectives, and such an administrator will be pleased to offer instructors an opportunity to teach their research specialty. But therein lies the challenge: no instructor can possibly specialize in the whole field, because it is too diverse. And if instruction is to happen at an advanced level, it may be difficult, expensive or even impossible to offer training in specialized skills. The history of the book is an attractive subject and (as this chapter has argued) one that can be made accessible to students who lack any prior awareness of it. Nevertheless there are times when very specialized knowledge is required, and that expertise is held by only a handful of scholars in the whole world. The answer, in this case, is to bring the students to the instructor for a short period of time, rather than put the instructor regularly in front of students but only in his or her own institution. The concept of a Rare Book School was initiated by the American rare-book librarian Terry Belanger, who hired a series of experts to teach five-day non-credit courses on subjects relating to the history of the book and rare-book librarianship. Belanger's successors have developed variations on the basic concept which now flourish around the world.[10] The demand for intensive summer courses, workshops and master classes is fuelled by the introductory courses which create a demand that non-specialist instructors cannot fill. The participants are not only academics, but also librarians, antiquarian booksellers, conservators and archivists, as well as enthusiastic amateurs. Rare Book Schools are also places where the relevant digital knowledge of the present generation is put into conversation with the bibliographical knowledge drawn from the recent past. This model is of particular importance as the skills of the bibliographer, and associated skills, are no longer routinely taught in institutions of higher learning. Practitioners and educators keep vital knowledge alive and pass it on to the next generation.

The history of the book in the educated imagination

The slick brochure, the plausible website, the over-hyped bestseller – each of these carries evidence inherent its own design. Not all of them are books, but each of them is nevertheless part of the history of the book. People who have studied that history know something their fellow-citizens don't. It is possible, actually, to judge quite a lot about a book by its cover. And what has been learned about old books can be applied to new ones, as well as to other media both old and new. A chronologically oriented progression through the history of the book in various world cultures concludes, for most teachers and learners, with the subject's application to contemporary media. In some cases there may be an extensive analysis of the publishing industry and its commercial and cultural practices. But even if their investigation has been limited to the past, students still take away an awareness of how books and texts are separate, but comingled; of how they change, with changing times and in response to the entangled interests of those who publish, use and compose them. It is useful to know, taking a well-known example, how badly Shakespeare's plays were printed in his own time, and further distorted by printers throughout the following decades and centuries; how they have been disentangled with varying degrees of success by scholarship, including bibliographical scholarship; how the plays became part of mass culture in the nineteenth century; and how they were incorporated into the twentieth-century schoolroom and the twenty-first-century media culture.[11] Even if the details are forgotten, the underlying message is not. Knowledge of the history of the book, conceptualized thus, is an essential component of what is sometimes called 'media literacy'. Like the latter, it incorporates concepts of critical thinking, identification of bias and recognition of how commercial interests intersect with political and cultural representations.

Unlike a media literacy oriented primarily to the 'new' and inherently visual media of internet and television, however, the history of the book inculcates an attitude of scepticism towards the myth of a solitary authorial genius. That myth is the notion that Shakespeare or Newton, Dickens or Darwin, was the sole source of the world-changing ideas that were, and continue to be, published under that author's name. The myth rests on the fact that knowledge or artistry can have such a powerful effect on the human intellect and imagination that they seem to exist in an unmediated trajectory between the 'genius' author's mind and the experience of the reader. The gatekeeping agency of publishers, the textual intervention of printers and editors, the collaboration of spouses and colleagues, the typographical and spatial messages created by book designers – all these and more are invisible, except to the trained eye of research. Not only that. Since the seventeenth century at least, books and periodicals have been designed consciously to promulgate this myth of authorial authority, to create the effect that the book is a work of literary, scholarly or scientific brilliance. Undermining the myth of the solitary *scientific* genius has been the work of historians of science, who have shown that the inventions and discoveries of the past were only possible in the context of other kinds of knowledge in circulation at the time, and were inherently collaborative. The unsung work of laboratory assistants is being recognized, along with that of the printers and publishers who also, quite consciously, acted to present certain figures as lone inventors.

One of the dominant conversations of our own time is the one about the imminent death of the book and the obsolescence of libraries. The producers of various kinds of electronic devices designed chiefly for leisure reading want their product and service to be the dominant model. But so did the proprietors of circulating libraries in the nineteenth century. The providers of databases and digital texts to public and research libraries, similarly and understandably, market their services in terms of making older materials obsolete. So did the manufacturers of microfilm, only a few decades ago. The educated person who knows a bit about how books (and other media) travel and transform, and hence that it is not technology, but human choices, behind the changes that take place, is armed with the ability to read the message of the material form. She or he will not be persuaded by apocalyptic statements, and will know how to value the library as a cultural institution that survives and flourishes by changing, along with the books it collects.

NOTES

1. C. A. Reed, *Gutenberg in Shanghai: Chinese Print Capitalism, 1876–1937* (Vancouver: University of British Columbia Press, 2004).
2. C. Haynes, 'Reassessing "Genius" in Studies of Authorship: The State of the Discipline', *Book History* 8 (2005), 288.
3. J. B. Friskney, *New Canadian Library: The Ross-McClelland Years 1952–1978* (University of Toronto Press, 2007), 152–84.
4. J. A. Sutherland, *Victorian Novelists and Publishers* (University of Chicago Press, 1976), 6.
5. M. Esbester, 'Nineteenth-century Timetables and the History of Reading', *Book History* 12 (2009), 156–85.
6. For some practical guidance of this sort see A. R. Hawkins, *Teaching Bibliography, Textual Criticism, and Book History* (London: Pickering and Chatto, 2006).
7. J. D. Groves, 'Dramatising the Familiar: Showing Students what they Don't Know about Books', *SHARP News* 6:1 (1997), 2–4.
8. N. Waite, 'Private Printing', in P. Griffith, R. Harvey and K. Maslen (eds.), *Book and Print in New Zealand: A Guide to Print Culture in Aotearoa* (Victoria University of Wellington, 1997), 83–4; P. Gaskell, 'The Bibliographical Press Movement', *Journal of the Printing Historical Society* 1 (1965), 1–13.
9. J. Dane, *The Myth of Print Culture* (University of Toronto Press, 2003, 32–5; A. Grafton, E. L. Eisenstein and A. Johns, 'AHR Forum: How Revolutionary was the Print Revolution', *American Historical Review* 107 (2002), 84–128.
10. There are Rare Book Schools and similar short-term programmes operating in England (London), France (Lyons), New Zealand (Wellington and Dunedin), the US (Charlottesville, Los Angeles, College Station Texas, Urbana and Colorado Springs) and elsewhere. For an up-to-date listing, see www.rarebookschool.org/related.
11. L. Erne, *Shakespeare and the Book Trade* (Cambridge University Press, 2013).

GLOSSARY OF TECHNICAL TERMS USED BY BIBLIOGRAPHERS AND HISTORIANS OF THE BOOK

Scholarship in the history of the book often uses specialized terminology. This glossary is intended to help newcomers to interpret what they are reading, by providing brief definitions of such terms. However it is important to note that much more extensive definitions are available. A standard work on the subject is *ABC for Book Collectors* (by John Carter, revised edition published by Oak Knoll Press, 1995 and also available online). Many of the entries below consist of quotations from the *Oxford Companion to the Book* (Oxford University Press, 2010), abbreviated as *OCB*. See volume 1 of *OCB* for a list of editors and contributors of individual entries.

alphabet, printer's Defined by *OCB* as a 'set of types kept in upper case, lower case and small capitals within a fount. It originally excluded j (represented by i), u (represented by v), and w (represented by vv), but included accented letters and ligatures'.

bibliography, analytical Described by *OCB* as 'the practice of reconstructing the physical processes by which printed books came to be produced'.

bibliography, descriptive Described by *OCB* as being 'concerned with books as material objects [but unlike analytical bibliography having] the single goal of describing the physical structure of books in a clear and concise way'.

bibliography, enumerative Its 'basic function' as described by *OCB* is 'to list all titles of books that fall within specified parameters: geographic, linguistic, chronological, thematic or some combination thereof'.

bibliography, historical *OCB*: 'as a term it has been displaced by "history of the book" or histoire du livre'.

bibliography, textual *OCB*: 'any bibliographical endeavor that attempts to reconstruct the transmission of texts, with the possible goal of establishing or editing a specific work'.

Book of Hours A prayer book in the Christian tradition, organized around the eight canonical hours of the day.

bookplate A label (usually printed) to be attached inside a book as a record of ownership.

bookseller A retail bookseller sells copies of books; until around 1800 in Britain and America the term 'bookseller' referred to an entrepreneur who undertook the functions now described as 'publishing'. See also 'stationer'.

broadsheet A newspaper with large folded sheets; larger than a 'tabloid' and in journalism terms expected to be taken more seriously.

broadside A sheet of paper printed on one side and publicly posted as a notice.

codex Defined by *OCB* as 'a book made from hinged leaves, in contrast to a roll (or scroll)'; these came into use in Europe between the second and fourth centuries CE.

codicology The study of the text and materials making up a manuscript codex (as opposed to the scroll or roll).

collation A complex term used in bibliography, but also referring to processes taking place in the printing house. Refers to the correct ordering and orientation of gatherings of printed sheets.

communication(s) circuit Theoretical concept proposed by Robert Darnton in 1982 as a model of the ways in which a written text moves from author to publisher (plus editor and others) to printer (and binder and other production workers) to shipper to bookseller and on to the reader; the circuit is completed when the reader becomes an author.

diplomatics (or diplomatic) Defined by *OCB* as: 'the study of the authenticity, provenance and effects of such documents as legal records, charters, decrees, property deeds, accounts, registers, or any such historical documents of interest'.

Duodecimo: 12° or 12mo Defined by *OCB* as 'format ... whereby a sheet is folded either twice across the longer side and thrice across the shorter, or ("long 12mo") once across the shorter side and five times across the longer, producing a gathering of twelve leaves'. See also 'format', 'leaf' and 'sheet'.

edition Defined by *OCB* as 'the total number of copies of a book printed, at any time, from substantially the same setting of type ... The identification of different editions requires specialized bibliographical analysis and close examination of the differences between copies ... With the advent of automated printing techniques in the machine-press period, the longevity of an edition has greatly expanded'.

edition binding Defined by *OCB* as 'the issuing of whole editions of books, or significant portions of them, in identical bindings as part of the publication process'.

GLOSSARY OF TECHNICAL TERMS

folio or 2o Defined by OCB as 'format whereby a sheet is folded once across the longer side, giving two leaves (four pages)'. See also 'format', 'leaf' and 'sheet'.

format According to OCB: 'Often used in a generic fashion to describe the size and appearance of a book, "format" is the technical and bibliographical term for the shape of the book, defined by the number of times each sheet has been folded'.

forme Defined by OCB as 'the chase and its contents (type, blocks, etc.) prepared for printing'. The chase is the 'solid frame of wood or (more commonly) iron into which the type and other matter making up a forme are locked'.

fount (font) Defined by OCB as 'type acquired or consistently used as a single entity: letterpress and most bit-mapped founts generate one size, film or outline founts a range of sizes ... Founts are products, while typefaces are abstractions: one produces, sells, buys and downloads founts, but designs (and sells rights to) typefaces'.

gathering Defined by OCB as 'a group of one or more conjugate leaves sewn together before binding. Depending on format, a gathering is made from one folded sheet, from a fraction of a sheet, or from several folded sheets tucked one inside another (i.e. quired)'.

impression Defined by OCB as 'all copies of an edition printed at any one time' and also as 'the art or process ("taking an impression") or the quality (a "good", "bad", "light" or "heavy impression") of printing, usually letterpress'.

imprint Identification of the person(s) responsible for producing a printed book, usually giving place of publication, name of publisher and date of publication.

incunable (plural: incunabula) A book printed with moveable type, in Europe, between the mid-1450s and 1501. The term refers to the 'cradle' and hence to the earliest experiments with the new technology.

leaf Defined by OCB as a 'double-sided piece of paper, parchment or similar material capable of being written or printed on, comprising two pages, recto and verso'.

legal deposit Defined by OCB as 'a statutory obligation on publishers to deposit in designated libraries a copy of each publication'.

letterpress OCB defines this as 'a term used by scholars and the trade, equivalent to relief. As a noun, "letterpress" means relief, rather than intaglio or planographic, printing; as an adjective, it modifies "machines" (letterpress machines are for relief printing), "plates" (letterpress plates print relief) or output (letterpress text means printed by type)'.

lithography A method of printing using a smooth plate (or a stone) and based on chemicals; widely used throughout the twentieth century.

metadata Data about data – such as the information in a library catalogue record which identifies a book or article.

MS (plural MSS) Abbreviation for 'manuscript(s)' often used in citations referring to archival or library collections.

Octavo: 8° or 8vo Defined by *OCB* as 'format whereby a sheet is folded thrice, giving eight leaves (sixteen pages)'. See also 'format', 'leaf' and 'sheet'.

offset printing *OCB*: 'Unlike printing directly from an inked surface, offset printing is indirect. The inked surface delivers its ink to a second surface, which in turn transfers the ink to the third and final surface, usually paper ... Its practical application has been for lithography'.

paleography Defined by *OCB* as 'the study of the handwriting of previous centuries ... [The] paleographer teaches both how to read the text and how to interpret the MS'.

plate Defined by *OCB* as 'a printing surface, usually made of one solid piece, rather than a set of individual components that have been forced together (such as a forme of type)'. Also refers to 'a leaf that is not integral to a gathering, but is printed separately and added when gathering ... [M]ost plates are illustrations'.

Quarto: 4° or 4to Defined by *OCB* as 'format whereby a sheet is folded twice, giving four squarish leaves (eight pages)'. See also 'format', 'leaf' and 'sheet'.

recto Defined by *OCB* as 'front side of a single leaf or right-hand page of an opening in a codex'.

serial A periodical publication. But 'serialization' refers (per *OCB*) 'to the practice of dividing longer works for inclusion in newspapers or magazines, or publishing them separately as parts, issued over a long period'.

sheet Defined by *OCB* as 'the printer's unit of paper, manufactured in various sizes, weights and qualities. A sheet in the handpress period printed two folio leaves, four quarto leaves, eight octavo and so forth ... Sheets were sold in quires and reams, with a ream comprising twenty quires of 24 or 25 sheets each'.

signature Defined by *OCB* as 'alpha-numeric indicator for the binder of the gathering and its bifolia ("pairs of conjugate leaves joined at a central fold") – and of the gathering's place in the sequence of gatherings'. However the term is often used informally to refer to a folded sheet or set of sheets.

stationer In the book trade, someone who sells books (and pamphlets, periodicals etc.) by retail from a shop or fixed stall.

stereotyping Defined by *OCB* as 'the process of making cast-metal copies of a relief printing surface, such as a forme of type or a woodblock illustration'.

verso Defined by *OCB* as 'reverse side of a single leaf or left-hand page of an opening in a codex'.

woodblock printing Defined by *OCB* as 'printing images, text, or patterns by means of wooden blocks, usually inked on the relief surface'.

GUIDE TO FURTHER READING

Altick, R., *The Scholar Adventurers* (Columbus: Ohio State University Press, 1987).
Atiyeh, G. N. (ed.), *The Book in the Islamic World: The Written Word and Communication in the Middle East* (Albany: State University of New York Press, 1995).
Ballantyne, T., *Webs of Empire: Locating New Zealand's Colonial Past* (Wellington: Bridget William Books, 2012).
Bannet, E. T., *Transatlantic Stories and the History of Reading, 1720–1810: Migrant Fictions* (Cambridge University Press, 2011).
Barnard, J., D. F. McKenzie, D. McKitterick and I. Willison (eds.), *The Cambridge History of the Book in Britain* (7 vols.) (Cambridge University Press, 1999–).
Beal, P., *In Praise of Scribes: Manuscripts and their Makers in Seventeenth-Century England* (Oxford: The Clarendon Press, 1998).
Belanger, T., 'Descriptive Bibliography', in J. Peters (ed.), *Book Collecting: A Modern Guide* (New York and London: R. R. Bowker, 1977), 97–115.
Birkerts, S., *The Gutenberg Elegies: The Fate of Reading in an Electronic Age* (New York: Fawcett Columbine, 1994).
Blayney, P., *The Stationers' Company and the Printers of London, 1501–1557* (2 vols.) (Cambridge University Press, 2014).
Blouen, F. and W. G. Rosenberg, *Processing the Past: Contesting Authority in History and the Archives* (Oxford University Press, 2011).
Bode, K., *Reading by Numbers: Recalibrating the Literary Field* (London: Anthem Press, 2012).
Bolter, J. D., *Writing Space: The Computer, Hypertext, and the History of Writing* (Mahwah, NJ: Erlbaum Associates, 1990).
Bowers, F., *Principles of Bibliographical Description* (New Castle, DE: Oak Knoll Press, 1994).
Brokaw, C. J. and K. Chow (eds.), *Printing and Book Culture in Late Imperial China* (Berkeley: University of California Press, 2005).
Burrows, S. and M. Curran, *The French Book Trade in Enlightenment Europe Database, 1769–1794*, available at http://fbtee.uws.edu.au.
Burton, A. (ed.), *After the Imperial Turn: Thinking With and Through the Nation* (Durham and London: Duke University Press, 2003).
Cambridge History of Libraries in Britain and Ireland (3 vols.), Vol. I: *To 1640*, E. Leedham-Green and T. Webber (eds.); Vol. II: *1640–1850*, G. Mandelbrote and K. A. Manley (eds.); Vol. III: *1850–2000*, A. Black and P. Hoare (eds.) (Cambridge University Press, 2006).

Cavallo, G. and R. Chartier (eds.), *A History of Reading in the West: Studies in Print Culture and the History of the Book* (Amherst: University of Massachussets Press, 1999).
Chambers, A., *Godly Reading: Print, Manuscript and Puritanism in England, 1580–1720* (Cambridge University Press, 2011).
Chartier, R., *The Order of Books: Readers, Authors, and Libraries in Europe between the Fourteenth and Eighteenth Centuries* (Cambridge: Polity Press; Stanford, CA: Stanford University Press, 1994).
Chatterjee, P., *Nationalist Thought and the Colonial World: A Derivative Discourse* (Minneapolis: University of Minnesota Press, 1993).
Cheah, P. and J. D. Culler (eds.), *Grounds of Comparison: Around the Work of Benedict Anderson* (New York: Routledge, 2003).
Chow, K., *Publishing, Culture, and Power in Early Modern China* (Stanford University Press, 2004).
Clark, J. W., *The Care of Books: An Essay on the Development of Libraries and their Fittings, from the Earliest Times to the End of the Eighteenth Century* (Cambridge University Press, 1902; repr. 2009).
Clegg, C. S., *Press Censorship in Elizabethan England* (Cambridge University Press, 1997).
 Press Censorship in Jacobean England (Cambridge University Press, 2002).
 Press Censorship in Caroline England (Cambridge University Press, 2008).
Crone, R., *Violent Victorians: Popular Entertainment in Nineteenth-Century London* (Manchester University Press, 2012).
Dane, J. A., *The Myth of Print Culture: Essays on Evidence, Textuality, and Bibliographical Method* (University of Toronto Press, 2003).
Darnton, R., *The Business of Enlightenment: A Publishing History of the Encyclopédie 1775–1800* (Cambridge, MA: The Belknap Press of Harvard University Press, 1979).
 The Kiss of Lamourette: Reflections in Cultural History (New York: Norton, 1990).
 The Forbidden Best-Sellers of Pre-Revolutionary France (New York: Norton, 1995).
Darnton, R. and D. Roche (eds.), *Revolution in Print: The Press in France 1775–1800* (Berkeley: University of California Press, 1989).
de Hamel, C., *The Book: A History of the Bible* (London and New York: Phaidon, 2001).
 The British Library Guide to Manuscript Illumination: History and Techniques (University of Toronto Press, 2001).
Derrida, J., *Archive Fever: A Freudian Impression.* Trans. Eric Prenowitz (University of Chicago Press, 1996).
Dick, A. L., *The Hidden History of South Africa's Book and Reading Cultures* (University of Toronto Press, 2012).
Driscoll, M. J., *The Unwashed Children of Eve: The Production, Dissemination and Reception of Popular Literature in Post-Reformation Iceland* (Enfield Lock: Hisarlik Press, 1997).
Eisenstein, E., *The Printing Press as an Agent of Change: Communications and Cultural Transformations in Early Modern Europe* (2 vols.) (Cambridge University Press, 1979).

Eliot, S., *Some Patterns and Trends in British Publishing 1800–1919*. Occasional Papers, no. 8 (London: Bibliographical Society, 1994).

Eliot, S. and J. Rose (eds.), *A Companion to the History of the Book* (Chichester: Wiley Blackwell, 2009).

Erickson, L., *The Economy of Literary Form: English Literature and the Industrialization of Publishing, 1800–1850* (Baltimore, MD: The Johns Hopkins University Press, 1996).

Ezell, M. J. M., *Social Authorship and the Advent of Print* (Baltimore, MD: The Johns Hopkins University Press, 2003).

  'Invisible Books', in P. Rogers and L. Runge (eds.), *Producing the Eighteenth-Century Book: Writers and Publishers in England, 1650–1800* (University of Delaware Press, 2009).

Febvre, L. and H-J. Martin, *The Coming of the Book: The Impact of Printing 1450–1800*. Trans. D. Gerard. First published 1958 (London: NLB; New York: Schocken, 1976).

Finkelstein, D. and A. McCleery, *The Book History Reader* (London: Routledge, 2002; 2nd edn. 2013).

  An Introduction to Book History (London: Routledge, 2005).

Fleming, P. and Lamonde, Y. (eds.), *History of the Book in Canada* (3 vols.) (University of Toronto Press, 2004–7).

Fraser, R., *Book History Through Postcolonial Eyes: Rewriting the Script* (London: Routledge, 2008).

Fraser, R. and M. Hammond (eds.), *Books Without Borders*. Vol. I: *The Cross-National Dimension in Print Culture*; Vol. II: *Perspectives from South Asia* (Basingstoke and New York: Palgrave Macmillan, 2008).

Freitag, U. and A. von Oppen (eds.), *Translocality: The Study of Globalising Processes from a Southern Perspective* (Leiden: Brill, 2010).

Frost, S. and R. W. Rix (eds.), *Moveable Type, Mobile Nations: Interactions in Transnational Book History. Angles on the English-Speaking World*, Vol. X (Copenhagen: Museum Tusculanum Press, 2010).

Gadd, I., S. Eliot and W. R. Louis (eds.), *History of Oxford University Press* (3 vols.) (Oxford University Press, 2013).

Gaskell, P., *A New Introduction to Bibliography* (Oxford University Press, 1972).

Gaur, A., *A History of Writing* (London: The British Library, 1984).

Grafton, A., *Forgers and Critics: Creativity and Duplicity in Western Scholarship* (Princeton University Press, 1990).

Greetham, D. C., 'Describing the Text: Descriptive Bibliography', in *Textual Scholarship: An Introduction* (London: Routledge, 1994), 153–68.

Grenby, M. O., *The Child Reader, 1700–1840* (Cambridge University Press, 2011).

Griffin, C., *Journeymen-Printers, Heresy, and the Inquisition in Sixteenth-century Spain* (Oxford University Press, 2005).

Griffiths, J. and D. Pearsall (eds.), *Book Production and Publishing in Britain 1375–1475* (Cambridge University Press, 1989).

Hall, D. D., *Ways of Writing: The Practice and Politics of Text-making in Seventeenth-Century New England* (University of Pennsylvania Press, 2008).

  (ed.), *The History of the Book in America* (5 vols.) (University of North Carolina Press, 2010).

Halsey, K., *Jane Austen and Her Readers, 1786–1945* (London: Anthem Press, 2012).
Havelock, E., *Origins of Western Literacy* (Toronto: Ontario Institute for Studies in Education, 1976).
Hemmungs Wirtén, E., *No Trespassing: Authorship, Intellectual Property Rights and the Boundaries of Globalization* (University of Toronto Press, 2004).
  Terms Of Use: Negotiating the Jungle of the Intellectual Commons (University of Toronto Press, 2008).
Hirschler, K., *The Written Word in the Medieval Arabic Lands: A Social and Cultural History of Reading Practices* (Edinburgh University Press, 2012).
Histoire des Bibliothèques Françaises (4 vols.), *Vol. I: Les Bibliothèques Médiévales: du VIe siècle à 1530*, A. Vernet (ed.); *Vol. II: Les Bibliothèques sous l'Ancien Régime: 1530–1789*, C. Jolly (ed.); *Vol. III: Les Bibliothèques de la Révolution et du XIXe siècle: 1789–1914*, D. Varry (ed.); *Vol. IV: Les Bibliothèques au XXe siècle: 1914–1990*, M. Poulain (ed.) (Paris: Promodis, 1988–91).
Hobbs, M., *Early Seventeenth-Century Verse Miscellany Manuscripts* (Aldershot: Ashgate, 1992).
Hofmeyr, I., *The Portable Bunyan: A Transnational History of* The Pilgrim's Progress (Princeton University Press, 2004).
  Gandhi's Printing Press: Experiments in Slow Reading (Johannesburg: Wits University Press, 2013).
Howard-Hill, T. H., 'Enumerative and Descriptive Bibliography', in P. Davison (ed.), *The Book Encompassed* (Cambridge University Press, 1992), 122–9.
Howsam, L., *Cheap Bibles: Nineteenth Century Publishing and the British and Foreign Bible Society* (Cambridge University Press, 1991).
  Old Books and New Histories: an Orientation to Studies in Book and Print Culture (University of Toronto Press, 2006).
Hunter, D., *Papermaking: The History and Technique of an Ancient Craft* (New York: A. A. Knopf, 1947).
Iriye, A. and P.-Y. Saunier (eds.), *The Palgrave Dictionary of Transnational History* (Basingstoke: Palgrave Macmillan, 2009).
Jackson, H. J., *Marginalia: Readers Writing in Books* (New Haven, CT: Yale University Press, 2001).
  Romantic Readers: the Evidence of Marginalia (New Haven, CT: Yale University Press, 2005).
Jarausch, K. H. and K. A. Hardy, *Quantitative Methods for Historians: A Guide to Research, Data, and Statistics* (Chapel Hill: The University of North Carolina Press, 1991).
Jardine, L., *Erasmus, Man of Letters: The Construction of Charisma in Print* (Princeton University Press, 1993).
Johns, A., *The Nature of the Book: Print and Knowledge in the Making* (University of Chicago Press, 1998).
  Piracy: The Intellectual Property Wars from Gutenberg to Gates (University of Chicago Press, 2009).
Joshi, P., *In Another Country: Colonialism, Culture, and the English Novel in India* (New York: Columbia University Press, 2002).
Kirschenbaum, M., *Mechanisms: New Media and the Forensic Imagination* (Cambridge, MA: MIT Press, 2009).

König, J., K. Oikonomopolou and G. Woolf (eds.), *Ancient Libraries* (Cambridge University Press, 2013).
Krummel, D. W., 'On Degressive Music Bibliography', *Music Library Association Notes* 56:4 (June 2000), 867–78.
Landow, G. P., *Hypertext: The Convergence of Contemporary Critical Theory and Technology* (Baltimore, MD: The Johns Hopkins University Press, 1992).
Lee, A. J., *The Origins of the Popular Press in England, 1855–1914* (London: Croom Helm, 1976).
Lerner, F., *The Story of Libraries from the Invention of Printing to the Computer Age* (2nd edn) (New Haven, CT: Continuum, 2009).
Love, H., *Scribal Publication in Seventeenth-Century England* (Oxford University Press, 1993).
  English Clandestine Satire 1660–1702 (Oxford University Press, 2004).
Lowry, M., *The World of Aldus Manutius: Business and Scholarship in Renaissance Venice* (Ithaca: Cornell University Press, 1979).
Maclean, I., *Scholarship, Commerce, Religion: The Learned Book in the Age of Confessions, 1560–1630* (Cambridge, MA: Harvard University Press, 2012).
Manguel, A., *A History of Reading* (New York: Viking 1996).
Manoff, M., 'Theories of the Archive from Across the Disciplines', *Portal: Libraries and the Academy* 4.1 (2004), 9–25.
Marotti, A. F., *Manuscript, Print, and the English Renaissance Lyric* (Ithaca: Cornell University Press, 1995).
Marotti, A. F. and M. D. Bristol (eds.), *Print, Manuscript, Performance: The Changing Relations of the Media in Early Modern England* (Columbus, OH: Ohio State University Press, 2000).
Martin, H-J. (ed.), *L'Histoire de l'édition française* (4 vols.) (Paris: Promodis, 1983–6).
May, S. W., *The Elizabethan Courtier Poets: the Poems and their Contexts* (Columbia: University of Missouri Press, 1991).
Mazrui, A. A. and Mazrui, A. M., *The Power of Babel: Language and Governance in the African Experience* (Oxford and Chicago: J. Currey and University of Chicago Press, 1998).
McCormick, J. (ed.), *George Santayana's Marginalia: A Critical Selection* (2 vols.) (Cambridge, MA: MIT Press, 2011).
McGann, J. J., 'The Rationale of Hypertext', *Text* 9 (1996), 11–32.
McGill, M. L., *American Literature and the Culture of Reprinting, 1834–1853* (Philadelphia: University of Pennsylvania Press, 2003).
McKenzie, D. F., 'The Sociology of a Text: Orality, Literacy and Print in Early New Zealand', *The Library* Sixth Series 6 (1984), 333–65. Repr. in D. F. McKenzie, *Bibliography and the Sociology of Texts* (Cambridge University Press, 1999).
  Bibliography and the Sociology of Texts. The Panizzi Lectures, 1985. London: The British Library (1986). Repr. in D. F. McKenzie, *Bibliography and the Sociology of Texts* (Cambridge University Press, 1999).

McKitterick, D., *Print, Manuscript and the Search for Order 1450–1830* (Cambridge University Press, 2003).
  (ed.), *The Cambridge History of the Book in Britain: Volume VI, 1830–1914* (Cambridge, 2011).
McLuhan, M., *The Gutenberg Galaxy* (University of Toronto Press, 1962).
Miller, C. L., *Nationalists and Nomads: Essays on Francophone African Literature and Culture* (University of Chicago Press, 1998).
Mollier, J.-Y., *Louis Hachette (1800–1864): Le fondateur d'un Empire* (Paris: Fayard, 1999).
Moretti, F., *Graphs, Maps, Trees: Abstract Models for a Literary History* (London: Verso, 2005).
Myers, R. and M. Harris (eds.), *A Millennium of the Book: Production, Design and Illustration in Manuscript and Print 900–1900* (Winchester: St Paul's Bibliographies, 1994).
Ólafsson, D., *Wordmongers: Manuscript Culture in the Age of Print and the Case of Nineteenth-Century Iceland* (Ithaca: Cornell University Library Press, 2012).
Olson, D. R., *The World on Paper: The Conceptual and Cognitive Implications of Writing and Reading* (Cambridge University Press, 1994).
Ong, W., *Orality and Literacy: The Technologizing of the Word* (London: Methuen, 1982).
Pearson, D., *Provenance Research in Book History: A Handbook* (2nd edn) (London: British Library and New Castle, DE: Oak Knoll, 1998).
  Books as History: The Importance of Books beyond their Texts (London: British Library and New Castle, DE: Oak Knoll, 2008).
Pollock, S., *The Language of the Gods in the World of Men: Sanskrit, Culture, and Power in Premodern India* (Berkeley: University of California Press, 2006).
Potter, S. J., *News and the British World: The Emergence of an Imperial Press System, 1876–1922* (Oxford University Press, 2003).
Radway, J., *Reading the Romance: Women, Patriarchy, and Popular Literature* (Chapel Hill: University of North Carolina Press, 1984).
Raven, J. (ed.), *Lost Libraries: The Destruction of Great Book Collections since Antiquity* (Basingstoke: Palgrave Macmillan, 2004).
  The Business of Books: Booksellers and the English Book Trade, 1450–1850 (London and New Haven, 2007).
  Bookscape: Geographies of Printing and Publishing in London before 1800 (London and Chicago: The British Library and University of Chicago Press, 2014).
Reed, C. A., *Gutenberg in Shanghai: Chinese Print Capitalism, 1876–1937* (Honolulu: University of Hawai'i Press; Vancouver: University of British Columbia Press, 2004).
Rehberg Sedo, D. (ed.), *Reading Communities from Salons to Cyberspace* (Basingstoke: Palgrave Macmillan, 2011).
Richardson, B., *Printing, Writing and Reading in Renaissance Italy* (Cambridge University Press, 1995).
Roberts, C. H. and T. C. Skeat, *The Birth of the Codex* (Oxford University Press, 1983).

Rose, J., *The Intellectual Life of the British Working Classes* (New Haven: Yale University Press, 2001).

Round, P. H., *Removable Type: Histories of the Book in Indian Country, 1663–1880* (Chapel Hill: University of North Carolina Press, 2010).

Salter, E., *Popular Reading in English, c. 1400–1600* (Manchester University Press, 2012).

Secord, J. A., *Victorian Sensation: The Extraordinary Publication, Reception, and Secret Authorship of* Vestiges of the Natural History of Creation (University of Chicago Press, 2000).

Seyed-Gorab, A. A. (ed.), *The Great 'Umar Khayyam: A Global Reception of the Rubaiyat* (Leiden University Press, 2012).

Sharpe, K., *Reading Revolutions: The Politics of Reading in Early Modern England* (New Haven: Yale University Press, 2000).

Siemens, R., M. Timney, C. Leitch, C. Koolen and A. Garnett, 'Toward Modeling the Social Edition: An Approach to Understanding the Electronic Scholarly Edition in the Context of New and Emerging Social Media', *Literary and Linguistic Computing* 27:4 (2012), 445–61.

Smith, H., *'Grossly Material Things': Women and Book Production in Early Modern England* (Oxford University Press, 2012).

Squires, C., *Marketing Literature: the Making of Contemporary Writing in Britain* (Basingstoke: Palgrave Macmillan, 2009).

St Clair, W., *The Reading Nation in the Romantic Period* (Cambridge University Press, 2004).

Stam, D. H. (ed.), *International Dictionary of Library Histories* (2 vols.) (Chicago and London: Fitzroy Dearborn, 2001).

Stoicheff, P. and A. Taylor (eds.), *The Future of the Page* (University of Toronto Press, 2004).

Suarez, M. and H. R. Woudhuysen (eds.), *the Oxford Companion to the Book* (Oxford University Press, 2010); abridged edition, *The Book: A Global History* (2013).

Tanselle, G. T., 'The Arrangement of Descriptive Bibliographies', *Studies in Bibliography* 37 (1984), 1–38.

  'A Sample Bibliographical Description with Commentary', *Studies in Bibliography* 40 (1987), 1–30.

  'A Description of Descriptive Bibliography', *Studies in Bibliography* 45 (1992), 1–30.

Thompson, J. B., *Merchants of Culture: The Publishing Business in the Twenty-first Century* (Cambridge: Polity Press, 2010).

Towheed, S., R. Crone and K. Halsey (eds.), *The History of Reading* (London: Routledge, 2010).

Tschichold, J., *The Form of the Book: Essays on the Morality of Good Design* (Washington: Hartley and Marks, 1991).

Turner, E. G., *The Typology of the Early Codex* (Philadelphia: University of Pennsylvania Press, 1977).

Vander Meulen, D. L., 'General Methods', in his 'A Descriptive Bibliography of Alexander Pope's *Dunciad*, 1728–1751', unpublished PhD thesis, University of Wisconsin (1981), 17–40.

Voet, L., *The Golden Compass: A History and Evaluation of the Printing and Publishing Activities of the Officina Plantiniana at Antwerp* (2 vols.) (Amsterdam: Van Gendt; New York: Abner Schram, 1969–72).

Watts, J. W. (ed.), *Iconic Books and Texts* (Sheffield: Equinox Books, 2013).

Weedon, A., *Victorian Publishing: The Economics of Book Production for a Mass Market 1836–1916* (Aldershot: Ashgate, 2003).

'The Uses of Quantification', in S. Eliot and J. Rose (eds.), *A Companion to the History of the Book* (Chichester: Wiley Blackwell, 2009), 33–49.

West, J. L. W., *Making the Archives Talk: New and Selected Essays in Bibliography, Editing, and Book History* (Philadelphia: University of Pennsylvania Press, 2011).

Williams, W. P. and C. S. Abbott, 'Descriptive Bibliography', in their *An Introduction to Bibliographical and Textual Studies* (2009), 11–12, 36–56.

Woudhuysen, H. R., *Sir Philip Sidney and the Circulation of Manuscripts 1558–1640* (Oxford: The Clarendon Press, 1996).

INDEX

Africa, 10, 39, 43, 44, 45, 48, 59, 159, 173
African American readers, 223, 239
Albatross, 86, 165, 167
Alexandria, 18, 27, 29, 32, 56, 76, 185
Amazon.com, 88, 173, 181, 184, 240
Anderson, B., 10, 36, 39–43, 45, 46, 47, 51, 61, 176, 262, 263
Annales, 5
annotation, 94, 121, 193, 208, 241
anthologies, 97, 103, 200
antiquarian book trade. *See* bookselling
archives, 5, 187, 219
   as mediated entities, 224, 229
   booksellers', 10, 94, 220, 221, 222, 223, 225, 248
   digital, 191, 234
   government records, 228
   library records, 34, 190, 220, 222, 227
   publishers', 10, 200, 216, 221, 223, 225
archivists, 224, 265
Asia, 7, 39, 43, 54, 143, 254
Austen, J., 213, 243, 250
Australia, 10, 54, 58, 61, 170, 171, 224, 227, 231, 232, 240, 245
authors and authorship, 9, 87, 117, 134, 214–16

Barthes, R., 249
Bertelsmann, 163, 167, 168
bibles and bible societies, 55, 57–8, 59, 78, 80, 81, 91, 102, 128, 158, 238, 250
bibliographers, 187, 200, 226, 265
bibliographical presses, 261
bibliographies, 24, 227
   degressive principle, 210–13
   descriptive, 201
bibliography, 188
   as a discipline, 2, 8, 90, 108
   legitimating effect of, 209
binding, 25, 58, 79, 84, 86, 94, 112, 147, 192, 201, 208, 215, 260
blockbooks, 26, 110, 122

Bodleian Library, 18, 25, 32
book
   definitions of the, 2–3, 5, 257, 258
   predictions of its demise, 182, 185, 187, 257, 266
book clubs, 154, 168, 207, 223, 240
Book-of-the-Month Club, 6, 222
books
   as gifts, 19, 91, 95, 96, 101, 215
   mutability of, 6, 9, 55, 65
Books of Hours, 80, 91
booksellers, 101, 118, 133, 151
bookselling, 1, 61, 155, 257
   antiquarian, 146, 212, 216, 265
   as distinct from publishing, 5, 144, 153
botanical books. *See* illustration
Bourdieu, P., 65, 262
brands and branding, 155, 165, 166, 207, 243
Britain, 10, 20, 33, 48, 148, 149, 153, 155, 156, 227
British Library, 19, 26, 32, 231

Cambridge University Library, 28, 32
Canada, 3, 10, 58, 158, 170, 171, 227
censorship, 32, 90, 126, 129, 137, 149, 241
Chartier, R., 54, 125, 135, 211
Chatterjee, P., 47, 51
cheap books, 28, 30, 57–8, 84, 85–6, 143, 151, 153, 154, 158, 244
children's books, 157, 173, 177, 246
China, 3, 45, 55, 75, 80, 143, 145, 146, 149, 159, 172
clay tablets, 3, 17, 75, 241
collectors and collecting, 6, 27, 201, 209, 212, 216, 234
colonial editions, 56, 58, 158, 206
colonialism and postcolonialism, 10, 46, 59–62, 176, 241
commonplace books, 6, 97, 245
communication circuit. *See* Darnton, R.
contracts, 157, 170, 200, 221, 224

281

INDEX

copyright, 55, 108, 117, 127, 148, 149, 157, 158, 166, 167–8, 171, 184, 226, 233
cultural exception, 173, 177, 178

Darnton, R., 64, 118, 125, 226, 227, 229, 231, 237, 262
Dickens, C., 4, 58, 85, 152, 240, 266
digital humanities, 190–2, 233, 259
digitization, 1, 21, 29, 75, 231–2
dime novels. *See* cheap books
distribution, 58, 118, 146, 150, 159, 164, 183

edition size, 83, 84, 111, 150, 151, 153, 164, 207, 215
editors and editorship, 120, 136, 139, 172, 193, 201, 210, 212, 221, 225, 255
educational books. *See* textbooks
Egypt, 21, 29, 74, 75, 77, 170, 248
Eisenstein, E., 36–9, 134, 135, 186, 263
electronic books, 87, 181, 182–5, 187, 242
Eliot, S., 225, 229, 230
emotional responses, 6, 239, 262
England, 10, 26, 28, 84, 93, 97, 117, 126, 128, 145, 147, 149, 205, 239
English language, hegemony of, 163, 168, 172, 177
engraving, 110, 147, 210

fairs, 114, 226
  Frankfurt, 55, 118, 165
Febvre, L. and Martin, H.-J., 36, 44, 107
financing of book publication, 109, 111, 117, 118, 119, 144, 150, 157
fixity of print, apparent, 54, 92, 134, 135, 139–40, 182, 186, 257
folding printed or manuscript sheets, 79, 83, 213, 214
forbidden books. *See* censorship
France, 5, 10, 31, 73, 86, 117, 129, 145, 148, 156, 158, 174, 177

Gandhi, M., 59, 241
Genette, G., 4
genres, 2, 10, 42, 159
  literary categories, 6
  of the material book, 80, 83, 120, 257
  publishing and marketing categories, 171–2, 203, 249
  scholarly and academic categories, 199
Germany, 24, 33, 38, 86, 134, 145, 149, 164–6, 168, 174, 177

global history. *See* transnational history of the book
globalization, 43, 51, 63, 157, 175–8
Google, Inc., 21, 184, 231
government records. *See* archives
guilds, 115, 116–18, 126, 149, 226
Gutenberg J. myth of, 36, 48, 51
Gutenberg, J., 3, 7, 54, 80–1, 107, 109–12, 123, 186, 256–7
Gutenberg press. *See* printing, origin of

Hachette, 150, 157–8, 167, 174–5
Harlequin, 164, 171–2, 176
history as academic discipline, 2, 8, 108
history of the book
  as interdisciplinary formation, 2, 8–9
  models and theories, 5, 7–8, 48–51, 64–7, 140–1, 163, 248–50, 262–3
  relationship to bibliography, 203–5
  relationship to library history, 34
  relationship to national history, 36–9, 45–8, 136, 140–1
  research methods. *See* research methods
Hofmeyr, I., 10, 59
Houghton Mifflin, 175, 215, 216
humanism, 80, 112, 129, 135–7
hybrid books (combining manuscript and print), 93–101

Iceland, 102–3
illustration, 58, 94, 209–10, 234
imagined communities. *See* Anderson, B.
incunabula, 19, 21, 30, 92, 263
India, 3, 44, 46, 48, 53, 58, 59, 61, 158, 206, 227–9, 248
indigenous peoples, 7, 46, 47, 73–4, 172
inscription, 73, 79, 80, 189, 254
interdisciplinarity, 2, 8–9, 188, 262, 263
Ireland, 10, 26, 145
Iser, W., 249

Jackson, H. J., 6, 247
Japan, 146, 149, 159
Johns, A., 133–5, 136, 192, 263
Joyce, M., 87, 183

King's Printer, 117
Kirschenbaum, M., 188, 190, 192
Korea, 3, 54

legal deposit. *See* libraries
libels, 101, 125, 140

282

INDEX

libraries, 5, 122, 146, 184
  academic, 18, 28, 32, 253
  access to collections, 27, 253
  buildings, 20, 29
  cataloguing, 25, 225, 226
  commercial circulating, 19, 20, 28, 85, 150, 154, 243, 266
  ecclesiastical, 18, 27, 34, 56, 91
  legal deposit, 21, 23, 31–2
  loss or destruction, 29–34, 56
  public, 19, 20, 25, 26, 28, 32, 85, 227, 233, 241
  shipboard, 56
library and information studies as academic discipline, 2, 264
Library of Congress, 19, 23, 29, 33, 224, 226
library records. *See* archives
linotype, 148
literacy, 56, 74, 256
  alphabetic, 60
  media, 266
  rates, 81, 102, 239, 242
  working-class, 159, 239
literary agents, 220, 221
literary criticism, 4, 8, 67, 159, 166, 201, 212, 249
lithography, 45, 93, 146, 147
Luther, M., 54, 130, 256

Macmillan, 150, 155, 157, 168
manuscript books, 10, 19, 91–3, 95, 98, 101–3
Manutius, A., 27, 92, 112, 120, 126, 135, 144
marginalia, 93, 130, 190, 247
marketing. *See* publishing: as a business
Marx and Marxism, 27, 32, 50
McGann, J., 181, 184, 191, 211
McKenzie, D. F., 4, 53, 187, 188, 190, 204, 208, 211, 220, 262
McKitterick, D., 192
McLuhan, M., 36, 185
Mesopotamia, 3, 6, 18, 21
modernity and modernization, 38, 45–8, 49–50, 107–9, 148–9, 256
monopolies, 126–8, 167, 170, 176, 184
monotype, 148
Muslim book culture, 18, 45, 48

net book agreements, 155, 172
New Zealand, 57, 58, 245
newspapers, 30, 43, 57, 58, 82, 84, 86, 103, 148, 152–3, 216, 242, 257

novels, 7, 28, 58, 83, 84–6, 87, 171, 204, 239, 255, 259

oral communication, 50, 60, 73, 187, 254, 255
Oxford Companion to the Book, 48–50

paper, 151
  electronic, 184
  invention of, 80
  machine-made, 5, 58, 84, 146, 152, 214
  rag-based, 3, 214
  wood-pulp, 82–3, 87
paperbacks, 86, 164, 165–6, 171–2, 174
papyrus, 3, 75–6, 77, 248
paratext, 4, 94, 135, 244
parchment, 3, 77–8, 79, 80, 248
Patten, R. L., 4, 221
pecia, 79, 80
Penguin, 86, 163, 166
periodicals, 4, 125, 154, 241, 257
petroglyphs and pictographs. *See* stone as substrate
Pettegree, A., 109, 134, 136
piracy, 133, 134, 136, 149, 215
Plantin, C., 113, 128, 144
Pocket Books, 166–7
preservation, 29–32, 248
print capitalism. *See* Anderson, B.
print culture, 43–5, 137, 220, 233, 257
print run. *See* edition size
printers, 155–6, 261
  master, role or function of, 5, 38, 112–13
  travelling, as a mobile workforce, 57–8
printing
  colour, 147
  dissemination of, 82, 114–19, 128–30, 143–6
  origin of, 92–3, 108–12, 122–3, 254, 256–7
  practices, 113–14
  steam-press, 84, 146–7, 149, 152
Project Gutenberg, 183
publishing, 1, 5, 214, 261
  as a business, 149–51, 155–9, 209
  as distinct from printing, 117, 144–5, 149
  conglomerates, 163, 172–3
  paperback. *See* paperbacks
  transnational, 164, 170–2
publishing studies, 2, 65

Radway, J., 222, 240
Rare Book Schools, 258, 265
Raven, J., 204, 223

283

INDEX

readers and reading
  as subversive, 125
  effect on human brain, 250
  experience, 5–6, 201, 243–6
  practices and spaces, 55–6, 67, 87, 186, 213, 222–3, 238–40, 240–2
  protocols, 120, 121, 202
  women, 28
reception. *See* readers and reading
Reclam, 148, 165, 166, 167
Reed, C., 44, 254
remediation, 9, 53, 178, 188, 191, 192
reprints and reprinting, 4, 25, 83, 118, 131, 144, 153, 158, 166, 172, 200, 205–6
research methods for the history of the book
  qualitative, 223–5
  quantitative or statistical, 225–8, 231
Rose, J., 227, 240
Rowling, J. K., 9, 176, 177, 178
royalties. *See* contracts
Russia, 19, 32, 103

sacred books, 3, 45, 136, 238, 257
Sammelbände. *See* hybrid books
Scotland, 10, 132, 233
scribes and scriptoria, 5, 78–9, 91, 96, 102, 112
serialization, 154, 200
Shakespeare, W., 212, 266
South Africa, 59, 170
St Clair, W., 222, 226, 230

stationers, 5, 144
Stationers' Company, 116, 127–8, 137, 156, 226, 232
stereotype, 83, 147, 205, 215
stone as substrate, 73–4, 146, 248
Suarez, M., 31, 228, 230

Tauchnitz, 86, 158, 167
textbooks, 20, 31, 60, 150, 153, 155, 163, 174, 177, 256
textual studies as academic discipline, 90, 137, 188, 192, 193, 209, 254
translation, 30, 55, 60, 136, 164, 172, 177, 200
transnational history of the book, 10–11, 50, 59–62, 163, 254
type and typesetting, 54, 57, 81, 83, 92, 111, 143, 148, 201, 214, 261

United Kingdom. *See* Britain
United States, 10, 153, 158
university presses, 61, 65, 114, 117, 150, 170

vellum. *See* parchment
visualization, 5, 230, 232–3

Wales, 27, 152
wampum, 3, 74
wax tablets as substrate, 76
women, 8, 28, 91, 226, 239

Cambridge Companions to...

AUTHORS

Edward Albee edited by Stephen J. Bottoms
Margaret Atwood edited by Coral Ann Howells
W. H. Auden edited by Stan Smith
Jane Austen edited by Edward Copeland and Juliet McMaster (second edition)
Beckett edited by John Pilling
Bede edited by Scott DeGregorio
Aphra Behn edited by Derek Hughes and Janet Todd
Walter Benjamin edited by David S. Ferris
William Blake edited by Morris Eaves
Jorge Luis Borges edited by Edwin Williamson
Brecht edited by Peter Thomson and Glendyr Sacks (second edition)
The Brontës edited by Heather Glen
Bunyan edited by Anne Dunan-Page
Frances Burney edited by Peter Sabor
Byron edited by Drummond Bone
Albert Camus edited by Edward J. Hughes
Willa Cather edited by Marilee Lindemann
Cervantes edited by Anthony J. Cascardi
Chaucer edited by Piero Boitani and Jill Mann (second edition)
Chekhov edited by Vera Gottlieb and Paul Allain
Kate Chopin edited by Janet Beer
Caryl Churchill edited by Elaine Aston and Elin Diamond
Cicero edited by Catherine Steel
Coleridge edited by Lucy Newlyn
Wilkie Collins edited by Jenny Bourne Taylor
Joseph Conrad edited by J. H. Stape
H. D. edited by Nephie J. Christodoulides and Polina Mackay
Dante edited by Rachel Jacoff (second edition)
Daniel Defoe edited by John Richetti
Don DeLillo edited by John N. Duvall
Charles Dickens edited by John O. Jordan
Emily Dickinson edited by Wendy Martin
John Donne edited by Achsah Guibbory
Dostoevskii edited by W. J. Leatherbarrow
Theodore Dreiser edited by Leonard Cassuto and Claire Virginia Eby
John Dryden edited by Steven N. Zwicker
W. E. B. Du Bois edited by Shamoon Zamir
George Eliot edited by George Levine

T. S. Eliot edited by A. David Moody
Ralph Ellison edited by Ross Posnock
Ralph Waldo Emerson edited by Joel Porte and Saundra Morris
William Faulkner edited by Philip M. Weinstein
Henry Fielding edited by Claude Rawson
F. Scott Fitzgerald edited by Ruth Prigozy
Flaubert edited by Timothy Unwin
E. M. Forster edited by David Bradshaw
Benjamin Franklin edited by Carla Mulford
Brian Friel edited by Anthony Roche
Robert Frost edited by Robert Faggen
Gabriel García Márquez edited by Philip Swanson
Elizabeth Gaskell edited by Jill L. Matus
Goethe edited by Lesley Sharpe
Günter Grass edited by Stuart Taberner
Thomas Hardy edited by Dale Kramer
David Hare edited by Richard Boon
Nathaniel Hawthorne edited by Richard Millington
Seamus Heaney edited by Bernard O'Donoghue
Ernest Hemingway edited by Scott Donaldson
Homer edited by Robert Fowler
Horace edited by Stephen Harrison
Ted Hughes edited by Terry Gifford
Ibsen edited by James McFarlane
Henry James edited by Jonathan Freedman
Samuel Johnson edited by Greg Clingham
Ben Jonson edited by Richard Harp and Stanley Stewart
James Joyce edited by Derek Attridge (second edition)
Kafka edited by Julian Preece
Keats edited by Susan J. Wolfson
Rudyard Kipling edited by Howard J. Booth
Lacan edited by Jean-Michel Rabaté
D. H. Lawrence edited by Anne Fernihough
Primo Levi edited by Robert Gordon
Lucretius edited by Stuart Gillespie and Philip Hardie
Machiavelli edited by John M. Najemy
David Mamet edited by Christopher Bigsby
Thomas Mann edited by Ritchie Robertson
Christopher Marlowe edited by Patrick Cheney

Andrew Marvell edited by Derek Hirst and Steven N. Zwicker
Herman Melville edited by Robert S. Levine
Arthur Miller edited by Christopher Bigsby (second edition)
Milton edited by Dennis Danielson (second edition)
Molière edited by David Bradby and Andrew Calder
Toni Morrison edited by Justine Tally
Nabokov edited by Julian W. Connolly
Eugene O'Neill edited by Michael Manheim
George Orwell edited by John Rodden
Ovid edited by Philip Hardie
Harold Pinter edited by Peter Raby (second edition)
Sylvia Plath edited by Jo Gill
Edgar Allan Poe edited by Kevin J. Hayes
Alexander Pope edited by Pat Rogers
Ezra Pound edited by Ira B. Nadel
Proust edited by Richard Bales
Pushkin edited by Andrew Kahn
Rabelais edited by John O'Brien
Rilke edited by Karen Leeder and Robert Vilain
Philip Roth edited by Timothy Parrish
Salman Rushdie edited by Abdulrazak Gurnah
Shakespeare edited by Margareta de Grazia and Stanley Wells (second edition)
Shakespearean Comedy edited by Alexander Leggatt
Shakespeare and Contemporary Dramatists edited by Ton Hoenselaars
Shakespeare and Popular Culture edited by Robert Shaughnessy
Shakespearean Tragedy edited by Claire McEachern (second edition)
Shakespeare on Film edited by Russell Jackson (second edition)
Shakespeare on Stage edited by Stanley Wells and Sarah Stanton
Shakespeare's History Plays edited by Michael Hattaway
Shakespeare's Last Plays edited by Catherine M. S. Alexander

Shakespeare's Poetry edited by Patrick Cheney
George Bernard Shaw edited by Christopher Innes
Shelley edited by Timothy Morton
Mary Shelley edited by Esther Schor
Sam Shepard edited by Matthew C. Roudané
Spenser edited by Andrew Hadfield
Laurence Sterne edited by Thomas Keymer
Wallace Stevens edited by John N. Serio
Tom Stoppard edited by Katherine E. Kelly
Harriet Beecher Stowe edited by Cindy Weinstein
August Strindberg edited by Michael Robinson
Jonathan Swift edited by Christopher Fox
J. M. Synge edited by P. J. Mathews
Tacitus edited by A. J. Woodman
Henry David Thoreau edited by Joel Myerson
Tolstoy edited by Donna Tussing Orwin
Anthony Trollope edited by Carolyn Dever and Lisa Niles
Mark Twain edited by Forrest G. Robinson
John Updike edited by Stacey Olster
Mario Vargas Llosa edited by Efrain Kristal and John King
Virgil edited by Charles Martindale
Voltaire edited by Nicholas Cronk
Edith Wharton edited by Millicent Bell
Walt Whitman edited by Ezra Greenspan
Oscar Wilde edited by Peter Raby
Tennessee Williams edited by Matthew C. Roudané
August Wilson edited by Christopher Bigsby
Mary Wollstonecraft edited by Claudia L. Johnson
Virginia Woolf edited by Susan Sellers (second edition)
Wordsworth edited by Stephen Gill
W. B. Yeats edited by Marjorie Howes and John Kelly
Zola edited by Brian Nelson

TOPICS

The Actress edited by Maggie B. Gale and John Stokes
The African American Novel edited by Maryemma Graham
The African American Slave Narrative edited by Audrey A. Fisch
African American Theatre by Harvey Young

Allegory edited by Rita Copeland and Peter Struck

American Crime Fiction edited by Catherine Ross Nickerson

American Modernism edited by Walter Kalaidjian

American Poetry Since 1945 edited by Jennifer Ashton

American Realism and Naturalism edited by Donald Pizer

American Travel Writing edited by Alfred Bendixen and Judith Hamera

American Women Playwrights edited by Brenda Murphy

Ancient Rhetoric edited by Erik Gunderson

Arthurian Legend edited by Elizabeth Archibald and Ad Putter

Australian Literature edited by Elizabeth Webby

British Literature of the French Revolution edited by Pamela Clemit

British Romanticism edited by Stuart Curran (second edition)

British Romantic Poetry edited by James Chandler and Maureen N. McLane

British Theatre, 1730–1830 edited by Jane Moody and Daniel O'Quinn

Canadian Literature edited by Eva-Marie Kröller

Children's Literature edited by M. O. Grenby and Andrea Immel

The Classic Russian Novel edited by Malcolm V. Jones and Robin Feuer Miller

Contemporary Irish Poetry edited by Matthew Campbell

Creative Writing edited by David Morley and Philip Neilsen

Crime Fiction edited by Martin Priestman

Early Modern Women's Writing edited by Laura Lunger Knoppers

The Eighteenth-Century Novel edited by John Richetti

Eighteenth-Century Poetry edited by John Sitter

English Literature, 1500–1600 edited by Arthur F. Kinney

English Literature, 1650–1740 edited by Steven N. Zwicker

English Literature, 1740–1830 edited by Thomas Keymer and Jon Mee

English Literature, 1830–1914 edited by Joanne Shattock

English Novelists edited by Adrian Poole

English Poetry, Donne to Marvell edited by Thomas N. Corns

English Poets edited by Claude Rawson

English Renaissance Drama edited by A. R. Braunmuller and Michael Hattaway (second edition)

English Renaissance Tragedy edited by Emma Smith and Garrett A. Sullivan Jr

English Restoration Theatre edited by Deborah C. Payne Fisk

The Epic edited by Catherine Bates

European Modernism edited by Pericles Lewis

European Novelists edited by Michael Bell

Fairy Tales edited by Maria Tatar

Fantasy Literature edited by Edward James and Farah Mendlesohn

Feminist Literary Theory edited by Ellen Rooney

Fiction in the Romantic Period edited by Richard Maxwell and Katie Trumpener

The Fin de Siècle edited by Gail Marshall

The French Enlightenment edited by Daniel Brewer

The French Novel: from 1800 to the Present edited by Timothy Unwin

Gay and Lesbian Writing edited by Hugh Stevens

German Romanticism edited by Nicholas Saul

Gothic Fiction edited by Jerrold E. Hogle

The Greek and Roman Novel edited by Tim Whitmarsh

Greek and Roman Theatre edited by Marianne McDonald and J. Michael Walton

Greek Comedy edited by Martin Revermann

Greek Lyric edited by Felix Budelmann

Greek Mythology edited by Roger D. Woodard

Greek Tragedy edited by P. E. Easterling

The Harlem Renaissance edited by George Hutchinson

The History of the Book edited by Leslie Howsam

The Irish Novel edited by John Wilson Foster

The Italian Novel edited by Peter Bondanella and Andrea Ciccarelli

The Italian Renaissance edited by Michael Wyatt

Jewish American Literature edited by Hana Wirth-Nesher and Michael P. Kramer

The Latin American Novel edited by Efraín Kristal

The Literature of the First World War edited by Vincent Sherry

The Literature of London edited by Lawrence Manley

The Literature of Los Angeles edited by Kevin R. McNamara

The Literature of New York edited by Cyrus Patell and Bryan Waterman

The Literature of Paris edited by
Anna-Louise Milne

The Literature of World War II edited by
Marina MacKay

Literature on Screen edited by Deborah Cartmell
and Imelda Whelehan

Medieval English Culture edited by
Andrew Galloway

Medieval English Literature edited by
Larry Scanlon

Medieval English Mysticism edited by
Samuel Fanous and Vincent Gillespie

Medieval English Theatre edited by
Richard Beadle and Alan J. Fletcher
(second edition)

Medieval French Literature edited by
Simon Gaunt and Sarah Kay

Medieval Romance edited by
Roberta L. Krueger

Medieval Women's Writing edited by
Carolyn Dinshaw and David Wallace

Modern American Culture edited by
Christopher Bigsby

Modern British Women Playwrights edited by
Elaine Aston and Janelle Reinelt

Modern French Culture edited by
Nicholas Hewitt

Modern German Culture edited by Eva Kolinsky
and Wilfried van der Will

The Modern German Novel edited by
Graham Bartram

The Modern Gothic edited by Jerrold E. Hogle

Modern Irish Culture edited by Joe Cleary
and Claire Connolly

Modern Italian Culture edited by
Zygmunt G. Baranski and Rebecca J. West

Modern Latin American Culture edited
by John King

Modern Russian Culture edited by
Nicholas Rzhevsky

Modern Spanish Culture edited by
David T. Gies

Modernism edited by Michael Levenson
(second edition)

The Modernist Novel edited by Morag Shiach

Modernist Poetry edited by Alex Davis and
Lee M. Jenkins

Modernist Women Writers edited by
Maren Tova Linett

Narrative edited by David Herman

Native American Literature edited by Joy Porter
and Kenneth M. Roemer

Nineteenth-Century American Women's Writing
edited by Dale M. Bauer and Philip Gould

Old English Literature edited by
Malcolm Godden and Michael Lapidge
(second edition)

Performance Studies edited by Tracy C. Davis

Piers Plowman edited by Andrew Cole
and Andrew Galloway

Popular Fiction edited by David Glover
and Scott McCracken

Postcolonial Literary Studies edited by
Neil Lazarus

Postmodernism edited by Steven Connor

The Pre-Raphaelites edited by
Elizabeth Prettejohn

Pride and Prejudice edited by Janet Todd

Renaissance Humanism edited by Jill Kraye

The Roman Historians edited by
Andrew Feldherr

Roman Satire edited by Kirk Freudenburg

Science Fiction edited by Edward James and
Farah Mendlesohn

Scottish Literature edited by Gerald Carruthers
and Liam McIlvanney

Sensation Fiction edited by Andrew Mangham

The Sonnet edited by A. D. Cousins and
Peter Howarth

The Spanish Novel: from 1600 to the Present
edited by Harriet Turner and
Adelaida López de Martínez

Theatre History by David Wiles
and Christine Dymkowski

Textual Scholarship edited by Neil Fraistat
and Julia Flanders

Travel Writing edited by Peter Hulme and
Tim Youngs

*Twentieth-Century British and Irish Women's
Poetry* edited by Jane Dowson

The Twentieth-Century English Novel
edited by Robert L. Caserio

Twentieth-Century English Poetry edited by
Neil Corcoran

Twentieth-Century Irish Drama edited by
Shaun Richards

Twentieth-Century Russian Literature edited by
Marina Balina and Evgeny Dobrenko

Utopian Literature edited by Gregory Claeys

Victorian and Edwardian Theatre edited by
Kerry Powell

The Victorian Novel edited by Deirdre David
(second edition)

Victorian Poetry edited by Joseph Bristow

War Writing edited by Kate McLoughlin

Writing of the English Revolution edited by
N. H. Keeble